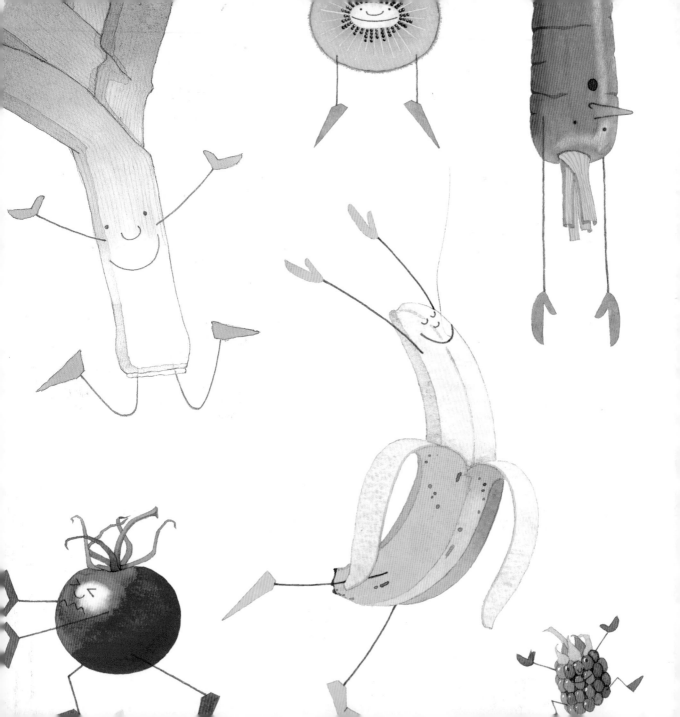

Annabel Karmel's
Baby-Led Weaning Recipe Book

120 recipes to let your baby take the lead

PINDOCK
PUBLISHING

CONTENTS

INTRODUCTION

For over 25 years, my delicious, nutritious baby and toddler recipes have graced the tables (and quite probably the walls and floors) of millions of households. Tales of proud weaning conquests regularly flood my inbox, and I take great pleasure in seeing snaps and videos of babies demolishing my recipes.

So what's my recipe for success in getting millions of babies and children eating well? My mantra is simple: experiment with a wide variety of healthy foods, flavours and textures early on in a baby's weaning journey.

Lots of parents find themselves feeling apprehensive about weaning and that's only natural. After all, you've finally found your comfort zone with the milk feeds! You ask yourself, what foods should I start with? How much should they be having? Should I be trying baby-led weaning, and what if they choke?

While lots of parents start out with smooth purees for spoon feeding, baby-led weaning (BLW) is fast growing in popularity. Some feel a need to go with one method or the other, but you don't have to choose. At around six months, you have the freedom to combine an element of baby-led weaning alongside spoon feeding if you feel that's right for you and your baby. The key is to go at your baby's pace and give her the opportunity to explore lots of different tastes and textures. Combining purees and soft finger foods at the beginning is appealing to lots of families.

And that's why I've devised my *Baby-Led Weaning Recipe Book* – to be used on its own for those wanting to explore BLW, or to be used as a companion cookbook to my bestselling *New Complete Baby & Toddler Meal Planner* which contains my favourite puree recipes.

Whichever approach you adopt, I'll be there to support you and your baby along the way with delicious, nutritious recipes, simple methods and clear advice for giving your child the very best start.

What is BLW and how does it differ to feeding purees?

There are two ways of weaning: spoon-feeding purees and BLW. Most mums know me for my failsafe puree recipes, starting out with smooth textures and simple flavours, then introducing new tastes and textures, and soft, cooked finger foods around six months, or as soon as your baby is able to pick up food and bring it to her mouth.

The philosophy behind BLW is to let your baby feed herself from six months, leaving out purees and spoon feeding altogether. It gives babies the opportunity to explore a variety of different tastes and textures from the beginning, helping them to eat a wide range of foods and develop good eating habits from the start.

Signs that your baby is ready to feed themselves

Look out for these signs that indicate your baby is ready to start feeding herself soft lumps and textures:
* She can sit up unassisted.
* She has lost the tongue-thrust reflex (automatically pushing solids out of her mouth with her tongue).
* She has developed sufficient hand-to-eye coordination to pick up food and put it in her mouth.
* She is able to chew, even if she has few or no teeth.
* She shows that she wants to join in family mealtimes.

At first, your baby may just play with the food you give them, but this is all part of their development. They will soon progress to sucking, chewing and swallowing.

Premature babies are advised to begin weaning earlier than the recommended 26 weeks, so are not suitable for BLW from the outset. They often have delays in their development, which mean that, by six months, they may not be able to sit up unassisted or be able to pick up and interact with food.

Milk feeds

It is important to remember when starting your baby on solids that milk is still the best and most natural food for growing babies and it contains all the nutrients your baby needs for the first six months. Breastmilk is best and if there is a history of allergy in the family it is particularly important to try and breastfeed exclusively for six months before introducing solids. Babies should be given breast or formula milk for the whole of the first year. Between six months and a year babies need 500–600 ml of breastmilk or formula each day.

What are the advantages of BLW?

BLW encourages shared and social eating, with your baby enjoying family meals from the beginning of her food journey. While busy family schedules don't always allow time for eating together, it's a positive principle to adopt, albeit if only a few times a week.

Regularly offering a variety of family meals (without added salt or sugar) encourages babies to adopt good eating habits, as these foods, which often offer a wider variety of tastes and textures than a spoon-fed diet, become a regular part of their diet. Babies that are only offered a limited variety of foods could develop fussiness, whereas babies and young children that are given foods such as curries, casseroles and tagines tend to accept new foods more willingly. Also, spices add flavour to food without the need for added salt.

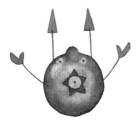

What are the advantages of spoon-fed purees?

While Department of Health recommend-ations state that babies should not begin weaning before six months and should be exclusively breastfed for the first six months, babies do develop at their own pace. If your baby is showing signs of being ready to move on from breastfeeding or formula milk, you can try giving simple solids from 17 weeks, but not before as your baby's digestive system will not be sufficiently developed to cope with food other than breast or formula milk.

Before six months, babies tend not to have developed the hand-to-eye coordination which is essential in BLW and therefore it should not be attempted. Purees or well-mashed food are an obvious bridge between liquid and solid foods and it's easy for you to see how much your baby is eating if you spoon-feed her.

When your baby reaches six months, the Department of Health, the European Union, the World Health Organisation and the British Dietetic Association all recommend giving your baby well-mashed or pureed foods at the beginning of weaning, as well as soft finger foods.

From six months, your baby starts to need iron from food, as breastmilk alone won't give him enough. If your baby is just starting out weaning at six months, giving iron-rich foods such as chicken or meat without some form of pureeing or mashing can make it difficult for babies to eat, which could mean they are missing out on essential nutrients. Some young babies also don't cope as well as others with lumpy food and need a more gradual transition from milk to solids.

A flexible approach to weaning

I believe there is a third way to weaning which involves giving purees when a baby is ready for first foods (particularly if slightly earlier than six months), with the introduction of finger foods and family meals from around six months.

Official advice advocates giving a mix of purees and soft finger foods at the start, and in speaking to parents, dietitians and healthcare professionals about weaning, this flexible approach is now a preferred option, and one that many are finding the most realistic to adopt.

What's important is that there is no right or wrong to weaning. It's about what works for you and your family. The key is to go at your baby's pace and give her the opportunity to explore lots of different tastes and textures. Combining purees and finger foods is, for many families, a good compromise.

With this flexible approach in mind, my *Baby-Led Weaning Recipe Book* has been designed as the ultimate companion book to my classic *New Complete Baby & Toddler Meal Planner*. It uses everyday mealtime ingredients that your baby can feed themselves, and paired with my Meal Planner (which starts out with purees) it

will help you and your baby to get the very best out of both weaning methods.

As with BLW, purees can also fit into the family routine. If you are preparing a cottage pie or lasagne for the family, simply skip the added salt and blend your baby's portion to the desired texture.

And, whether you choose purees, BLW or a mix of both, it's important to realise that your baby will instinctively tell you whether they like something or not, whether they are hungry or full, or whether they are ready to move onto something new. However you want to feed them, they will take the lead.

Registered dietician and consultant nutritionist Sarah Almond Bushell says: 'My advice would be to give your baby well-mashed or pureed foods at the beginning of weaning, as well as offering finger foods which dissolve easily in the mouth. As a trusted expert in feeding, Annabel's new baby-led weaning recipes are a great addition to her puree recipes. Parents often feel pressured to try baby-led weaning, but actually it's probably better to combine the two, that way you ensure optimum nutrition while helping your baby to develop the important motor skills as well as being included in sociable family mealtimes.'

How to get started with baby feeding herself

＊Ensure you have a safe place for your baby to sit. A highchair is the best option. Your baby should be able to sit upright unassisted. Then you need appropriate finger foods. The key is to take your baby's lead and feed them solids once a day to start with, gradually increasing quantities as she shows she wants more.

＊Make mealtimes a fun experience. Even if eating together at the same time doesn't work for your family, perhaps sit down and eat a snack with her while she eats so that mealtimes don't become an isolating experience.

＊Baby's first finger foods at six months should be soft and easy to swallow; fresh fruits, soft, cooked vegetables, healthy carbohydrates, and fats. Your role as the parent is to provide a variety of healthy foods that in combination provide a good balance of nutrients.

Safety

However your baby is fed, they should never be left alone while eating, and they must always be supported in an upright position.

It's understandable to worry about your baby choking. It's important to note that a baby who is struggling to get food into her mouth probably isn't quite ready to eat, so take your baby's lead. Whether you are feeding purees or finger foods (or both), your baby's own developmental abilities are what ensure that the transition to solid foods takes place at the right time for her, reducing the risk of choking. That's why it's important to start weaning only when your baby shows signs she is ready.

It's also important to differentiate between gagging and choking. Gagging is a safety mechanism that prevents choking by pushing food away from the airway if it is too big to be swallowed. The gag reflex in babies is triggered towards the front of the tongue (unlike adults where this is much further back). That's why finger foods are recommended from six months as your baby learns to chew and swallow when this reflex is safely close to the front of the mouth.

Choking occurs when the airway is completely or partially blocked. A baby who is choking is usually silent rather than coughing and spluttering, as no air is getting past the blockage. In this rare instance, your baby will need help in dislodging the lump using standard First Aid measures. If her airway is only partially blocked, your baby will usually cough to clear the blockage.

It is important to note that babies can store food in their mouth for quite some time after eating, so do check that your baby has swallowed her food.

Avoid these foods that could cause choking

* Whole grapes*
* Whole cherry tomatoes*
* Whole or chopped nuts
* Fruits with stones such as cherries and lychees
* Bony fish (make sure you check for bones)

*Small round fruits are better cut up.

How much food should I give?

Feeding purees as well as solids takes some of the anxiety out of knowing whether your child is getting enough to eat.

Breastmilk (or formula) should provide all of your baby's nutritional needs for the first six months. After that, milk alone will not provide all or your baby's needs. It is important to include iron-rich foods such as meat and chicken as babies are born with an iron store that starts to run out at around six months, and iron deficiency is the most common nutritional deficiency in young children.

The benefit of offering purees as well as finger foods is that it allows you to take back some control, particularly if you are not sure that your baby is meeting her nutritional needs through BLW alone.

Gradually increase the quantity of food you give your baby, and offer full-fat rather than low-fat dairy foods (low in added sugar), as these are a better source of vitamin A, and provide extra calories which babies need for growth and development.

Cooking oils

*Unsaturated fats are the best fats to cook with for babies and adults alike and occur naturally in plant foods such as nuts, seeds and vegetables. They can either be polyunsaturated (sunflower, soya, corn and sesame oils) or monounsaturated (rapeseed or olive oils). Monounsaturated oils have the added benefit of being good for heart heath as they have the ability to produce the HDL cholesterol (the good cholesterol). Try to avoid cooking with products that contain high levels of saturated fat, such as coconut oil, palm oil, butter, ghee, lard, suet or dripping, which can increase the risk of heart disease.

*Coconut oil has gained popularity in recent years, but there's not enough evidence as yet to suggest that coconut oil is anything other than detrimental to heart health.

*Omega-3 oils found in oily fish are great, too. Natural sources found in oily fish are the most bioavailable for a baby's growth and brain development.

Salt

Don't season your baby's food with salt before the age of one. Salt is present in some foods, such as bread, breakfast cereals and cheese, which can be added to your baby's diet from six months and give them all the sodium their body needs.

Do check the labels of shop-bought sauces and ready-meals for salt content before serving them to your baby. Stock cubes and stock powders can also be very salty and are best avoided. Instead, make your own stock, or choose a low-salt variety (dilute it well) or an unsalted variety.

Up to the age of one, babies should consume less than 1 g salt (0.4 g sodium) a day. From 1–3 years of age, the maximum daily salt intake is 2 g salt (0.8g sodium), and from four–six years of age, children should not consume more than 3 g salt (1.2g sodium) a day.

Dairy and eggs

Full-fat cow's milk can be used in cooking from six months onwards.

Feed your child full-fat dairy products (yoghurt, cheese etc.) for the first two years to help fuel his rapid growth.

Babies can eat whole cooked eggs, including the yolk, from six months. For the latest cooking guidelines, refer to www.nhs.uk. In the UK, ensure you buy British Lion eggs as they are produced to the highest standards of hygiene and food safety.

Fibre

Babies shouldn't have too much insoluble fibre (such as bran and wholemeal foods) in their diet as this can deplete their bodies of vital nutrients such as iron and zinc, by binding to them and affecting their absorption. Soluble fibre, on the other hand, such as that found in oats, beans, lentils and vegetables, does not bind to these nutrients. Ideally, give your baby a mixture of white and wholemeal bread, pasta and rice. Babies need proportionately more fat and less fibre in their diet than adults.

Sugar

There is no need to add sugar to your baby's food as it offers no nutritional benefits, unless you occasionally want to add a little to muffins or cookies to improve their flavour, or a pinch to a tomato sauce to reduce its acidity. You can sweeten food naturally using fruit and fruit purees.

Allergies

If you are introducing family meals to your baby, keep a close eye on potential allergens and limit the addition of salt and sugar, especially if using ready-made foods such as pasta sauces.

Food allergies are more common among babies and children from families with a history of allergy. This can be any type of allergy and is not just associated with food allergy, from pollen to animal hair. Babies who suffer from eczema are also at risk of suffering from food allergies. Babies who develop severe eczema before the age of three months are at very high risk, so you need to be particularly cautious when introducing new foods.

Most serious food allergies start in infancy and early childhood. They are caused by a relatively small number of different foods. Milk, soya and egg allergy are the most common and tend to disappear during childhood.

Until recently, parents were encouraged to delay the introduction of allergenic foods such as milk, eggs or peanuts, but in fact, there is now substantial evidence to suggest that early introduction of eggs and peanuts can reduce the risk of a child forming an allergy. In some countries, such as Israel for example, peanut is used in a snack called Bamba which is given to infants. This early weaning with a peanut product seems to relate to a corresponding low level of peanut allergy, even among children at high-risk of allergy. In 2016, doctors at St Thomas' Hospital in London were able to show that children who ate products containing ground peanuts between the ages of four and eleven months, and regularly thereafter, had a 70% reduced risk of developing an allergy to peanuts, compared with children who ate them for the first time when they were older.

Diagnosing food allergies relies on a careful analysis of medical history, examination and tests. The best treatment for a food allergy is to completely avoid the problem food. Speak to your doctor and ask for a referral to a paediatric dietitian before avoiding food groups as you do not want to cut out nutrients without replacing them with other food sources. Your doctor will ask about the symptoms of the reaction and whether they happen every time the food is eaten.

With immediate type allergies, testing can be done by a blood test or by a 'skin prick' test, where food extracts are placed on the skin of the arm and gently pricked. The results of either test can be very helpful in confirming if the allergy is present.

What to do if your child chokes

I encourage all new parents to become familiar with First Aid procedures for children, especially if they are concerned about choking risks when they start weaning. Refer to the Red Cross or NHS websites, which have instructional step-by-step videos, or ask your GP about local First Aid courses.

High-risk foods to avoid for babies under 12 months

* Honey
* Mould-ripened soft cheeses
* Added salt and sugar
* Whole cow's milk (or goat's / sheep's milk) as a main drink. You can introduce a little into your baby's foods from six months, once she's started on solids
* Shark, swordfish or marlin (due to high mercury levels)
* High choking-risk foods like whole grapes and whole/chopped nuts (although nut butters can be given at six months)
* Stimulants such as chocolate or sugar
* Unhealthy and processed foods such as battered foods, sugary breakfast cereals, chips, and other foods that contain sugar
* Caffeinated drinks such as tea, coffee, hot chocolate and cola

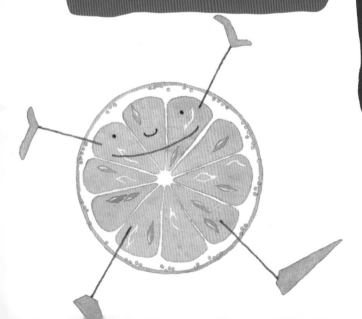

Giving you the means to find your own way

What I'm suggesting is a hybrid approach to feeding: provide your baby with a variety of nutrient-packed purees at the very beginning, along with soft finger foods and nutritious family meals that your baby can experiment with herself. It's all about finding out what works for you and your baby.

All the recipes in this book are suitable for the whole family and can be scaled up accordingly.

❄ Suitable for freezing

 Dairy-free recipes (other recipes can be made dairy-free by substituting butter for a dairy-free margarine. There are also lots of dairy-free alternatives to cow's milk made from soy, coconut, oat and almond)

What parents say about using a flexible approach

'The general consensus among my mum friends is that you can do a bit of both. My daughter showed strong signs of wanting food at 5½ months, so I started her on purees, then introduced finger foods just after six months which worked really well for her. I don't think you have to follow baby-led weaning exclusively.'
KatieMarch

'I did start out with baby-led weaning, but my son wasn't getting enough food, so I resorted to giving more milk. I felt that having the option of purees took the pressure off me, and whilst I know that a mix of the two methods isn't true baby-led weaning, it is working for us as he is getting the nutrients he needs, whilst also enjoying experimenting with finger foods.'
Loubymama

TOP TIPS FOR INTRODUCING FINGER FOODS AND FAMILY MEALS

1 Babies around six months tend to use their whole hand to pick things up. They need to be able to close their hand around the food, so avoid making the pieces too wide. Start with pieces that are big enough for your baby to hold in their fist with some sticking out. Fairly long pieces stand a better chance of being picked up. I would suggest cutting food into 5–6cm batons or sticks so that half is held in a baby's hand and the other half sticks out.

2 Start with softer fingers foods such as cooked sticks of carrot, broccoli and sweet potato, and chunks of banana, avocado and cucumber. First tastes like steamed carrots should be cooked until soft but not too mushy so that they can grab it with their fist. It's best to wait until your baby has teeth before you offer harder foods like raw carrot.

3 Let your baby pick up food with their fingers when they start baby-led weaning. Babies must learn to move foods safely around their mouths, so don't put food in their mouth. That way they will only pick up foods they can manage.

4 Brace yourself for a messy experience! It may be easier just to place the food straight onto their highchair tray rather than a plate. Choose an easy-clean highchair with a wide tray. Alternatively, choose a highchair without a tray and bring it up to the table.

5 Invest in a wipe-clean bib and a splash mat for the floor. Shower curtains are a great option and can be bought cheaply.

6 BLW is about making family mealtimes a social experience. While finger foods are important (particularly soft foods at the beginning), there's no reason why you can't serve them a portion of cottage pie, spaghetti Bolognese or roast chicken. Just be sure to leave out the salt.

7 Don't worry if your baby doesn't like certain foods – it's important that they explore a wide variety of foods independently. Although don't put too much on the highchair tray at the one time, as this could be a little overwhelming. Just a couple of pieces of food, or a small portion of a family meal will be adequate.

8 It's important to be aware of the foods which your baby shouldn't eat under the age of 12 months. Refer to page 14 for foods to avoid.

9 Wait until your baby is ready. She should be able to sit in a highchair unassisted.

10 Don't rush your baby or encourage her to eat a set amount or specific food. She chooses what, how much, and how quickly to eat.

Banana

Cheese, cut into
sticks or chunks

Whole eggs
(including the yolk)

GOOD FINGER FOODS AT SIX MONTHS

Start with pieces of food that are big enough for your baby to hold in their clenched fist with
some sticking out. They need to be able to close their hand around the food, so don't make
it too wide. Fairly long pieces of food stand a better chance of being picked up, and as
a general rule of thumb, a stick of food should be around 5cm long.

Dried fruit

Mango

Cooked pasta

Cooked sticks or chunks of carrot, broccoli, potato, sweet potato, butternut squash or apple

Pieces of poultry (dark meat is best) or meat

Pieces of cooked fish

Cubes or fingers of bread, toast and pitta bread

Low-salt rice cakes

Low-salt breadsticks

Wholegrain cereal

Citrus fruits

Raw slices or chunks of soft foods such as avocado, cucumber, peaches, pears and strawberries

Breakfast

Nectarine, Strawberry and Banana Smoothie

MAKES 2 CHILD PORTIONS

1 small frozen banana,
  cut into chunks
2 large juicy nectarines or
  peaches, skinned, halved,
  stoned and chopped
4 fresh strawberries, hulled
  and halved
125 ml/4½ fl oz orange juice
125 g/4½ oz vanilla yoghurt

Babies love bananas and they are a great first food as they are soft and bursting with nutrients. Combining banana with juicy sweet nectarines, strawberries and fresh orange juice, this smoothie packs a nutritious punch with its vitamin C and antioxidants.

• •

Peel the banana and cut it into chunks. Place all of the ingredients in a blender and blitz until smooth.

Tips

★ If you have any overripe bananas languishing in your fruit bowl, peel, slice and freeze them in a plastic bag. Then you have them ready and waiting for your next smoothie or homemade ice-cream.
★ You can freeze any leftover smoothie mixture in lolly moulds, if you wish.

Fruit Smoothie with Oats and Almond Milk

DAIRY FREE

MAKES 2 CHILD PORTIONS
1 banana
150 g/5 oz fresh strawberries,
    hulled and halved
150 g/5 oz fresh raspberries
150 ml/5 fl oz almond milk
2 tablespoons porridge oats
1–2 tablespoons maple syrup

Almond milk is very much having its 'superfood' moment. Now widely available, it's a good source of calcium and vitamin E and is an effective substitute for cow's milk if your toddler has a dairy allergy or intolerance.

Place all of the ingredients in a blender and blitz until smooth.

My Favourite Granola

DAIRY FREE

175 g/6 oz porridge oats
70 g/3 oz pecan nuts,
   finely chopped
20 g/¾ oz desiccated coconut
¼ teaspoon fine salt
50 g/2 oz light soft brown sugar
2 tablespoons sunflower
   or rapeseed oil, plus extra
   for greasing
4 tablespoons maple syrup
50 g/2 oz raisins

Make this and you'll never want shop-bought granola again. It's super-easy to make, too. I like to serve it with natural set yoghurt, fresh berries and a drizzle of maple syrup. Choose full-fat yoghurt for children under 2, to fuel their rapid growth.

• •

Preheat the oven to 150°C/300°F/Gas 2 and lightly grease a baking tray with oil. Combine the oats, pecans, desiccated coconut, salt and sugar in a large bowl.

Whisk the oil and maple syrup together in a jug or small bowl, then pour the mixture over the dry ingredients and mix well. Spread out the granola mixture on the oiled baking tray and bake in the middle of the oven for 40 minutes, stirring every 10 minutes. Remove from the oven, transfer to a bowl, stir in the raisins and leave to cool.

Scrambled Eggs with Toppings

MAKES 2 CHILD PORTIONS
a knob of butter
3 large eggs
2 tablespoons milk
a little salt and pepper (for babies over 12 months old)

Toppings
SPRING ONION, TOMATO AND CHEESE
1 teaspoon light olive oil
3 spring onions, sliced
1 tomato, chopped
1 tablespoon grated Cheddar cheese
a small pinch of salt (for babies over 12 months old)

MUSHROOM, CHIVE AND CHEESE
1 teaspoon light olive oil
75 g/3 oz button mushrooms, sliced
1 teaspoon chopped chives
1 tablespoon grated Cheddar cheese
a small pinch of salt (for babies over 12 months old)

Eggs are a fantastic food for the whole family and are packed full of nutrients. It's fine to give whole cooked eggs to babies, including the yolk, and the great thing is that you often have them to hand so you can rustle up a quick, nutritious breakfast in no time.

For the latest cooking guidelines on eggs, refer to www.nhs.co.uk.

• •

Melt the butter in a frying pan. Beat the eggs, milk and seasoning (if using) together in a bowl then pour it into the pan. Stir over a medium heat until scrambled and cooked through, then remove from the heat and make your chosen topping.

Spring Onion, Tomato and Cheese Heat the oil in a frying pan. Add the spring onions and fry for 1 minute, then add the tomato and fry for a further 2 minutes. Season with the salt (if using). Spoon the tomato and spring onion mixture on top of the scrambled eggs and sprinkle with the cheese.

Mushroom, Chive and Cheese Heat the oil in a frying pan. Add the mushrooms and fry over a high heat for 3–4 minutes until golden. Season with the salt (if using). Spoon the mushrooms on top of the scrambled eggs and sprinkle with the chives and cheese.

Almond Milk Porridge with Berries

MAKES 3 CHILD PORTIONS
80 g/3 oz blueberries
1 tablespoon maple syrup
80 g/3 oz raspberries
apple, banana, blueberries
   and strawberries, to decorate
   (optional)

Porridge
40 g/1½ oz porridge oats
300 ml/10 fl oz almond milk
1 tablespoon maple syrup

The king of all breakfasts! A bowl of porridge makes for a great start to the day, and will give you and your baby long-lasting reserves of energy thanks to the slow release of complex carbs. Sweetening it with fresh fruit and a drizzle of maple syrup gives it extra appeal.

• •

Put the blueberries in a small saucepan with the maple syrup. Stir over the heat for a few minutes until the blueberries are just starting to soften, then remove from the heat and add the raspberries. Set aside.

Place the oats in a small saucepan with the almond milk. Bring to the boil over a medium heat then reduce the heat and simmer for 4–5 minutes until thickened. Add the maple syrup.

Spoon the porridge into bowls and top with the warm fruits.

If you like, create an owl face by topping each portion with two apple slices for wings, sliced halves of banana for feathers, wedge of strawberry for a nose, and slices of bananas topped with blueberries for eyes.

Banana, Carrot and Seed Bread ❊

MAKES 1 LOAF

150 g/5 oz softened unsalted
    butter
2 large eggs
200 g/7 oz ripe bananas,
    peeled and mashed
125 g/4½ oz grated carrot
25 g/1 oz sultanas
125 g/4½ oz soft dark brown sugar
225 g/8 oz self-raising flour
½ teaspoon ground cinnamon
1 teaspoon mixed spice
1 teaspoon ground ginger
25 g/1 oz pumpkin seeds
25 g/1 oz sunflower seeds
butter, for spreading
    and greasing

Topping
1 tablespoon pumpkin seeds
1 tablespoon sunflower seeds
icing sugar, for dusting (optional)

Who doesn't love banana bread? Packed full of grated carrots, sultanas and seeds, this is a delicious breakfast or snack and a great way to use up overripe bananas.

• •

Preheat the oven to 170°C/340°F/Gas 3, grease a 900 g/2 lb loaf tin and line it with baking parchment.

Place all of the ingredients, except the topping, in a large mixing bowl. Whisk together with an electric hand-held whisk for 1-2 minutes until light and fluffy. Alternatively, use a stand mixer fitted with the paddle or whisk attachment.

Spoon the mixture into the tin and level out the top.

Sprinkle with the extra seeds and bake for 1–1¼ hours until golden, well risen and a skewer inserted comes out clean.

Remove from the oven and leave to cool on a wire rack, then remove from the tin. Dust with icing sugar (if using), cut into slices, spread with butter and serve.

Banana Muffins

MAKES 24 MINI MUFFINS

150 g/5 oz ripe bananas,
   peeled and mashed
100 g/4 oz softened unsalted
   butter
2 eggs
100 g/4 oz soft dark brown sugar
150 g/5 oz self-raising flour
1 teaspoon baking powder
1 teaspoon ground cinnamon
1 teaspoon vanilla extract
50 g/2 oz raisins

Give your little one an energy boost with these mini banana muffins – the perfect finger food for little hands.

Preheat the oven to 180°C/350°F/Gas 4 and line a 24-hole mini muffin tin with mini muffin paper cases.

Place the mashed banana, butter , eggs, sugar, flour, baking powder, cinnamon and vanilla in a large mixing bowl. Whisk together with an electric hand-held whisk for 1 minute until light and fluffy, then stir in the raisins. Alternatively, use a stand mixer fitted with the paddle or whisk attachment.

Divide the mixture evenly between the paper cases and bake for 15–18 minutes until well risen and lightly golden. Remove from the oven and leave to cool on a wire rack.

French Toast

MAKES 2 CHILD PORTIONS
1–2 slices white bread, raisin
   bread or French bread
1 egg
2 tablespoons whole milk
a generous knob of unsalted
   butter or a little vegetable oil,
   for frying

SAVOURY FRENCH TOAST
Marmite or Promite, for spreading
   (optional)

SWEET FRENCH TOAST
sugar and/or ground cinnamon,
   to serve (optional)
fresh berries or other fruit,
   to serve (optional)

French toast served with some fresh berries is a real treat for breakfast. Sprinkle with a little cinnamon and serve with your baby's favourite fruit, or for babies over one you can add a very thin layer of Marmite for a savoury version.

● ●

Remove the crusts from the bread slices and cut each slice into four triangles or into fingers.

For a savoury version, spread a thin layer of Marmite or Promite on the bread.

Beat the egg and milk together in a shallow bowl and soak the bread triangles or fingers in this mixture for a few seconds. Drain on kitchen paper. Heat the butter or oil in a frying pan and fry the soaked bread for 1–2 minutes on each side until lightly golden.

For a sweet version, add a pinch of sugar or a pinch of ground cinnamon (or both) to the egg mixture and sprinkle a little more sugar on the toast after frying. Serve immediately, with your choice of fruit.

Snacks

Trio of Finger Sandwiches

MAKES 9 FINGER SANDWICHES
(ENOUGH FOR 3 LUNCHBOXES)
3 slices wholemeal bread
3 slices white bread
a little margarine or butter,
    for spreading

**TUNA MAYONNAISE
WITH SWEETCORN**
60 g/2½ oz tinned tuna
1 tablespoon mayonnaise
1 tablespoon tinned sweetcorn
6 slices cucumber

CLUB SANDWICH
1 tablespoon mayonnaise
¼ cooked chicken breast, sliced
iceberg lettuce, shredded
2 slices Gruyère cheese
½ tomato, sliced
1 hard-boiled egg, sliced

**TOMATO, CREAM CHEESE
AND CHIVE**
1 tablespoon cream cheese
1 teaspoon chopped chives
½ tomato, sliced

A true lunchbox favourite, sandwiches are the perfect way to start your little ones experimenting with different textures and flavours. Explore these tried-and-tested flavour combos on hungry tums.

•●•●•●•●•●•●•●•●•●•●•●•●•●•●•●•●•

Spread all the slices of bread with margarine or butter and arrange them on a board.

For the tuna mayonnaise and sweetcorn sandwich, mix the tuna, mayonnaise and sweetcorn together in a bowl. Spread the mixture over one slice of wholemeal bread. Top with the cucumber, then sandwich together with a slice of white bread. Remove the crusts and cut into 3 fingers.

For the club sandwich, spread one slice of wholemeal bread with the mayonnaise. Top with the chicken, lettuce, cheese, tomato and egg. Sandwich together with a slice of white bread. Remove the crusts and cut into 3 fingers.

For the tomato, cream cheese and chive sandwich, combine the cream cheese and chives. Spread the mixture over one slice of wholemeal bread. Top with the sliced tomato. Sandwich together with a slice of white bread. Remove the crusts and cut into 3 fingers.

Dips

Serve these delicious dips with breadsticks, cucumber, carrot, sweet red or yellow pepper sticks, pitta bread and cherry tomatoes and try offering some more unusual vegetables, such as sweet sugar snap peas, too.

• •

Sweet Chilli and Cream Cheese Dip

100 g/4 oz light cream cheese
1 teaspoon chopped chives
1 teaspoon sweet chilli sauce

Mix the cream cheese and chives together and put them in a ramekin. Spoon over the chilli sauce or mix it into the cream cheese if you prefer.

Thousand Island Dip

2 tablespoons Greek yoghurt
2 tablespoons mayonnaise
2 teaspoons tomato ketchup
½ teaspoon lemon juice
1–2 drops of Worcestershire sauce

Mix the ingredients together and put them in a ramekin.

Ranch Dip

3 tablespoons sour cream
2 tablespoons mayonnaise
1 teaspoon lime or lemon juice (optional)
1 teaspoon chopped coriander
1 teaspoon chopped chives

Mix the ingredients together and put them in a ramekin.

Mango and Cream Cheese Dip

4 tablespoons light cream cheese
3 tablespoons natural yoghurt
1½ tablespoons mango chutney
1 tablespoon lemon juice
a pinch of curry powder

Mix all the ingredients together and put them in a ramekin.

Cottage Cheese Dip

125 g/4½ oz cottage cheese
2 tablespoons mayonnaise
4 teaspoons tomato ketchup
squeeze of lemon juice
a tiny drop of Worcestershire sauce (optional)

Blitz the ingredients in a food processor until smooth. Chill in the fridge until ready to serve.

My Favourite Cobb Salad

MAKES 8 CHILD PORTIONS
2 Little Gem lettuces, shredded
150 g/5 oz Gruyère cheese, diced
1–2 ripe avocados, halved, stoned,
   peeled and chopped
3 eggs, hard-boiled and peeled
4 tomatoes, deseeded
   and chopped
2 cooked chicken breasts, diced
2 rashers of streaky smoked
   bacon, grilled and chopped
   (optional)
sprig of basil, to serve

Dressing
1 tablespoon Dijon mustard
2 tablespoons rice wine vinegar
2 tablespoons mirin
2 teaspoons runny honey or
   maple syrup
6 tablespoons light olive oil
   (or whatever olive oil you
   have to hand)

Little ones love finely chopped salads, and this amazing salad is one of my all-time favourites. It's good as a light lunch, picnic or snack. Use maple syrup instead of honey in the dressing, if serving to babies under 12 months, and leave out the bacon.

• •

Arrange all the salad ingredients on a round plate or serving board. Garnish with the basil in the centre.

Place all the dressing ingredients in a jug or jar, and whisk or shake until well blended. Serve the dressing alongside the salad.

Sweet Potato and Parsnip Crisps

MAKES 2–3 CHILD PORTIONS
1 small parsnip, peeled
1 small sweet potato, peeled
1 tablespoon olive oil
a small pinch of flaky sea salt
    (for babies over 12 months old)

It's no secret that children love crisps, so it's a good idea to introduce healthier alternatives early on in their weaning journey. Sweet potatoes and parsnips have a natural sweetness and baking them in the oven caramelises them, intensifying that sweetness.

• •

Preheat the oven to 200°C/400°F/Gas 6 and line two large baking sheets with baking parchment.

Use a swivel peeler to peel thin strips from the parsnip. Put the strips in a bowl and toss with half the oil. Spread them out in a single layer on one of the lined baking sheets.

Repeat the process with the sweet potato, spreading the strips on the second baking sheet.

Bake the parsnip and sweet potato crisps for 10 minutes, then swap the baking sheets around so that the one on the higher oven shelf is moved to a lower shelf. You may find that the parsnip cooks slightly faster than the sweet potato, so keep an eye on them as they brown very quickly. Bake for a further 5 minutes, or until crisp and browned at the edges, then remove from the oven.

Transfer the crisps to a bowl and sprinkle with salt, if using. These are best served the day they are made.

Cheat's Spring Rolls

MAKES 4 SMALL WRAPS

1 tablespoon sunflower oil

2 boneless skinless chicken
   breasts, cut into very thin strips

1 medium carrot, peeled and
   coarsely grated

2 handfuls of beansprouts

2 spring onions, thinly sliced

1 teaspoon dark soy sauce

2 tablespoons plum sauce

4 small wheat tortilla wraps

Chinese spring rolls are so yummy, but takeaway versions are often deep-fried, making them an unhealthy treat. So, I've come up with a healthy, but just as tasty, grilled version that you can make at home.

● ●

Preheat the grill to high. Heat the oil in a wok or large frying pan, add the chicken and stir-fry it for 2 minutes. Add the vegetables and stir-fry for a further 2 minutes, until the chicken has cooked through and the vegetables have softened slightly (but aren't completely soft). Stir in the soy sauce and 1 teaspoon of the plum sauce, and remove from the heat.

Spread the remaining plum sauce over the four wraps. Divide the chicken and vegetable filling between the wraps, spooning it on to the lower half of each wrap. Fold the left- and right-hand sides of the wrap over the filling then roll the wraps up from the bottom, so that the filling is completely enclosed.

Carefully transfer the filled wraps to a grill pan, sitting them seam side down. Place under the grill for 1–1½ minutes, until the tops are crisp and starting to brown then turn them over and grill for a further 1–1½ minutes. Watch carefully as the wrap can scorch easily. Remove from the grill and serve immediately.

Tip

★ If the rolls won't stay wrapped, secure them with cocktail sticks before you grill them. Remove the cocktail sticks before serving.

Falafel with Minty Yoghurt Dressing ❉

MAKES 4–6 CHILD PORTIONS
(12 FALAFELS IN TOTAL)

1 tablespoon olive oil
1 small onion, finely chopped
1 small garlic clove, crushed
¼–½ teaspoon ground cumin
¼–½ teaspoon ground coriander
400 g/14 oz tin chickpeas,
    drained and rinsed
½ tablespoon chopped parsley
finely grated zest of 1 small
    unwaxed lemon
3 tablespoons hummus
1 tablespoon plain flour
3 tablespoons sunflower oil
    for frying
4–6 pitta breads or wraps,
    shredded lettuce, lemon
    wedges, to serve (optional)

Minty Yoghurt Dressing
6 tablespoons Greek yoghurt
1 teaspoon chopped fresh mint
    (10–12 leaves)
1 teaspoon lemon juice
a pinch of salt

The key to a healthy vegetarian diet is to eat a wide range of foods. Apart from a few foods like quinoa and tofu, most plant proteins are not complete and only by eating a variety of foods can you optimise your protein intake. Falafel are equally delicious cold so they are a good lunchbox option. Chickpeas are also a good source of vegetable protein.

• •

Heat the olive oil in a frying pan then add the onion and sauté for 8–10 minutes, until soft. Add the garlic, cumin and coriander and cook for a further 2 minutes.

Tip the chickpeas onto kitchen paper and rub them dry, then transfer them to a bowl, leaving behind as many of the papery skins as possible. Mash the chickpeas with a potato masher then stir in the onion mixture, parsley, lemon zest and hummus. Divide the mixture into 12 and squash it firmly into balls, then press each ball lightly to make small burger shapes. Dust with the flour and pat off any excess.

Fry the falafel in the sunflower oil for 1–1½ minutes each side, until golden. Drain on kitchen paper.

Mix together all the dressing ingredients in a bowl.

Toast and split the pittas, if using. Spread a tablespoon of the dressing in each pitta or wrap and add two or three falafel, and a little lettuce (if using). Serve with lemon wedges to squeeze over, if you like.

Turkey and Cucumber Wraps

MAKES 2 WRAPS

2 small tortilla wraps
2 tablespoons mayonnaise
2 teaspoons sweet chilli sauce
4 thin slices cooked turkey
8 thin cucumber matchsticks

★ You could swap the turkey for cooked chicken (perhaps leftovers from my Roast Chicken on page 126) or shredded roast duck.

Quick and easy to prepare, these wraps are a snack saviour. Turkey is a fantastic source of protein and zinc which is important for a healthy immune system. The mayonnaise and sweet chilli sauce gives the roll-ups a great flavour, too. If you want to try something different, swap the sweet chilli sauce for 1½ teaspoons of plum sauce.

· ·

Warm the tortilla wraps in the microwave for 20 seconds, then place them on a board.

Combine the mayonnaise and chilli sauce and spread the mixture over the wraps. Top each wrap with two turkey slices, put four strips of cucumber next to the turkey, then roll up the wraps so the cucumber is in the middle.

Slice each wrap into bite-sized pieces.

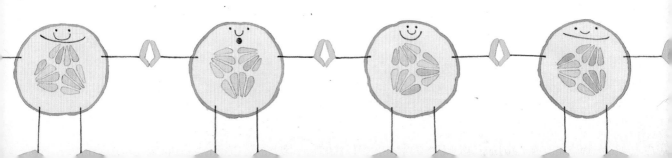

Kebabs

Sometimes the simplest ideas are the most effective in tempting little ones to eat well. Threading colourful bite-sized pieces of food onto a straw or skewer not only makes it fun for children, it offers them a wide variety of nutritious vegetables, too. (If using wooden skewers, remove them before serving to babies and young childen.)

• •

Chicken Kebabs

MAKES 4 KEBABS

100 g/4 oz cooked chicken breast,
    cut into 4 large bite-sized pieces
4 thin slices Gruyère cheese
4 cherry tomatoes
¼ cucumber, halved, deseeded and
    cut into 4 large chunks

You will also need: 4 plastic straws
    or wooden skewers

Thread a piece of chicken onto a straw. Add a slice of rolled up cheese, a cherry tomato and a chunk of cucumber. Repeat, threading the chicken, cheese, tomato and cucumber onto the remaining straws.

Salad Kebabs

MAKES 4 KEBABS

1 Little Gem lettuce, cut into bite-sized pieces
½ sweet red pepper, deseeded and
    cut into 2cm chunks
¼ cucumber, halved, deseeded and
    cut into 2cm chunks
8 cherry tomatoes

Creamy Dressing
2 tablespoons rice wine vinegar
1 tablespoon apple juice
100 ml/4 fl oz light olive oil
2 tablespoons mayonnaise
1 tablespoon cold water
1 tablespoon grated Parmesan cheese

You will also need: 4 plastic straws
    or wooden skewers

Thread a piece of lettuce onto a straw then add a piece of pepper, cucumber and a cherry tomato. Repeat so you have two pieces of each vegetable on the kebab, then thread the remaining vegetables onto the remaining three straws.

Whisk the dressing ingredients in a bowl and drizzle the dressing over the kebabs.

Serve as a snack with fruit and yoghurt, or in a wrap or sandwich for lunch.

Arancini ❄

MAKES 12–15 BALLS
10 g/¼ oz butter
1 shallot, finely chopped
1 small garlic clove, crushed
100 g/4 oz risotto rice
250 ml/9 fl oz unsalted
   or weak chicken stock
25 g/1 oz grated Parmesan cheese
5 tablespoons plain flour
1 egg, beaten
60 g/2½ oz dried or Panko
   breadcrumbs
sunflower oil for deep frying

Quick Tomato Sauce
olive oil
1 shallot, finely diced
1 garlic clove, crushed
400 g/14 oz tin chopped tomatoes
½ teaspoon soft light brown sugar
1 tablespoon tomato ketchup
a little salt and pepper (for
   babies over 12 months old)

These are perfect finger food. The soft middle and crispy breadcrumb coating makes them a great way to introduce different textures.

• •

Melt the butter in a saucepan, add the shallot and sauté for a few minutes until softened, then add the garlic and rice and stir for 1 minute. Add the stock, bring to the boil and stir. Cover and simmer for 15–20 minutes until the rice is just cooked and the stock has been absorbed.

Remove from the heat. Stir in the Parmesan and transfer the risotto to a plate to cool. Once cool, cover and chill in the fridge for 1 hour.

Heat a little oil for the tomato sauce in a large frying pan, add the shallot and garlic and sauté for 2 minutes. Add the remaining sauce ingredients and bring to the boil, then simmer for 15 minutes, stirring occasionally, until thickened. Season to taste (if using).

Place the flour, beaten egg and breadcrumbs in three separate bowls. Shape the cold risotto into 12–15 balls and coat the balls one at a time, first in the flour, then the egg and finally rolling them in the breadcrumbs.

Heat some sunflower oil in a deep-sided frying pan until hot. Fry the balls for about 3 minutes, in batches of 3–4 at a time, until golden and hot through, then drain on kitchen paper and serve.

Speedy Crostini

MAKES 12–15 CROSTINI

1 small part-baked baguette

1 tablespoon olive oil

6 tablespoons chopped
  fresh tomatoes

1½ tablespoons sun-dried
  tomato paste

5 basil leaves, chopped

10 cherry tomatoes, sliced

40 g/1½ oz grated Cheddar
  cheese

a little salt and pepper (for
  babies over 12 months old)

Who doesn't love crostini? This simple classic is easy to make at home and sure to be a hit. Why not get your child involved in adding the fresh cherry and basil topping.

• •

Preheat the oven to 180°C/350°F/Gas 4 and line a baking sheet with baking parchment.

Remove the ends of the baguette and cut it into roughly 1.5 cm /¾ in slices, then brush the slices with olive oil and place them on the baking sheet. Bake for 10 minutes until lightly golden and crisp.

Mix the tomatoes, sundried tomato paste and some seasoning (if using) together in a bowl. Spoon the mixture on top of the baked bread slices and arrange the basil, cherry tomatoes and cheese on top. Bake for 10–12 minutes until golden and the cheese has melted.

Topping Variations

Avocado and tomato: Mash 1 ripe avocado on the toasted baguette slices and top with chopped cherry tomatoes.

Chicken and pesto: Combine 1 chopped chicken breast with 2 tablespoons of mayonnaise and 1 teaspoon of pesto and spread over the baguette slices.

Salmon and cream cheese: Spread cream cheese on the baguette slices and top with strips of smoked salmon.

Vegetables

Cauliflower in Panko Breadcrumbs

1 large cauliflower, cut into florets
50 g/2 oz plain flour
2 eggs, beaten
2 tablespoons milk
75 g/3 oz dried or Panko
    breadcrumbs
30 g/1 oz finely grated
    Parmesan cheese
1 tablespoon chopped fresh thyme
    (optional)
a little salt and pepper (for
    babies over 12 months old)

Roasted cauliflower florets with a crisp cheesy coating is an irresistible melt-in-the-mouth combination. Sometimes, the key to encouraging a child to accept certain foods is about preparing them in different ways. For example, a lot of kids I know wouldn't eat boiled cauliflower, but roasting it changes everything!

Preheat the oven to 200°C/400°F/Gas 6 and line a baking sheet with baking parchment.

Put the flour in a large plastic bag and add some seasoning (if using). Add the cauliflower florets and shake to coat them in the seasoned flour.

Beat the eggs and milk together in a bowl, and put the breadcrumbs, cheese and thyme (if using) in another plastic bag, shaking the bag to combine the ingredients. Remove the cauliflower florets from the bag and dip them into the egg. Add the cauliflower to the bag of breadcrumbs and shake to coat in the crumbs.

Place the cauliflower florets on the lined baking sheet and roast for 25–30 minutes, until golden and crisp. Remove from the oven and serve straight away. I like to serve them with fish goujons (see my Krispie Fish Fingers recipe on page 147), chicken fingers, mini meatballs, chicken balls or salmon balls (see my Salmon, Quinoa and Spinach Balls recipe on page 158).

Green Macaroni ❄

130 g/4½ oz macaroni pasta
15 g/½ oz butter
15 g/½ oz plain flour
300 ml/10 fl oz milk, warmed
½ teaspoon Dijon mustard
50 g/2 oz grated mature
   Cheddar cheese
50 g/2 oz fresh spinach,
   finely chopped

Fussiness often strikes when it comes to serving up anything green. However, my special green macaroni always wins over the 'that's yucky' brigade.

Cook the macaroni according to the packet instructions, then drain.

Melt the butter in a saucepan. Add the flour and stir over the heat for 1 minute, then gradually add the milk, whisking constantly, until you have a smooth, thick sauce. Remove from the heat, add the mustard, cheese and spinach and stir until the cheese has melted.

Add the cooked macaroni and stir until heated through. Serve with salad or cucumber and carrot sticks.

Parmesan Roasted Sweet Potato Wedges

MAKES 4 CHILD PORTIONS
800 g/1 lb 8 oz sweet potatoes,
   scrubbed and cut into thick
   wedges or chips
2 tablespoons olive oil
1 tablespoon cornflour
2 tablespoons finely grated
   Parmesan cheese
3 large sage leaves, chopped
   (optional)
a little salt and pepper (for
   babies over 12 months old)

Babies love the flavour of these baked sweet potato batons coated with Parmesan and sage. Roasting sweet potato intensifies the natural sweetness. Make sure they are cut large enough for a child to hold easily in their fist so that one end sticks out. This recipe can be lightly seasoned.

• •

Preheat the oven to 200°C/400°F/Gas 6.

Place the sweet potato wedges or chips on a baking tray. Add the oil and cornflour and toss together. Season with salt and pepper (if using).

Roast for 20 minutes, turning them over after 15 minutes. Add the Parmesan and sage (if using) and put them back in the oven for 3–4 minutes until the cheese has melted.

I like to serve these with fish goujons (see my Krispie Fish Fingers recipe on page 147), chicken fingers, mini meatballs, chicken balls or salmon balls (see my Salmon, Quinoa and Spinach Balls recipe on page 158).

Lentil Dahl ❄

MAKES 6 CHILD PORTIONS

2 tablespoons sunflower oil
1 large onion, chopped
3 small carrots, peeled and diced
1 sweet red pepper, deseeded
   and diced
3 garlic cloves, crushed
a pinch of dried chilli flakes
2 teaspoons mild curry paste
2 teaspoons garam masala
100 g/4 oz yellow split peas
750 ml/1¼ pints unsalted
   or weak vegetable stock
50 g/2 oz frozen peas
2 tablespoons crème fraîche
squeeze of lemon

It's important to introduce a world of flavour to your baby early on, so this recipe is the perfect introduction to curry and mild spice. Lentils are also a good source of protein, iron and fibre, all of which are important for your baby's development. It's quite thick and sticks to the spoon which is helpful when a baby's aim isn't always perfect first time!

• •

Heat the oil in a saucepan, add the onion, carrot and pepper and fry for 2–3 minutes until softened. Add the garlic, chilli flakes, curry paste and garam masala. Stir-fry for 30 seconds, then add the split peas and stock.

Cover with a lid and bring to the boil, then reduce the heat and simmer for 1 hour, or until the lentils are soft. Add the peas, crème fraîche and lemon juice, stir and simmer for 4 minutes.

Remove from the heat and serve with vegetable sticks and pitta bread, and perhaps some salad.

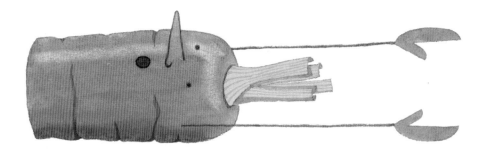

Kale and Root Veg Mash ❄

MAKES 6 CHILD PORTIONS

2 teaspoons sunflower oil
100 g/4 oz onions, chopped
150 g/5 oz carrots, peeled
    and diced
200 g/7 oz potato, peeled
    and diced
30 g/1 oz celery, finely chopped
50 g/2 oz parsnip, peeled
    and diced
350 ml/12 fl oz unsalted or
    weak vegetable stock
2 teaspoons chopped fresh thyme
    (or ¼ teaspoon dried thyme)
40 g/1½ oz trimmed kale,
    roughly chopped

Kale is a culinary superhero, full of essential vitamins and minerals like iron and potassium. A good starting point with leafy greens is to combine them with sweet root veggies or a cheese sauce.

Heat the oil in a saucepan, add the onion, carrot, potato, celery and parsnip. Cook, stirring, for 2–3 minutes, until softened, then add the stock and thyme. Cover with a lid, bring to the boil, then lower the heat and simmer for 15 minutes.

Add the kale and simmer for a further 5 minutes. Remove from the heat and mash it.

I like to serve the mash with Chicken and Sweetcorn Croquettes (see page 134), Swedish Meatballs (see page 175) or Chicken and Kale Balls (see page 113).

My Quinoa Salad

MAKES 6 CHILD PORTIONS

250 g/9 oz cooked red and
   white quinoa (or 150 g/
   5 oz dried quinoa)
198 g/7 oz tin sweetcorn, drained
½ sweet red pepper, deseeded
   and diced
4 spring onions, finely sliced
4 tablespoons chopped cashew
   nuts (optional)
30 g/1 oz sultanas or raisins
freshly chopped parsley, to
   garnish
a little salt and pepper (for
   babies over 12 months old)

Dressing
2 tablespoons balsamic vinegar
½ garlic clove, crushed
a pinch of sugar
6 tablespoons light olive oil

If using dried quinoa, rinse it in a sieve under cold running water before following the instructions on the packet. Once it is cooked and all the water has been absorbed, remove from the heat and leave uncovered for about 5 minutes, then fluff up the quinoa with a fork.

• •

Add the remaining ingredients to the quinoa and season with salt and pepper (if using).

Mix all of the dressing ingredients together in a bowl, pour it over the salad and mix to combine.

Chill for 30 minutes then garnish with parsley to serve.

I like to serve this salad with my Sweetcorn Fritters (see page 72) or Grilled Vegetable Kebabs (see page 79).

Tomato and Vegetable Soup with Orzo Pasta ❄

MAKES 6 CHILD PORTIONS

1 tablespoon olive oil
100 g/4 oz carrots, peeled
  and diced
150 g/5 oz butternut squash,
  peeled and diced
1 onion, chopped
1 garlic clove, crushed
1 tablespoon tomato puree
400 g/14 oz tin chopped tomatoes
500 ml/18 fl oz unsalted or
  weak vegetable stock
2–3 tablespoons apple juice
3 tablespoons double cream
50 g/2 oz orzo pasta
a little salt and pepper (for
  babies over 12 months old)

This is a delicious way to disguise veggies! The orzo (rice-shaped pasta) adds texture to the tasty tomato soup while also remaining nice and soft, so easy for your baby to chew.

● ●

Heat the oil in a saucepan. Add the carrot, squash and onion and fry for 3–4 minutes, then add the garlic and fry for 30 seconds.

Add the tomato puree, chopped tomatoes, stock and apple juice. Cover with a lid, bring to the boil and simmer for 15 minutes or until all the vegetables are tender. Remove from the heat and blend until smooth using a stick blender. Add the cream and salt and pepper (if using).

Cook the orzo according to the packet instructions until al dente. Drain and sprinkle it on top of the soup to serve.

Serve with salad and fresh bread.

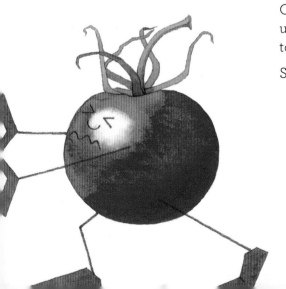

Fusillli with Spinach and Spring Vegetables

MAKES 4 CHILD PORTIONS
100 g/4 oz mini fusilli pasta
50 g/2 oz broccoli florets
1 tablespoon olive oil
½ onion, finely chopped
100 g/4 oz courgette, diced
50 g/2 oz sweet red pepper,
   deseeded and diced
1 garlic clove, crushed
50 g/2 oz baby spinach, chopped
100 ml/4 fl oz unsalted or weak
   vegetable stock
3 tablespoons double cream
25 g/1 oz grated Parmesan cheese
1 tablespoon chopped basil
a little salt and pepper (for
   babies over 12 months old)

This simple dish is brimming with veggies and will help towards your family's 5-a-day! If you are bringing up your baby on a vegetarian diet, check the Parmesan you use is made with animal-free rennet. Alternatively, choose another Italian-style hard cheese without animal rennet.

● ●

Cook the pasta according to the packet instructions. Add the broccoli florets for the last 2 minutes of cooking time and drain.

Heat the oil in a frying pan. Add the onion, courgette, pepper and garlic and fry for 3–4 minutes. Add the spinach, cooked pasta and broccoli and toss together. Add the stock and cream, bring to the boil, then remove from the heat.

Add the Parmesan and gently fold it through. Sprinkle with the chopped basil to serve and season to taste (if using).

Thai Rice Veggie Wraps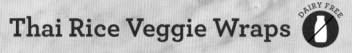

MAKES 6 WRAPS

6 Thai rice paper wraps

2 x 2 cm/¾ in lengths
   of cucumber, finely
   sliced lengthways

2 x 2 cm/¾ in lengths of peeled
   carrot, finely sliced lengthways

¼ sweet red pepper, finely
   sliced lengthways into
   2 cm/¾ in strips

1 spring onion, cut into
   2 cm/¾ in lengths and
   finely sliced lengthways

½ small tub mustard cress

Dip

½ teaspoon fish sauce

2 teaspoons sweet chilli sauce

1 tablespoon sunflower oil

2 teaspoons rice wine vinegar

¼ teaspoon grated fresh
   root ginger

Don't be afraid to try out new tastes on your child.
These rice paper wraps are full of crunchy veggies
and the dipping sauce is a fantastic introduction
to Thai-style flavours. Rice paper wraps are
available in most large supermarkets.

Soak the wraps in warm water for a few seconds,
one at a time, then place them on a dry plate.

Arrange a mixture of sliced vegetables and mustard
cress in the middle of one of the wraps. Carefully
fold in the sides and roll up the wraps to make a neat
package. Repeat with the remaining five wraps.

Combine all of the dip ingredients in a small bowl
and mix well.

Cheese and Cherry Tomato Muffins ❄

MAKES 12 MUFFINS
225 g/8 oz self-raising flour
1 teaspoon baking powder
1 tablespoon snipped chives
5 spring onions, finely sliced
70 g/2¾ oz grated mature
   Cheddar cheese
40 g/1½ oz grated
   Parmesan cheese
30 g/1 oz feta cheese, crumbled
1 large egg
200 ml/7 fl oz buttermilk
75 ml/3 fl oz sunflower oil
10 cherry tomatoes,
   roughly chopped
freshly ground black pepper

This is a fantastic quick and easy savoury muffin recipe, great for a snack on the go or a delicious lunch. Cheese is a good source of calcium, protein and vitamins A, D and B12.

Preheat the oven to 160°C/325°F/Gas 3 and line a 12-hole muffin tray with paper cases.

Sift the flour and baking powder into a bowl and add the chives, spring onion and cheeses. Season with a little pepper.

Mix the egg, buttermilk and oil together in a jug.

Add the wet ingredients to the bowl of dry ingredients and gently mix.

Divide the muffin mixture evenly between the paper cases, top with the chopped tomatoes and bake for 25–30 minutes until well risen and lightly golden.

Remove from the oven and transfer the muffins in their paper cases to a wire rack to cool (they will deflate slightly). Store in an airtight container for up to 2 days.

Sweetcorn Fritters

MAKES ABOUT
20 SMALL FRITTERS
198 g/7 oz tin sweetcorn, drained
100 g/4 oz wholemeal flour
1 teaspoon baking powder
2 large eggs
3 tablespoons sweet chilli sauce
4 spring onions, roughly chopped
handful of basil, chopped
10 cherry tomatoes,
    roughly chopped
100 g/4 oz grated halloumi cheese
sunflower oil for frying
a little salt and pepper (for
    babies over 12 months old)

★ These are best served straight
away but you can save half the
batter and keep it in the fridge
to cook the next day.

Fritters are a firm family favourite and a great way to
encourage kids to eat their veggies. Halloumi cheese
has a very high melting point so it works well in a
fritter. The fresh basil and sweet chilli sauce gives
these a delicious flavour.

Blend 100 g/4 oz of the sweetcorn in the bowl of
a food processor, or in a mixing bowl with a stick
blender, until finely chopped.

Combine the flour, baking powder and eggs in
a bowl. Whisk in the sweet chilli sauce and finely
chopped sweetcorn. Add the remaining ingredients
including the remaining whole, unblended
sweetcorn kernels. Season to taste (if using).

Heat a little oil in a frying pan. When hot, fry heaped
tablespoonfuls of the fritter mixture for 1–2 minutes on
each side until golden and cooked through. Transfer
to kitchen paper, fry the remaining batter, then serve
with salad, such as My Quinoa Salad on page 65.

Curried Vegetable Fritters

**MAKES ABOUT
20 SMALL FRITTERS**

200 g/7 oz sweet potato,
   coarsely grated
175 g/6 oz carrot, peeled
   and coarsely grated
4 spring onions, chopped
8 tablespoons cooked quinoa
1 tablespoon chopped coriander
2 eggs, beaten
6 tablespoons plain flour
1 tablespoon korma curry powder
sunflower oil for frying
a little salt and pepper (for
   babies over 12 months old)

These fritters are so easy to make and are very moreish. The korma curry powder adds a lovely mild, spicy flavour.

• •

Combine the grated sweet potato and carrot in a bowl with the spring onion, quinoa and coriander and season with salt and pepper (if using). Add the eggs, then add the flour and curry powder and mix together until combined.

Heat a little oil in a frying pan. When hot, fry heaped tablespoonfuls of the mixture for 2 minutes on each side, flattening the mixture down with a palette knife, until each side until golden.

Transfer to kitchen paper, fry the remaining batter, then serve with a salad, such as My Quinoa Salad (see page 65), or Sweet Dijon Chicken Kebabs (see page 112).

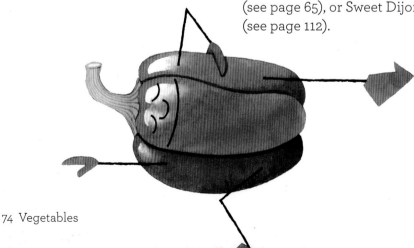

Hidden Vegetable Frittata

MAKES 6 CHILD PORTIONS
175 g/6 oz courgettes,
    topped, tailed, and diced
60 g/2½ oz sweet red pepper,
    deseeded and diced
100 g/4 oz broccoli, chopped
    (including trimmed stalks)
4 spring onions, sliced
5 large eggs
4 tablespoons milk
40 g/1½ oz grated Parmesan
    cheese
1 tablespoon chopped fresh basil
a knob of butter
2 tablespoons sunflower oil
a little salt and pepper (for
    babies over 12 months old)

Eggs form the base of this family-friendly frittata, making it an excellent source of protein, iron and zinc. Packed full of colourful veggies, my children (now all grown up) used to love – and still love – this frittata. As well as adding bags of flavour, the Parmesan seasons the dish.

• •

Put all the vegetables in the bowl of a food processor and blitz until finely chopped.

Mix the eggs, milk, Parmesan, basil, and a little salt and pepper (if using) together in a large bowl.

Add the finely chopped vegetables to the egg mixture and stir to combine.

Preheat the grill to high.

Melt the butter and oil in a medium frying pan. Once the butter starts to foam, add the frittata mixture. Cook, without stirring, until the egg starts to set around the edges, then transfer the pan to the grill. Grill for 8–10 minutes until the frittata is set in the middle.

Slide the frittata onto a plate and cut it into wedges. Serve with halved cherry tomatoes and cucumber sticks.

Kale and Tomato Omelette

30 g/1 oz trimmed kale,
   roughly chopped
a knob of butter
3 spring onions, sliced
3 large eggs
2 tablespoons milk
2 tomatoes, diced
2 tablespoons grated
   Parmesan cheese

The combination of eggs, kale and tomatoes in this omelette packs a nutritious punch, and it works well as a breakfast, lunch or light dinner.

Blanch the kale in boiling water for 4 minutes, then drain and refresh under cold running water. Drain and squeeze out the water.

Heat a non-stick omelette pan or small frying pan until hot. Add the butter and, as soon as it starts to foam, add the spring onions and blanched kale and fry for 2 minutes.

Beat the eggs and milk together, then add them to the pan. Stir until the mixture is set underneath. Sprinkle with the tomatoes and cheese, cook for about 1 minute, then fold in half.

Cook for a further 3–4 minutes, until the inside is cooked through and the outside is lightly golden.

Remove from the pan and cut into 4 pieces. Serve straight away.

Aubergine Pasta ❄

MAKES 6 CHILD PORTIONS
250 g/9 oz fusilli pasta
2 tablespoons sunflower oil
1 red onion, chopped
2 garlic cloves, crushed
1 red chilli, deseeded and diced
    (optional)
1 aubergine, cubed
400 g/14 oz tin chopped tomatoes
1 tablespoon tomato puree
200 ml/7 fl oz unsalted or weak
    vegetable stock
a pinch of sugar
a handful of fresh basil, chopped
50 g/2 oz grated Parmesan cheese

Aubergines are rich in antioxidants and are a great source of dietary fibre. With a hint of chilli and a sprinkling of Parmesan this pasta dish is comfort food at its best.

• •

Cook the pasta according to the packet instructions, then drain.

While the pasta is cooking, heat the oil in a frying pan, add the onion, garlic and chilli (if using) and fry for 2–3 minutes until the onion and garlic have softened. Add the aubergine and fry over a high heat for a further 4–5 minutes, then add the chopped tomatoes, tomato puree and stock. Simmer for 5 minutes.

Remove the pan from the heat and add the cooked pasta along with the basil and Parmesan, and toss together. Serve with cucumber and carrot sticks.

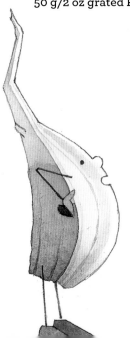

Grilled Vegetable Kebabs

DAIRY FREE

MAKES 4 KEBABS

1 garlic clove, crushed

½ teaspoon soy sauce

½ teaspoon maple syrup

2 teaspoons chopped fresh thyme

1 tablespoon light olive oil, plus extra for greasing

8 small cauliflower florets

8 cherry tomatoes

4 baby courgettes, each cut into 4 pieces

½ sweet red pepper, deseeded and cut into 8 pieces

8 button mushrooms

You will also need: 4 wooden skewers, soaked in warm water for 30 minutes

The trick to making these kebabs super-tasty is my marinade. Using a little soy, thyme and maple syrup makes them sweet, sticky and succulent.

Preheat the grill to high. Line a baking sheet with foil and lightly grease it with oil.

Combine the garlic, soy sauce, maple syrup, thyme and oil in a bowl. Add the vegetables and coat them in the marinade then set aside to marinate for 5 minutes.

Thread the vegetables onto the soaked skewers and arrange them on the baking sheet. Place under the grill for 5 minutes on each side until lightly golden and cooked through. Remove from the grill and leave to cool slightly before serving, removing the skewers for smaller children.

Tasty Veggie Burrito

MAKES 1 BURRITO
(2 CHILD PORTIONS)

1 soft tortilla wrap (about
   20 cm/8 in diameter)

1 egg

15 g/½ oz butter

½ red onion, finely chopped

½ sweet red pepper, deseeded
   and diced

leaves from 1 sprig of thyme

a pinch of paprika

1 tomato, deseeded and diced

2–3 drops of Tabasco sauce
   (optional)

25 g/1 oz grated Cheddar cheese

1 tablespoon sour cream, to serve
   (optional)

a little salt and pepper (for
   babies over 12 months old)

★ If you prefer, cut the omelette
into little strips and mix it in
with the cooked onion and red
pepper mixture.

It's good to get together at mealtimes, and my
veggie-packed burritos can easily be doubled in
quantity to serve the whole family: simply make two
separate omelettes and double the filling quantities.

· ·

Put the tortilla wrap on a large plate. Beat the egg
with 1 teaspoon of water and a little salt and pepper.

Heat half of the butter in a 20 cm/8 in non-stick frying
pan. Add the egg and tilt the pan to help the egg
spread out and make a thin omelette. Cook for
2–3 minutes, until the omelette has set, then slide
it onto the tortilla.

Heat the remaining butter in the frying pan and, once
it starts to foam, add the onion, red pepper, thyme and
paprika and sauté for 5 minutes, until the onion and
pepper are soft. Add the tomato and cook for a further
2 minutes, until the tomato is soft.

Add the Tabasco sauce (if using) and season with
salt and pepper (if using). Remove from the heat
and set aside for a moment.

Heat the tortilla and omelette for 10–20 seconds
in a microwave, spoon the pepper and onion mixture
over the centre, sprinkle over the cheese and roll
it up. Serve immediately with a spoonful of sour
cream, if you like.

Veggie Balls ❄

MAKES 15 VEGGIE BALLS
1 large white potato
  (about 440 g/15 oz)
40 g/1½ oz dried or Panko
  breadcrumbs
50 g/2 oz carrot, grated
4 spring onions, chopped
50 g/2 oz brown mushrooms,
  chopped
40 g/1½ oz grated Parmesan
  cheese
1 tablespoon chopped fresh basil
1 teaspoon chopped fresh thyme
2 teaspoons soy sauce
1 teaspoon sweet chilli sauce
1–2 tablespoons plain flour
2 tablespoons sunflower oil
a little salt and pepper (for
  babies over 12 months old)

These little balls are a fantastic way to pack in veggies and are ideal finger food. They are also ideal for batch-cooking and freezing, in readiness for those busy days. Just pop them in a plastic freezer box, separating each layer with greaseproof paper, and reheat from frozen in the oven or microwave.

Prick the potato and bake it in the microwave for 7–10 minutes until soft. Leave to cool, then cut it in half and scoop out the flesh – you will need 250 g/9 oz potato.

Put the cool potato and remaining ingredients (except the flour and the oil) in the bowl of a food processor and blitz until chopped. Transfer the mixture to a bowl, season lightly with salt and pepper (if using) and shape it into 15 equal-sized balls.

Place the flour in a bowl and lightly coat the balls in flour. Transfer them to plate and chill for 15 minutes.

Heat the oil in a frying pan until hot. Fry the balls for about 2 minutes until golden all over and heated through. Serve with cucumber sticks and halved cherry tomatoes, or a mayonnaise dip with sweet chilli sauce.

Rice and Vegetable Croquettes

MAKES 12 CROQUETTES
150 g/5 oz cold cooked white
    or brown rice
50 g/2 oz carrot, peeled
    and grated
25 g/1 oz sweet red pepper,
    deseeded and finely diced
25 g/1 oz courgette, grated
5 spring onions, chopped
30 g/1 oz grated Parmesan cheese
1 small egg, beaten
20 g/¾ oz dried or Panko
    breadcrumbs, plus extra
    for dusting
2 teaspoons sweet chilli sauce
1 tablespoon chopped fresh basil
1 teaspoon soy sauce
2 tablespoons light olive oil
a little salt and pepper (for
    babies over 12 months old)

These croquettes can be made with leftover rice and are a great way to ensure your little one gets their five-a-day.

• •

Put the rice, carrot, pepper, courgette, spring onion and Parmesan in the bowl of a food processor and blitz until roughly chopped. Add the egg and breadcrumbs, sweet chilli sauce, basil and soy sauce. Blitz again until finely chopped.

Transfer the mixture to a bowl, season lightly with salt and pepper (if using) and shape into 12 equal-sized croquettes. Place some extra breadcrumbs on a large plate and coat the croquettes with the breadcrumbs. Chill the croquettes if you have time, to help them keep their shape (this is not essential).

Heat the oil in a frying pan until hot. Fry the croquettes for 2 minutes on each side until lightly golden and crisp, and heated through. Serve with a chopped salad or crudités with a dip (see page 41 for dip ideas).

Roasted Veg Ratatouille

MAKES 4–6 CHILD PORTIONS

½ eating apple, peeled, cored and diced
1 large courgette, topped, tailed and diced
1 sweet red pepper, deseeded and diced
2 tablespoons olive oil
1 red onion, chopped
1 garlic clove, crushed
400 g/14 oz tin chopped tomatoes
2 teaspoons tomato puree
½ teaspoon maple syrup
1 tablespoon chopped fresh basil (optional)
a little salt and pepper (for babies over 12 months old)

Roasting vegetables intensifies their natural sweetness and this is a delicious way to get your baby loving those veggies.

•••••••••••••••••••••••••••••••••••••

Preheat the oven to 180°C/350°F/Gas 4.

Put the apple, courgette and pepper in a roasting tin, drizzle with half the oil and toss together. Roast for 15 minutes.

Meanwhile, heat the remaining oil in a saucepan, add the onion and garlic and fry for 2 minutes until softened. Add the tomatoes, tomato puree, 100 ml/ 4 fl oz water and the maple syrup and bring to the boil. Add the roasted vegetables, cover and simmer for 15 minutes until reduced and softened.

Remove from the heat, season with salt and pepper (if using) and add the basil to serve, if you wish.

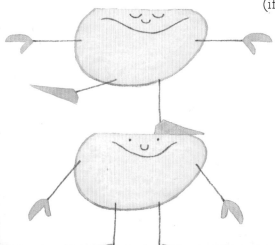

Squash, Spinach and Ricotta Risotto

MAKES 4 CHILD PORTIONS

200 g/7 oz peeled butternut
    squash, cut into small cubes
½ tablespoon chopped fresh
    thyme
2 tablespoons olive oil
1 onion, finely diced
1 garlic clove, crushed
100 g/4 oz risotto rice
2 teaspoons white wine vinegar
400 ml/14 fl oz unsalted or weak
    hot vegetable stock
50 g/2 oz spinach, chopped
a pinch of grated nutmeg
25 g/1 oz grated Parmesan cheese
1 tablespoon ricotta cheese
a little salt and pepper (for
    babies over 12 months old)

Combining cooked rice and vegetables make a soft meal, and is a good way to introduce texture to your baby's food. Butternut squash is rich in vitamin A, calcium, and potassium, and its natural sweetness paired with creamy ricotta and fresh thyme is a match made in heaven.

• •

Preheat the oven to 200°C/400°F/Gas 6.

Toss the squash with the thyme and 1 tablespoon of the oil in a roasting tin and roast it for 20 minutes, or until soft and golden.

Heat the rest of the oil in a saucepan, add the onion and fry for 5 minutes until softened, then add the garlic and fry for 30 seconds. Add the rice and stir to coat it in the oil, then add the vinegar and stir for 10 seconds. Add the stock, bring to the boil, cover with a lid and simmer gently for 15 minutes until the rice is just cooked and all the stock has been absorbed.

Add the spinach, nutmeg, ricotta, cheeses and roasted squash to the pan while it's still over the heat. Lightly season with salt and pepper (if using) and stir until the spinach has wilted.

Serve straight away with steamed vegetables, such as broccoli florets.

Scrummy Rice with Butternut Squash

MAKES 4 CHILD PORTIONS

25 g/1 oz butter
50 g/2 oz onion, finely chopped
1 garlic clove, crushed
100 g/4 oz basmati rice
450 ml/16 fl oz boiling water
150 g/5 oz peeled butternut
    squash, cubed
3 ripe tomatoes (about 225 g/
    8 oz), skinned, deseeded
    and chopped
50 g/2 oz grated Cheddar cheese
1 tablespoon chopped fresh basil

A simple but delicious rice dish with butternut squash and a fresh tomato and cheese sauce.

● ●

Heat half the butter in a saucepan, add the onion and sauté for 3–4 minutes until softened, then add the garlic and cook for a further 30 seconds. Add the rice and stir to coat it in the butter. Pour over the boiling water, cover with a lid and cook for 8 minutes over a high heat. Stir in the chopped butternut squash, reduce the heat and cook, covered, for a further 12 minutes or until all the water has been absorbed.

Meanwhile, melt the remaining butter in a small pan, add the chopped tomatoes and sauté for 2–3 minutes. Stir in the cheese until melted, then add the cheese and tomato mixture to the rice and stir it through.

Serve with steamed broccoli florets or Cauliflower in Panko Breadcrumbs (see page 58).

Pasta

Chicken Pasta Salad

MAKES 4 CHILD PORTIONS
150 g/5 oz edamame (soya beans)
200 g/7 oz cooked baby
   shell pasta
150 g/5 oz cherry tomatoes,
   quartered
150 g/5 oz drained tinned
   sweetcorn
150 g/5 oz cooked chicken
   breast, diced

Dressing
2 tablespoons rice wine vinegar
1 tablespoon runny honey
   or maple syrup
1 tablespoon soy sauce
4 tablespoons mild olive oil

This recipe is an all-round winner; babies love the bright colours and the size of the veg and mini pasta. This looks great in layers but for little ones it's best to mix the ingredients together and serve it in a child-safe bowl (not glass). Broccoli florets make a good alternative to the edamame, if you fancy switching the ingredients. Use maple syrup in the dressing instead of honey if serving to babies under 12 months old.

• •

Cook the edamame in a pan of boiling water for 5 minutes until tender. Drain and refresh under cold running water.

Layer the ingredients in jars or bowls, starting with the cooked pasta, followed by the tomatoes, sweetcorn, cooked edamame and, finally, the diced chicken.

Mix the dressing ingredients together in a small bowl or jug and serve it with the salad.

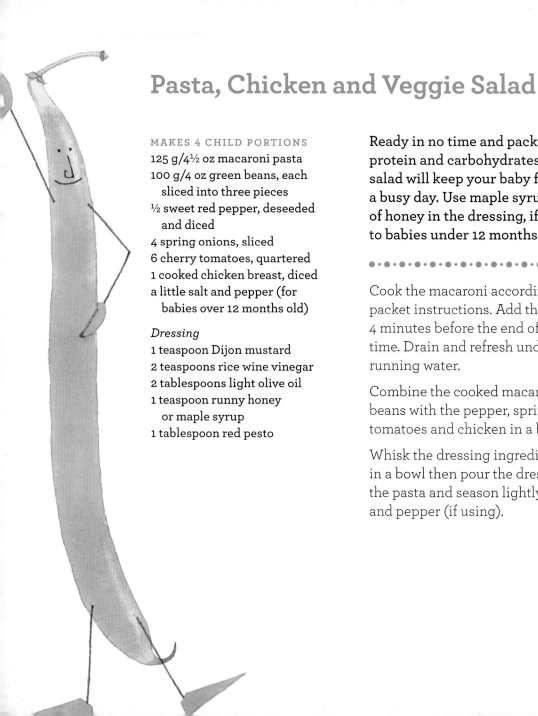

Pasta, Chicken and Veggie Salad

MAKES 4 CHILD PORTIONS

125 g/4½ oz macaroni pasta
100 g/4 oz green beans, each
  sliced into three pieces
½ sweet red pepper, deseeded
  and diced
4 spring onions, sliced
6 cherry tomatoes, quartered
1 cooked chicken breast, diced
a little salt and pepper (for
  babies over 12 months old)

Dressing
1 teaspoon Dijon mustard
2 teaspoons rice wine vinegar
2 tablespoons light olive oil
1 teaspoon runny honey
  or maple syrup
1 tablespoon red pesto

Ready in no time and packed with protein and carbohydrates, this salad will keep your baby fuelled for a busy day. Use maple syrup instead of honey in the dressing, if serving to babies under 12 months.

• •

Cook the macaroni according to the packet instructions. Add the beans 4 minutes before the end of the cooking time. Drain and refresh under cold running water.

Combine the cooked macaroni and beans with the pepper, spring onions, tomatoes and chicken in a bowl.

Whisk the dressing ingredients together in a bowl then pour the dressing over the pasta and season lightly with salt and pepper (if using).

Wholemeal Pasta with Ham and Broccoli

MAKES 4 CHILD PORTIONS
100 g/4 oz wholemeal fusilli
   pasta or other pasta shape
80 g/3 oz broccoli florets
70 g/2¾ oz thick ham, diced
50 g/2 oz mini mozzarella balls
6 cherry tomatoes, quartered
¼ cucumber, peeled and diced
a little salt and pepper (for
   babies over 12 months old)

Dressing
1½ tablespoons rice wine vinegar
3 tablespoons light olive oil
1 teaspoon soy sauce
1 teaspoon maple syrup

Wholemeal pasta is a good source of complex carbs; it's digested at a slower pace so helps sustain energy levels for longer. Little ones will also love the tasty ham and mini mozzarella balls in this dish. You could add diced Gruyère cheese instead of mozzarella if your child prefers it.

• •

Cook the pasta according to the packet instructions. Add the broccoli florets 3 minutes before the end of the cooking time. Drain and refresh under cold running water.

Mix the cooled, cooked pasta and broccoli in a serving bowl with the ham, mozzarella, tomatoes and cucumber.

Whisk the dressing ingredients together in a bowl then pour the dressing over the pasta. Season with a little salt and pepper (if using).

Hidden Vegetable Tomato Sauce

MAKES 4–5 CHILD PORTIONS

2 teaspoons rapeseed,
   sunflower or olive oil
75 g/3 oz carrot, peeled
   and chopped
50 g/2 oz courgette, topped,
   tailed and chopped
100 g/4 oz onion, chopped
½ apple, peeled, cored and diced
2 garlic cloves
600 g/1 lb 3 oz tinned chopped
   tomatoes (1½ x 400 g/14 oz cans)
1 tablespoon sun-dried
   tomato paste
1 tablespoon tomato puree
200 ml/7 fl oz unsalted or weak
   vegetable stock
100 ml/4 fl oz apple juice
1 tablespoon torn fresh
   basil leaves

Pasta with a tomato sauce is always a winner –
my secret ingredient is the apple, which brings
out a hint of sweetness in the tomato sauce and
takes away any acidity. I blend the ingredients here
for reluctant veggie eaters, as what they can't see,
they can't pick out. This also makes a great sauce
to go with my Swedish Meatballs or Chicken and
Kale Balls (see pages 175 and 113).

Heat the oil in a saucepan, add the vegetables, apple
and garlic and fry for about 4 minutes, until softened.
Add the tomatoes, stock and apple juice. Bring to the
boil, then reduce the heat and simmer for 20 minutes,
stirring occasionally, until the vegetables are tender.
Remove from the heat, add the basil and blitz until
smooth using a stick blender.

Serve with pasta.

Animal Pasta with Broccoli

MAKES 6 CHILD PORTIONS

- 100 g/4 oz animal pasta shapes (or letters or stars)
- 80 g/3 oz broccoli florets
- 1 tablespoon olive oil
- ½ large courgette, diced
- 1 garlic clove, peeled and crushed
- 4 ripe tomatoes, quartered
- 2 tablespoons tinned drained sweetcorn
- 10 g/¼ oz butter
- 30 g/1 oz grated Parmesan cheese

Sometimes it can be a challenge to get fussy eaters to eat anything other than pasta with a little butter and grated cheese, but if anything will persuade them to eat their veg, this simple recipe – with the addition of little broccoli 'trees' and colourful veggies – will.

Cook the pasta according to the packet instructions, adding the broccoli florets 3 minutes before the end of the cooking time. Reserve 6 tablespoons of the cooking water before draining the pasta.

Heat the oil in a small frying pan. Add the courgette and garlic and fry for 3 minutes, making sure the garlic doesn't burn, then add the tomatoes and sweetcorn. Add the pasta and broccoli and toss together. Add the reserved pasta cooking water, then remove the pan from the heat and set it aside for 3–4 minutes. Add the butter and cheese and gently mix through until melted.

Pasta with Tomato and Mascarpone Sauce ❄

1 tablespoon olive oil
1 red onion, chopped
30 g/1 oz carrot, peeled and diced
30 g/1 oz courgette, diced
15 g/½ oz celery stalk, diced
1 garlic clove, crushed
50 g/2 oz button mushrooms, chopped
400 g/14 oz passata (sieved tomatoes) or 400 g/14 oz tin chopped tomatoes
2 tablespoons apple juice
60 g/2½ oz mini pasta shells
2 tablespoons torn basil leaves (optional)
3 tablespoons mascarpone
3 tablespoons grated Parmesan cheese

★ If freezing, freeze the sauce separately, before you mix it with the pasta.

Five different vegetables are blended into this tasty tomato sauce. Passata is simply sieved tomatoes, and you can buy it in any supermarket, usually in jars. Mascarpone is good for babies as they need proportionately more fat in their diets than adults due to their rapid growth rate. If you don't have any, use double cream or full-fat cream cheese instead.

Heat the oil in a saucepan, add the onion, carrot, courgette and celery and sauté for 5 minutes. Add the garlic and sauté for a further minute, then add the mushrooms and sauté for 2 minutes. Stir in the passata or chopped tomatoes with the apple juice, cover and simmer for 10 minutes, stirring occasionally.

Meanwhile, cook the pasta shells according to the packet instructions, then drain.

Remove the tomato sauce from the heat, add the basil (if using), leave to cool slightly then blend in a food processor or in the pan with a stick blender. Return to the pan (if using the food processor) and stir in the mascarpone and Parmesan. Stir the sauce into the drained pasta and serve. This dish goes well with my Chicken and Kale Balls (see page 113).

Variation: Chicken, tomato and mascarpone sauce

To make a creamy tomato and chicken sauce, simply add 75 g/3 oz diced cooked chicken breast at the same time as the mushrooms.

Tomato, Sweet Potato and Cheese Sauce with Pasta Shells ❄

MAKES 4 CHILD PORTIONS

1 tablespoon olive oil

1 onion, chopped

1 garlic clove, chopped

225 g/8 oz sweet potatoes, peeled and chopped

2 medium carrots, peeled and sliced (about 125 g/4½ oz)

400 g/14 oz tin chopped tomatoes

200 ml/7 fl oz unsalted or weak vegetable stock, or water

100 g/4 oz organic mini shell pasta

60 g/2½ oz grated Cheddar cheese

★ If freezing, freeze the sauce separately, before you mix it with the pasta.

This delicious tomato sauce is enriched with vegetables. It is very versatile; you can mix it with pasta, as here, or combine it with cooked fish or chicken.

Heat the oil in a saucepan, add the onion and sauté for about 4 minutes until softened. Add the garlic and sauté for a minute, then stir in the sweet potato and carrot, followed by the chopped tomatoes and vegetable stock or water. Bring to the boil, stirring frequently, then cover the pan with a lid and simmer for about 30 minutes until the vegetables are tender.

Meanwhile, cook the pasta according to the packet instructions, then drain.

Once cooked, allow the sauce to cool slightly, then blend the sauce to a puree in a food processor, or in the pan with a stick blender, then stir in the cheese until melted. Mix the drained pasta with the sauce and serve.

I like to serve this with the Salmon, Quinoa and Spinach Balls (see page 158) or Salmon Rissoles (see page 160).

Mushroom and Spinach Pasta

60 g/2½ oz mini pasta shells
10 g/¼ oz butter
50 g/2 oz onion, finely diced
50 g/2 oz chestnut mushrooms,
   finely diced
1 garlic clove, crushed
10 g/¼ oz plain flour
250 ml/9 fl oz whole milk
¼ teaspoon chopped fresh thyme
30 g/1 oz grated Parmesan cheese
30 g/1 oz baby spinach,
   finely chopped

Mini pasta shells or orzo pasta are the perfect size to encourage little ones to chew. Mushrooms provide vitamin B, vitamin D, fibre and essential minerals like potassium – finely chopping them gives them a more appealing texture for babies.

Cook the pasta according to the packet instructions, then drain.

Melt the butter in a saucepan, add the onion, cover with a lid and sauté for 4 minutes, stirring every now and then, until softened. Add the mushrooms and fry for 3 minutes. Add the garlic and fry for 2 minutes. Add the flour and cook for 1 minute, then gradually add the milk, stirring for 1–2 minutes until thickened. Remove the pan from the heat, add the thyme, Parmesan and spinach and stir until wilted. Stir in the drained pasta and serve.

Baby Vegetable Pasta

MAKES 4 CHILD PORTIONS
50 g/2 oz mini shell pasta
10 g/¼ oz butter
50 g/2 oz onion, finely chopped
30 g/1½ oz carrot, peeled and
  finely diced
30 g/1½ oz sweet red pepper,
  deseeded and finely diced
30 g/1½ oz frozen sweetcorn
30 g/1½ oz frozen peas
10 g/ ¼ oz plain flour
250 ml/9 fl oz hot unsalted
  or weak vegetable stock
2 tablespoons chopped fresh basil
1 teaspoon lemon juice
30 g/1 oz grated Parmesan cheese

As your baby gets older it is important to encourage him to chew, so dice vegetables instead of pureeing them. Frozen peas and sweetcorn are always a good standby to keep in your freezer.

• •

Cook the pasta according to the packet instructions, then drain.

Melt the butter in a saucepan. Add the onion, carrot and pepper, cover with a lid and sauté for 10 minutes until nearly soft, then add the sweetcorn and peas and sauté for a further 2 minutes. Add the flour, cook for 1 minute, then gradually add the stock, stirring until thickened. Simmer for 3 minutes, then stir in the basil, lemon juice and Parmesan.

Stir in the drained pasta and serve.

Macaroni Cheese ❄

MAKES 4–5 CHILD PORTIONS
150 g/5 oz macaroni pasta
600 ml/1 pint whole milk
3 tablespoons cornflour
75 g/3 oz grated mature
   Cheddar cheese
75 g/3 oz grated Gruyère cheese
50 g/2½ oz grated Parmesan
   cheese
125 g/4½ oz mascarpone
¼ teaspoon Dijon mustard
a little salt and pepper (for
   babies over 12 months old)

Topping
25 g/1 oz fresh or dried
   breadcrumbs
20 g/¾ oz grated Parmesan
   cheese

This is my best-ever macaroni recipe made with three cheeses. Every generation will love this classic dish.

• •

Cook the macaroni according to the packet instructions, then drain and rinse under cold running water. Heat 500 ml/17 fl oz of the milk in a pan until it just reaches boiling point.

Mix the cornflour and the remaining 100 ml/4 fl oz milk together then whisk the mixture into the hot milk. Cook, whisking constantly, for about 2 minutes, until the sauce thickens and comes to the boil.

Remove from the heat and whisk in the grated cheeses until melted, followed by the mascarpone and Dijon mustard.

Stir in the cooked pasta and season to taste with salt and pepper (if using). Transfer to a baking dish. Mix together the breadcrumbs and Parmesan cheese and sprinkle them over the top and place under the grill until golden and bubbling.

Remove from the grill and serve with steamed vegetables, such as broccoli florets.

Poultry

Krispie Chicken Nuggets

2 tablespoons sunflower oil
45 g/1½ oz Rice Krispies
1 tablespoon finely grated
    mature Cheddar cheese
1 tablespoon grated
    Parmesan cheese
1 egg
1 tablespoon milk
4 tablespoons plain flour
200 g/7 oz skinless, boneless
    chicken breasts, cut into
    1.5 cm/½ in cubes
dips, to serve (optional)
a little salt and pepper (for
    babies over 12 months old)

★ Alternatively, you can fry the
Krispie chicken nuggets instead of
baking them. Put 3–4 tablespoons
of sunflower oil in a large pan over
a medium heat. Fry the nuggets for
2–3 minutes each side, until golden
and crisp. Drain on kitchen paper
and cool slightly before serving.

**It will be hard to go back to shop-bought nuggets after
you have tasted these.**

Preheat the oven to 200°C/400°F/Gas 6.

Place half the oil in the bowl of a food processor with
the Rice Krispies and grated cheeses and blitz to evenly
combine (you may need to stop and scrape the mixture
down from the sides of the bowl a couple of times).
Alternatively, crush them in a plastic bag with a rolling
pin. Transfer the Krispie mixture to a wide, shallow bowl
or a large plate. Whisk the egg in a small bowl with
the milk and mix the flour with a little salt and pepper
(if using) and spread it out on a large plate. Grease
a baking sheet with the remaining oil.

Toss the chicken cubes in the flour, dip them in
the egg, then coat them in the Krispie coating.
Lay them on the baking sheet and bake for 15 minutes,
or until cooked through and crispy, turning them
over halfway. Serve immediately, with dips
if you wish (mayonnaise, ketchup, or
one of my dip recipes on page 41).

Sweet Dijon Chicken Kebabs

MAKES 4 KEBABS

1 tablespoon runny honey
   or maple syrup
½ teaspoon Dijon mustard
½ small garlic clove, crushed
1 teaspoon olive oil
½ teaspoon lemon juice
4 chicken mini fillets (about
   110 g/4¼ oz total weight)
   or 1 small boneless, skinless
   chicken breast, sliced
   lengthways into 4 strips,
   or into 2 cm/¾ in cubes

You will also need: 4 wooden
   skewers, soaked in warm
   water for 30 minutes

I love honey mustard, and this was the inspiration for the marinade. You can use wholegrain mustard instead if your children like spicier foods, but I find it has a little too much heat for smaller children. Use maple syrup instead of honey if serving to babies under 12 months.

Combine the honey or maple syrup, mustard, garlic, olive oil and lemon juice in a small bowl. Add the chicken and toss to coat, then cover the bowl with clingfilm and leave to marinate in the fridge overnight.

Preheat the grill to high and line a grill pan or baking sheet with foil. Remove the chicken from the marinade and thread each piece onto a skewer. Lay the skewers on the foil and spoon over any marinade left in the bowl. Place under the grill for 3–4 minutes on each side, until the chicken has cooked through.

Remove from the grill and allow to cool slightly before serving. Remove the skewers for smaller children. Serve with cooked rice and steamed vegetables, such as broccoli florets.

Chicken and Kale Balls

MAKES 25 BALLS
(ABOUT 5 CHILD PORTIONS)

50 g/2 oz trimmed kale
100 g/4 oz fresh breadcrumbs
500 g/1 lb 1 oz skinless, boneless
  chicken thighs, chopped
100 g/4 oz carrots, peeled
  and grated
1½ teaspoons grated fresh
  root ginger
1 tablespoon sweet chilli sauce
1 teaspoon Chinese five spice
1 teaspoon soy sauce
4 tablespoons plain flour
3 tablespoons rapeseed,
  sunflower or light olive oil

Tip

★ To make your own fresh
breadcrumbs, simply blitz some
stale bread in a food processor.
You can store the breadcrumbs
in a sealed bag in the freezer –
they are great to have to hand
for coating goujons or arancini.

When my son Nicholas was little and very fussy,
my solution to encourage him to eat chicken was
to blitz it in a food processor with other ingredients
such as apple and form it into mini chicken balls.
This is a twist on my signature Chicken and Apple
Balls recipe in my *New Complete Baby & Toddler
Meal Planner*, but this time using carrot and kale
and adding some mild oriental flavours.

• •

Cook the kale in a pan of boiling water for 4 minutes,
then drain and refresh under cold running water.
Squeeze out the water and finely chop the kale.

Place the chicken thighs in the bowl of a food
processor with the breadcrumbs and blitz until
roughly chopped (you don't want it too fine).

Transfer to a bowl, add the chopped kale and the
remaining ingredients and stir to combine. Shape
the mixture into 25 equal-sized balls.

Place the flour on a large plate and roll each ball in
the flour. Heat the oil in a frying pan and fry the balls
for 8–10 minutes (in 2–3 batches) until golden and
cooked through.

Courgetti with Pesto, Tomato, Basil and Chicken

MAKES 4 CHILD PORTIONS

3 tablespoons olive oil

4 spring onions, finely sliced

2 garlic cloves, crushed

4 large tomatoes, skinned, deseeded and roughly chopped

2 tablespoons fresh green pesto

150 g/5 oz cooked chicken breast, finely diced

1 tablespoon chopped fresh basil leaves

2–3 large courgettes

30 g/1 oz finely grated Parmesan cheese

a little salt and pepper (for babies over 12 months old)

It only takes minutes to transform veggies into spaghetti using a spiraliser. I'm not usually one for kitchen gadgets, however this is one is essential for anyone with a reluctant veggie eater. It's so simple and works with other veggies too, such as sweet potato and carrot.

To make the sauce, heat 1 tablespoon of the oil in a saucepan, add the spring onions and fry for 2 minutes. Add the garlic and fry for 30 seconds, then add the tomatoes, stir, and simmer for 4 minutes until softened. Season lightly with salt and pepper (if using) and add the pesto, chicken and basil. Stir gently and simmer for 2 minutes, then remove from the heat.

Make the courgetti using a spiralizer to make long spaghetti shapes.

Heat a large frying pan until hot. Add the remaining oil and half the courgetti to the pan. Quickly fry for 2 minutes until just softened, then remove from the heat and add the remaining courgette. Toss together in a bowl.

Add the sauce and mix thoroughly. Sprinkle with the Parmesan and serve.

Chicken, Cherry Tomato and Sweetcorn Quesadillas

MAKES 4 QUESADILLAS
(6 CHILD PORTIONS)

2 tablespoons olive oil
1 boneless, skinless chicken
    breast, cut into strips
1 teaspoon runny honey
    or maple syrup
1 onion, finely sliced
1 teaspoon chopped fresh
    thyme leaves
100 g/4 oz fresh cherry
    tomatoes, chopped
50 g/2 oz tinned drained
    sweetcorn
1 teaspoon balsamic vinegar
50 g/2 oz grated Cheddar cheese
6 small tortilla wraps
yoghurt, for drizzling
a pinch of paprika (optional)

Quick to prepare, my quesadillas have instant child (and adult) appeal with a yummy chicken filling sandwiched between tortillas and topped with grated Cheddar cheese. Simply fry them on both sides until the cheese has melted. Use maple syrup instead of honey if serving to babies under 12 months old.

• •

Heat half the oil in a frying pan, add the chicken and honey and fry for 3–4 minutes until golden and cooked through. Remove the chicken from the pan and set aside.

Add the remaining oil to the pan. Add the onion and thyme and fry for 5 minutes until soft. Add the tomatoes, sweetcorn, balsamic vinegar and chicken and cook for 2 minutes, then transfer to a bowl.

Wipe the frying pan clean. Add one of the wraps to the pan. Spoon a third of the chicken mixture on top, sprinkle with a third of the grated cheese and place another wrap on top.

Push down and fry for 2 minutes, then flip over and cook for another 2 minutes. Slice into wedges.

Repeat with the remaining tortillas, filling and cheese and serve the wedges, drizzled with yoghurt and if you like sprinkled with the paprika.

Chicken Teriyaki Sausages

MAKES 25 CHICKEN SAUSAGES

1 onion, chopped
400 g/14 oz skinless, boneless
   chicken thighs, diced
150 g/5 oz carrots, peeled
   and grated
1 garlic clove, crushed
2 tablespoons soy sauce
1 teaspoon runny honey
   or maple syrup
50 g/2 oz dried or Panko
   breadcrumbs, plus extra
   for coating
2–3 tablespoons rapeseed
   or sunflower oil

Yoghurt Dip
6 tablespoons plain full-fat
   yoghurt
1 teaspoon snipped chives
   or chopped flat-leaf parlsey
¼ cucumber, deseeded and
   coarsely grated

Here's how to make your own super-succulent sausages. The addition of soy sauce makes them extra moreish! Use plenty of brown meat from the chicken as this contains more iron than the white breast meat. Use maple syrup instead of honey if serving to babies under 12 months.

Put the onion in the bowl of a food processor and blitz until finely chopped. Add the chicken and briefly blitz again. Add the remaining ingredients and blitz until everything is finely chopped.

Transfer the mixture to a bowl and shape it into 25 equal-sized sausages. Place some extra breadcrumbs on a plate and roll the sausages in the breadcrumbs to coat them.

Heat the oil in a frying pan and fry the sausages in 2 batches for about 10 minutes until golden and cooked through.

Combine the ingredients for the dip in a bowl and serve the sausages with the dip.

Chicken with Tomatoes and Orzo ❄

MAKES 4 CHILD PORTIONS

3 tablespoons olive oil
1 red onion, diced
1 sweet red pepper, deseeded
    and finely diced
2 garlic cloves, crushed
1 teaspoon sweet smoked paprika
1 teaspoon soft brown sugar
1 teaspoon balsamic vinegar
125 g/4½ oz orzo pasta
450 ml/16 fl oz hot unsalted
    or weak chicken stock
250 g/9 oz passata
    (sieved tomatoes)
1 teaspoon chopped fresh thyme
10 cherry tomatoes, quartered
2 boneless, skinless chicken
    breasts, cut into strips or 2
    ready cooked chicken breasts
a little salt and pepper (for
    babies over 12 months old)
a handful of basil leaves (optional)

Is it pasta? Is it rice? If you haven't used orzo before it looks like rice but it is in fact pasta and has a soft texture which is perfect for little ones. Sweet smoked paprika, balsamic vinegar and fresh thyme make this a tasty meal for the whole family.

• •

Heat 1 tablespoon of the oil in a deep frying pan, add the onion and pepper and fry for 3–4 minutes.

Add the garlic and paprika and fry for 30 seconds, then add the sugar, balsamic vinegar and orzo. Stir to coat the pasta in the mixture, then add the stock and passata. Bring to the boil, cover and simmer for 15–20 minutes, until the pasta is cooked and most of the liquid has been absorbed. Add the thyme and cherry tomatoes and stir until the tomatoes have softened slightly.

Season the chicken strips with salt and pepper (if using) and fry them in the remaining oil until lightly golden and cooked through. Alternatively add the ready cooked chicken cut into strips and heat through. Add them to the pasta and serve with steamed broccoli florets and baby carrots. Chop the basil leaves and add with the chicken (if using)

Broccoli, Chicken and Potato Bites ❄

MAKES 8 BITES

75 g/3 oz broccoli florets
110 g/4¼ oz cooked mashed
    potato (cold)
25 g/1 oz grated Parmesan cheese
60 g/2½ oz cooked chicken, diced
40 g/1½ oz dried or Panko
    breadcrumbs
1 egg, beaten
2 spring onions, finely sliced
2 tablespoons rapeseed or
    sunflower oil
a little salt and pepper (for
    babies over 12 months old)

These bites have been very popular on my Instagram. They have received comments like, 'Never mind the kids, I wouldn't mind gobbling these up!' They are so easy to make and you can freeze them once cooked and cooled, simply reheating them in the oven when needed. This is also a great leftovers recipe, for those days when you're lucky enough to have some cooked meat in the fridge left over from a roast (see my Roast Chicken on page 126).

Steam the broccoli florets for 5–6 minutes until tender, then set aside until they are completely cool. Once cool, chop them finely.

Mix together the cold mashed potato, chopped broccoli, grated cheese, chicken, half the breadcrumbs, half the beaten egg and the spring onions. Season with salt and pepper (if using).

Shape the mixture into 8 sausage shapes, then coat them in the remaining egg and roll them in the remaining breadcrumbs. Transfer to a lined plate or tray and chill for 30 minutes.

Heat the oil in a frying pan. Fry until golden and heated through. Serve with ketchup or a dip of your choice (see my dips on page 41).

Griddled Chicken with Three Quick Sauces

MAKES 4 CHILD PORTIONS
2 skinless, boneless chicken breasts
1 tablespoon olive or sunflower oil
1 garlic clove, peeled and halved
a little salt and pepper

Three Quick Sauces
MILD CURRY
2 tablespoons mayonnaise
2 tablespoons Greek yoghurt
1½ teaspoons mild korma
   curry paste
1 teaspoon runny honey
2–3 drops of lemon juice

EASY BARBECUE
3 tablespoons tomato ketchup
1 tablespoon runny honey
¼ teaspoon soy sauce
¼ teaspoon lemon juice
2 teaspoons water

SPICY TOMATO
3 tablespoons tomato ketchup
1 tablespoon sweet chilli sauce
1 tablespoon water
¼ teaspoon soy sauce

Chicken without a breadcrumb or batter coating can still be super tasty. Simply marinate it and cook it on a griddle or in a frying pan and serve it with one of these three delicious sauces.

Cover the chicken breasts with clingfilm and bash them with a mallet or rolling pin to flatten them.

Brush the fillets with oil, then rub one of the cut sides of the garlic clove over them. Season with a little salt and pepper.

Brush a griddle pan with oil and when it is very hot cook the chicken on one side for 2–3 minutes, then turn the heat down a little and cook for a further 3 minutes. Turn the chicken breasts over and repeat on the other side, until cooked through.

Cut the chicken into strips and follow one of the quick sauce recipes to make tasty dipping sauces for the chicken. Serve with steamed vegetables, such as petits pois, sugar snap peas, baby carrots and broccoli florets.

For the Three Quick Sauces: Simply mix all the ingredients together for your sauce of choice and serve alongside the griddled chicken.

Cherub's Chicken Couscous

MAKES 4 CHILD PORTIONS
200 ml/7 fl oz unsalted
  or weak chicken stock
80 g/3 oz couscous
15 g/½ oz unsalted butter
½ small onion, finely chopped
50 g/2 oz courgette, diced
½ garlic clove, crushed
2 plum tomatoes, deseeded
  and chopped
70 g/2¾ oz cooked chicken, diced
1 tablespoon chopped basil
1 tablespoon grated Parmesan
  cheese
a little salt and pepper (for
  babies over 12 months old)

Couscous has a soft texture which makes it perfect for babies who are lacking in teeth, although you'll be surprised what gums can get through! I love to add fresh herbs to baby food to maximise flavour, and here I've used basil.

• •

Bring the stock to the boil in a pan. Put the couscous in a heatproof bowl. Pour over the hot stock, stir and cover with clingfilm, then set aside for 15 minutes to absorb the liquid.

Meanwhile, melt the butter in a saucepan, add the onion and sauté for 2 minutes, then add the diced courgette and garlic and sauté for a further 3 minutes. Add the tomatoes and cook for 1 minute, and finally add the chicken and basil.

Add the chicken mixture to the couscous, season lightly with salt and pepper (if using), then add the Parmesan and mix gently before serving.

Roast Chicken with Vegetables and Gravy

MAKES 5 ADULT PORTIONS
OR 10 CHILD PORTIONS

1 x 1.5 kg/3 lb 3 oz large
  free-range chicken
1 tablespoon chopped
  fresh rosemary
3 garlic cloves, crushed
2 tablespoons olive oil
1 tablespoon runny honey
  (or maple syrup, if serving
  to babies under 12 months old)
a little salt and pepper (for
  babies over 12 months old)

Roast Vegetables
800 g/1 lb 8 oz floury potatoes,
  peeled and cut into large pieces
6 tablespoons sunflower oil
3 parsnips, peeled and sliced
  into batons
500 g/1 lb 1 oz baby carrots

Gravy
3 tablespoons plain flour
450 ml/16 fl oz hot chicken stock
Worcestershire sauce to taste

Making one meal for the whole family not only saves time, but it encourages everyone to eat together, which I love. Here is my favourite roast chicken recipe, that's also suitable for sharing with your baby. I have come up with five different delicious and baby-friendly ways to use up the leftover roast chicken, which follow on from this recipe.

• •

Preheat the oven to 180°C/350°F/Gas 4.

Put the chicken in a roasting tin.

Mix the rosemary, garlic and oil together in a bowl. Pour over the chicken and season with salt and pepper (if using). Roast for 1¼ hours until golden brown and cooked through. To test if it's ready, push a sharp knife into the thickest part of one of the thighs, and if the juices run clear, it's done.

Put the potatoes in a saucepan, cover with cold salted water, bring to the boil and cook for 5 minutes. Drain thoroughly. Drizzle 4 tablespoons of the oil into a roasting tin and heat it in the oven. Once it's hot, add the potatoes and coat them in the oil. Roast for 30–40 minutes, turning them once, until golden and crispy.

Put the parsnips and carrots in a large roasting tin.

Drizzle over the remaining oil and season with salt and pepper (if using). Roast for 30 minutes, tossing them halfway through the cooking time, until golden and cooked through.

Drizzle the honey or maple syrup over the chicken 15 minutes before the end of the cooking time.

Transfer the chicken to a large serving plate, cover loosely with foil and leave it to rest while you make the gravy.

To make the gravy, skim 3 tablespoons of fat off the cooking juices. Add the flour to the roasting pan and whisk it over the heat for 1 minute. Whisk in the stock, Worcestershire sauce and chicken juices and cook, stirring, until thickened and bubbling.

Serve the roast chicken, gravy and roast vegetables with steamed broccoli.

Chicken and Sweetcorn Soup

MAKES 6 CHILD PORTIONS

1 tablespoon sunflower oil
1 onion, finely chopped
1 teaspoon grated fresh
   root ginger
2 garlic cloves, sliced
1 x 198g tin sweetcorn, drained
650 ml unsalted or weak
   chicken stock
1½ tablespoons cornflour
a pinch of chilli flakes (optional)
2 teaspoons soy sauce
5 spring onions, thinly sliced
a pinch of sugar
juice of ½ lemon
150 g/5 oz cooked chicken meat,
   finely chopped
sesame oil to taste (optional)
a little salt and pepper (for
   babies over 12 months old)

Here's a creamy chicken soup that gives any Chinese takeaway a run for its money. You can set aside your baby's portion before adding the soy sauce.

● ●

Heat the oil in a saucepan, add the onion, ginger and garlic and fry for 4–5 minutes, then add the sweetcorn and stir over the heat for 30 seconds.

Add the chicken stock, cover and simmer for 5–8 minutes, then remove from the heat and blend until smooth with a stick blender.

Mix the cornflour with a little cold water and add it to the soup then cook over a medium heat, stirring, until thickened.

Add the remaining ingredients to the soup. Season with salt and pepper (if using) and simmer for 1 minute until the chicken is heated through. Serve with fresh bread.

Chicken Curry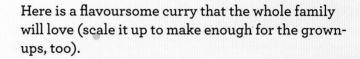

MAKES 2 CHILD PORTIONS

1 teaspoon rapeseed or
   sunflower oil
75 g/3 oz onions, chopped
50 g/2 oz grated apple
1 garlic clove, crushed
1 teaspoon korma curry paste
2 teaspoons plain flour
300 ml/10 fl oz hot unsalted
   or weak chicken stock
1 teaspoon soy sauce
1 teaspoon mango chutney
100 g/4 oz cooked chicken
   meat, diced
cooked rice, to serve

Here is a flavoursome curry that the whole family
will love (scale it up to make enough for the grown-
ups, too).

• •

Heat the oil in a saucepan, add the onion, apple and
garlic and fry for 2–3 minutes, then add the korma
paste and flour and stir over the heat for 1 minute.
Stir in the stock, soy sauce and mango chutney.
Bring to the boil, cover and simmer for 5–8 minutes.

Remove from the heat and blend to the desired
consistency then stir in the chicken and serve
with cooked rice and steamed vegetables.

Chicken and Sweetcorn Croquettes ❄

MAKES 20 CROQUETTES

100 g/4 oz fresh breadcrumbs
5 spring onions, roughly chopped
100 g/4 oz carrots, peeled
   and grated
150 g/5 oz tinned sweetcorn
10 g/¼ oz fresh basil leaves
130 g/4½ oz cooked chicken,
   diced
1–2 tablespoons sweet chilli sauce
50 g/2 oz grated mature
   Cheddar cheese
1 egg yolk
2 tablespoons plain flour, plus
   extra for coating
2 tablespoons sunflower oil
a little salt and pepper (for
   babies over 12 months old)

Leftover Roast Chicken

Spice up your child's dinner time and use up all those leftovers with these tasty and nourishing croquettes. Once cooked, you can freeze the croquettes in a plastic container, separated by greaseproof paper. Reheat in a microwave from frozen or in an oven preheated to 180°C/350°F/Gas 4 for about 15 minutes or until hot throughout.

• •

Place the breadcrumbs, spring onions, carrot, sweetcorn, basil and chicken in a food processor and and blitz until finely chopped. Add the sweet chilli sauce, cheese, egg yolk and flour. Blitz again for 2 seconds. Season with salt and pepper (if using).

Transfer the mixture to a bowl, then shape the mixture into 20 equal-sized croquettes. Place some extra flour on a plate and roll the croquettes in the flour, then transfer them to a tray and chill in the fridge for at least 10 minutes (or up to 24 hours before you are ready to cook them).

When ready to serve, heat the oil in a frying pan. Fry the croquettes for 3–4 minutes (in 2 batches) until golden all over. Transfer to a plate lined with kitchen paper. Leave for a few minutes to firm up before serving with roasted vegetables, such as sweet potato wedges, and some steamed vegetables.

Little Chicken and Leek Pies ❄

MAKES 4 CHILD PORTIONS

225 g/8 oz potatoes, peeled
   and diced
225 g/8 oz carrots, peeled
   and diced
20 g/¾ oz butter
2 small leeks, trimmed and
   roughly chopped
185 g/6 oz cooked chicken meat,
   cubed (or 2 skinless, boneless
   chicken breasts, cut into
   2 cm/¾ in cubes)
3 mushrooms, thinly sliced
2 tablespoons plain flour
200 ml/7 fl oz whole milk
50 g/2 oz grated Cheddar cheese
25 g/1 oz tinned drained
   sweetcorn
a little salt and pepper (for
   babies over 12 months old)

Leftover Roast Chicken

Individual ramekins are the perfect size for your little one and look so much more appealing than serving small portions on a big plate.

•·•

Put the potatoes and carrots in a saucepan of water, bring to the boil and simmer for 10–12 minutes until soft. Drain, then mash until smooth.

Melt the butter in a saucepan. Add the leeks and sauté for 5 minutes, until just soft, then add the chicken and fry for 2 minutes. Next, add the mushrooms and cook for 2 minutes. Sprinkle over the plain flour, stir for 1 minute, then gradually stir in the milk and bring to the boil. Simmer gently for 5 minutes, until the chicken is cooked. While it's simmering, preheat the grill.

Add three-quarters of the grated cheese to the sauce, season with salt and pepper (if using) and add the sweetcorn. Divide the mixture between 4 ramekins. Spoon the potato and carrot mash on top and sprinkle with the remaining cheese.

Place under the grill for 4–5 minutes, until lightly golden on top and bubbling around the edges. Serve with peas.

Rice 'N' Easy ❄

MAKES 3–4 CHILD PORTIONS
100 g/4 oz long-grain rice
1 tablespoon olive oil
1 small onion, finely chopped
70 g/2¾ oz courgette, finely diced
½ sweet red pepper, deseeded
   and finely diced
1 garlic clove, crushed
150 g/5 oz passata (sieved
   tomatoes)
1 tablespoon red pesto
70 g/2¾ oz cooked chicken
   meat, diced
1 tablespoon chopped basil leaves
1 teaspoon balsamic vinegar

Leftover Roast Chicken

Here's a recipe approved by my children! The smart combo of red pesto, fresh basil and sweet balsamic vinegar give rice the ultimate flavour boost.

• •

Cook the rice according to the packet instructions, then drain.

Heat the oil in a saucepan, add the onion, courgette and pepper and sauté for 5 minutes, then add the garlic and fry for a further 30 seconds. Add the passata and simmer for 10 minutes until reduced and thickened, then add the pesto, chicken, basil, vinegar and cooked rice. Mix well and serve.

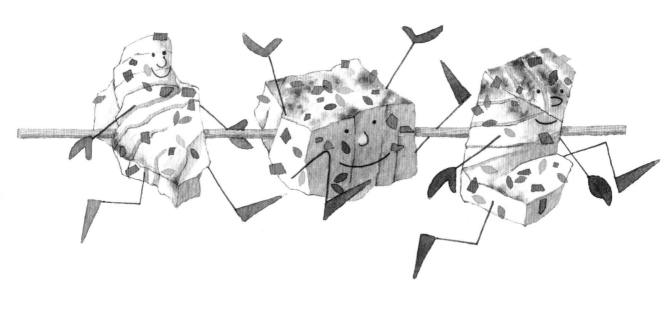

Fish

Monkfish Kebabs

MAKES 4 KEBABS

500 g/1 lb 1oz monkfish tail
4 tablespoons olive oil
1 teaspoon chopped fresh thyme
juice of ½ lemon
a pinch of finely diced red
   chilli (optional)
½ small garlic clove, crushed
1 small courgette, cut into
   0.5 cm/¼ inch-thick rounds

You will also need: 4 wooden
skewers, soaked in warm
water for 30 minutes

Being a slightly more robust and firm-fleshed fish, monkfish is a good option to serve to enthusiastic young hands. I'd recommend leaving out the chilli for young babies.

• •

Remove the monkfish fillets from the bone, trim away any membrane, and cut the fish into bite-sized pieces.

Combine half the oil with the thyme, lemon juice, chilli and garlic in a bowl. Add the fish pieces, coat them in the marinade, then set aside to marinate for 5 minutes.

Thread the courgette and marinated monkfish pieces onto the soaked skewers.

Heat a large frying pan or griddle pan until hot and fry the kebabs in the remaining oil for 2–3 minutes on each side until golden and cooked through. Remove from the heat and leave to cool slightly before serving, remove the skewers before giving to young children.

Scrummy Fish Chowder ❄

MAKES 6 CHILD PORTIONS
2 teaspoons sunflower oil
150 g/5 oz leeks, trimmed
and chopped
125 g/4½ oz carrots, peeled
and diced
250 g/9 oz floury potatoes,
peeled and diced

I love this deconstructed fish pie. The tender cubes
of fish and vegetables mingle in a light cheesy sauce
flavoured with fresh dill.

Heat the oil in a saucepan. Add the leek and carrots
and stir over the heat for 2 minutes, then cover with
a lid and cook gently for 5 minutes until soft.

200 ml/7 fl oz unsalted
  or weak fish stock
150 ml/5 fl oz whole milk
250 g/9 oz mix of diced skinless
  and boneless cod and salmon
  (or just white fish)
60 g/2½ oz frozen peas
1 tablespoon chopped fresh dill
2 tablespoons grated Parmesan

Remove the lid and add the potatoes and stock. Bring to the boil, cover and simmer for 10–12 minutes, until the potatoes are cooked through, then add the milk, fish and peas. Simmer for 5 minutes until the fish is cooked through. Remove from the heat, stir in the dill and Parmesan and serve.

Scrumptious Salmon Fishcakes ❄

MAKES 18–20 MINI FISHCAKES

250 g/9 oz floury potato
  (about 1 potato)
2 tablespoons mayonnaise
1½ tablespoons sweet chilli sauce
1 teaspoon lemon juice
4 spring onions, finely sliced
40 g/1½ oz Cheddar cheese,
  grated
2 tablespoons tomato ketchup
250 g/9 oz raw skinless, boneless
  salmon, cut into small cubes
2 teaspoons chopped fresh dill
100 g/4 oz fresh breadcrumbs
3–4 tablespoons sunflower oil
  for frying
a little salt and pepper (for
  babies over 12 months old)

These deliciously moist salmon fishcakes are flavoured with a little sweet chilli sauce, Cheddar and fresh dill. You can keep the breadcrumb-coated (but uncooked) fishcakes in the fridge overnight if you don't want to cook them all on the same day, or freeze them.

· ·

Prick the potato with a fork and cook it in the microwave on High for 10 minutes until soft (or in a 200°C/400°F/Gas 6 oven for 1 hour, or until soft). As soon as the potato is cool enough to handle, cut it in half, scoop out the fluffy potato into a bowl and mash it with a fork. Leave to cool for a few minutes.

Add the mayonnaise, sweet chilli sauce, lemon juice, spring onion, grated cheese and ketchup to the mashed potato and roughly combine.

Stir in the cubes of salmon, dill and 50 g/2 oz of the breadcrumbs and season lightly with salt and pepper (if using).

Using your hands, form the mixture into about 8 fishcakes. Tip the remaining breadcrumbs onto a large plate and coat the fishcakes in the crumbs.

Heat the oil in a large frying pan and fry the fishcakes for about 5 minutes on each side until golden. Drain on kitchen paper then serve.

Salmon and Cod Fish Pie ❄

MAKES 6 CHILD PORTIONS

150 g/5 oz carrots,
    peeled and diced
500 g/1 lb 1 oz potatoes,
    peeled and diced
40 g/1½ oz butter, plus a knob
    for the mash
1 large onion, finely chopped
40 g/1½ oz plain flour
400 ml/14 fl oz whole milk, plus
    2 tablespoons for the mash
1 teaspoon Dijon mustard
2 teaspoons lemon juice
1½ teaspoons rice wine vinegar
50 g/2 oz grated Cheddar cheese
25 g/1 oz grated Parmesan cheese
1½ tablespoons chopped fresh dill
200 g/7 oz boneless, skinless
    salmon fillet, cubed
200 g/7 oz boneless, skinless
    cod fillet, cubed
1 egg, lightly beaten

Who says my fish pie is just for kids? Yes, you can make small portions for your little one but I've met lots of mums and dads who proudly serve it up at their dinner parties. The fish, added just before it is baked with the topping, stays lovely and moist. Oily fish such as salmon is a great source of Omega-3 oils, which are very important for your baby's brain and visual development. Here, the veggie content is given a boost with a tasty carrot and potato mash topping.

Preheat the oven to 200°C/400°F/Gas 6.

Boil the carrots in a pan of water for 8 minutes, then add the diced potatoes and boil for a further 12–15 minutes until soft. Drain, mash and mix with the knob of butter and the 2 tablespoons of milk.

Melt the rest of the butter in a pan, add the onion and sauté for 5–6 minutes until soft. Add the flour, stir over the heat for a minute, then gradually whisk in the milk. Add the Dijon mustard, lemon juice and vinegar and stir for a few minutes over a low heat until thickened. Remove from the heat and add the cheeses, dill and fish. Spoon the mixture into an ovenproof dish and pipe or spoon the potato and carrot mash on top. Brush the top with beaten egg and bake for 30 minutes until bubbling and golden on top. Serve with peas.

Krispie Fish Fingers

45 g/1½ oz Rice Krispies
3 tablespoons grated
    Parmesan cheese
¼ teaspoon paprika
1 egg
2 tablespoons plain flour
225 g/8 oz skinless, boneless
    sole or plaice fillets, cut into
    little finger-sized strips
2–3 tablespoons sunflower oil
a little salt and pepper (for
    babies over 12 months old)

Dip
2 tablespoons mayonnaise
2 tablespoons Greek yoghurt
1 teaspoon fresh lemon juice
a pinch of salt (optional)

★ To freeze, lay the coated but
uncooked pieces of fish on a lined
baking sheet and freeze uncovered.
Once frozen, transfer to a plastic
freezer box.

Rice Krispies make a tasty, crunchy coating for fish. These goujons cook quickly and can be cooked from frozen. Crushed cornflakes make a good alternative coating: coat the fish in flour and egg, as below, then roll them in crushed cornflakes instead of Krispies.

Put the Rice Krispies, Parmesan and paprika in the bowl of a food processor and blitz to form fine crumbs. Transfer to a large plate and stir in some salt and pepper (if using). Beat the egg in a bowl with a pinch of salt (if using). Place the flour on a separate plate.

Toss 3–4 fish pieces in the flour, dip them in the egg, then coat them in the Krispie coating. Lay the coated fish pieces on a clean plate and continue with remaining fish. Cook immediately or freeze (see Tip).

Heat the oil in a large frying pan and fry the fish fingers for 1½–2 minutes on each side, until golden and cooked through. Transfer to a paper-lined plate to cool slightly before serving.

Alternatively, place the fish fingers on a greased non-stick baking tray, drizzle with a little oil, and bake for 12 minutes in an oven preheated to 200°C/400°F/Gas 6.

To make the dip, combine the ingredients in a bowl and season with salt (if you wish). Serve the fish fingers with the dip and some peas.

Jambalaya

DAIRY FREE

MAKES 4 CHILD PORTIONS
1 tablespoon olive oil
1 onion, finely chopped
1 medium carrot, peeled and diced
¼ sweet red pepper, deseeded and diced
½ celery stalk, diced
1 garlic clove, crushed
½ teaspoon chopped fresh thyme
¼ teaspoon paprika
200 g/7 oz basmati or long-grain rice
400 g/14 oz tin chopped tomatoes
250 ml/9 fl oz unsalted or weak chicken stock
4–6 drops of Tabasco, or to taste
1 large cooked skinless chicken breast (about 120 g/4½ oz), cubed
100 g/4 oz cooked prawns
75 g/3 oz frozen peas
150 g/5 oz tinned drained sweetcorn
a little salt and pepper (for babies over 12 months old)

The beauty of this dish is that you can substitute or add any ingredients you wish, so it's a great way of using up leftovers, particularly leftover roast chicken (see page 126). If you like spicy food, sauté 50 g/2 oz diced chorizo with the vegetables and remove the paprika.

Heat the oil in a large saucepan or wok with a lid. Add the onion, carrot, pepper and celery and sauté for 8–10 minutes until soft.

Add the garlic, thyme and paprika and cook for 1 minute, then add the rice, tomatoes, stock and Tabasco and bring to the boil. Cover with a lid and simmer for 15 minutes, or until the rice is just tender.

Remove the lid and add the chicken, prawns, peas and sweetcorn. Reduce the heat to low, cover and cook for a further 5 minutes, until everything is hot. Season with salt and pepper (if using) and stir through with a fork. Serve with extra Tabasco, if you wish.

Tuna Muffin Melts

MAKES 2 CHILD PORTIONS
170 g/6 oz tin tuna in oil, drained
1 spring onion, finely chopped
2 tablespoons Greek yoghurt
2 tablespoons tomato ketchup
¼ teaspoon lemon juice
2 dashes of Worcestershire sauce
   (optional)
2 muffins, split in half
40 g/1½ oz grated Cheddar
   cheese
a little salt and pepper (for
   babies over 12 months old)

Halved and toasted muffins are an ideal size for smaller children to pick up and eat. If you have more tuna filling than you need, don't worry – it will keep well, covered, in the fridge for 2–3 days and makes a great sandwich or quesadilla filling.

• •

Preheat the grill to high.

Put the tuna and spring onion in a bowl and stir in the yoghurt, ketchup, lemon juice and Worcestershire sauce (if using). Season to taste with salt and pepper (if using).

Lightly toast the muffin halves then pile the tuna mix onto the four cut sides. Scatter over the grated cheese and place under the grill for 1–2 minutes, until the cheese has melted. Cool slightly then serve cut in half or into quarters. Serve with salad, or hummus or avocado dip with breadsticks, carrot and cucumber sticks.

Variation: Tuna Quesadilla

Spread half of the tuna mix over a wheat tortilla wrap, scatter over 20 g/¾ oz grated cheese and top with a second wrap then dry-fry or grill for around 2 minutes on each side, until crisp.

Bow-Tie Pasta Salad with Tuna

MAKES 4 CHILD PORTIONS

Salad
150 g/5 oz pasta bows
1 shallot, finely chopped
200 g/7 oz tin tuna in oil,
   drained and flaked
4 cherry tomatoes
50 g/2 oz cooked frozen or
   canned sweetcorn
1 small avocado, halved, stoned,
   peeled and cut into small cubes

Dressing
2 tablespoons mayonnaise
2 tablespoons olive oil
2 teaspoons lemon juice
a pinch of cayenne pepper
   (optional)

Bow-tie pasta is an easy shape for little ones to pick up. Lots of babies and toddlers love it with a little melted butter and grated Parmesan. Alternatively, you can make into a delicious tuna salad, leaving out the cayenne pepper for young babies.

• •

Cook the pasta bows according to the packet instructions.

Mix together all the ingredients for the salad in a bowl (except the avocado – add this just before serving or it will discolour).

Combine the dressing ingredients. Drain the pasta, leave to cool, then mix with the salad, add the avocado and toss in the dressing.

Mini Baked Potatoes with Tuna and Sweetcorn

MAKES 3 CHILD PORTIONS
6 large new potatoes
80 g/3 oz tinned drained tuna
2 tablespoons tinned drained
sweetcorn
2 tablespoons mayonnaise
4 cherry tomatoes, quartered
1 tablespoon grated Cheddar
cheese

This easy recipe makes the perfect delicious standby meal, as it uses budget-friendly ingredients that are staple foods in most households.

● · ● · ● · ● · ● · ● · ● · ● · ● · ● · ● · ● · ● · ● · ● · ● · ● · ● · ● · ●

Preheat the oven to 200°C/400°F/Gas 6.

Prick the potatoes and place them on a baking tray and bake for 30–35 minutes. Alternatively, cook the pricked potatoes in the microwave for 7–10 minutes until soft.

As soon as they are cool enough to handle, slice halfway through the cooked potatoes (not all the way through). Mix the drained tuna, sweetcorn, mayonnaise, tomatoes and cheese together and spoon the mixture onto the potatoes.

Tuna Tortilla Tartlets ❄

MAKES 12 TUNA TARTLETS
a little sunflower oil for greasing
3 mini tortilla wraps
25 g/1 oz tinned tuna in oil,
    drained
25 g/1 oz tinned drained
    sweetcorn
3 cherry tomatoes, quartered
1 egg
3 tablespoons sour cream
2 tablespoons finely grated
    Parmesan cheese
a little cress, to garnish
a little salt and pepper (for
    babies over 12 months old)

Transform tortillas into these tasty tartlets by cutting them into circles using a pastry cutter and pressing them into a muffin tin.

Preheat the oven to 180°C/350°F/Gas 4 and grease a 12-hole mini muffin tin with oil.

Stamp out twelve 7 cm/3 in circles from the 3 wraps.

Push the tortilla discs into the muffin tin holes to make 12 little cases. Divide the tuna, sweetcorn and tomatoes between the cases.

Mix the egg and sour cream together in a small bowl or jug, season lightly with salt and pepper (if using) and divide it evenly between the cases. Sprinkle with the cheese. Bake for 15–18 minutes until golden on top and set in the middle. Remove from the oven, sprinkle with cress and serve with carrot and cucumber sticks, and sugar snap peas.

Tuna and Broccoli Pasta

MAKES 8 CHILD PORTIONS

250 g/9 oz mini shell pasta
150 g/5 oz broccoli florets
50 g/2 oz butter
50 g/2 oz plain flour
700 ml/1.2 pints whole
   milk, warmed
2 teaspoons Dijon mustard
50 g/2 oz grated Cheddar cheese
30 g/1 oz grated Parmesan cheese
160 g/6 oz tin tuna in oil, drained
75 g/3 oz cherry tomatoes,
   quartered

Those little green trees which little ones often love to hate make a great finger food. Try this recipe and they'll soon be eating entire forests!

Cook the pasta according to the packet instructions. Add the broccoli florets 3 minutes before the end of the cooking time. Reserve 50 ml/2 fl oz of the pasta cooking water before draining.

Melt the butter in a saucepan, add the flour and stir over the heat for a minute, then gradually whisk in the milk, stirring until thickened. Add the mustard and grated cheeses. Remove from the heat and add the cooked pasta, broccoli, tuna and tomatoes, plus the reserved pasta cooking water, and stir together.

Serve with raw vegetables and a dip, if you wish.

★ To avoid a lumpy white sauce, always heat the milk before adding it to the flour and butter (the roux).

Cod Fillet with Herb Butter

MAKES 8 CHILD PORTIONS

25 g/1 oz softened butter
2 tablespoons chopped fresh
  mixed herbs e.g. parsley,
  thyme, oregano
1 tablespoon lemon juice
450 g/1 lb thick skinless,
  boneless fillets of cod
a little salt and pepper (for
  babies over 12 months old)

Give white fish a lift with a squeeze of lemon, fresh herbs and butter. You can also make this recipe with lemon sole, hake, plaice or pollock.

• •

Preheat the oven to 180°C/350°F/Gas 4.

Mix the softened butter with the chopped herbs and lemon juice. Place the fish in a small ovenproof dish, season with salt and pepper (if using) and spread the herb butter over the top.

Place in the oven and bake for 8–10 minutes until the fish is cooked through. Remove from the oven and flake the cooked fish with a fork, checking to make sure that there are no bones, and serve it with Parmesan Roasted Sweet Potato Wedges (see page 61).

Salmon, Quinoa and Spinach Balls ❄

MAKES 20 BALLS

75 g/3 oz quinoa
1 sweet potato
85 g/3½ oz fresh white breadcrumbs
175 g/6 oz skinless, boneless
  salmon fillet, sliced
40 g/1½ oz spinach, roughly
  chopped
30 g/1 oz grated Parmesan cheese
5 spring onions, sliced
1 teaspoon fish sauce
1 tablespoon sweet chilli sauce
2 tablespoons plain flour
sunflower oil for frying
a little salt and pepper (for
  babies over 12 months old)

Dill Sauce
2 teaspoons sunflower oil
1 large leek, trimmed and
  finely chopped
½ teaspoon white wine vinegar
4 teaspoons plain flour
300 ml/10 fl oz unsalted
  or weak fish stock
100 ml/4 fl oz milk
½ teaspoon Dijon mustard
20 g/¾ oz grated Parmesan cheese
50 ml/2 fl oz single cream
1 teaspoon lemon juice
1 teaspoon fresh chopped dill

We ran a competition to find the cover star for this book. I made a big batch of these balls for the finalists' photoshoot and couldn't believe how quickly they were gobbled up! They're so easy, and are just perfect for little fingers.

● ●

Cook the quinoa in a pan of lightly salted boiling water for 15 minutes until tender. Drain, rinse, then leave to drain in a sieve for about 10 minutes.

Prick the sweet potato with a fork and cook it in the microwave for 7–10 minutes or bake at 200°C/400°F/ Gas 6 for 45 minutes. Once cool, remove the skin.

To make the dill sauce, sauté the leek in the oil for 4–5 minutes until softened. Stir in the vinegar and cook for 30 seconds, then stir in the flour and cook for 1 minute. Add the fish stock, milk and mustard and cook, stirring, for about 5 minutes until thickened. Remove from the heat, stir in the Parmesan until melted then add the cream, lemon juice and dill.

Blitz the sweet potato in a food processor with the quinoa, breadcrumbs, salmon, spinach, Parmesan, spring onions, fish sauce and chilli sauce, and some seasoning (if using), until finely chopped.

Shape the mixture into 20 equal-sized balls. Lightly coat the balls in the flour. Heat a little oil in a frying pan and fry the balls in batches for 5–6 minutes until golden and cooked through. Serve with the dill sauce.

Salmon Rissoles

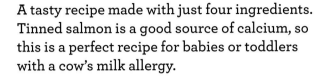

MAKES 6 RISSOLES

1 x 215 g/7½ oz tin red salmon in oil, drained
2 tablespoons dried or Panko breadcrumbs, plus extra for coating
2 tablespoons tomato ketchup
3 spring onions, finely chopped
2 tablespoons sunflower oil

A tasty recipe made with just four ingredients. Tinned salmon is a good source of calcium, so this is a perfect recipe for babies or toddlers with a cow's milk allergy.

• •

Tip the tinned salmon into a bowl. Add the remaining ingredients (except the oil), flake the salmon with a fork and mix everything together with a spoon. Shape the mixture into 6 rissoles.

Spread a few tablespoons of breadcrumbs on a large plate and coat the rissoles in the breadcrumbs.

Heat the oil in a frying pan and fry the rissoles for 2–3 minutes, turning them once, until golden and cooked through. Serve with Kale and Root Veg Mash (see page 63).

Pasta Shells with Salmon and Veggies in a Light Cheese Sauce ❋

MAKES 6 CHILD PORTIONS

200 g/7 oz skinless,
  boneless salmon fillet
a knob of butter
150 g/5 oz mini shell pasta
150 g/5 oz broccoli florets
2 tablespoons olive oil
1 large onion, thinly sliced
1 garlic clove, crushed
200 g/7 oz peeled butternut
  squash, deseeded and diced
250 ml/9 fl oz unsalted
  or weak vegetable stock
200 g/7 oz full-fat crème fraîche
150 g/5 oz cherry tomatoes,
  halved or quartered if large
50 g/2 oz grated Parmesan cheese
a squeeze of lemon juice
a little salt and pepper (for
  babies over 12 months old)

Let me introduce you to my Cheat's Cheese Sauce. It's lighter than a roux-based sauce as it is made with vegetable stock. You can leave out the salmon and add extra veggies for a vegetarian version.

Preheat the oven to 180°C/350°F/Gas 4.

Put the salmon in the centre of a piece of foil, top with the butter and season with salt and pepper (if using). Fold the foil over the fish to make parcel, place it on a baking sheet and bake for 15 minutes until cooked through. Remove from the oven, unwrap and flake the fish into large pieces.

Cook the pasta according to the packet instructions, adding the broccoli florets 2 minutes before the end of the cooking time.

While the pasta is cooking, make the sauce. Heat the oil in a deep frying pan, add the onion, garlic and squash and fry for 5 minutes, then add the stock, cover and simmer for 5 minutes or until the squash is tender. Remove the lid and stir in the crème fraîche and salmon. Stir in the pasta and broccoli until heated through, then remove from the heat. Add the tomatoes, Parmesan and lemon juice and serve.

Sesame-coated Salmon

MAKES 4 CHILD PORTIONS
1 teaspoon grated fresh
    root ginger
1 tablespoon soy sauce
1 tablespoon sweet chilli sauce,
    plus extra to serve
2 skinless, boneless salmon fillets,
    cut into bite-sized chunks
    (about 4 chunks per fillet)
1 tablespoon sesame seeds
60 g/2½ oz cooked noodles
wedges of lime, to serve
sweet chilli sauce, to serve
    (optional)

Transform salmon in a matter of minutes with this finger-licking marinade. If your child has a gluten or egg allergy, you could use rice noodles instead of egg noodles. Sesame seeds should be safe for your baby from 6 months. However, very occasionally, babies can have a sesame allergy. If your baby has severe eczema then you may need to be cautious as there is an increased risk of food allergy.

• •

Preheat the oven to 180°C/350°F/Gas 4 and line a baking sheet with baking parchment.

Place the ginger, soy sauce and sweet chilli sauce in a bowl. Add the salmon chunks, coat them in the marinade and set aside for 10 minutes.

Place the marinated salmon pieces on the lined baking sheet and sprinkle them with the sesame seeds.

Roast for 7 minutes, until lightly golden and cooked through.

Serve with the noodles, wedges of lime and a small bowl of sweet chilli sauce for dipping (if you wish).

Meat

Bolognese Sauce ❄

MAKES 8–10 CHILD PORTIONS
2 tablespoons olive oil
2 onions, finely diced
100 g/4 oz carrots, peeled
   and finely diced
100 g/4 oz courgette, diced
30 g/1 oz sweet red pepper,
   deseeded and finely diced
30 g/1 oz celery stalk, diced
2 garlic cloves, crushed
2 x 400 g/14 oz tins
   chopped tomatoes
1 tablespoon sun-dried
   tomato paste
2 teaspoons chopped fresh thyme
500 g/1 lb 1oz lean minced beef
150 ml/5 fl oz unsalted
   or weak beef stock
350 g/12 oz spaghetti, to serve
grated Parmesan cheese, to serve
1 tablespoon chopped fresh basil,
   to serve

Garlic Bread (optional)
1 small baguette
25 g/1 oz soft butter
1 garlic clove, crushed
2 teaspoons chopped
   flat-leaf parsley

You can't go wrong with this classic bolognese recipe. It's important to introduce red meat into your baby's diet from 6 months as the iron reserves they are born with start to run out – red meat provides the best and most easily absorbed source of iron.

• •

Heat half the oil in a saucepan, add the onions, carrots, courgette, red pepper and celery and sauté for 5 minutes, then add the garlic and sauté for a further 30 seconds. Add the tinned tomatoes, tomato paste and thyme, bring to the boil, then reduce the heat, cover and simmer for 20 minutes. Remove from the heat and blend until smooth using a stick blender.

Heat the remaining oil in a frying pan over a high heat, add the minced beef and fry it (in batches if necessary) until browned, breaking up any lumps with a wooden spoon. Add the beef to the tomato sauce with the stock. Return the pan to the heat and simmer for 30 minutes.

Cook the spaghetti according to the packet instructions, then drain. Serve the bolognaise with spaghetti and sprinkled with grated Parmesan and basil.

For the garlic bread (if serving), preheat the oven to 180°C/350°F/Gas 4. Cut 6 shallow slices in the baton. Combine the butter, garlic and parsley and spread it into the slits and over the top of the bread. Wrap it in foil, place on a baking sheet and bake for 10 minutes, then unwrap and bake for a further 5 minutes.

Bolognese Pasta Bake ❄

MAKES 4–6 CHILD PORTIONS
150 g/5 oz fusilli pasta
450 g/1 lb Bolognese Sauce

Cheese Sauce
20 g/¾ oz butter
2 tablespoons plain flour
250 ml/9 fl oz whole milk, warmed
1 teaspoon Dijon mustard
40 g/1½ oz grated Parmesan
    cheese

Leftover Bolognese

This pasta bake is a good introduction to beef for your baby. A cheesy sauce often helps encourage them to give something a try.

• •

Cook the pasta according to the packet instructions, then drain.

Mix the Bolognese Sauce and cooked pasta together and spoon the mixture into a baking dish. Preheat the grill to high.

To make the cheese sauce, melt the butter in a saucepan. Add the flour and stir over the heat for a minute, then gradually add the milk, whisking continuously, until thickened. Remove from the heat, add the mustard and Parmesan, stir until the cheese has melted, then spoon the sauce on top of the pasta.

Place under the hot grill for 10 minutes until bubbling.

Cottage Pie ❄

MAKES 4 CHILD PORTIONS

400 g/14 oz floury potatoes,
    peeled and diced
2 tablespoons milk
a small knob of butter
300 g/11 oz Bolognese Sauce
cooked peas and carrot stars,
    to serve (optional)

Leftover Bolognese

Cottage pie is the ultimate comfort food and the perfect winter warmer. Why not divide portions between mini ramekins. Serving it like this is more appealing to children as they feel like they have their own very special dinner.

● ●

Preheat the grill to high. Put the potatoes in a pan of cold salted water, bring to the boil, then reduce the heat and simmer for about 15 minutes, until tender. Drain and mash with the milk and butter.

Divide the Bolognese Sauce between 4 small heatproof dishes and spoon the mash on top.

Place under the hot grill for 5–8 minutes until bubbling and golden on top. Remove from the grill, leave to cool slightly and garnish with cooked peas and carrot stars.

Sweet Potato Boats

MAKES 2 SWEET POTATO BOATS
(2 CHILD PORTIONS)

1 small sweet potato
3 tablespoons Bolognese Sauce
2 tablespoons grated mature
   Cheddar cheese

An excellent source of vitamin A, sweet potato is packed full of goodness and acts as a fun and healthy 'boat' for your bolognese. The quantities below can easily be doubled or tripled to serve a whole family.

Prick the sweet potato with a fork several times and cook it in the microwave for 7–10 minutes until soft in the middle, or bake in the oven at 200°C/400°F/ Gas 6 for about 45 minutes, or until soft and cooked through.

Preheat the grill to high. As soon as the potato is cool enough to handle, slice it in half and scoop out some of the potato into a bowl. Mix it with the Bolognese Sauce and spoon it back into the boats. Sprinkle with the cheese.

Place under a hot grill for 5 minutes until the cheese has melted.

Serve with steamed broccoli florets.

Lamb Chops with Thyme, Garlic and Lemon

DAIRY FREE

MAKES 4 CHILD PORTIONS
leaves from 4 sprigs fresh thyme
2 teaspoons lemon juice
1 garlic clove, crushed
2 tablespoons olive oil
4 lamb chops

These marinated lamb chops are beautifully tender. Cut into strips, the tender meat makes great finger food for young babies, or you can give them the chops whole, trimming off the fat and wrapping the bone to make it easier for them to hold.

Put the thyme sprigs in a bowl with the lemon juice, garlic and oil. Add the lamb chops and coat them in the marinade. Marinate for at least 1 hour (ideally overnight).

Preheat the grill to high. Put the marinated chops on a baking sheet and grill about 20 cm/8 in away from a hot grill for 8–10 minutes, turning them over halfway through the cooking time. This makes a 'pink' medium-cooked chop. For a well done chop, cook it under the grill for 12–15 minutes.

Remove from the grill, leave to rest for a few minutes, and serve with couscous (try my Cherub's Chicken Couscous, without the chicken, on page 125).

Swedish Meatballs ❄

MAKES 20 MEATBALLS
(4–5 CHILD PORTIONS)

Meatballs
300 g/11 oz lean minced beef
30 g/1 oz dried or Panko
    breadcrumbs
30 g/1 oz finely grated
    Parmesan cheese
1½ teaspoons chopped
    fresh thyme
1 egg, beaten
a few dashes of Worcestershire
    sauce
2–3 tablespoons rapeseed
    or sunflower oil
chopped fresh parsley to
    garnish (optional)

Sauce
2 tablespoons sunflower oil
2 leeks, trimmed and finely sliced
1 garlic clove, crushed
250 ml/9 fl oz unsalted or
    weak beef stock
200 g/7 oz sour cream
a few drops of Worcestershire
    sauce
1 teaspoon balsamic vinegar
a little salt and pepper (for
    babies over 12 months old)

Nothing beats homemade Swedish meatballs smothered in a creamy gravy sauce. This is a family favourite in my house.

• •

To make the meatballs, combine all the ingredients (except the oil and parsley) in a mixing bowl. Season with salt and pepper (if using), mix well, then shape the mixture into 20 equal-sized balls.

Heat the oil in a frying pan. Fry the meatballs (in batches if necessary) for 4–5 minutes, turning them occasionally, until golden on all sides but not completely cooked through. Set aside.

Now, make the sauce. Heat the oil in a saucepan, add the leeks and cook gently over a low heat until they are completely soft. Add the garlic and fry for a few minutes, then add the stock. Simmer the sauce for 3–4 minutes until it has reduced by a third. Add the meatballs and simmer for a further 10 minutes until the meatballs are cooked through.

Stir in the sour cream, Worcestershire sauce and vinegar, and heat through until bubbling, then serve with mash (such as my carrot and potato mash pie topping on page 145), sprinkling the meatballs with parsley if you wish.

Minty Lamb Koftas 1+ year ❄

**MAKES 8 KOFTAS
(8 CHILD PORTIONS)**

1 tablespoon olive oil
1 small red onion, finely chopped
1 garlic clove, crushed
½ teaspoon ground cumin
225 g/8 oz minced lamb
20 g/¾ oz fresh breadcrumbs
2 teaspoons chopped
    fresh mint leaves
1 teaspoon runny honey
1 egg yolk
8 small pitta breads, to serve
4 tablespoons Greek yoghurt,
    to serve
sliced tomato and cucumber,
    to serve
a little salt and pepper

You will also need: 8 wooden
    skewers, soaked in warm
    water for 30 minutes

Children love to eat things on sticks, but these koftas are just as good stuffed into pittas or wraps (remove the skewer first), or you can use the mince mixture to make larger lamb burgers. Try them with my Minty Yoghurt Dressing (see page 48).

• •

Heat the oil in a frying pan, add the onion and sauté for 5–6 minutes, until soft. Add the garlic and cumin, and cook for a further minute, then transfer to a bowl. Add the remaining ingredients (except the pitta, yoghurt, tomato and cucumber), season with salt and pepper and mix thoroughly. For a finer texture pulse everything in the bowl of a food processor.

Divide the mixture into eight and form into balls. Thread a skewer through each ball and use your hand to firmly form each ball into a patty shape on the skewer. If you have time, chill the koftas on a plate in the fridge for 1–2 hours.

Preheat the grill to high. Grill the koftas on a grill rack for 8–10 minutes, turning halfway, until cooked through. Cool slightly before serving and remove the skewers for smaller children. Split the pittas and stuff a kofta into each pitta, along with some yoghurt, tomato and cucumber.

Tasty Beef Quesadillas

MAKES 12 WEDGES
(6 CHILD PORTIONS)
1 tablespoon sunflower oil
4 spring onions, sliced
75 g/3 oz courgette, finely diced
½ sweet red pepper, deseeded
  and finely diced
110 g/4¼ oz lean minced beef
1 garlic clove, crushed
3 tablespoons drained
  tinned sweetcorn
1½ teaspoons korma curry paste
1 teaspoon sun-dried tomato paste
40 g/1½ oz grated Cheddar
  cheese
4 small tortilla wraps

Children will love to help prepare their very own quesadilla creations.

Heat the oil in a frying pan, add the spring onion, courgette and pepper and sauté for 2 minutes.

Add the beef and fry with the vegetables until browned, breaking up any lumps of mince with a wooden spoon. Add the garlic, sweetcorn, curry paste and sundried tomato paste. Stir and simmer for 4 minutes.

Put a tortilla on a board. Spoon half of the mixture on top and spread it out to the edges. Sprinkle with half of the cheese. Top with another tortilla. Make the second quesadilla with the remaining tortillas and filling.

Heat a large frying pan until hot. Add a quesadilla and fry for 1 minute on each side, until golden, crisp and the cheese has melted. Remove from the pan and repeat with the second quesadilla.

Remove from the heat and slice each quesadilla into 6 wedges. Serve with crudités and dips (see my dip recipes on pages 41).

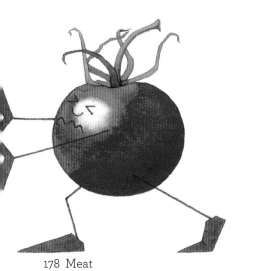

Steak with Roasted Vegetables

MAKES 4 CHILD PORTIONS

300 g/11 oz sirloin steak

½ teaspoon chopped
rosemary leaves

1 tablespoon plus 1 teaspoon
light olive oil

Roasted Vegetables

175 g/6 oz new potatoes, halved

1 small sweet potato, scrubbed
and cut into thin wedges
or chips

1 sweet yellow pepper, deseeded
and cut into strips

½ sweet red pepper, deseeded
and cut into strips

1 tablespoon olive oil

1 teaspoon finely chopped
rosemary leaves

1 teaspoon balsamic vinegar

6 button mushrooms,
halved if large

Red meat is good for young children as it provides the best source of iron. Serve with lots of sweet roasted veggie fingers for a nutritious mini adult meal.

• •

Put the rosemary and 1 teaspoon of the light olive oil in a bowl, and add the steak, coating it in the aromatic oil.

Preheat the oven to 200°C/400°F/Gas 6. Put the potatoes (new and sweet) and peppers in a roasting tin. Add the oil and rosemary and roast for 20 minutes until golden. Add the balsamic vinegar and the mushrooms and roast for a further 10 minutes.

Heat a frying pan until hot, add the remaining light olive oil and fry the steak for 2 minutes on each side, then remove from the pan and leave to rest for 5 minutes. Slice the rested steak into strips and serve it with the roasted vegetables.

Mini Burgers ❄

MAKES 20 MINI BURGERS

75 g/3 oz fresh breadcrumbs
1 small red onion, chopped
100 g/4 oz peeled and
    grated carrot
50 g/2 oz peeled, cored
    and grated apple
250 g/9 oz lean minced beef
1 small garlic clove, crushed
1 teaspoon chopped fresh thyme
25 g/1 oz grated Parmesan cheese
canapé-style mini burger rolls
    (optional)
carrot sticks, halved cherry
    tomatoes and tomato ketchup,
    to serve

Grated apple is the secret ingredient here. It makes the burgers succulent and tender, giving them a flavour that babies love. Simply blitz all the ingredients together in a blender and you're good to go. Freeze any leftover cooked burgers so you know you have a home-cooked meal ready and waiting on those busy days.

• •

Place the breadcrumbs in the bowl of a food processor with the onion, carrot, apple, minced beef, garlic, thyme and Parmesan and blitz until finely chopped.

Transfer the burger mixture to a bowl and use your hands to shape it into 20 mini burgers.

Preheat the grill to high.

Line a baking sheet with foil and lightly grease the foil.

Place the burgers on the baking sheet and place under the grill for 5 minutes. Turn over and grill for a further 3–5 minutes until lightly golden and cooked through.

Serve in mini burger rolls, if you wish, with carrot sticks, cherry tomatoes and ketchup.

Roast Beef

MAKES 5 ADULT PORTIONS
OR 10 CHILD PORTIONS

1 kg/2 lb 2oz topside
roasting joint
1 tablespoon olive oil
fresh thyme leaves from 3 sprigs
a little salt and pepper (for
babies over 12 months old)

Yorkshire Puddings
sunflower oil
120 g/4¼ oz plain flour
3 eggs
150 ml/5 fl oz whole milk

Gravy
2 tablespoons sunflower oil
2 tablespoons plain flour
500 ml/18 fl oz unsalted or
weak beef stock
½ teaspoon Worcestershire sauce
1 teaspoon tomato puree

Who doesn't love a roast? This is the ultimate family
Sunday lunch. Cut the beef into strips for your baby
and serve it with a little gravy and some roasted
vegetables like sweet potato and parsnip. I have also
come up with two tasty recipes using leftover roast
beef for your little one.

Preheat the oven to 180°C/350°F/Gas 4.

Put the beef in a small roasting tin, drizzle with the
oil, season with salt and pepper (if using) and scatter
with thyme leaves. Roast for 50 minutes–1 hour (for
medium doneness), until golden and firm to the touch.
Remove from the oven, cover with foil and leave to
rest for 20 minutes.

While the beef is resting, make the Yorkshire puddings.
Increase the oven temperature to 200°C/400°F/Gas 6.
Put a 12-hole deep muffin tin in the oven to get hot,
then pour a thin layer of sunflower oil into each hole.
Put the tin back into the oven for 5 minutes.

Place the flour in a bowl, make a well in the middle,
add the eggs then gradually pour in the milk, whisking
continuously, until you have a smooth batter.

Ladle the batter into the 12 holes of the hot tin and put into the oven for 15–18 minutes until well risen, golden and crisp.

Place the beef on a board. Pour the cooking juices into a jug. Add 2 tablespoons of oil to the tin the beef was roasted in and put the tin on the hob. Sprinkle in the flour and whisk over the heat for a few seconds before gradually whisking in the stock, until you have a thick and smooth mixture. Add the Worcestershire sauce, tomato puree and some salt and pepper (if using), together with any beef cooking juices. Boil, then simmer and reduce until you have a gravy consistency.

Carve the rested beef and serve it with the gravy and Yorkshire puddings, and green vegetables of your choice.

My First Beef Curry ❄ 1+ year

MAKES 4 CHILD PORTIONS

1 tablespoon sunflower oil
1 shallot, finely chopped
1 sweet red pepper,
   deseeded and diced
2 garlic cloves, crushed
1 tablespoon korma curry paste
1 teaspoon garam masala
300 ml/10 fl oz unsalted or
   weak beef stock
1–2 teaspoons mango chutney
1 tablespoon apple juice
2 teaspoons cornflour
40 g/1½ oz frozen peas
2–3 tablespoons double cream
120 g/4½ oz leftover roast
   beef, diced
cooked basmati rice, to serve

Leftover Roast Beef

Here's a great recipe for introducing new tastes and textures to your little one. Babies are often open to accepting new tastes between the age of 6 and 12 months but can become more fussy towards the end of the first year, so take the opportunity to introduce lots of flavour combinations before their first birthday. The korma paste and garam masala here act as a pleasant, subtle introduction to spice.

Heat the oil in a wok or frying pan, add the shallot, pepper and garlic and fry for 3 minutes, then add the curry paste and garam masala and fry for a few seconds.

Stir in the stock, mango chutney and apple juice, bring to the boil, and simmer for 5 minutes. Mix the cornflour with a little water and stir it into the curry sauce. Add the peas, cream and diced beef and stir until thickened and heated through. Serve with basmati rice.

Tasty Beef with Rice and Tomato Sauce ❄

MAKES 6 CHILD PORTIONS

1 tablespoon sunflower oil

2 shallots, chopped

2 garlic cloves, crushed

400 g/14 oz tin chopped tomatoes

150 ml/5 fl oz unsalted or
    weak beef stock

1 tablespoon chopped fresh thyme

2 tablespoons apple juice

150 g/5 oz leftover roast
    beef, diced

35 g/1 oz frozen peas

2 tablespoons drained
    tinned sweetcorn

100 g/4 oz brown or white
    long-grain rice

2 tablespoons grated
    Parmesan cheese

Leftover
Roast Beef

This is a great way to use up leftover roast beef, and little ones will love the bright colours of the added peas and sweetcorn which make it all the more enticing.

• •

Heat the oil in a saucepan, add the shallots and garlic and fry for 2–3 minutes. Add the tomatoes, stock, thyme and apple juice, bring to the boil, then simmer for 10 minutes.

Add the beef, peas and sweetcorn and simmer for 3 minutes, then remove from the heat.

Cook the rice according to the packet instructions, then drain well and add it to the sauce along with the Parmesan to serve.

Sweet Things

Carrot and Banana Cookies

MAKES 15 COOKIES

250 g/9 oz peeled bananas, chopped

115 g/4½ oz carrots, peeled and grated

100 g/4 oz raisins

2 heaped tablespoons smooth peanut butter

2 tablespoons sunflower oil

2–3 tablespoons agave syrup, maple syrup or honey

½ teaspoon ground cinnamon

1 teaspoon mixed spice

125 g/4½ oz porridge oats

Here's a guilt-free sweet treat! Carrots, bananas, raisins and oats make this a far healthier snack than most shop-bought treats, as it doesn't contain refined sugar. Only use honey if serving to babies over 12 months old.

• •

Preheat the oven to 180°C/350°F/Gas 4 and line a baking sheet with baking parchment.

Place the bananas in the bowl of a food processor and blitz until smooth. Add the remaining ingredients and pulse a few times to roughly combine.

Transfer the mixture to a bowl, then divide it into 15 equal-sized balls.

Place the balls on the lined baking sheet and, using wet hands, slightly flatten each ball. Bake in the oven for 20 minutes, or until light golden brown. Remove from the oven, leave to cool on the tray for a few minutes, then transfer to a wire rack to cool completely.

Peanut Butter Cookies

MAKES 15 COOKIES

165 g/6 oz smooth peanut butter
50 g/2 oz ground almonds
55 g/2 oz sultanas
40 g/1½ oz desiccated coconut
1 teaspoon vanilla extract
2 tablespoons maple syrup
a pinch of salt
2 tablespoons buckwheat flour
   or plain flour
25 g/1 oz chocolate chips
   (for dairy free, use dairy
   free chocolate chips)

Babies are less likely to develop allergies if they are introduced to certain foods early on (see page 13). Peanut butter and finely ground nuts can be introduced from 6 months and these cookies are a tasty way to bring new flavours into your child's diet.

• •

Preheat the oven to 160°C/325°F/Gas 3 and line two baking sheets with baking parchment.

Place all the ingredients, except the chocolate chips, in the bowl of a food processor and blitz until roughly chopped and the mixture has come together.

Transfer the cookie mixture to a bowl and add the chocolate chips.

Shape the cookie dough into 15 equal-sized balls and place the balls on the lined trays. Flatten them slightly and press the prongs of a fork gently onto each one. Bake for 12 minutes until lightly golden, then remove from the oven, leave to cool slightly on the trays, then transfer to a wire rack to cool completely.

Little Red Jellies

DAIRY FREE

MAKES 6–8 CHILD PORTIONS
3 gelatine leaves
150 ml/5 fl oz strawberry or
  raspberry cordial
150 g/5 oz fresh raspberries

I've always loved jelly and it's so simple to make your own. You can use any cordial, such as elderflower or blackberry, to make your child's favourite flavour.

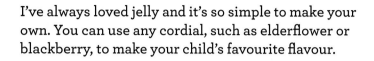

Place the gelatine leaves in a bowl of cold water and leave to soak for 5 minutes until soft.

Meanwhile, put the cordial in a saucepan. Add 200 ml/ 7 fl oz water and heat until hot but not boiling. Remove from the heat.

Remove the gelatine leaves from the bowl, squeeze out any excess water and add them to the hot cordial. Stir until the gelatine has dissolved.

Divide the raspberries between 6–8 little heatproof pots. Pour the jelly mixture on top and chill for 4 hours, or until set.

Spiced Apple and Date Squares

MAKES 20 SQUARES

200 g/7 oz porridge oats
50 g/2 oz desiccated coconut
50 g/2 oz pecans, finely chopped
75 g/3 oz pitted dates,
   roughly chopped
150 ml/5 fl oz boiling water
100 ml/4 fl oz sunflower oil
1 teaspoon vanilla extract
115 g/4¼ oz runny honey
1 teaspoon ground cinnamon
¼ teaspoon mixed spice
75 g/3 oz dried apple,
   finely chopped

Dried fruit is a good source of fibre, iron and energy. Adding a little spice to these snacks will intrigue your little one and pairing the spice and oats with apple, date and coconut transforms this healthy bake into an irresistible treat.

• •

Preheat the oven to 200°C/400°F/Gas 6 and line a 20 cm/8 in square cake tin with clingfilm.

Combine the oats, coconut and pecans in a bowl, then spread them out on a baking sheet. Bake for 10–15 minutes, stirring halfway through, until lightly toasted. Remove from the oven and leave to cool.

Put the dates and boiling water in the bowl of a small blender or processor and blend until smooth.

Place the oil, vanilla, honey and date mixture in a saucepan and heat until runny. Remove from the heat, add the toasted oat mixture, spices and apple and stir until combined.

Spoon the mixture into the cake tin and level the surface. Chill in the fridge for 2 hours before turning out, removing the clingfilm and cutting into 20 squares. The squares will keep well, in an airtight container, for 2–3 days.

Strawberry and Rhubarb Crumble

MAKES 6 CHILD PORTIONS
25 g/1 oz ground almonds
400 g/14 oz trimmed rhubarb,
    cut into 1.5 cm/¾ in lengths
100 g/4 oz fresh strawberries,
    hulled and halved
4 tablespoons caster sugar

Crumble
150 g/5 oz plain flour
a generous pinch of fine salt
100 g/4 oz cold butter, cubed
75 g/3 oz demerara sugar
50 g/2 oz ground almonds

A good crumble is comfort food at its best, and I love the combination of rhubarb and strawberries. Sprinkle ground almonds over the base of the dish to soak up some of the juices from the fruit, so that they don't bubble up over the top when it's cooking.

· ·

Preheat the oven to 200°C/400°F/Gas 6.

To make the topping, mix the flour with the salt in a bowl and rub in the butter using your fingertips until the mixture resembles breadcrumbs, then stir in the demerara sugar and ground almonds. Alternatively, place the ingredients in a food processor and blitz briefly.

Sprinkle the ground almonds over the base of an ovenproof dish (about 17 cm/7 in diameter). Mix the rhubarb and strawberries with the sugar and tip them into the dish.

Cover the fruit with the crumble topping and sprinkle over a tablespoon of water (this will help to make the topping crispy). Bake for about 25 minutes, until the crumble topping is golden brown.

Remove from the oven and allow to cool slightly before serving.

Courgette, Orange and Spice Muffins ❄

MAKES 18 MINI MUFFINS
OR 10 REGULAR MUFFINS

165 g/6 oz self-raising flour
½ teaspoon baking powder
½ teaspoon bicarbonate of soda
½ teaspoon mixed spice
a pinch of fine salt
100 ml/4 fl oz freshly squeezed
   orange juice
grated zest of 1 medium orange
45 g/1½ oz butter, melted
1 egg
60 g/2½ oz soft light brown sugar
1 courgette, finely grated
   (about 125 g/4½ oz)
60 g/2½ oz sultanas

Tip

★ To reheat frozen muffins,
remove them from the freezer
container and leave to to defrost
at room temperature overnight.
Alternatively, reheat straight from
frozen in the oven at 180°C/350°F/
Gas 4 for 10–15 minutes (or for less
time if reheating mini muffins).

Here's a tasty way to eat your greens! These
deliciously moist bakes are low in sugar, too, and
you can make them as mini muffins or regular
muffins. Either way, they freeze well, so are an
excellent snack to have to hand.

•••

Preheat the oven to 180°C/350°F/Gas 4 and line
two 12-hole mini muffin tins with 18 mini muffin
paper cases, or one regular 12-hole muffin tin with
10 paper cases.

Sift the flour, baking powder, bicarbonate of soda, mixed
spice and salt into a large bowl and stir to combine.

Whisk the orange juice, zest, melted butter, egg and
sugar together in a jug or bowl until well combined.

Stir the wet ingredients into the dry ingredients, then
fold in the grated courgette and sultanas. Spoon the
muffin mixture into the muffin cases and bake for
12–15 minutes for mini muffins or 22–25 minutes for
regular muffins, until a skewer inserted into one
of the muffins comes out clean.

Remove from the oven and leave to cool on a
wire rack.

Carrot, Maple and Sultana Muffins

MAKES 24 MINI MUFFINS

2 eggs
100 g/4 oz softened unsalted butter
75 g/3 oz soft dark brown sugar
2 tablespoons maple syrup
1 teaspoon mixed spice
1 teaspoon baking powder
100 g/4 oz self-raising flour
50 g/2 oz peeled and grated carrot
50 g/2 oz sultanas
4½ tablespoons cream cheese
24 fresh raspberries
icing sugar, to dust

Carrot works so well in muffins, keeping the mixture moist and moreish, and mini versions are the perfect size for busy little fingers.

• •

Preheat the oven to 160°C/325°F/Gas 3 and line a large mini-muffin tin with 24 mini-muffin cases.

Place all the ingredients (except the cream cheese, raspberries and icing sugar) in a mixing bowl and whisk with an electric hand-held whisk. Alternatively, use a stand mixer.

Divide the mixture evenly between the paper cases and bake for 18 minutes, or until well risen and lightly golden. Remove from the oven and leave to cool on a wire rack.

To serve, spread each cooled muffin with a teaspoon of cream cheese, garnish with a raspberry and dust with icing sugar.

Mini Energy Balls

MAKES 25 BALLS
200 g/7 oz pitted dates
3 tablespoons smooth
    peanut butter
3 tablespoons sunflower oil
40 g/1½ oz desiccated coconut
3 tablespoons sunflower seeds
125 g/4½ oz porridge oats
40 g/1½ oz raisins
20 g/¾ oz pecans, very
    finely chopped
1 tablespoon chia seeds
20 g/¾ oz Rice Krispies
a pinch of salt (for babies
    over 12 months old)

Try these delicious healthy snacks to give you or your child a mid-morning or afternoon energy boost.

• •

Put the dates in a saucepan with 100 ml/4 fl oz boiling water. Cover with a lid, bring to the boil and simmer for 2 minutes, then remove from the heat and set aside for 5 minutes.

Transfer the soaked date mixture to a blender or food processor and blitz until smooth (or blend in a bowl using a stick blender).

Place the peanut butter and date mixture in a saucepan and melt over a low heat until smooth. Remove from the heat and add the remaining ingredients to the pan. Mix well, then shape into 30 equal-sized little balls. Place the balls on a plate and chill for 1 hour before eating.

The balls will keep in the fridge, stored in an airtight container, for up to 5 days.

Strawberry Rice Pudding

MAKES 6 CHILD PORTIONS
50 g/2 oz pudding rice
600 ml/1 pint whole milk
¼ teaspoon vanilla extract
1½ tablespoons caster sugar
a knob of unsalted butter,
   plus extra for greasing
strawberry jam, to serve

This is a quick and tasty way to cook rice pudding, and kids love it. Stir in some strawberry jam for an added fruity flavour (use sugar-free strawberry jam for babies under one).

• •

Preheat the oven to 150°C/300°F/Gas 2 and grease an ovenproof dish with butter.

Place the rice, milk, vanilla extract and sugar in the dish and stir well. Dot the surface with butter then bake the pudding for 30 minutes. Remove from the oven and stir, then continue to bake for 1–1½ hours until the rice is cooked. Remove the dish from the oven, let it cool slightly and serve each portion topped with a little strawberry jam.

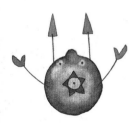

Rice Krispie, Oat and Peanut Butter Bars

MAKES 12 BARS
50 g/2 oz soft light brown sugar
160 g/6 oz smooth peanut butter
75 ml/3 fl oz maple syrup
75 ml/3 fl oz sunflower oil
50 g/2 oz Rice Krispies
50 g/2 oz porridge oats
60 g/2½ oz pecans,
   roughly chopped
50 g/2 oz sultanas
50 g/2 oz dried apricots,
   finely chopped
a pinch of salt (optional)

This is a peanut butter-lover's dream treat. It's so good and so simple to make, and a good recipe to make with budding little chefs.

• •

Line a 20 cm/8 in square baking tin with clingfilm, allowing it to overhang the sides of the tin.

Place the sugar, peanut butter, maple syrup and sunflower oil in a saucepan and gently warm it through over a low heat until the mixture is runny and smooth.

Remove the pan from the heat and add the remaining ingredients (including the pinch of salt, if using). Stir to combine, then spoon into the square baking tin. Press it down firmly and evenly (I use a potato masher), cover with clingfilm and chill for 3–4 hours until firm.

Once firm, turn out, remove the clingfilm and cut into 12 bars. The bars will keep well in an airtight container in the fridge for 4–5 days.

Carrot, Coconut and Raisin Bites

DAIRY FREE

MAKES 20 BITES

75 g/3 oz pitted dates
100 ml/4 fl oz boiling water
50 g/2 oz pecans
50 g/2 oz desiccated coconut
100 g/4 oz carrots, peeled
    and grated
½ teaspoon mixed spice
30 g/1 oz raisins
2 tablespoons sunflower oil
50 g/2 oz porridge oats
a good pinch of salt (for
    babies over 12 months old)

These make the perfect healthy snack for little ones. They contain no refined sugar and the natural sweetness comes from the dates, carrots and raisins.

• •

Put the dates in a saucepan with the boiling water. Cover with a lid, bring to the boil and simmer for 2 minutes, then remove from the heat and set aside for 5 minutes.

Put the pecans in a food processor and blitz until finely chopped, then set aside.

Put the soaked dates and 2 tablespoons of the soaking liquid in the processor. Blitz until smooth, then add the remaining ingredients, including the chopped pecans. Blitz again briefly, until the mixture has come together but is still coarse.

Shape the mixture into 20 balls, place the balls on a plate and chill them in the fridge for at least 1 hour before eating. The balls will keep in the fridge for up to 2 days.

Summer Fruit Yoghurt Ice Cream

MAKES 6 CHILD PORTIONS

300 g/11 oz mixed frozen
   summer fruits e.g. raspberries,
   blackberries, blueberries,
   thawed at room temperature
   or heated gently in a pan
   or microwave
400 g/14 oz natural yoghurt
200 ml/7 fl oz double cream
75 g/3 oz caster sugar

Making frozen yoghurt is easier than you might think – it can be made without an ice-cream maker.

• •

Puree and sift half the summer fruits.

Stir the yoghurt if it is set yoghurt and lightly whisk the cream in a bowl until it forms soft peaks. Fold together the yoghurt, cream, caster sugar and the summer fruit puree.

Freeze in an ice-cream machine, following the manufacturer's instructions. When frozen but still with a soft texture, mix the remaining summer fruits with the remaining tablespoon of caster sugar and stir them into the ice cream mixture.

Alternatively, spoon the ice cream mixture into a suitable container and put it in the freezer. When half frozen, remove from the freezer and beat well until smooth, either with a electric hand-held whisk or in a food processor, to break down the ice crystals. Mix the rest of the fruit with the tablespoon of caster sugar and stir it into the yoghurt ice cream. Return to the freezer and stir one or two more times during the freezing process to get a smooth ice cream.

Chocolate Beetroot Brownies

MAKES 25 SQUARES

200 g/7 oz dark chocolate,
   chopped
100 g/4 oz unsalted butter, cubed
3 large eggs
1 teaspoon vanilla extract
225 g/8 oz caster sugar
100 g/4 oz self-raising flour
20 g/¾ oz cocoa powder
300 g/11 oz cooked beetroot,
   grated

These brownies are chocolate heaven, and what a great way to boost your 5-a-day!

Preheat the oven to 160°C/325°F/Gas 3 and line a 20 cm/8 in square cake tin with baking parchment.

Melt the chocolate and butter together in a large heatproof bowl over a pan of simmering water.

Remove the bowl from the pan, let the mixture cool slightly, then add the eggs, vanilla extract and sugar and whisk using an electric hand-held whisk until well mixed, then add the flour, cocoa and beetroot. Whisk again, then spoon the mixture into the tin. Bake for 30 minutes until the cake is set and just firm in the middle. Remove from the oven, leave to cool, then remove from the tin and cut into 25 squares. Store in an airtight container in the fridge, or at room temperature, for up to 2 days.

Peach, Apple and Berry Crumble ✻

MAKES 6 CHILD PORTIONS
25 g/1 oz butter
2 Pink Lady apples (or
   other sweet eating apple),
   peeled, cored and diced
2 ripe peaches, skinned,
   stoned and diced
4 tablespoons soft light
   brown sugar
100 g/4 oz fresh blueberries
150 g/5 oz fresh raspberries

Crumble
150 g/5 oz plain flour
25 g/1 oz porridge oats
75 g/3 oz cold butter, cubed
4 tablespoons soft light
   brown sugar

This light crumble is bursting with a gooey peach, berry and apple filling. It's full of antioxidants from the berries and fibre from the peach and apple, and is an easy way to get your child eating and enjoying more fruit.

● ●

Preheat the oven to 180°C/350°F/Gas 4.

To make the fruit filling, melt the butter in a saucepan. Add the diced apple and peach and sauté for 3 minutes, then add the sugar. Remove from the heat, stir in the berries and spoon the mixture into a 20 cm/8 in ovenproof dish or 6 individual ramekins.

Mix all of the crumble topping ingredients together in a bowl. Rub in the butter using your fingertips until the mixture resembles coarse breadcrumbs. Alternatively, place the ingredients in a food processor and blitz briefly.

Scatter the topping over the fruit and bake until bubbling and golden on top (25–30 minutes if using a large dish, 20 minutes for ramekins).

Remove from the oven and allow to cool slightly before serving.

Egg and Dairy-free Chocolate Cake

MAKES 10 CHILD PORTIONS
Chocolate Cake
175 ml/6 fl oz sunflower oil
75 g/3 oz golden syrup
2 teaspoons vanilla extract
500 ml/18 fl oz boiling water
60 g/2½ oz cocoa powder
450 g/1 lb self-raising flour
200 g/7 oz caster sugar
1 teaspoon baking powder
2 teaspoons bicarbonate
  of soda

Chocolate Icing and Filling
75 g/3 oz dairy-free margarine
75 g/3 oz soya soft cheese
150 g/5 oz icing sugar,
  plus extra to dust
50 g/2 oz cocoa powder
1 teaspoon vanilla extract
125 g/4½ oz dairy-free chocolate,
  chopped, plus extra to
  grate and decorate
8 tablespoons seedless
  raspberry jam, warmed
  until runny

Just because you have an allergy doesn't mean you can't enjoy a good cake ... This crowd-pleaser is great for children's parties.

• •

Preheat the oven to 160°C/325°F/Gas 3 and grease and line the bases of 2 x 20 cm/8 in round sandwich tins.

Stir the oil, syrup, vanilla and boiling water together in a large bowl until well mixed. Sift in the cocoa powder and flour, then add the sugar, baking powder and bicarbonate of soda and whisk until light and fluffy. Divide the mixture between the tins. Bake for 30–35 minutes until risen and firm in the middle. Remove from the oven and transfer to a wire rack to cool.

For the icing, whisk the margarine, soft cheese and icing sugar together in a bowl until light and fluffy. Stir in the cocoa powder and vanilla extract. Melt the chocolate in a heatproof bowl over a pan of simmering water, then leave to cool before adding it to the bowl. Whisk the icing until it thickens.

Put one of the cakes on a cake stand. Brush the warm jam over the cake. Spread a third of the icing on top, right to the edges. Place the second cake on top and brush it with more jam. Completely coat the top and sides of the cake with the remaining icing. Decorate with chocolate and dust with icing sugar.

INDEX

Cookbook-inspired meals for toddlers & children

Busy days still deserve the best mealtimes. That's why Annabel has transformed her most popular recipes into super-quick and nutritionally balanced meals. Ideal for toddlers and children aged one to four, Annabel's chilled and frozen ranges are low in salt and a tasty way towards their 5-a-day.

Visit **www.annabelkarmel.com** to discover where you can stock up on Annabel's delicious meals.

The must-have recipe app

Mums everywhere rely on Annabel's award-winning Baby & Toddler Recipe App. Filled with more than 220 delicious, nutritious recipes, simple planners, shopping lists, and more, it's the handiest of guides for easy mealtime inspiration – whether you're cooking for baby, toddler or the whole family.

Available on iPhone and Android.

Be a part of the AK Club

Join the AK Club for free today and discover exclusive recipes and special content, insider news, competitions, plus a host of great offers. You can also be a part of Annabel's world on social media too.

www.annabelkarmel.com

 annabelkarmeluk   annabelkarmel    annabelkarmel

The New Complete Baby & Toddler Meal Planner

The ultimate companion to Annabel's Baby-Led Weaning Recipes

If you are looking to explore spoon-led feeding alongside baby-led weaning, Annabel's *New Complete Baby & Toddler Meal Planner* makes for the perfect companion to this book.

A global bestseller, this is the No.1 cookbook for babies and toddlers, with over 4 million copies sold. Annabel's special 25th Anniversary edition is filled with new recipes, timeless classics, advice, planners and a handy weaning chart.

www.annabelkarmel.com

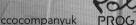

Thanks to:

Sarah Louise Smith, Lucinda
McCord, Dave King, Emma Smith,
Laura Nickoll, Sarah Almond
Bushell MPhill, BSc RD, Dr Adam
Fox MA, Nadine Wickenden,
Jonathan Lloyd, Tamsin Weston,
Maud Eden, Kostas Stavrinos,
Lucy Staley, Lara Karmel,
Chloe Leeser, Marina Magpoc,
Ebury.

A special thank you to our
cover-star finalists: Darcy
Beresford, Harlen Bodhi White,
Evie Lilly Gallacher, Milan
McIntyre and Lola Sokeyo.

First published in 2017 by Annabel Karmel.

Annabel Karmel Foods Ltd.
18A Pindock Mews, London W9 2PY

www.annabelkarmel.com

20 19 18 17 16 15 14 13 12 11 10 9 8 7 6 5 4 3 2

ISBN: 9781786750846

Photography: Dave King
Design: Smith & Gilmour, London
Project management: Laura Nickoll

Printed and bound in the EU by PALAZZO, London SW13 9HE

TIPPU

Abigail Pizer with David Day

Piccadilly Press • London

Tippu and his sister live with their family on a wide grassy plain in Africa.

They eat lots of fresh grass and leaves.

One morning trucks roar across the plain. The hunters have come in search of the elephants. They want elephant tusks for ivory jewellery. Guns are fired and the elephants flee in terror.

Tippu and his sister become lost. Then a friendly white stork arrives to help them.

'Come with me,' says the stork. 'I know a place that is safe for animals.'

The young elephants follow the stork for many miles. Eventually, they come to a land that is scorched and black.

'Men have burned all the grass, and the trees, and they have dammed up the river. Animals cannot live here now,' explains the stork.

After leaving the scorched land, Tippu and his sister come across a
sad little leopard.
'Hunters were here too,' explains the leopard. 'They wanted
leopard skins to make into fur coats.'

'Come with us,' says Tippu. 'We are going to a place that is safe for animals.'

The animals find a little rhinoceros standing by a dry river. 'The hunters were here,' says the little rhinoceros. 'They wanted rhinoceros horn to make into medicine.'

'Come with us,' says the leopard. 'We are going to a place that is safe for animals.'

The elephants, the leopard, and the little rhinoceros all follow the stork. Then trucks appear, and a helicopter whirrs overhead. The animals start to run.

Tippu hears shots. His legs feel weak, and he finds himself tumbling to the ground.

Tippu awakes in the truck with the other animals. The truck stops, and men gently lead the animals down to the grassy plain.

This place is safe for animals. Tippu begins to understand that not all men try to hurt animals. Some are good and gentle and helpful.

The little rhinoceros sees six other rhinoceros wading in the water-hole. He is so happy to see them, he runs over and rubs horns.

A moment later, the leopard sees a family of leopards resting beneath a big tree. She runs over to play with the other baby leopard.

Tippu and his sister hear a loud trumpeting sound. Standing out on the plain is a herd of elephants. One of them is calling.

They have found their family. They are safe.

Vaginal and Laparoscopic Vaginal Surgery

Vaginal and Laparoscopic Vaginal Surgery

Daniel Dargent MD
Professor of Gynecology and Obstetrics
Claude Bernard University, Lyon
Head, Department of Gynecology and Obstetrics
Hopital Édouard Herriot
Lyon
France

Denis Querleu MD
Professor of Oncology
University Paul Sabiter, Toulouse and
Head of Department of Surgery
Institut Claudius Regaud
Toulouse
France

Marie Plante MD
Gynecology Service
L'Hôtel-Dieu de Québec
Laval University
Quebec City
Canada

Karina Reynolds MD FRCS MRCOG
Senior Lecturer and Honorary Consultant
Department of Gynaecological Oncology
St Bartholemew's Hospital and Queen Mary University
London
UK

Taylor & Francis
Taylor & Francis Group

LONDON AND NEW YORK

A MARTIN DUNITZ BOOK

First published in the United Kingdom in 2004
by Taylor & Francis, an imprint of the Taylor & Francis Group,
2 Park Square, Milton Park, Abingdon, Oxon OX14 4RN

Tel.:	+44 (0) 20 7017 6000
Fax.:	+44 (0) 20 7017 6699
E-mail:	info.medicine@tandf.co.uk
Website:	www.tandf.co.uk/medicine

Reprinted 2005

A CIP record for this book is available from the British Library.

Library of Congress Cataloging-in-Publication Data

Data available on application

ISBN 1 84184 244 3

Distributed in North and South America by
Taylor & Francis
2000 NW Corporate Blvd
Boca Raton, FL 33431, USA
Within Continental USA
Tel.: 800 272 7737; Fax.: 800 374 3401
Outside Continental USA
Tel.: 561 994 0555; Fax.: 561 361 6018
E-mail: orders@crcpress.com

Distributed in the rest of the world by
Thomson Publishing Services
Cheriton House
North Way
Andover, Hampshire SP10 5BE, UK
Tel.:   +44 (0)1264 332424
E-mail: salesorder.tandf@thomsonpublishingservices.co.uk

Composition by Newgen Imaging Systems (P) Ltd, Chennai, India

Printed and bound in Italy by Grafos SA

Contents

Preface

The vaginal approach to abdominal surgery first emerged in the late 1820s but it was only towards the end of the nineteenth century that further attempts were made, and the technique began to be established. This vaginal approach has subsequently been in competition with laparotomy and, more recently, laparoscopy, to gain favor as the method of choice. The aim of this book is to guide surgeons through some of the core techniques in vaginal surgery, and to highlight situations where taking a joint laparoscopic vaginal approach can be most beneficial to the patient.

This book is the surgical counterpart of the leaflets distributed by some furniture dealers who sell their commodities in "flat packs" to be assembled by the consumer at home. The difference between such leaflets and this book of *Vaginal and Laparoscopic Vaginal Surgery* is that the latter works: every surgeon with basic training will be able, after reading this book, to perform the vaginal and laparoscopic vaginal operations herein.

To increase the chances of success for the reader who desires to enter or re-enter the field of this "renewed ancient surgery," selected operations are featured and are described in complete and full detail so that every surgeon, including those with no previous training in vaginal surgery, is able to become a "vaginalist." The figures do not skip any surgical steps of the operations presented and the figure legends clarify the surgical procedures as the reader progresses from one figure to the next. Thus the book can be read as an abundantly illustrated textbook or as a "comic strip" integrated with a comprehensive text on operative gynecology.

Acknowledgments

Mr Nacer Youcef deserves more than a mere mention in "Acknowledgments" even if he is at the top of the list. He took more than 95% of the photographs in this textbook. He is therefore the first editor of this tome, which aims to demonstrate in a precise way the details of each of the described operations. We are also grateful to Professor Michel Roy who provided the pictures for the chapter on "Laparoscopic vaginal radical trachelectomy"; to Professor Georges Mellier who provided the pictures for the "inverted Burch procedure"; and to Mr Vincent Dargent who took the great photographs of the instruments.

Dr Francois Saunier who revised Chapter 4, and Dr Jo Osborne who translated Chapter 7 (initially written in French), deserve our gratitude, as does Ms Martine Arnaud who typed and laid out the initial manuscript.

Mr Dominique Duval produced all the drawings and did a job of outstanding quality. He belongs to the very select group of true medical artists that still operate today in this new hi-tech world. Many thanks go to him.

ERBE Elektromedizin GmbH, Tubingen, Germany is thanked for its sponsorship.

We are indebted to the Royal College of Surgeons of Edinburgh who awarded the Autosuture Travelling Fellowship in Minimally Invasive Surgery to Karina Reynolds in 1998, thus supporting her numerous visits to Lyon, Paris, Lille and Toulouse.

1 Introduction

Vaginal surgery is the mother of abdominal surgery. Over past centuries, the only operations not resulting in patient death were those performed through the vaginal route on the female reproductive organs. These were also the only operations that could improve patient welfare at that time. This approach to surgery was empirical until the French surgeon Joseph Recamier performed the first well-standardized vaginal hysterectomy on July 26, 1829 at Hotel Dieu in Paris. The patient was a 50-year-old woman with a bulky cervical cancer. Recamier incised the anterior fornix of the vagina transversely, then the vesicouterine peritoneal cul de sac and drew the fundus downward. He divided the broad ligaments and then, having put ligatures around them, divided the uterine arteries and the paracervical ligaments before separating the uterus from the posterior fornix of the vagina. It was the first time an intra-abdominal organ was removed following principles that remain the basis of extirpative surgery today. The patient survived the surgery, was discharged after 20 days and was still alive 1 year later.

The first success of Recamier was followed by a series of failures and it is only at the end of that (nineteenth) century that new attempts were made. At about the same time, chloroform and antisepsis encouraged renewed surgical boldness and the abdominal approach for hysterectomy was introduced (Freund 1878). This was in competition with the vaginal approach, which French surgeons continued to use electively (Pean, Second, Doyen, Richelot and others). Casualties were three times lower in the case series gathered by the vaginalists (10 versus 30%). Nevertheless, vaginal surgery, which was at the beginning the procedure of choice, progressively lost its place as postoperative casualties became fewer and fewer thus making the difference between techniques less obvious to the individual surgeon assessing his own practice.

Nowadays the difference between the vaginal and abdominal approaches has not disappeared. This was mirrored in the national survey undertaken in the USA at the end of the twentieth century. The difference in mortality rates persists but is no longer at the percent level but rather estimated in units in ten thousands (1 in 10 000 versus 1 in 30 000). It is obviously a strong argument for favoring vaginal surgery. But this argument is not the only one. Vaginal surgery is not only less dangerous; it is also more patient-friendly.

Vaginal surgery not only reduces the risk of casualty but also significantly diminishes postoperative morbidity. Furthermore, it improves postoperative recovery, which is less painful, shorter and has the advantage of leaving no visible scars. This advantage can appear trivial but in fact from both the psychological and medical viewpoints is not. Preservation of body image is an important aspect of global welfare. On the other hand laparotomy is itself a source of rare but awkward complications such as seroma, hematoma, abscess, wound leakage and incisional hernia.

Today, laparoscopy is taking the place of laparotomy as a competitor of vaginal surgery. After laparoscopic surgery, recovery is fast and there is no alteration in body image. Incisional problems are few. However, other types of problems due to either the approach itself (introduction of trocars) or to the insufflation of CO_2 it necessitates (hypercapnia, hemodynamic problems) can occur. The Austrian surgeon Kurt Richter used to say that the risk of performing hysterectomy by laparotomy was equivalent to adding up the risks of two operations: laparotomy and hysterectomy. This aphorism applies to laparoscopy as well. The risks of laparoscopy differ from the risks of laparotomy. They are few and their prevention is possible but they will never be totally erased. At the end of the day, the vaginal approach, in all situations where it can be used, is surely the best choice for the patient: training in this ancestral surgery must continue.

The ambition of this book is neither to compile the descriptions one can find in the numerous textbooks that fill the libraries of our venerable universities nor to encourage the reader to believe that the descriptions herein are the fruit of an original personal elaboration. The techniques we describe are the ones the oldest of the editors has selected after having deeply scrutinized the ancient literature and, above all, having personally visited the giants who maintained the vaginal tradition in middle Europe after the Second World War: Navratil in Graz, Centaro in Padova, Käser in Bâle, Novak in Ljubjana, Richter in Bruck an der Mur and then in Munich and others. The youngest members of the editorial staff have adopted these techniques, consolidated over almost four decades. These are the only ones that will be described, but they will be described in full detail and, thanks to the liberal generosity of the publisher, illustrated with numerous photographs. We think that this editorial approach will be of most use to the reader.

In spite of our belief in the immutability of the rules of vaginal surgery, we will not ignore the benefits one can gain from the application of the latest technologies. The best example is the new bipolar coagulation technology that improves vaginal surgery in the field where laparoscopy is the more competitive, i.e. less tissue damage and less postoperative pain. On the other hand an important place will be devoted to laparoscopy in its role of assisting vaginal surgery. In fact, the laparoscopically assisted vaginal hysterectomy, which is the paradigm of so-called laparoscopic vaginal surgery, has only a limited place today. In the current state of the art, if one chooses to use the laparoscope in a patient with poor vaginal access, it is best to perform the operation from beginning to end under laparoscopic guidance. But there are circumstances where neither the purely laparoscopic approach nor the purely vaginal approach is adequate. The management of uterine cancer is an example. Other situations do exist which make the laparoscopic vaginal approach the approach of choice. These situations are tackled and the technical details are presented in the following chapters.

2 Anatomy

There is no question of describing here the anatomy of the female genital organs in the same way as it is described in textbooks devoted to human anatomy. The aim of this "fake" text of anatomy is two-fold: first, to describe the anatomy as it appears to the eye of the gynecologist, and second, to describe the anatomy as the surgeon transforms it.

Since Vesale (1514–1564), anatomy is described as it is seen when the subject is placed in the supine position in front of the anatomist: the urinary bladder is in front of the vagina, the uterus is above the bladder and so on. For gynecologists assessing the anatomy of a subject lying on a table in the so-called lithotomy position, the classical terminology is no longer appropriate; for this reason one has to replace the terms "in front of" and "behind," i.e. the adjectives "anterior" and "posterior" by the adjectives "ventral" and "dorsal." Likewise, the words "above" and "below," i.e. the adjectives "superior" and "inferior" by the adjectives "cephalic" or "cranial" and "podalic" or "caudal." We will, in this text, try not to forget this, but occasionally we will, bad habits being more difficult to lose than good ones.

The anatomy the surgeon is confronted with is quite different from classical anatomy. The live organs are different from organs congealed by fixation or by freezing and thawing. Moreover as soon as the first incision is made the relationship between the different anatomical structures changes. As far as vaginal surgery is concerned the transformation starts even before this moment: the relationship between the pelvic organs changes as soon as the retractors are put in place. The moment the cervix is placed under traction the anatomical architecture is almost inverted. Then incisions and subsequent maneuvers completely transform the situation.

The description we give in the following paragraphs is focused on the uterus because hysterectomy is the most commonly performed operation in the vaginal surgery repertoire and the uterus is often identified as the keystone of "pelvic organ harmony." First, we describe the organ itself and the relationship between it and neighboring organs. Then we move to a description of the anatomically preformed free spaces (the so-called avascular spaces) one has to identify and use as working spaces in order to isolate the organs from each other. We then finish with a description of the so-called ligaments one must identify in order to either divide them if one intends to remove the uterus or to repair them if one intends to restore the pelvic architecture. In each of these sections the static anatomy is described first followed by the modifications that surgery imposes on this anatomy (Figures 2.1–2.3). And finally, the text ends with a description of the urogenital and pelvic diaphragms, which provide the surgeon with the approach to the uterus and to neighboring organs.

Anatomy of the uterus and the organs situated close to it

The corpus of the uterus is totally intraperitoneal. In the usual anteverted position it lies in contact with the bladder dome from which it is separated by the vesicouterine cul de sac of the pelvic peritoneum. The uterine leaf of the cul de sac is adherent to the isthmus. The vesical leaf is separated from the bladder by loose cellular tissue. The opposite aspect of the uterus is separated from the rectum by the rectouterine peritoneal cul de sac, which is occupied by the free part of the sigmoid colon, the last ileal loops and, occasionally, the very first part of the cecum. The uterine leaf of the peritoneal cul de sac is adherent to the myometrium. It also covers the dorsal part of the isthmus, the dorsal surface of the cervix and the dorsal vaginal fornix before reflecting onto the ventral surface of the rectum to which it is strongly adherent. It is only at the very bottom of the cul de sac that a loose cellular tissue covers the fascia delineating the outside surface of the peritoneum.

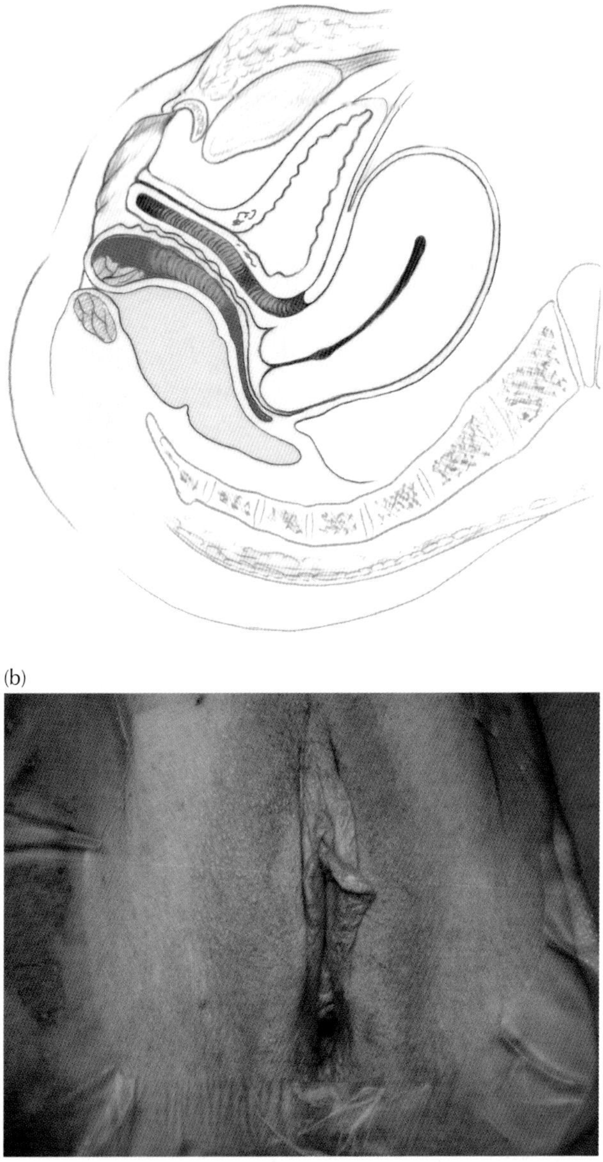

(a)

(a)

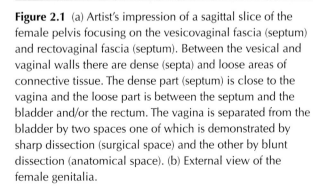

(b)

(b)

Figure 2.1 (a) Artist's impression of a sagittal slice of the female pelvis focusing on the vesicovaginal fascia (septum) and rectovaginal fascia (septum). Between the vesical and vaginal walls there are dense (septa) and loose areas of connective tissue. The dense part (septum) is close to the vagina and the loose part is between the septum and the bladder and/or the rectum. The vagina is separated from the bladder by two spaces one of which is demonstrated by sharp dissection (surgical space) and the other by blunt dissection (anatomical space). (b) External view of the female genitalia.

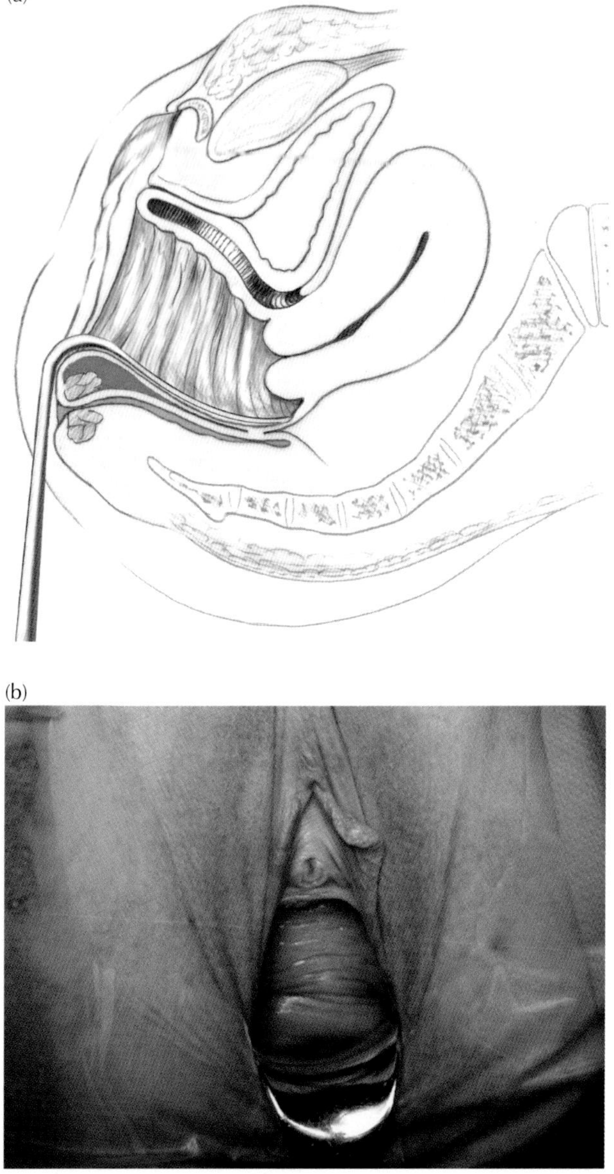

Figure 2.2 (a) Retracting the perineal body with an appropriate retractor (Chapter 3), the ventral vaginal wall and the ventral lip of the uterine cervix become visible. The loose part of the connective tissue interposed between the vesicovaginal septum and the bladder wall involves three areas that are more dense: one dorsal to the urethra, one at the level of the inter-ureteric line and one just below the base of the utero-vesical fold of peritoneum. (b) External view of the female genitalia having retracted the perineal body.

The cervix is partly intraperitoneal and supravaginal and partly retroperitoneal and intravaginal. The ventral lip of the cervix is in contact with the dorsal aspect of the bladder floor. This contact is direct with the two deepest thirds (see later) of the cervix as the lowest third is separated from the bladder by the ventral fornix of the vagina. The dorsal lip of the cervix is intravaginal in its lower two-thirds as the insertion of the vagina onto the cervix is situated 3 cm higher dorsally than it is ventrally.

(a)

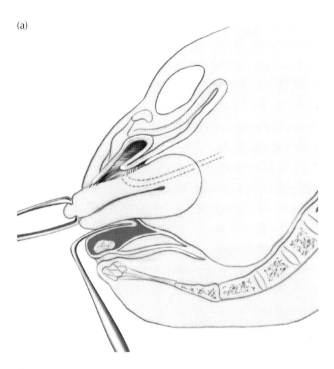

(b)

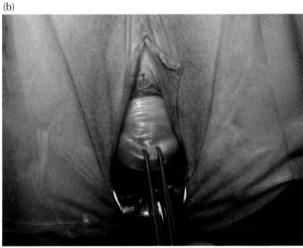

Figure 2.3 (a) and (b) Pulling on the ventral lip of the cervix with a grasping forceps, the bladder descends with the uterus due to the dense parts of the connective tissue interposed between the two organs. The intermediate part of this tissue becomes a "true" pseudo-aponeurosis, the supravaginal septum (see Chapter 7).

The uterine arteries originate from the internal iliac arteries by means of a common trunk including the superior vesical artery; this common trunk later becomes the obliterated umbilical artery or umbilical ligament. The first segment of each of the uterine arteries is oblique, almost parallel to the superior vesical artery. The second segment is transverse and runs from the pelvic side wall to the uterus, which it meets at the level of the isthmus where it takes a hairpin-shaped course, the so-called arch of the uterine artery.

The pelvic parts of the ureters run under the uterine arteries from back to front. This crossing takes place 1.5–2.0 cm from the side of the uterus and 1.5–2.0 cm from the top of the vaginal fornix. The artery crosses the ureter cranially. The veins generally cross it caudally but one or two of them can cross it cranially. The collaterals of the artery and veins, the so-called cervicovaginal vessels branch medial to the crossing point.

The vagina has two parts. The first, for the surgeon operating from below, is the caudal one. In patients lying in the lithotomy position it is situated in a horizontal position. The second, the cranial one, is oblique and almost frontal. The "cape" corresponds to the projection of the perineal body, which is drawn ventrally by the puborectalis muscles. The outside aspect of the ventral vaginal wall is in contact with the urethra, the urethrovesical junction (bladder neck) and the bladder floor. The outside aspect of the dorsal vaginal wall is in contact with the perineal body, the anorectal junction and the rectal ampulla. The "cape" separating the two parts of the vagina corresponds to the urethrovesical junction ventrally and to the anorectal junction dorsally.

By positioning the perineal retractor (which opens the vulval orifice and pushes the perineal body dorsally) the bisegmental shape of the ventral wall of the vagina becomes apparent. The ventral lip of the cervix can be grasped and traction exerted on this by pulling forceps markedly modifies the anatomical architecture particularly in parous women assessed under effective pharmacological relaxation. The tip of the ventral lip of the cervix can be drawn down to the level of the vulval orifice (do not confuse this normal finding with uterine prolapse). The cranial part of the anterior wall of the vagina follows. The bladder floor and ureters come down at the same time. After the first incision is performed for vaginal hysterectomy (i.e. once the ventral vaginal wall has been separated from the cervix) the downward movement becomes exaggerated. The bladder floor and ureters come down a little more but the uterine arteries come down even more, which results in the crossing point between the two elements becoming more distant from the lateral side of the isthmus (Figure 2.4(a) and (b)). The arch of the uterine artery appears more acute. The length of its afferent or descending branch becomes longer: 3–4 cm instead of 1.5–2 cm. This dramatically reduces the risk of ureteric injury when managing the uterine artery during vaginal hysterectomy. The facts are quite different if division of the ventral vaginal wall is made some distance from the cervix as is done in radical vaginal hysterectomy (Figure 2.5(a) and (b)). The surgical implications of this difference are tackled in Chapters 11 and 12. These differences are due to the arrangement of the structures that both separate and connect the pelvic organs.

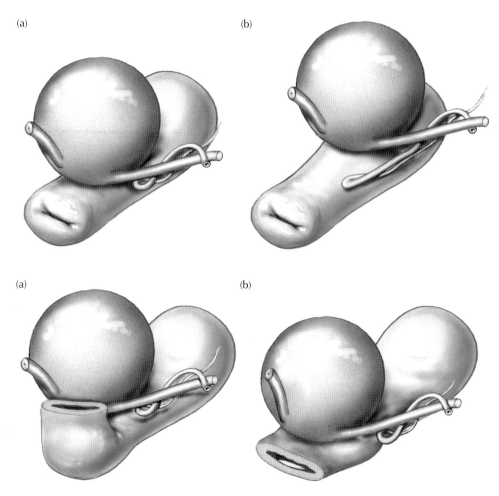

Figure 2.4 (a) and (b) Modification of the relationship between the vaginal floor and the uterus during simple vaginal hysterectomy. The bladder floor moves only minimally downward as do the ureters. In contrast, the arch of the uterine artery is dramatically displaced downward. Thus the risk of injury to the bladder and ureters during simple vaginal hysterectomy is very low.

Figure 2.5 (a) and (b) Modification of the relationship between the vaginal floor and the uterus during radical vaginal hysterectomy. Traction on the so-called vaginal cuff forces the bladder floor and ureters to move dramatically downward while the position of the uterine arteries is almost constant. Access to the uterine arteries is the most difficult step of the Schauta operation.

Fascia and free spaces between the genital organs and the organs located close to them

The pelvic organs are separated from each other and separated from the walls of the pelvis by cellular tissue that is embryologically considered to be a derivative of the fascia covering the outer aspect of the pelvic peritoneum. The mechanical qualities of this tissue are exceptional. It ensures the stability of the organs while allowing them relative mobility at the same time (as David Nichols said, the manufacturer who could manage to develop and produce such a tissue would be an industrial mogul!). The mobility-preserving characteristics of the tissue are greatest in the loose areas, whereas the stability-ensuring characteristics of the tissue are best in the dense areas. This tissue allows mobility where it is loose but ensures stability where it is dense.

The vesicovaginal spaces – the vesicovaginal fascia

The ventral wall of the vagina is separated from the bladder by a space whose width varies from bottom to top. At the bottom, i.e. at the level of the caudal third of the vagina, the space is virtual which means that the urethra is in direct contact with the vagina. Arriving at the level of the intermediate third, i.e. at the level of the bladder neck, the space becomes wider and wider up to the level of the ventral vaginal fornix, i.e. the level of the dorsal edge of the bladder floor (the interureteric line). Afterwards the space extends into the space situated between the bladder dome and the anterior leaf of the vesicouterine peritoneal cul de sac. Another way to express these anatomical facts is to say that the connective tissue separating the urinary tract and the ventral wall of the vagina is as dense at the level of the urethra as it is loose at the level of the bladder floor. From the surgical viewpoint sharp dissection is needed to separate the urethra from the vagina whereas blunt dissection is adequate to mobilize the bladder floor.

Most surgeons believe that there is a fascia interposed between the urinary tract and the ventral wall of the vagina. This fascia is denominated by various names including pubo-urethro-vesico-uterine fascia, septum vesicovaginalis and Halban's fascia. The embryological significance and the anatomical nature of this fascia have been disputed for decades. Some anatomists consider it to be an autonomous structure resulting from a condensation of the pelvic cellular tissue underneath the vesicouterine peritoneal cul de sac. Others, us included, consider this fascia to be the deepest part of the vaginal wall. This wall has three constituent layers. The first layer is the mucosa, which is made up of a paramalpighian epithelium lying on a stratum of connective fibers, mostly elastic fibers, called the lamina propria. The second layer is the muscularis that conveys a vascular web whose density of veins is noteworthy. The third layer is the adventitia, which is relatively thin and made up of connective fibers only. This adventitia is the true anatomical fascia vaginalis. It has nothing to do with the fascia identified by the surgeon that corresponds in fact to the two deepest layers, which can be detached en bloc from the superficial layer by sharp dissection.

For the surgeons who defend the concept of an autonomous vesicovaginal fascia, a space does exist between it and the vaginal wall (spatium septo vaginale). It is narrow and can only be identified by sharp dissection starting from a midline colpotomy that must not be too deep. The surgeons who do not share this concept consider that this dissection introduces a surgical artefact. The so-called "spatium septo vaginale" can thus be called the "surgical vesicovaginal space" as opposed to the "anatomical vesicovaginal space". Access to this "anatomical vesicovaginal space" must be found in another way. As described before, traction exerted on the cervix after the first incision performed for vaginal hysterectomy draws the bladder floor downward. This is due to the density of the connective fibers occupying the vesicovaginal space. Under traction, these fibers that invert the normal anatomical relationship, gather together in the shape of an aponeurosis called the supravaginal septum. The opening of this septum allows access either to the space situated between the bladder dome and the vesicouterine peritoneal cul de sac (see Chapter 7) or to the space situated between the bladder floor and the inner aspect of the so-called septum vesicovaginale (see Chapter 8).

The rectovaginal spaces – the rectovaginal fascia

The relationship between the dorsal wall of the vagina and the lower intestinal tract is anatomically quite similar to the relationship between the ventral wall and the lower urinary tract. An anatomically preformed rectovaginal space exists that is virtual at the level of the perineal body and then gets wider and wider until it reaches the bottom of the retrouterine peritoneal cul de sac. Most surgeons believe that an autonomous fascia is interposed between the rectum and the vagina: the rectovaginal fascia, septum rectovaginalis, Denonvilliers fascia and so on. Others think that this fascia is made up of the two deeper layers of the vaginal wall that one can detach from the mucosa en bloc by sharp dissection giving access to the superficial aspect of the fascia. To get access to the deep surface, one has to identify and open the dorsal supravaginal septum (see Chapter 7). Alternatively, one may open the rectovaginal ligaments and enter the two pararectal spaces (see Chapter 8).

Ligaments and free spaces between the pelvic organs and the pelvic walls

The pelvic organs whose solidarity is ensured by the so-called vesicovaginal and rectovaginal fascia share the same system of fixity that is provided by the so-called ligaments and aponeuroses joining them to the pelvic walls. Actually the pelvic cellular tissue interposed between the three organs and the pelvic walls includes both loose and dense areas (Figure 2.6). The loose areas ensure relative mobility of the visceral contents of the pelvis whereas the dense areas ensure attachment to each other and relative stability.

The ligaments and aponeuroses

The term "ligament," which is used to designate the structures fastening the pelvic organs to the pelvic walls, is anatomically inappropriate. These are in fact only condensations of pelvic cellular tissue around vessels and nerves ensuring the blood supply and nervous supply of these organs. The uterus being the organ whose blood and nervous appetites are the most important, or at least the organ that is programmed to be the most greedy, is the first beneficiary of the so-called ligamentous system. This system has two constituent parts: the so-called cardinal ligaments and the so-called uterosacral ligaments.

The term cardinal ligament has several synonyms such as "parametrium," the most frequently used by clinicians, or "web," frequently used by surgeons. The most appropriate term, perhaps, is the one used by the French anatomists who speak of the "gaine hypogastrique." As a matter of fact the cardinal

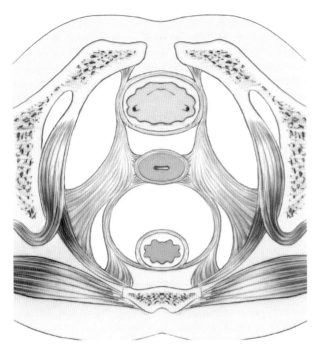

Figure 2.6 Artist's impression of a cranial horizontal slice of the female pelvis (an interpretation of the famous Amreich drawing). The loose midline spaces (retropubic prevesical space, vesicouterine space, rectouterine space, presacral retrorectal space) and the loose lateral spaces (paravesical and pararectal spaces) are separated by fascia and ligaments. The paracervical ligaments have three constituent parts. The first is the paracervix itself. The second is the so-called bladder pillar, which is made up of a ventral extension of the paracervix and by a so-called vesicouterine ligament (lateral and medial parts of the bladder pillar). The third is the so-called rectal pillar, which is made up of the sacrouterine ligament and the rectouterine ligament.

ligament corresponds to the web of elastic fibers surrounding the collaterals of the internal iliac artery and vein once called the hypogastric artery and vein. These vessels are mainly devoted to the uterus and to the vagina but vessels devoted to the urinary and intestinal tracts are also included.

The cardinal ligament is often described as a transverse structure going from the pelvic sidewall to the uterovaginal junction. Actually the origin of the vessels branching from the internal iliac artery and vein is more dorsal than lateral. It is located on the sacral side of the sacroiliac joint. For this reason the direction of the ligament is not transverse but is oblique from back to front and from outside to inside. On the other hand the insertion of the ligament on the pelvic wall is not frontal but oblique from back to front and from top to bottom. Another detail worth emphasizing is that the thickness of the insertion increases from top to bottom, the thickest part being situated at the level of the ischial spine, which is often considered to be the central knot of the

ligamentous system fastening the pelvic organs in place. This point, in fact, is the point where the vascular web is the richest: the vascular network being relatively simple at the top of the ligament (superior vesical artery and uterine artery branching together from the internal iliac artery) becomes plexoid at the level of its base (sponge-like arterial and, above all, venous plexus). The attachment of the cardinal ligament to the ischial spine is situated lateral to the cervix and to the vaginal fornix.

The so-called pelvic aponeurosis or endopelvic fasciae pelvis is the ventral continuation of the cardinal ligament. This insertion onto the pelvic sidewall draws a line extending the attachment of the pelvic insertion of the paracervix ventrally (Figure 2.7). The line of fasciae pelvis insertion is described as the "arcus tendineus pelvici." This structure often (but not always) appears as a pseudo-tendon (Figure 2.8) attached to the lowest part of the posterior aspect of the pubis. This attachment is 1 cm lateral to the midline and runs dorsally to the ischial spine where it merges with the arcus tendineus levator ani (the fibrous bundle crossing the inner surface of the obturator internus muscle and serving as the insertion of the ilio-coccygeal part of the levator ani muscle). The connections of the endopelvic fascia with the arcus tendineus are easy to collapse except at their most ventral extremity where they are reinforced by the so-called urethrotendineus ligament or posterior pubourethral ligament.

The endopelvic fascia has the same significance as the cardinal ligament. It is the vessel holder of the collaterals of the internal iliac vessels devoted to supplying and draining the sheath of the vagina and the base of the bladder, i.e. the vaginal arteries and veins and the inferior vesical arteries and veins that are collaterals of the former. The difference is that the vessels become more distant from the pelvic wall and closer to the organs of their destination as one goes from the ischial spine to the pubic bone. For this reason the paracolpos can be detached from the pelvic wall without dividing any vessels whereas the cardinal ligament cannot be detached from the pelvic wall without dividing the vessels it conveys.

The uterosacral ligament is made up of two constituent parts. The preeminent part of the uterosacral ligament or ligament proper is inserted onto the periosteum of the sacral concavity next to the ventral orifices of the sacrum. Bilaterally it circumscribes the lateral aspect of the rectal ampulla and finishes on each side of the midline on the dorsal surface of the cervix and of the vagina. This produces a fan-shaped ligament that converges toward its uterine and vaginal insertions. The most caudal fibers inserted onto the anterior surface of the coccyx cross closer to the rectum before reaching the uterus and the vagina.

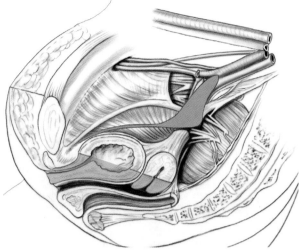

Figure 2.8 Insertion (in red) of the paracervix and of the endopelvic fascia onto the pelvic sidewall. The paracervix is a condensation of the pelvic cellular tissue around the collaterals of the internal iliac vessels and, in its most caudal and dorsal part, around the branches of the Frankenhauser nervous plexus. The endopelvic fascia is a condensation of the pelvic cellular tissue around the vessels devoted to the vagina.

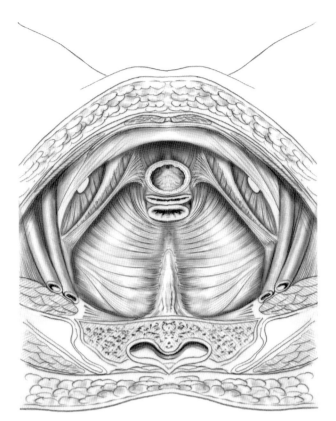

Figure 2.7 Artist's impression of a caudal horizontal slice of the female pelvis. The arcus tendineus musculi levator ani and the arcus tendineus fascia pelvici are visible. The former crosses the internal obturator muscle and provides an insertion for the iliococcygeus part of the levator ani muscle. The latter is the insertion of the endopelvic fascia onto the pelvic sidewall and is medial to the former.

the lateral surface of the bladder while giving off branches organized like the rungs of a ladder to the uterus, the vaginal fornix, the base of the bladder and to the sheath of the vagina. Most of these fibers are situated in the caudal part of the cardinal ligament (the so-called nervous part of the cardinal ligament).

The free spaces

The loose pelvic cellular tissue interposed between the visceral centro-pelvic complex and the pelvic walls is arranged into two parts. The prevesical and retropubic and the presacral or retrorectal spaces separate the viscera from the pelvic walls on the midline. The paravesical and pararectal spaces do the same on each side. Only these last are described. They are situated ventral and dorsal respectively to the cardinal ligaments, which make a strong boundary between them. As said before the cardinal ligament is essentially made up of a network of blood vessels. The paravesical and pararectal spaces are free of significant blood vessels: they are often called "dry spaces." They are actually virtual spaces. The surgeon creates them. Creating them is the key to accessing the ligaments and aponeuroses.

The paravesical space is situated between the lateral aspect of the bladder corpus and the medial surface of the pelvic sidewall. Operating from above, i.e. at laparotomy or laparoscopy, one finds the entrance to this space by pushing the obliterated umbilical artery

These latter parts of the ligament are called rectouterine and rectovaginal ligaments respectively. They are less strong than the uterosacral ligament proper. These ligaments are rich in connective and glatt muscular fibers to which one attributes their great properties of adherence and are closer to being genuine ligaments than the cardinal ligaments.

Actually, there is no fundamental difference between the uterosacral and cardinal ligaments. The uterosacral ligaments transmit the sympathetic and parasympathetic nervous fibers that merge on the lateral surface of the rectum in the Frankenhauser plexus or inferior hypogastric plexus. The roots of this plexus are formed from the sympathetic fibers of the hypogastric nerves that branch on each side of the midline from the superior or presacral hypogastric plexus. These fibers mix with the parasympathetic fibers originating from successive roots of the sciatic plexus. The Frankenhauser plexus is separated from the rectum by the musculo-connective parts of the uterosacral ligaments (and by the rectal fascia). It gives rise to the pelvic nerves that cross the lateral fornix of the vagina and run ventrally to medially. This vessel is the continuation of the first branch of the internal iliac artery and runs medial and almost parallel to the external iliac vessels. Simple pressure exerted with one or two closed instruments working divergently along the axis of the pelvic sidewall rapidly provides access to the bottom of the space. The floor of this space is made up of the pelvic aponeurosis attached to the arcus tendineus fascia pelvici. As said before it is easy to collapse this aponeurosis, which means that access to the paravesical space can be obtained without difficulty using the vaginal approach. Access is quite different if one tries to reach either the ventrocaudal or dorsocranial part of the space.

Transvaginal access to the ventrocaudal part of the paravesical space is sought in the vaginal operation for genital prolapse (see Chapter 8). A midline colpotomy allows separation of the vaginal wall from the base of the bladder allowing access to the paravesical space. If separation is achieved in the "surgical vesicovaginal space" one is led to the "linea vasorum," i.e. to the vascular bundle delineating the lateral border of the fascia vesicovaginalis. The fascia is collapsed opening up the paravesical space. Separation can also be performed in the "anatomical vesicovaginal space." Whatever the approach to achieve separation it is easily achieved dorsally and becomes progressively more difficult as one moves ventrally (here the pelvic aponeurosis is reinforced by the posterior pubourethral or urethrotendineus ligaments). Actually separation is easiest just in front of the bladder neck, i.e. before the area where the pubourethral ligaments provide reinforcement. Once the paravesical space is opened the avascular part of the subperitoneal aspect of the corpus of the bladder becomes visible at the same time as the arcus tendineus fasciae pelvis situated facing it on the same side.

Transvaginal access to the dorsocranial part of the paravesical space is required in vaginal radical hysterectomy (see Chapter 12). As opposed to simple hysterectomy, this radical operation involves removal of the upper part of the vagina. Circular transection of the vagina is performed at a distance from its insertion onto the cervix. Pulling on the ventral wall of the vagina draws the bladder floor downward and the ureters, like the arches of the uterine arteries, remain in a cranial position. This phenomenon, which is opposite to that observed at simple vaginal hysterectomy, is due to the presence of the so-called vesicouterine ligaments that are the vesical equivalents of the so-called rectouterine ligaments: they are located on either side of the midline and join, in a sagittal plane, the ventral surface of the cervix and of the vaginal fornix to the bladder floor. The vesicouterine ligaments are identified by first incising the supravaginal septum and opening the vesicouterine

space. Then one of the paravesical spaces is opened by collapsing the pelvic aponeurosis medial to the vaginal flap turned inside out thanks to a grasping forceps placed on its edge. Once the paravesical space has been entered, the bladder pillar, which is situated between it and the vesicovaginal space, is identified. This pillar includes the vesicouterine ligament and a ventrolateral expansion of the cardinal ligament conveying the branches of the superior and inferior vesical arteries devoted to the bladder floor as well as the autonomic nervous branches of the inferior hypogastric plexus. The last part of the ureter runs inside the pillar effecting the shape of a curve (designated as the knee of the ureter). Both the fibers of the vasculonervous part of the pillar situated lateral to the ureter and the fibers of the fibrous part situated medial to the ureter must be divided. In this way one gains access to the uterine artery that arrives in the operative field inside the so-called knee of the ureter.

The pararectal space is situated between the lateral aspect of the rectum and the medial aspect of the most dorsal part of the pelvic sidewall. Operating from above one finds the entrance to the space while pushing the posterior sheet of the broad ligament medially. Here the retroligamentous part of the ureter runs almost parallel to the common iliac vessels that are prolonged ventrally by the internal iliac vessels. The point where the ureter crosses the uterine artery (branching from the internal iliac artery) is the ventromedial landmark of the entrance. This space is opened in the same way as the paravesical space except that this space is narrower and the tissue contained therein more dense.

Transvaginal access to the pararectal space is simpler than transvaginal access to the paravesical space. Access to the ventrocaudal part is obtained by a midline colpotomy (see Chapter 8) allowing separation of the vagina from the rectum either in the "surgical" or in the "anatomical" rectovaginal space. The caudal expansion of the rectouterine ligament is easily collapsed and the pararectal space entered. As far as the dorsocranial part of the space is concerned (see Chapter 12) it is easy, once the posterior supravaginal septum has been incised and the pouch of Douglas entered, to identify the rectouterine ligaments and to separate them from the dorsal surface of the cardinal ligaments with which they merge at the level of their insertion onto the dorsal fornix of the vagina.

Urogenital and pelvic diaphragms

The urogenital and pelvic diaphragms are the curtains hiding the stage where the vaginal surgeon must play. Their anatomy is the only anatomy that is commonly described in classical textbooks of anatomy in a way that is appropriate for vaginal surgeons. The following description and figures are merely summaries of well-known facts.

The urogenital diaphragm

The complex muscular and aponeurotic structures making up the urogenital diaphragm (Figure 2.9) are fragile and very often deeply distorted or destroyed in parous women even in the absence of genuine prolapse.

The so-called deep transverse perineal muscle is the centerpiece of the ensemble. It is a curtain made up of small bundles of striated muscular fibers mixed with fibro-connective tissue and arranged in a horizontal plane (a frontal plane for the surgeon operating from below). The lateral insertions of this musculo-aponeurotic structure are onto the ischio-pubic bones. The medial insertion is onto the so-called perineal body, i.e. the dense musculo-fibrous stone

separating the vulvar vestibule from the very last part of the intestine. The constrictor vulvae muscle and the superficial (striated) sphincter ani muscle constitute, on the midline, part of the musculo-aponeurotic ensemble. They mix their fibers with the fibers of the deep transverse perineal muscle at the level of the perineal body. The root(s) of the clitoris covered by the ischio-cavernosus muscles and the bulbs of the cavernous body covered by the bulbocavernosus muscles are applied to the external surface of the diaphragm and share the same aponeurotic blanket: the superficial urogenital aponeurosis. The dorsal limit of the diaphragm is marked by a fusiform reinforcement of its horizontally arranged muscular fibers. This reinforcement is known as the "superficial transverse perineal muscle." This muscle is the ventral limit of the entry to the ischio-rectal fossa.

The pelvic diaphragm

The pelvic diaphragm (Figure 2.10) is both simpler and stronger than the urogenital diaphragm. It is formed by the two levator ani muscles whose fibers

Figure 2.9 The urogenital diaphragm.

insert onto the deep surface of the ventral and lateral walls of the pelvis converging obliquely from their horseshoe-shaped insertion to the midline. The ensemble is shaped like the hull of a ship. The outer surface of the muscular wall is separated from the pelvic wall by the ischio-rectal fossa. The dorsal part of this fossa is found directly under the subcutaneous fascia of the ischial area while the ventral part is hidden by the urogenital diaphragm (one speaks about the ventral extension of the ischio-rectal fossa). The levator ani muscle has two constituent parts: the levator muscle itself and the ilio-coccygeus muscle.

The levator muscle inserts onto the dorsal aspect of the pubic bone. From here the fibers run in a sagittal plane before curving to join on the midline, behind the dorsal wall of the vagina, the fibers of the opposing muscular bundles, just as the more lateral fibers run dorsally to insert onto the lateral sides of the coccyx having partially mixed their fibers with the superficial sphincter ani muscle. The medial bundle is called the puborectalis muscle and the lateral bundle the pubococcygeus muscle. The midline

convergence of the dorsal extremities of the puborectalis and pubococcygeus muscles form two sling systems called the urogenital hiatus and anal hiatus, which are traversed by the urogenital tract and intestinal tract respectively. Tonic contraction of the muscles pull the viscera crossing the diaphragm in a cranial and ventral direction resulting in the angulation observed at the junction of the two caudal thirds of the vagina and at the junction of the rectum and the anal canal.

The iliococcygeus muscle inserts onto the arcus tendineus levator ani. This more or less developed pseudo-tendinous structure crosses the inner aspect of the internal obturator muscle obliquely from the ventral surface of the pubis to the ischial spine where it merges with the arcus tendineus fascia pelvici. The muscular bundles converge on the inner surface of the coccyx. The iliococcygeus muscle follows without interruption the pubococcygeus muscle and is prolonged dorsally by the sacrospinous muscle, which is the remnant of the muscle that operates the tail in quadruped animals. This nonactive muscle is richer in fibrous elements than it is in muscular

Figure 2.10 The pelvic diaphragm.

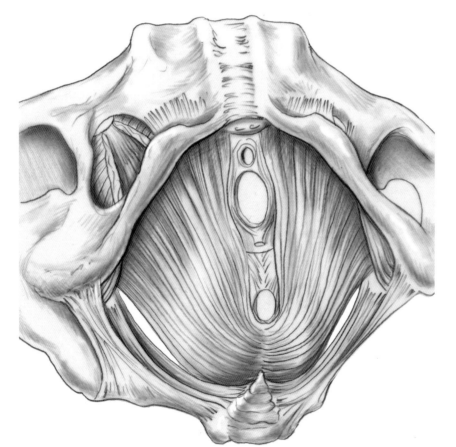

bundles. It is often called the sacrospinous ligament analogous to the sacrotuberous ligament, which is situated lateral to it running from the ischial tuberosity to the lateral edge of the sacrum.

The inside surface of the urogenital diaphragm and the inside surface of the levator ani are covered by an aponeurosis, which merges at the level of their midline insertion with the aponeurosis covering the organs that traverse the urogenital hiatus and the anal hiatus. The pelvic aponeurosis also participates in this cohesion, which is particularly developed at its ventral extremity where the pubourethral ligaments reinforce the hammock system. This system connects the urethra to the arch of the pubis more firmly than the muscular sling sustaining the vagina and the anorectal junction. The sling draws the organs ventrally while allowing plenty of distension.

The relative laxity of the muscular system connecting the vagina and the arch of the pubis allows placement of retractors and thus performance of surgical procedures on the genital organs and neighboring organs. If necessary, it is possible to improve access by making an episiotomy or paravaginal incision. Midline episiotomy involves the vulvar vestibule. Mediolateral episiotomy divides the urogenital diaphragm obliquely and opens the ventral extension of the ischiorectal space. The paravaginal incision divides the levator muscle and provides direct access to the pararectal space. However, these incisions rarely need to be done. In most cases the vagina provides direct access without leaving any scar.

3 Instruments

According to a French proverb *"there are no bad instruments, only bad workmen."* We prefer the sentence David Nichols wrote in the first paragraph of his text book: *"The carpenter is more important than his or her tools, but fine tools may help the good carpenter make one's good work even better."* The surgeon may be more important than the instruments he uses. However, the issues of adequate positioning of the patient on the table and the use of adequate and well-standardized instruments are at least as important as the techniques implemented. So-called laparoscopic assistance does not erase this fundamental axiom.

Positioning the patient on the table

To perform vaginal surgery properly, the patient must be placed in the so-called lithotomy position (the position adopted by surgeons of the Renaissance to remove urinary bladder stones through the perineum). The buttocks of the patient must hang over the end of the table a little. The thighs have to be bent at an angle of at least 90° and the lower legs should be extended. Multi-positional stirrups (Figure 3.1) allow the most adequate positioning while avoiding pressure on those parts of the lower limbs that are at risk (e.g. lateral surface of the knee). Ideal positioning of the patient can be difficult in cases of disorders of the hip and spine. These difficulties can be overcome under anesthesia but one has to refrain from using this type of "forced" positioning to avoid postoperative pain, which can last for weeks or months if not more. In these cases a trial positioning should be first performed before induction of anesthesia and the final position adopted under anesthesia must not be more extreme than the one achieved pre-anesthesia.

In addition to the surgeon, the operative team ideally includes two assistants and one scrub nurse. The surgeon is seated opposite the operative field. The two assistants stay on either side of the surgeon. The table

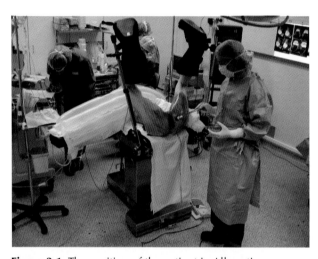

Figure 3.1 The position of the patient in Allen stirrups.

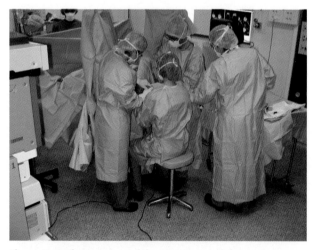

Figure 3.2 The position of the team around the patient.

should be level with the assistants' elbows and the seat of the surgeon must be adjusted to bring the shoulders of the surgeon level with the operative field. The nurse stays behind the right shoulder of the surgeon (if he or she is right-handed). She must share the same clear view of the operative field to follow the procedure and thus provide the right instrument at the right moment without the surgeon asking for it. In such an ideal set up (Figure 3.2) every one can play his or her role under comfortable conditions – the comfort of the team is in itself of no importance, except that it has an impact on the safety of the surgery!

The instruments and the way to use them

Our "vaginal surgery box" includes various instruments. Most of these belong to sets common to all pelvic surgery boxes while others are specific to the operations described in this book

The retractors

Appropriate retractors are the key to success in vaginal surgery. One must use retractors designed to retract the tissues at the right level without deepening the working area. Autostatic retractors (exact copies of the ones used in open surgery) do exist but they cannot replace elective retractors handled at the right moment by a skilled hand.

The perineal retractor most commonly used is the Martin weighted speculum. The surgeon puts it in place at the very beginning of the surgery and does not remove it until the end. We much prefer to use the Mangiagalli retractor (Figure 3.3) whose double curvature allows placement flush against the prominence of the perineal body. This makes the assistant's hand exercise appropriate pressure at the appropriate moment without interfering with the operative field. Two models of Mangiagalli retractors exist. To these one adds a longer right-angled retractor that is often required after the pouch of Douglas has been opened.

The vaginal retractors we use are the bayonet-shaped Breisky retractors. Thanks to this shape the hand

holding the instrument never obscures the operative field but is able to move the blade obliquely, i.e. without pushing into the depths of the tissue it retracts laterally and/or ventrally, a result that cannot be achieved using the standard right-angled Heney and Deaver retractors. We have 12 different types of Breisky retractor (Figure 3.4) in our vaginal surgery box whose blades vary from 70 to 135 mm in length and from 15 to 28 mm in width. Two more retractors 130 mm in length and 25 mm in width (Richter retractors) have to be added for the deeper steps of certain operations.

Two intermediate-sized retractors (80 and 90 mm in length and 28 and 32 mm in width) may be enough for performing standard vaginal hysterectomy but the complete set of retractors is essential for many other types of operation.

The grasping forceps

The cervix and other parts of the uterus are grasped by using the classical Pozzi forceps (tenaculum or bullet forceps) and Museux forceps (Figure 3.5).

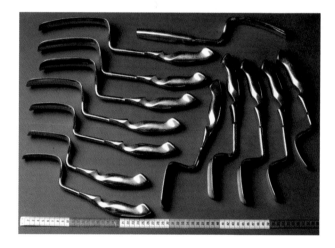

Figure 3.4 The Breisky retractors. Instruments manufactured by Landanger, Chaumont, France.

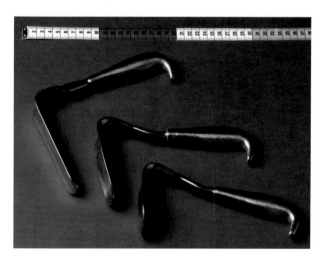

Figure 3.3 The perineal retractors. Instruments manufactured by Landanger, Chaumont, France.

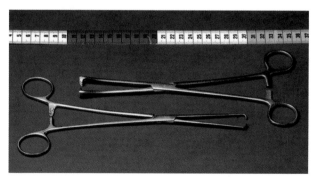

Figure 3.5 The Pozzi (bullet forceps or tenaculum) and the Museux forceps. Instruments manufactured by Landanger, Chaumont, France.

Grasping the vaginal flaps requires specific toothed forceps. Our preferences are the Chrobak forceps and Gaston Cotte forceps. The teeth, at the extremities of these forceps, are mouse-like, which means that they cross each other giving the instrument great grasping strength. The Chrobak forceps are electively used for vaginal radical hysterectomy. The Gaston Cotte forceps, which are copies of the former but half the size, are the best instruments for tightening the vaginal flaps during reconstructive surgery. They are more powerful than Allis forceps that continue to be very useful in many steps of reconstructive surgery and deserve to be kept in the vaginal surgery box alongside the Chrobak and Gaston Cotte forceps (Figure 3.6).

The other instruments

The use of the delicate atraumatic instruments of contemporary surgery is highly commendable when performing vaginal surgery. However as the specific qualities of vaginal surgery are simplicity and speed, the use of historical instruments continues in most instances to be the best choice.

The cold knife is not displaced by electrocautery for opening the vagina (Chapter 7) or by the most delicate scissors for sharp dissection of the vaginal flaps (Chapter 8). Our preference is the no. 23 blade. We only rarely use a no. 11 blade (e.g. de-epidermization of the vagina).

Delicate non-toothed forceps like the de Bakey forceps are not superior to classical toothed forceps. Our favorite instrument is the 20-cm-long Duval forceps with its three-toothed jaws, and also the 25-cm version. We strongly believe that taking tissues once with such a forceps, rather than three or more times with a so-called atraumatic forceps that unavoidably slips, reduces trauma.

Delicate scissors such as Metzenbaum scissors have their place in the vaginal surgery box but for the most part we use Mayo scissors, which are more appropriate for cutting vaginal flaps, uterine ligaments and so on. We also use strong curved or straight scissors for morcellating a big uterus. A special type of vaginal Mayo scissors is our preference for the very first part of the ventral preparation in vaginal hysterectomy (Figure 3.7) (see Chapter 7).

Dissecting forceps should not be excessively fine for fear of injuring the plexiform veins forming the skeleton of the pseudo-ligaments one has to isolate by dissection. Our preference is a curved dissecting clamp that is a copy of the Jean Louis Faure clamp but without toothed jaws. We also use the classical O'Shaughnessy right-angled dissecting forceps and our preference is the heaviest one, which is the least dangerous (Figure 3.8).

The atraumatic Rogers forceps is truly invaluable for clamping the paracervical ligaments. There are two versions in our vaginal surgery box: curved and slightly curved – we use them electively in vaginal radical hysterectomy (Chapters 12 and 13). However in all other circumstances we continue to use the three-toothed jaws of the Jean Louis Faure forceps and also the strong Kocher forceps (Figure 3.9).

Needling is mostly performed using atraumatic needles handled with the new generation of Tungsten needle holders. The needles we electively use are semicircular and 26 mm long. The tip of the needle is round which, in contemporary technology, does not jeopardize the power of penetration even through tougher tissues. The stitches we prefer are polyglycolic acid sutures that are absorbed without producing an inflammatory response while retaining

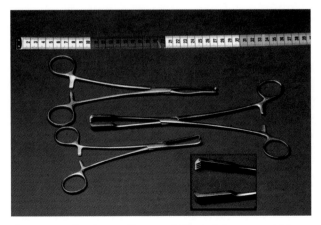

Figure 3.6 The Gaston Cotte and Chrobak forceps, which are "mouse-like" toothed and the classical Allis forceps. Instruments manufactured by Landanger, Chaumont, France.

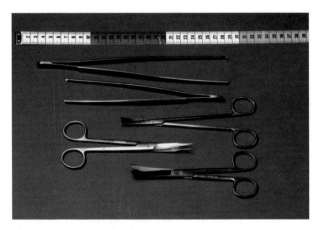

Figure 3.7 Surgical forceps and scissors. Note the very sharp Mayo scissors, which are used concurrently with the Metzenbaum and regular curved scissors in some steps of vaginal surgery. Instruments manufactured by Landanger, Chaumont, France.

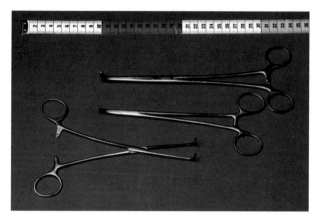

Figure 3.8 The dissecting forceps: strong and fine O'Shaughnessy forceps and "non-toothed" Jean Louis Faure forceps – equivalent to heavy Kelly forceps. Instruments manufactured by Landanger, Chaumont, France.

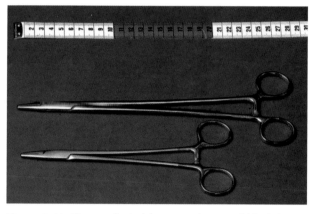

Figure 3.10 The needle holders, Vicryl 2-0 and black laser needle. Instruments manufactured by Landanger, Chaumont, France.

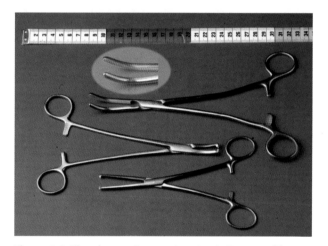

Figure 3.9 The clamps: Rogers, Jean Louis Faure and heavy Kocher. Instruments manufactured by Landanger, Chaumont, France.

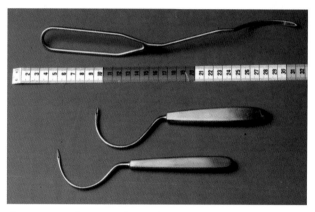

Figure 3.11 The vaginal Deschamps needle and Emmet needle. Instruments manufactured by Landanger, Chaumont, France.

significant tensile strength for long enough. This allows the use of smaller diameter threads ensuring more precise approximation. Our mascot needle is the 26-mm semicircular Black Laser® with 2-0 Vicryl®. We also use synthetic monofilament sutures like PDS (Figure 3.10).

Two historical needles complete our vaginal surgery box: the vaginal Deschamps needle and the Emmet needle. The vaginal Deschamps needle is a ligature carrier whose dissecting–penetrating part is in the extension of the handle (as opposed to the classical "abdominal" Deschamps needle whose needling part is perpendicular to the handle). The tip of the needle is sharp enough to penetrate the paraisthmic window but blunt enough to avoid injury to the vessels running alongside this anatomical space. In particular, the needle is used to place the lateral ligatures during

vaginal hysterectomy (see Chapter 7). The Emmet needle is a very ancient instrument that was designed to repair obstetric perineal lacerations. It remains the best instrument for the so-called dorsal levator plasty, because it allows one to take an adequate piece of the levator muscles and the perineal body during colpo-perineorrhaphy, and furthermore, it is one of the best tools for positioning (tension-free) mesh percutaneously in (the new) prolapse and incontinence surgery (Figure 3.11) (see Chapter 8).

One instrument is not shown in Figures 3.3–3.6. It is the hand of the surgeon. The skill of this hand counts more than all the instruments it handles. But this hand is also an instrument in itself. Palpation is in many instances the key to identifying the free spaces whose correct location is the basis of properly performed vaginal surgery.

4 Perioperative care

Perioperative care is not the business of the surgeon alone. It involves the whole team including the anesthesiologist. The role of the anesthesiologist in gynecological vaginal surgery is important at every level. It is he or she, every bit as much as the surgeon, who helps the patient recover, this being done as much through encouragement as it is through medical prescription. It is also he, obviously, who is in charge of the anesthetic during the operation, whether that is a general anesthetic or a loco-regional one. His presence is equally indispensable when one is operating under local anesthesia. These different functions are discussed below in turn.

Anesthesia

The organization of perioperative care

Everything must be done to optimize the health and well-being of the patient. All members of the team must strive to achieve this ultimate aim and it is the anesthesiologist who assists in organizing this team function. Furthermore, from the very first visit the anesthesiologist emphasizes to the patient that she also has a responsibility in optimizing her outcome.

On the morning of surgery we ask the patient to take a shower, to go up and down a flight of stairs if possible and to walk around to minimize venostasis. She then returns to her bed for premedication.

The afternoon after simple vaginal hysterectomy (which is taken here as the model operation for descriptive purposes) the patient is encouraged to sit on the edge of the bed and to get up for 2–3 min. She is encouraged to move her feet when she is sitting down again.

The day after surgery intravenous infusions are discontinued and if appropriate the urinary catheter is removed. For breakfast the patient has a choice of a little coffee or tea. It is important for her to leave her room three or four times and to start to go up and down stairs again. The day after, we encourage her to take a shower, to go up and down a flight of stairs at least three times and to walk between 100 and 150 m. The patients initially complain that they find this hard, but on the second and third days they begin to experience the benefits and appreciate the rapidity of their recovery. It is important to have the support of the patient's family during this period and to explain to them that the initial discomfort will be well worthwhile.

In fact, after most vaginal operations, patients could be discharged on the day following surgery. This is not the case in many countries, especially in France. However, one must simplify postoperative care as far as possible: whatever the healthcare system, convalescence begins in the hospital.

The anesthetic consultation

The anesthetic consultation is an important moment in the chain of events providing perioperative care. This consultation enables the practitioner to detect co-morbidities and to request special investigations if necessary. It also allows optimization of drug prescription if the patient is on long-term medication. Furthermore, it provides an opportunity for the patient and anesthesiologist to meet well in advance of the procedure allowing time to optimize the patient's condition as required. And, last but not least, it is a legal obligation (at least, it is in France).

Preoperative investigations

Preoperative investigations fall into two main categories: those that are routinely performed and those that are added as indicated by the patient's general condition and co-morbidities.

In all cases a full blood count is performed to check the hemoglobin level and a sample is sent to the laboratory for grouping and saving and to exclude or identify antibodies. Urea and electrolytes is performed in patients who are on diuretics, in diabetics and on those undergoing more radical procedures. A coagulation screen is performed on the latter. A random blood sugar check is conducted for all patients with diabetes and liver function tests are important in patients with malignancy. A chest X-ray is mandatory in the latter and is also indicated in older patients and in those with cardiorespiratory problems. An ECG is performed in older patients and those with cardiorespiratory problems. An echocardiogram or pulmonary function tests may be required if there is a history of cardiac or respiratory problems.

Pharmacological interactions

The anesthesiologist must know the type and dose of all medications currently being taken by the patient. If she is taking antihypertensives, cardiovascular medications, psychotropic drugs, she can for the most part take these right up to the morning of the surgery: it is better to operate on a stable patient than on one who has been destabilized by recently stopping important medication.

On the other hand certain types of medication will cause real problems for the anesthesiologist. Some of these need to be stopped between 1 and 3 weeks before the surgery and others can be accommodated by altering the anesthetic protocol. For example, it is, important to stop all mono-amine-oxidase inhibitors whereas the patient may continue to take Lithium or Digoxin as long as the serum levels are not in the toxic range. Warfarin must be stopped before proceeding with surgery and the patient heparinized. On the other hand it is important to continue treatment with beta-blockers right up to the time of surgery.

The different types of anesthesia

Vaginal surgery may be performed under general, loco-regional or local anesthetic. The choice depends not only on the type of procedure planned but also on the general health and psychological condition of the patient. The problems common to all types of anesthetic are discussed below followed by a presentation of the techniques themselves.

Problems common to all types of anesthetics
Premedication
Premedication reduces anxiety and facilitates induction of anesthesia. It is used and indicated irrespective of the type of anesthetic used.

For elective surgery, the anesthesiologist will want the patient to enter the operating room free of anxiety and sedated, but easily rousable and cooperative. Psychological preparation cannot accomplish everything and will not relieve all anxiety. In selecting the appropriate drugs for preoperative medication, the patient's psychological condition and physical status must be taken into consideration. The desired goals may be multiple and should be tailored to the needs of each patient: some of the goals, such as relief of anxiety and production of sedation, apply to almost every patient; whereas prophylaxis against allergic reactions, or against gastric fluid inhalation applies in only a few instances. Preoperative medication prevents preoperative elevation of plasma concentrations of beta-endorphins that normally accompanies the stress response.

We usually use a combination of sedative hypnotics and tranquillizers. A benzodiazepine, Alprazolam, 0.01 mg/kg, is used to produce anxiolysis, amnesia and sedation. This is added to a non-phenothiazine tranquillizer, Hydroxyzine, at a dose of 1 mg/kg, used for prophylaxis against histamine liberation. Hydroxyzine has a sedative action and anxiolytic and antiemetic properties. Oral premedication should be given 30–60 min before the patient's arrival in the operating room.

Finally, correct preoperative medication regimens have to produce sufficient obtundation (stupor) to be clinically significant in reducing anesthetic requirements.

Hemodilution
The technique of hemodilution is useful to limit blood transfusion and to reduce the risk of thromboembolism. For this reason some anesthesiologists recommend setting up an infusion of crystalloid 1.5–2 h before surgery.

Blood transfusion
The requirement for intraoperative blood transfusion during a vaginal procedure is generally rare unless that procedure is radical. The basic rules regarding risk management of transfusion are not described here. Suffice it to say that once transfusion exceeds four or five units it is important to consider fresh frozen plasma, platelets and cryoprecipitate.

Postoperative surveillance and analgesia
Postoperative surveillance in the recovery room and in the ward must be systematic. The length of surveillance in the recovery room will depend on the type of surgery performed and on the patient's condition. For most vaginal surgery other than radical procedures it is usually less than an hour.

Cardiac monitoring, blood pressure measurement, monitoring of oxygenation and spontaneous ventilation, including respiratory rate and pulse oximetry are routinely employed as a standard of care in the recovery room. Monitoring of urinary output is mandatory during this period. It is important to exclude abnormal bleeding: an agitated or shocked patient requires immediate and astute assessment. Correct fluid and electrolyte balance is maintained.

The problem of postoperative pain continues to be an issue but is somewhat less in patients undergoing vaginal surgery. Major analgesia in the form of morphine exposes the patient to the risks of respiratory complications and apnea. These complications are counterbalanced by the discomfort and the pain-related stress in an untreated patient. Therefore we use the current conventional methods of administration of morphine including Patient Controlled Analgesia. To enhance the analgesic effect, and therefore to minimize the dose of morphine we use infusions of minor analgesics as adjuvants (Nefopam chlorydrate, 1 mg/kg/24 h and Paracetamol). Minor analgesics such as nonsteroidal anti-inflammatories are regularly used but must be avoided in patients at risk of renal failure including pre-renal failure. They are also contraindicated in patients at risk of peptic ulcer. Epidural anesthesia is very effective and carries a minimal risk from a practical perspective. Good management of postoperative stress correlates with rapid recovery and good quality of sleep in the following days.

Individual anesthetic techniques

Whatever the technique used to induce anesthesia, common problems must be solved beforehand; these include positioning the patient on the operating table.

Positioning the patient

Positioning a patient for any type of surgical procedure is frequently a compromise between that which the anesthetized patient can tolerate anatomically and physiologically, and that which the surgical team require for access to the surgical field. After induction of anesthesia, positioning may need to be delayed until the patient is physiologically stable. Establishment of the intended surgical posture may need to be modified to match the patient's tolerance. If the exaggerated lithotomy position is chosen, this reduces perfusion gradients to and from the lower extremities. The lithotomy position produces an uphill gradient for arterial perfusion into the feet requiring careful avoidance of hypotension. This posture induces potential angulation and compression of the contents of the femoral canal by the inguinal ligament or stretch of the sciatic nerves, or both. An exaggerated lithotomy position stresses the lumbar spine, and may restrict

ventilation because of abdominal compression by bulky thighs. It can be tolerated under general anesthesia, but is sometimes difficult for the patient who is awake. Control of ventilation may be required. In cases of painful lumbar spinal disease, an alternative surgical position may need to be chosen beforehand to avoid severe postoperative exacerbation.

Frequently some degree of head down tilt is added to the lithotomy position, to induce a lithotomy plus Trendelenburg position. Depending on the degree of head depression, the addition of tilt to the lithotomy position combines the worst features of both the lithotomy and the Trendelenburg postures. The weight of abdominal viscera on the diaphragm adds to whatever abdominal compression is produced by the flexed thighs of an obese patient or of one placed in an exaggerated lithotomy position. Ventilation should be assisted or controlled in such cases.

General anesthesia

The general concept of stress-free anesthesia is inversely correlated with increased cardiac and respiratory complications, wound infections and nutritional and electrolyte disturbances, all of which correlate with increased morbidity rates in surgical patients.

In order to apply this concept of stress-free anesthesia, our preference is for intravenous induction of anesthesia. A preinduction dose of Midazolam (0.02 mg/kg) causes rapid changes in EEG rhythm, sedation and amnesia. Then intravenous induction with hypnotic doses of Propofol (2 mg/kg) or Etomidate (0.3 mg/kg) modifies CNS activity, alters consciousness, but causes respiratory depression, and, given with new, powerful opioids (Sufentanil, 0.5 µg/kg, or an infusion of Remifentanil) requires tracheal intubation and mechanical ventilation. Anesthesia can be maintained with an infusion of Propofol, or with inhalational anesthetics such as Sevoflurane or Desflurane.

We insist on good muscle relaxation at least in part to reduce intra-abdominal pressure. This is obtained thanks to a non-depolarizing agent, Atracurium (0.6 mg/kg) whose duration of action is at least 35 min, followed by reinjection of 0.1 mg/kg, if necessary, as monitoring of neuromuscular blockade is now systematically performed.

Loco-regional anesthesia

We will now discuss spinal, epidural and local anesthesia, outlining the advantages and disadvantages, and the indications and options available for each of these techniques.

Spinal anesthesia This is a rapid method of loco-regional anesthesia resulting in an effective block within 10–15 min. The level of anesthesia is determined by the nature of the surgery planned. It is essential in all cases to obtain an adequate "saddle" block. Having obtained this one can then also achieve a higher level of anesthesia by placing the patient in a horizontal position. This latter procedure is relatively contraindicated in older patients.

The length of anesthesia is dependent on the type of anesthetic used. All vaginal surgery can be performed under spinal anesthesia and the muscular relaxation obtained is perfect. It is ideal for short techniques. This approach is now coming back into vogue, particularly with the useful addition of adjuvants such as clonidine (0.5 µg/kg), which enhance the duration of the block, and intrathecal morphine (1 µg/kg), which can maintain effective postoperative analgesia for at least 12 h.

Epidural anesthesia Epidural anesthesia is appropriate for all vaginal surgery. However, there are two main objectives. In the first instance the local anesthetic injection must be inserted with the patient sitting up to achieve good perineal anesthesia. The patient must then be laid flat in slight Trendelenburg position to allow adequate anesthesia for intraperitoneal maneuvers. Of course the procedure takes longer than induction of general anesthesia. The local anesthetic most used is Ropivacaine 7.5 mg/ml as the cardiovascular and cerebral consequences are less than with Xilocaine 2%. Dolosal, 50 mg, does not carry a risk of apnea and its use is less dangerous than that of 0.25% Marcain. The various techniques of loco-regional anesthesia require adequate vascular filling to compensate for the pharmacological block of sympathetic innervation. It is therefore important to ensure that urinary output is maintained by inserting a urinary catheter before proceeding with surgery. The reduction in venous pressure (due to the pharmacological sympathectomy and the absence of artificial ventilation) reduces venous return and thus perioperative bleeding is diminished.

Loco-regional anesthetics are particularly useful in three types of patients:

1. Patients with respiratory problems
2. Patients with gross obesity
3. Patients (of course) who wish to remain conscious during the procedure.

Cardiac patients generally benefit from general anesthesia, as they do not tolerate well the psychological and pharmacological stresses of the loco-regional block. Advanced age is also a contraindication particularly among those who have hypertension. The risk of hypovolemia is a particular problem in these patients.

The use of loco-regional anesthesia is completely contraindicated in patients on anticoagulants because of the risk of hematoma formation. Neurological problems either central or peripheral are not absolute contraindications and each case must be assessed on its own merits. A long operation of more than 2 h duration is a contraindication.

Local anesthesia One can in theory perform everything under local anesthesia. This requires not only a courageous patient but also a courageous surgeon. From a practical perspective we only use local anesthesia for those cases that may be performed without retractors – i.e. procedures performed at the end of a speculum (e.g. dilatation of the cervix and curettage, conization of the cervix: see Chapter 5). We also use it for procedures performed exclusively on the perineum or on the prolapsed vagina, e.g. insertion of suburethral tapes and palliative prolapse surgery (see Chapter 8).

The choice of formulation used to provide local anesthesia is based on a balance of the risks and benefits of that particular drug. We generally use Lidocaine. The essential risk in using local anesthetics is that of a convulsive crisis. This is due to hematological diffusion of the product. To prevent this it is important when infiltrating the tissues to ensure that one is not injecting intravenously and it is also important to limit the dose (7 mg/kg should be the maximum): take care, before pushing the piston of the syringe, to withdraw, to confirm there is no reflux of blood. Addition of a vasoconstrictor is a recommended approach even if associated with a risk of side effects (palpitations): the potential drawbacks are more than outweighed by the potential benefits. From the practical point of view we prescribe the commercially available mixture of lidocaine and adrenaline.

Prevention of hemorrhage

One of the most important advantages of the vaginal approach is that it reduces intraoperative bleeding. This fact is demonstrated by many comparative trials, but is unlikely to be apparent to the observer as the surgery starts with an incision of the vaginal wall: the very step of gynecologic surgery that is the main source of bleeding. Once the inaugural colpotomy has been performed the bleeding stops, as long as the dissection is performed in the correct anatomical planes!

The rational use of vasoconstrictors

Appropriate use of vasoconstrictors can minimize perioperative bleeding. They must be appropriately chosen and used. Vasoconstrictors are practically indispensable when performing operations that involve resection of the cervix or uterine muscle (conizations, myomectomies). They are very useful for operations on the vagina (colpo-hysterectomies, vaginal repairs). They provide a certain comfort when performing other operations. There is thus a hierarchy of indications for their use.

Infiltrating with these vasoconstrictive substances can alter the anatomy. Injections into the cervix or into the myometrium do not cause any problems, but injections into the vagina, i.e. between the different layers of the vagina, make identification of the spaces separating them more difficult. Thus the whole procedure is more difficult and ultimately more hemorrhagic.

It must be understood that vasoconstrictors cannot replace sutures for the control of bleeding from wide caliber vessels. On the other hand they do have an effect on vessels of medium caliber, but this is temporary. Thus, because of the risk of postoperative hemorrhage, pharmacological hemostasis does not obviate the requirement for surgical hemostasis.

The choice of vasoconstrictor

For a long time catecholamines were the only product available to provide hemostasis through infiltration. Adrenaline and its homologs undoubtedly provide powerful vasoconstriction but equally provoke cardiovascular side effects (tachycardia and hypertension). Furthermore, metabolic acidosis develops at a tissue level under the effect of sustained vasoconstriction thus producing a secondary vasodilation.

This secondary vasodilation does not occur with the various synthetic vasopressins. Vasopressin produces a powerful vasoconstriction. It is rapid (less than 3 min) and prolonged (1.5–3 h). There is no "hemorrhagic rebound effect." The cardiovascular effects are rare and moderate (bradycardia and hyper or hypotension) if the product is used properly: injected exclusively into the tissues after appropriate dilution (5 units in 50–100 ml of saline – the latter is recommended). However if injected in error into the lumen of a blood vessel and/or used without previous dilution, severe bradycardia, hypotension and cardiac arrest can occur. Casualties have been reported and as a result the use of synthetic vasopressin for prevention of intraoperative bleeding is prohibited in many countries including France.

Respecting the rules of surgical anatomy

To avoid bleeding during vaginal surgery it is essential to know and be familiar with pelvic anatomy and to apply this knowledge while operating.

The vagina is organized from the surgical point of view into two main layers: the superficial layer (the skin) and the deep layer (the fascia). The deep layer is that which transmits the vessels. When one opens the vagina it is essential to pass either in front of or behind this fascia, but to avoid proceeding into the substance of the fascia.

The best example of this is taken from the technique of simple hysterectomy. For abdominal hysterectomy, most textbooks recommend using the intrafascial technique described by Aldridge: penetrating the periuterine fascia leads directly into the plane situated between the vaginal fascia and its skin, i.e. finally into the vaginal cavity. For vaginal hysterectomy penetrating the periuterine fascia leads into a bloody plane and prevents one entering the space situated between the uterus and the urinary bladder. The best option is opening the vagina itself and opening it at a distance from the uterus to enter directly into the space, which is practically free of significant blood vessels.

Occasionally hemorrhage occurs to warn the operator of a false move, e.g. unidentified damage to the bladder will result in hemorrhage. Although one of the aims of this book is to guide the operator, there is of course no substitute for observation, surgical apprenticeship and experience.

Prevention of thrombosis

The risk of thromboembolism is a significant concern in all types of gynecologic surgery. The pelvis is a vascular sponge whose morphology and function is modified by pregnancy and every gynecological surgeon is aware of the possibility of vascular thrombosis developing in association with pelvic surgery. In reality the available data show that the risk is relatively low. With vaginal surgery the risk is even lower than with the abdominal approach.

The risk of thromboembolism in vaginal surgery

It is very difficult to quote an exact figure for the true incidence of thromboembolic conditions associated with any particular type of surgery. Clinical impression is subject to error. The rate of inferior limb deep vein thrombosis is probably underestimated. The rate of pulmonary embolism is surely overestimated (half of the deaths clinically attributed to pulmonary embolism are, at autopsy, due to other causes). Investigative radiology searching for thrombosis of the lower limbs produces a high proportion of false positives. Furthermore it is not possible to perform this sort of investigation on every single patient undergoing surgery. Finally the risk of thrombosis varies from patient to patient and from procedure to procedure and the results of studies performed on one group of patients cannot necessarily be extrapolated to another.

For vaginal hysterectomy the rate of reported thromboembolic complications varies between 0 and 3% if defined by clinical criteria. Using systematic radiological assessment it can be as high as 10%. Whatever the criteria used, the risk is lower than it is for abdominal hysterectomy. The denominator ranges from 0 to 10 in the various comparative surveys reported.

Anticoagulants

Today anticoagulants hold a preeminent place in the prevention of postoperative thrombosis. This is most particularly true since the 1970s when Kakkar[1] demonstrated and reported that treatment with low doses of heparin drastically reduced the risk of deaths from embolism in the perioperative period. Kakkar showed that postoperative thrombosis actually started to develop on the operating table. Immobilization of the patient and trauma to the tissues and to the feeding vessels created favorable conditions for thrombosis (slowing of the circulation and liberation of thrombo-plastic substances). Although thrombosis starts intraoperatively it may manifest clinically a few days later. Heparin, which acts by reinforcing the action of anti-thrombin III, is able to inhibit these phenomena.

It is not necessary to use large doses and the efficacy is greater the sooner treatment is started. The original protocol of Kakkar recommended the administration of subcutaneous heparin at a dose of 7,500 units bd. The treatment was started 1 h before the procedure and continued for 6 days. It then became apparent that this protocol wasn't always sufficient and it was then suggested that three injections were required each day (5,000 units tds) and that treatment should continue for 10 days. Many specialists actually gave higher doses equivalent to therapeutic doses (40,000–60,000 U.I. each day). Of course, one cannot start such high doses in the immediate preoperative period. These higher doses require closer monitoring and are associated with a higher risk of complications.

More recently, the trend is toward using low molecular weight heparins that have the advantage of subcutaneous administration and also obviate the requirement for serum monitoring. Dalteparin sodium (Fragmin) is given subcutaneously as prophylaxis using a dose of 2,500. Theoretically, the treatment has to be started 1–2 h preoperatively but many teams delay this until the afternoon following surgery. For patients at moderate risk 2,500 units are then given

every 24 h for at least 5 days. High-risk patients require the same preoperative dose followed by 2,500 units 8–12 h later and then 5,000 units every 24 h for at least 5 days. Alternative preparations include enoxaparin (Clexane) and tinzaparan (Innohep).

Complications of anticoagulants are well known and include bleeding, hematoma formation and super infection. Across the board these are twice as frequent in patients receiving treatment. These risks are even more evident when the doses are higher and when treatment has been started earlier. In spite of these complications it is important to keep them in perspective remembering at all times the importance of avoiding fatal embolus.

Certain historical studies seem to indicate that heparin therapy does not protect against postoperative thromboembolism. For example Strobel[2], in a publication in 1981, showed that he had observed more thromboembolic incidents between 1952 and 1962 when he practiced systematic heparinization, than during the period 1962–1980 when he had abandoned it. Rather than doubting the effects of heparin therapy, these statistics should remind us that in recent years a number of other factors have resulted in a reduction in postoperative thromboembolism. It is possible that epidemiological conditions have changed with perhaps less venous insufficiency, and the like. Furthermore, operative techniques have developed. Not so much in their basic principles, but more in the way in which they are performed: more precise with less trauma. Finally, there are of course other methods of prevention that can be used.

Other methods of prevention of thromboembolism

Preventing postoperative thromboembolism begins at the time of the procedure, which should be as atraumatic as possible and during as short a period as possible. The techniques outlined in this book are designed to minimize trauma and time taken.

Postoperative physiotherapy is essential. This includes early mobilization and rising on the first postoperative evening appears to be most important. This event may take up to 15 min and requires the input of a motivated team, as does supervision of exercises, which should be performed during the inpatient postoperative period. We encourage patients to walk and to do exercises, which can be performed while lying on the bed. The day after surgery the patient is encouraged to negotiate a flight of stairs.

It is equally possible for patients who have had radical surgery to perform these procedures and one can encourage women who have had surgery for prolapse to do the same exercises as other patients. Patients who have had vaginal surgery have the advantage of not having wound pain. This encourages mobilization and deep breathing.

We encourage patients to start drinking the evening after surgery and within 48 h to take food. Again, this is of course easier in patients who have had vaginal surgery.

Therapeutic indications

Patients can be categorized into three main groups according to the risk of thromboembolism: women at high risk, women at risk and women who are not at risk.

Women at high risk

We consider the following to be patients at high risk:

- Women with a personal history of thromboembolism (associated with surgery or pregnancy/delivery)
- Women having surgery for a malignant tumor

For women considered to be at high risk we systematically prescribe heparin prophylaxis. We start preoperatively (unless there is an extremely high risk of intraoperative hemorrhage): enoxaparin 40 mg subcutaneously 12 h before surgery and then 40 mg every 24 h for 7–10 days. We also prescribe Aspirin (50 mg in 24 h) for 1–2 months.

Women at risk

We consider the following to be women at risk:

- Women with venous insufficiency
- Obese women
- Diabetic women
- Smokers
- All women over 50 years of age
- Women having a hysterectomy

In those women with two risk factors we use enoxaparin 20 mg subsutaneously 2 h before surgery and then 20 mg for 7–10 days. Finally, all women having a hysterectomy are now considered to be at risk and are given prophylaxis.

Women who are not at risk

Women who do not have any risk factors could be managed without any medication at all. However, judicial precedents mean that it is no longer possible to submit a patient to any surgical procedure involving opening the peritoneal cavity, however short and brief

(e.g. adnexal surgery through colpotomy), without perioperative anticoagulation.

As rare as they are thromboembolic complications do occur in women undergoing vaginal surgery. If thrombosis is confirmed, treatment must be instituted according to standard protocols.

Prevention of infection

Vaginal surgery has the reputation of being "more risky" as far as postoperative infectious complications are concerned. In fact in all surveys published before the era of modern antibiotic prophylaxis the rate of such complications appeared higher. This no longer applies today. These assertions summarize the following considerations.

The risk of infection following vaginal surgery

Whatever the adopted definition, postoperative infectious complications reported in surveys published before the 1970s were more frequent after vaginal hysterectomy than after abdominal hysterectomy e.g. global infectious morbidity (temperature 38 °C or more on two measurements 6 h apart, excluding the first postoperative 48 h) affected 40–70% of patients after vaginal surgery as opposed to 30–45% after abdominal surgery. Furthermore, the number of patients having further operations for postoperative peritonitis or pelvic abscess was twice as high.

Antibiotic prophylaxis has erased this difference if not actually inverted it. Before discussing the considerations relating to antibiotic prophylaxis, we briefly analyze below the data reporting that vaginal surgery is "more risky." This analysis provides the rationale for antibiotic prophylaxis while also demonstrating that other preventative measures are of equal importance.

The microorganisms responsible for postoperative infections

The microorganisms one finds in samples collected from patients affected by infectious complications after vaginal surgery are aerobic Gram-negative bacteria (*Escherichia coli, Proteus mirabilis*, streptococci and other species of enterobacteria) and anaerobes (*Bacteroides fragilis*, peptococci, anaerobic streptococci and other Gram-negative anaerobes). They can be isolated in vaginal discharge; in pus collected from a pyosalpinx, an ovarian abscess or other pelvic abscess; in peritoneal fluid or in blood in cases of peritonitis and/or septicemia. These microorganisms are not different from the microorganisms one finds in other types of pelvic infections (infectious complications following abdominal gynecologic operations, puerperal infections, venereal infections) and they belong to the normal commensal flora of the vaginal and cervical secretions.

In the field of genital pelvic infections, the difference between physiology and pathology is a quantitative one. The same microorganisms are detected but in the case of infection the concentrations for the same unit of volume are higher. For this reason the microorganisms are more easily detected and thus appear to be more frequently present. On the other hand mixed flora (the combination of aerobic Gram-negative and anaerobic organisms) are more commonly associated with infections following vaginal gynecologic operations as compared with other types of gynecologic pelvic infections and infections occurring after abdominal gynecologic procedures.

The causes of postoperative infections following vaginal surgery

As far as postoperative infections are concerned, surgical trauma kick-starts the multiplication of bacteria living peacefully at the surface of the vaginal and cervical mucosa. The anoxia and necrosis that are part of surgical trauma particularly favor the proliferation of anaerobes. The presence of foreign bodies such as suture material (even absorbable material) perpetrates the phenomenon. This applies to all gynecologic operations. The apparently higher frequency of infections after vaginal surgery is probably due to the fact that this type of surgery starts with direct trauma to the bacterial sanctuaries: the vaginal and cervical mucosa.

Once the mechanism of postoperative infection is understood, antibiotics appear to provide a logical prophylactic approach. They must be administered before trauma stimulates the chain of events leading to infection.

As stated before, vaginal surgery is associated with a greater risk of infection than abdominal surgery but in recent studies these proportions are inverted. This suggests that preventive measures (which are described below) are much more efficacious in cases of vaginal surgery as compared with cases of abdominal surgery. However, as in the past, the most serious infectious complications are more common in vaginal surgery. This indicates that specific measures have also to be taken during and after the operations particularly in those where the peritoneal cavity is opened (very few life threatening infections occur after extraperitoneal operations) and in patients with reduced resistance to infection (diabetics and obese women, anemic patients and patients on corticosteroids etc.).

In discussing the issue of prevention we start by defining the risk and comparing it as much as one can with the risk encountered when operating abdominally. The causes are discussed. The issue of preventative antibiotics is then analyzed and we finish by outlining preventive measures over and above pharmacological ones. We do not deal here with the issue of urinary infection.

Antibiotic prophylaxis

Prophylactic antibiotics
Theoretically there are pros and cons to prophylactic antibiotics. The cons include the concept that prophylactic antibiotics can encourage the proliferation of resistant strains, which can be dangerous not just for the patient but also for the hospital environment. On the other hand antibiotics, of themselves, carry their own risks (toxic effects, allergy, etc.). Thus the choice of antibiotic is of seminal importance.

The choice of antibiotic
The choice of antibiotic to be used for prophylaxis in cases of vaginal surgery should be determined by the activity of that antibiotic. One must select antibiotics that are active against a wide variety of organisms, i.e. the "normal" flora of the genital tract and the microorganisms that can be carried and transmitted by the operative team: Gram-positive aerobic and anaerobic cocci, Gram-negative aerobic and anaerobic bacilli (*Bacteroides fragilis* in particular). These organisms have different sensitivities.

A combination of penicillin and Metronidazole is theoretically satisfactory. Penicillin is very effective against Gram-positive aerobic and anaerobic cocci. On the other hand Metronidazole is the most effective agent when combating *Bacteroides fragilis*. Unfortunately penicillin is associated with allergic reactions and cannot be used for all patients. It acts on only a part of the spectrum of microorganisms involved in postoperative infections: its power against aerobic Gram-negative bacteria is low. But these microorganisms do not have the same pathogenicity if the other pathogenic flora is inhibited. The clinical results obtained are excellent.

Chloramphenicol and Clindamycin, which provide broad coverage, can be good alternatives. However, they are associated with toxicities that make their regular use impractical: agranulocytosis and ulcerative membranous enterocolitis.

Third generation cephalosporins have a spectrum that is almost ideal. Controlled trials have demonstrated their usefulness. From a theoretical perspective they don't provide absolute cover for *Bacteroides fragilis* and we have seen how important this organism is in the pathogenesis of postoperative infections in vaginal surgery. On the other hand, this raises the possibility of regular administration of these antibiotics producing resistant strains of the organism in the field of Gram-negative bacteria. It thus seems appropriate to reserve these antibiotics for the treatment of confirmed serious postoperative infection.

Now at the beginning of the twenty-first century, first generation cephalosporins are the preferred choice of most surgeons as their prophylactic efficiency is adequate, there are currently few resistant strains and they are cheap! They include cefalexin, cefradine and cefadroxil.

The mode of administration of antibiotics

The famous work of Burke[3] (1961) showed that prophylactic antibiotics were ineffective when their administration was delayed for more than 3 h after the time when contamination would occur. In his study, infection did not occur if prophylaxis was actually started before inoculation occurred. This experimental study corroborated by clinical observation shows that one must start prophylactic antibiotics before the inoculating procedure. On the basis of this work one can state that a bolus 30–60 min before surgical intervention is ideal.

Discussions are still ongoing about the necessity of giving a second and third injection during and after the preoperative bolus. Some trials show that these repeated injections are useful while others do not. The only certainty is that prolonged treatment is not appropriate.

The results of antibiotic prophylaxis

There is no doubt that antibiotic prophylaxis is efficacious in reducing postoperative morbidity following hysterectomy. Most of the prospective randomized trials available were published in the 1970s and 1980s. There are more than 20. Without exception, they demonstrated a significant reduction in postoperative infectious morbidity in patients given antibiotic prophylaxis, and this was independent of the prescribed drug (first generation cephalosporin in most instances). The strength of the evidence was such that studies on new antibiotic prophylaxis no longer had a placebo-only arm.

The triumph of antibiotic prophylaxis must not lead us to forget the side effects. We have already spoken of toxicity and the risk of allergic response. We have also mentioned the bacteriological risk of encouraging the development of resistant strains. Serious life-threatening infection is most problematic when caused by these strains. We now know from surveys published at the beginning of the era of antibiotic prophylaxis that the postoperative bacterial spectrum is not completely different when comparing patients who have received antibiotic prophylaxis with those who have not. This means that new strains develop to evade the action of the antibiotics prescribed. For this reason we believe that it is important that antibiotic prophylaxis is only used when indicated, as the only way to avoid resistant strains is to avoid the use of antibiotics!

Indications for antibiotic prophylaxis

It is therefore appropriate to prescribe antibiotic prophylaxis only in cases where it is indicated. As already mentioned certain procedures are at risk of postoperative infection, as are certain patients.

Operations at risk

Surgery that does not involve opening the peritoneal cavity (cone biopsy, vaginal repair and fistula repair) does not in general justify antibiotic prophylaxis.

In general, operations involving opening the peritoneal cavity justify antibiotic prophylaxis. Contamination of the peritoneal cavity can result in complications that are life threatening. However, in this category there are a large number of procedures with varying degrees of risk.

Hysterectomy in our opinion warrants antibiotic prophylaxis, as does hysterectomy associated with repair. Radical hysterectomy also warrants antibiotic prophylaxis.

Patients at risk

The concept of patients at risk takes second position when considering the indications for antibiotic prophylaxis. Obviously patients with chronic pelvic infection require antibiotics. All factors reducing resistance are indications for prophylactic antibiotics. These include patients on corticosteroids, diabetics, patients with anemia, obese patients and malnourished patients.

Other methods of prevention

Antibiotics are not the only approach to preventing postoperative infectious complications. Conversely one can actually state that antibiotics have an accessory role to the other preventative measures, which we classify in three categories according to the chronological order in which they occur.

Preoperative preparation

A long period of hospitalization before surgery increases the risk of postoperative infection – Cruse[4] in the giant survey (30,000 operative wounds) he published in 1977 has shown this in relation to general surgery where the risk of infection increases according to the period of preoperative hospitalization. This is the same for the postoperative stay: a shorter length of hospital stay is associated with a significantly lower risk of wound infection in the first 10 postoperative days. It is therefore imperative to ensure that as far as possible hospitalization is minimized.

Local antiseptic treatments in the days preceding surgery actually have a negative effect. We discovered this in our own practice when over a period of time we systematically treated the vagina with Povidone iodine for 10 days preoperatively. The rate of infectious complications during this period rose and the severity of the infections increased. A survey published in 1976 shows that after a single application of antiseptic the number of organisms per unit surface area diminishes in the first 15 min. After this period the number rapidly increases so that at 60 min the concentration is ten times the initial concentration. If one repeats the application each day the number of organisms increases day after day. This is the mechanism whereby the risk of postoperative infection is actually increased.

Bowel preparation given before vaginal surgery is not generally required. Nonetheless it is critical when treating a rectovaginal fistula. For other procedures we generally prescribe an enema to avoid fecal soiling during the procedure.

Intraoperative prevention

The way in which one operates and the measures one takes just before operating affects the risk of postoperative infection.

Shaving increases the risk of infection. Cruse has shown that postoperative infection can be reduced from 2.5% to 0.9% by avoiding shaving, and although these data relate to abdominal surgery there is no reason to presume that it will be different for vaginal surgery. We avoid shaving and cut hair only if it is absolutely essential to do so.

The use of a vaginal pessary given immediately before surgery has an important role. It dilutes the vaginal flora without throwing it out of balance. The addition of povidone iodine is a ritual that we find impossible to drop, even if it has been demonstrated that dilution is more important than bacteriolysis.

Careful and complete preparation of the operative field is important. We exclude the anal orifice and believe that this is a very important part of the preparation. Careful placing of the drapes is also important.

During surgery it is important to remember that all studies and in particular those of Cruse show that the risk of infection increases with the length of the operative procedure. Thus the longest operations, which are also the most difficult, are the most dangerous. Nonetheless time itself is an independent risk factor. It is important to move quickly but without taking risks. It is also clear that rough dissection must be more dangerous than careful slow dissection, which avoids devitalizing the tissues: "careful, gentle and meticulous surgical technique is the best prophylaxis against postoperative infection" (Halsted 1912).

Drainage

Drainage of the operative field continues to be a highly controversial issue in general surgery. The work of Cruse already cited shows that postoperative infectious morbidity is more common when one uses a drain: 1.5% of cases when no drain is used as compared to 2.3–3.9% of cases when a drain is used.

In fact, the main risk factor is hematoma formation. If the postoperative field is dry the risk is low and drainage only increases the risk. When the postoperative field is hemorrhagic a risk develops, which may be reduced by drainage. As far as vaginal hysterectomy is concerned the data we have at our disposal are contradictory.

A very nice survey was published at the end of the 1970s by a team in Manchester regarding vaginal hysterectomy combined with repair. In order to reduce infectious morbidity different antibiotic protocols were tried. The risk of complications dropped from more than 40% to less than 20%. Then a modification of the technique was tested: the vagina, which was previously closed at the end of the operation, was left partially open: the rate of complications fell to less than 5%. The drugs and protocols used were not today's drugs and protocols and therefore, the results of this trial could not be extrapolated for current application. However the study did show that drainage in itself is an efficient prophylactic tool.

More recent surveys do not give the same results and today we benefit from trials comprising two or more arms, which demonstrate that appropriate antibiotic prophylaxis works better than drainage either alone or combined with antibiotics. Drainage is necessary when hemostasis is not perfect. But drainage does not prevent infection and obviate the requirement for antibiotics. Hemostasis must be perfect, drainage is not recommended and antibiotics have to be given systematically.

Conclusion

It will never be possible to render the operative act completely inoffensive. Nonetheless it is essential to minimize the potential morbidity of surgery.

We have in this chapter outlined measures that in the current state of knowledge minimize the risk of anesthetic complications. We have also tried to outline the best approach to reducing the main postoperative complications. In the following chapters, under each intervention, we emphasize those approaches that are potentially morbid and encourage the use of approaches that minimize complications. We hope by so doing to assist those who read this book. Nonetheless the best way for each surgeon to minimize their morbidity is to keep an account of their own complication rates. The identification and registration of iatrogenic morbidity is a type of quality control that is essential for all those performing surgery.

References

1 Kakkar V.V. Low doses of heparin in the prevention of deep vein thrombosis. *Bull Schweiz Akad Med Wiss* 1973;29:235–43.
2 Strobel E. The mortality from thrombo-embolism following gynaecological operations without anticoagulation treatment (author's translation). *Geburtshilfe Frauenheilkd* 1981;41:749–53.
3 Burke J.F. and Morris P.J. Recent trends in surgical bacteriology. *J Surg Res* 1967;7:95–104.
4 Cruse P.J. and Foord R. The epidemiology of wound infection. A 10-year prospective study of 62,939 wounds. *Surg Clin North Am* 1980;60:27–40.

5 Surgery of the cervix: conization

The uterine cervix may be altered by various malformations or traumatic sequelae and/or affected by all sorts of diseases. Surgery can provide the solution to these problems. From a practical perspective, there are two types of operations: those aiming to reconstruct the cervix (on the basis that restoring the normal shape of the cervix restores its normal function too) and those aiming to remove just the damaged parts of the organ. In this book, we limit ourselves to those operations that aim to restore the functional role the cervicoisthmic continence system plays during pregnancy, and those operations that aim to remove the precancerous and cancerous lesions that can develop on the cervix. The first operations are described in Chapter 10 "Vaginal surgery in obstetrics." The second are the subject matter of this chapter.

The concept of precursors of cervical cancer was introduced at the beginning of the twentieth century and has changed quite a lot since that time. Initially, carcinoma *in situ* was the only recognized entity. Then, dysplasias were described some of which are close relatives of carcinoma *in situ*: the atypical dysplasias, morphologically similar to carcinoma *in situ* and considered to be at risk of transforming into cancer, albeit less so than carcinoma *in situ*. These atypical dysplasias were grouped with carcinoma *in situ* as members of the same family of Cervical Intraepithelial Neoplasia (CIN), which includes three grades, each of them being credited with a specific potential to transform into cancer. Nowadays, CIN3 and CIN2 are grouped together as High Grade Squamous Intraepithelial Lesions (SIL) as opposed to Low Grade SIL (CIN1 and flat condylomas). The same classification exists for Glandular Intraepithelial Lesions (GIL).

Cervical cancer precursors arise from the anatomical area that is located around the external orifice of the cervix. In cases where lesions of different grades occur in the same patient (one in three cases) the lowest-grade lesion generally develops on the outside and the highest-grade lesion in the center; but both are located above the original Squamo-Columnar junction (SC junction), which is the lower limit of the so-called Transformation Zone (TZ). The name TZ was launched by colposcopists who can identify the part of the ectocervix covered by native ectocervical squamous epithelium and the part covered by metaplastic squamous epithelium. The latter arises from transformation of the columnar epithelium that covers the endocervix but, through the physiological process of eversion, is exposed on the ectocervix (ectopy). The cancer precursors arise from the TZ that, in cases of cellular atypia, is called the ATZ (Atypical TZ). It is the ATZ that the surgeon must remove.

Carcinoma *in situ* was managed as invasive cancer in past decades. One spoke of Stage 0 cancer of the cervix and one either performed radical hysterectomy or gave radiotherapy. Later, more conservative approaches were introduced. Extrafascial hysterectomy and amputation of the cervix were the first steps on the path toward minimalization, then conization. Conization may be performed either using the cold knife or the monopolar wire loop. The so-called Large Loop Excision of the Transformation Zone (LLETZ) is generally considered less aggressive than cold knife conization. In actual fact, the use of each of these instruments has specific indications but the aim is the same, i.e. removal of the ATZ: all the ATZ but only the ATZ. A more conservative approach does exist, which involves ablating the ATZ either by cryo-dessication or laser vaporization. The indications for these blind techniques are mentioned but the techniques themselves are not described.

Technique

Large Loop Excision of the Transformation Zone

LLETZ is nothing more than an improvement on a very old technique used for assessing and curing (at the same time) procursors of cancer that had developed on the external surface of the cervix. The wire loops that were used before 1990 were small, did not include an insulated part and, above all, were linked to generators producing a so-called continuous sine wave cutting current. The procedure was bloody. Thermal damage to specimens was considerable and the specimens were small. Today one benefits from wire loops 2 cm in width and 1.4–2.0 cm in depth inserted on insulated straight bases (Figure 5.1). This configuration limits the so-called arcing phenomenon to the active part of the loop. At the same time, we also have the benefit of generators producing blended currents combining excellent cutting characteristics and hemostastic effect. These two technological improvements enable us to excise a relatively large specimen in a single pass with minimal bleeding and little thermal damage.

The large loop is connected to the generator, which at the same time must be connected to the return electrode (plate) attached to the patient's thigh (Figure 5.2). This generator is adjusted to produce a low voltage blended waveform current of 36 W with "rapid start" capacity (a microprocessor controls the power output and ensures that cutting commences as soon as the loop is activated). The control system can be activated either with a foot pedal or with a hand-piece.

The procedure can be performed under local anesthesia as an outpatient procedure. The first step of the procedure is to introduce a nonconducting speculum including a smoke evacuator (Figure 5.3). Local anesthesia is obtained in the simplest way by direct infiltration of the cervical connective tissue. The needle used is a 27-gauge needle attached to an aspirating syringe. The depth of infiltration is 2–3 mm and the mixture injected is 2% lidocaine with $1/10^5$ epinephrine. 1 ml is injected into each of the four quadrants at 6, 3, 9 and 12 o'clock (Figure 5.4). As soon as the bleeding from the puncture sites completely stops one can get started.

The electro-resection is performed either transversely from one fornix to the other (from the right fornix to the left fornix for a right-handed surgeon) or vertically from one lip to the other (from the upper to the lower lip: Figure 5.5). The electrode is activated (and the smoke evacuator) just before touching the cervical mucosa. Then it is moved across the cervix. The movement has to be slow but continuous. The depth required depends on preoperative colposcopic assessment. It is generally between 0.5 and 1.5 cm in the central part of the excision. Therefore, the loop is progressively pushed in deep and then pulled to the surface until it appears at the fornix opposite its

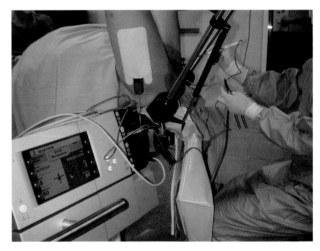

Figure 5.2 The generator and its connections to the patient and the loop.

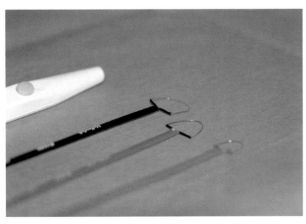

Figure 5.1 The wire loops.

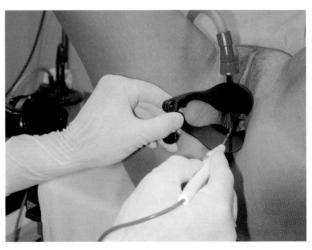

Figure 5.3 The protected speculum connected to suction.

Figure 5.4 Injecting the local anesthetic into the substance of the cervix at a depth of 5 mm. In all, six to eight injections are made around the circumference of the cervix.

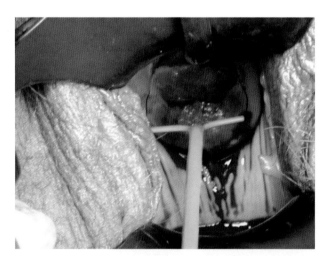

Figure 5.5 Having powered the loop it is then moved through the substance of the cervix from top to bottom aiming to remove the entire TZ.

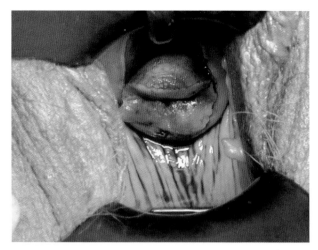

Figure 5.6 The specimen has been separated.

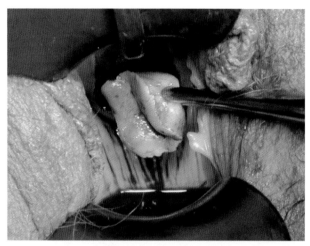

Figure 5.7 The specimen is removed.

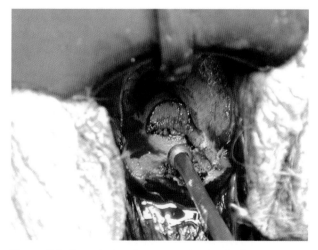

Figure 5.8 Coagulating the raw conization bed.

starting point (Figure 5.6). After the resection the raw area is generally bloodless (Figure 5.7). If not, bleeding can be controlled using a ball electrode (Figure 5.8) and coagulating current.

In some cases the cutting movement at a certain point appears difficult to complete. In such a case one has to stop and perform the excision from the opposite side until one meets the point where the first excision stopped. This problem is generally due to passing through the tissues too rapidly and/or stopping part way through (LLETZ is a simple procedure but a training curve does exist). It can also be due to inadequate assessment of the lesion: a large lesion developing on a large cervix and involving the deep endocervical canal cannot simply be removed with the large loop.

As far as lesions developing on a large cervix are concerned it is possible to resect them in two steps – posterior lip first and then anterior lip. As far as lesions involving most of the endocervix are concerned the same two-step procedure can be attempted: excision of the peripheral part with a curved loop of 2.0 × 1.5 cm and excision of the canal with a square loop 1.0 × 1.0 cm in size. We do not recommend this technique and prefer using cold knife conization for such cases.

Cold knife conization

Cold knife conization is no longer the radical procedure it once was, requiring in the past general anesthesia and hospitalization. Only the most anxious patients and those with unfavorable vaginal access are currently managed using the classical procedure. Other patients can have their operation done under local anesthesia with no hospitalization and, whatever the choice, only the ATZ is removed rather than the entire "field of endocervical glands" as was the case in the past.

Local anesthesia

If performed under local anesthesia the procedure has to be done without using standard vaginal surgery retractors as they cause pain. Adequate exposure is obtained using a Collin speculum.

The posterior lip of the cervix is held with a delicate bullet forceps applied transversely and pulled toward the pubis so that the first two injections involving the uterine extremity of the uterosacral ligaments can be performed. A 21-gauge needle is used and introduced through the posterior wall of the vagina at the 4 and 8 o'clock positions (Figure 5.9). After ensuring that the tip of the needle is not in a vascular space (aspiration) the injections are performed: 7 ml of fluid on each side.

For both subsequent infiltrations the bullet forceps is applied transversely to the anterior lip of the cervix and pulled axially. The punctures are made just outside the external orifice of the cervix (Figure 5.10). The needle is pushed in until it reaches the level of the internal os of the cervix: about 4 cm. The injections are performed while gradually pulling out the needle (do not forget to aspirate before injecting) – 7 ml fluid on each side.

(a)

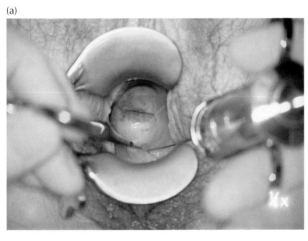

(b)

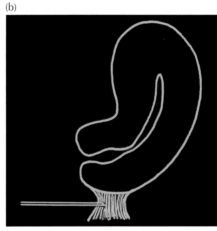

Figure 5.9 (a) and (b) Anesthetic/ hemostatic infiltration of the left uterosacral ligament.

(a)

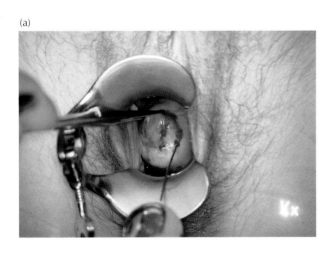

(b)

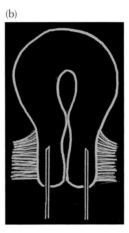

Figure 5.10 (a) and (b) Anesthetic/hemostatic infiltration of the lateral part of the upper cervix avoiding paracervical injecting and thus reducing the chance of intravascular injection of lidocaine and adrenaline.

After the first four injections that aim to interrupt the impulses transmitted by the paracervical nerves, four to six complementary injections into the cervical connective tissue must be performed. These are placed on a circular line, a few millimetres deep at 1 cm intervals. These injections aim to complete the anesthetic effect and to provide hemostasis.

The mixture we use is 2% lidocaine with $1/10^5$ epinephrine: 30–40 ml is injected. It is very important to check the position of the needle tip before injecting: use an aspirating syringe that allows easy withdrawal of the piston before each injection of fluid.

Resection

The resection can be started as soon as bleeding from the needle puncture sites completely stops. This takes about 3 min. The resection is performed inside the Collin speculum using two different knives (Figure 5.11): one no. 11 straight blade and one oblique blade (Rudolph Beaver, Waltham MA, USA). Two successive incisions are made.

For the first incision, made with the no. 11 straight blade, a delicate bullet forceps is inserted into the edge of the cervix at approximately 11 o'clock. The cervix is pulled axially. The incision must circumscribe the outer limit of the lesion. The incision must be circular or elliptical the radius being chosen to include the greatest diameter of the lesion and to leave a margin of approximately 3 mm. One commences at the 4 o'clock position (Figure 5.12). The blade penetrates to a depth of 4 mm and is handled axially as if to resect a cylinder rather than a cone. Going clockwise one finishes at the point where one started (Figure 5.13).

For the second incision the bullet forceps is moved and inserted into the connective tissue on the inside lip of the first incision at the 4 o'clock position and as

far as possible from the epithelial layer. Traction on the forceps broadens the wound and permits an oblique approach (Figure 5.14). The angle of the plane of incision is calculated based on the endocervical extension of the lesion, the goal being to have a

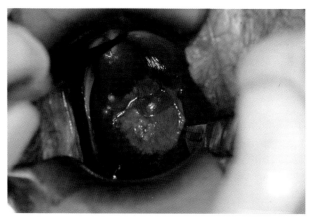

Figure 5.12 The first incision is made as though performing "cylinderalization" opposed to conization, i.e. the knife is held parallel to the long axis of the cervix at a depth of 4–5 mm.

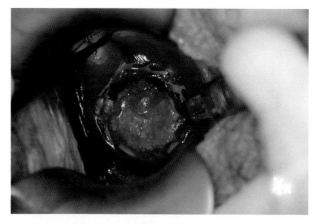

Figure 5.13 The first incision is complete.

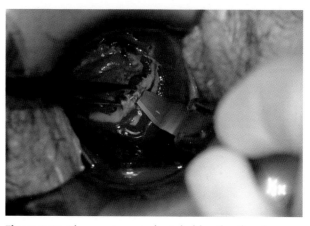

Figure 5.14 The specimen-to-be is held with a fine forceps applied to the substance of the cylinder at 4 o'clock. This opens up the first incision allowing the second, which is performed at an oblique angle.

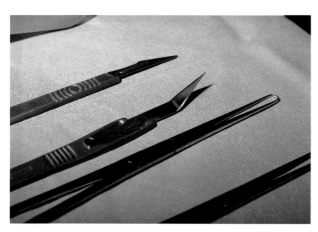

Figure 5.11 The two scalpels (a size 11 straight blade and oblique blade) and the fine tenaculum.

3 mm margin above the top of the lesion. The incision is performed clockwise. Once the posterior lip has been detached, the bullet forceps is moved to the anterior lip and left there until the specimen has been completely detached (Figure 5.15).

Sutures

Hemostasis and "reconstruction" may be achieved after conization by using electrocauterization. We prefer sutures because they are safer and do not impair cervical permeability as long as the procedure is performed correctly.

The technique we recommend is a modification of the Stürmdorf technique. Unlike the standard Stürmdorf technique we do not invaginate the peripheral cervical flap into the cervical canal but leave a free space around the orifice (Figure 5.16).

The Stürmdorf suture is inserted by stitching the outside flap to the inside deep down and close to the sagittal plane taking care that the tip of the needle enters the crater at a distance from the uterine orifice (Figure 5.17). The needle used is a 26 mm semicircular cutting needle. After the first stitch the flap is stitched again close to its free margins on the midline from inside to outside and then from outside to inside. The last stitch is another deep one starting on the inside at a distance from the uterine orifice and emerging at approximately 1 cm from the point where the first stitch was inserted. Tying the stitch invaginates the flap into the crater but leaves the orifice free (Figure 5.18).

After the two Stürmdorf sutures, two lateral sutures are inserted. The technique used is the "far and near" (or figure of 8) technique (Figure 5.19). These two sutures play an important role in hemostasis because the blood supply comes from the lateral aspects of the treated area. However, after suturing, cervical morphology is far from normal (Figure 5.20).

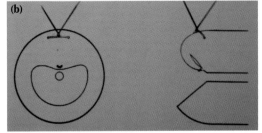

Figure 5.15 Detaching the cone.

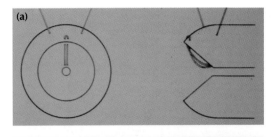

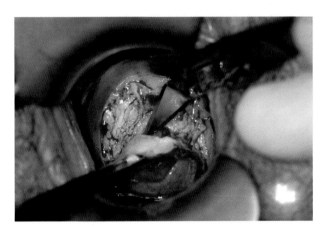

Figure 5.16 (a) and (b) The modified Stürmdorf suture. In contrast with the classical stitch the uterine canal is not dilated and the periphery of the raw area is not inverted. The orifice is not obliterated.

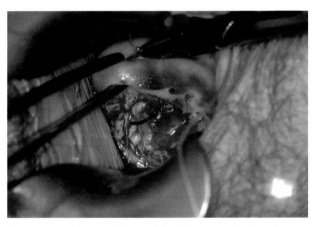

Figure 5.17 The initial step of the first Stürmdorf stitch. Note that the tip of the needle reappears 2 mm outside the uterine orifice and not inside it.

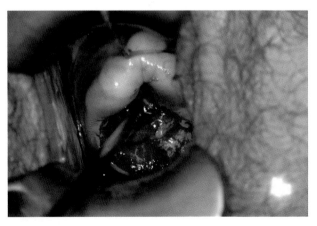

Figure 5.18 The first Stürmdorf stitch is complete. The uterine orifice is not obliterated as shown by the dilator.

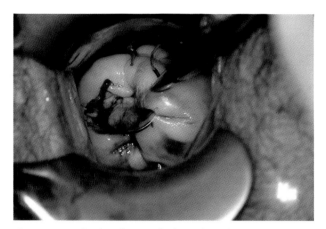

Figure 5.19 The first figure of 8 lateral stitch.

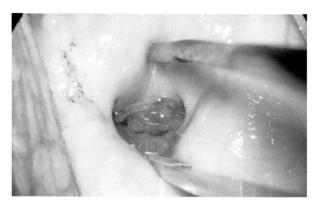

Figure 5.21 Appearance 2 months after cold knife conization. The squamocolumnar junction is slightly inverted but fully assessable.

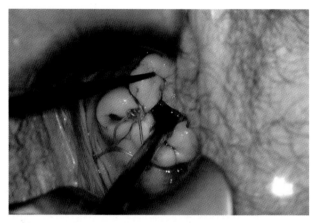

Figure 5.20 The final view after both Stürmdorf stitches and both lateral stitches have been placed: the appearance of the cervix is quite amazing. The suture used is carefully chosen. If absorbed too fast, hemorrhage occurs; if absorbed too slowly a bizarre scarred appearance results.

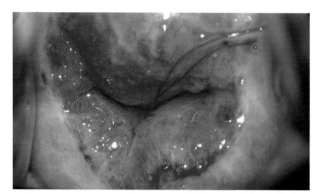

Figure 5.22 Appearance 2 months after LLETZ: the squamocolumnar junction is everted (ectopy).

The choice of suture is of great importance. We use O Monocryl as it has the best absorption properties: neither too fast, which could increase the risk of secondary hemorrhage, nor too slow, which could increase the risk of persistent cervical deformity.

Postoperative course and complications

LLETZ is performed as an ambulatory operation. The patient can go home immediately after the intervention. Cold knife conization is performed as an outpatient procedure. The patient can leave the hospital after 6 h. However, whatever the technique, one has to recommend avoiding professional activities, heavy housework and sport: sexual intercourse is prohibited until after postoperative assessment on day 14 or so. At the first postoperative visit, the cervical appearance is almost normal. Even after cold knife conization the loss of substance does not alter the appearance of the portio and the SC junction is fully visible (Figure 5.21). After LLETZ the junction is often frankly exteriorized resulting in an appearance somewhat similar to ectopy (Figure 5.22).

The perioperative and immediate postoperative complications are few. One has to quote injuries to bladder and rectum, and heavy perioperative bleeding due to direct injury to collaterals of the uterine arteries. All these complications are due to faulty maneuvers. They are more than exceptional. Postoperative bleeding is more common. It is related to the volume of specimen removed and, for this reason, is more frequent after cold knife conization than after LLETZ. Most cases can be resolved by packing alone during a short (1 day) hospital stay. Electrocauterization or suturing is not required in more than 1–3% of cases. Hemostatic hysterectomy is almost never indicated. Most postoperative bleeding occurs during the first 24 h after surgery. The incidence peaks again around day 10 after LLETZ. The risk completely disappears after 14 days. Other immediate complications are very rare: hematomas and infections. With regard to the latter, two points should be made: systematic removal of IUDs in patients with such a device (at the beginning of or, even better, before conization) is recommended, as is a delay of at least 6 weeks if hysterectomy is indicated as a result of histological assessment of the conization specimen (see later).

Late complications and sequelae are related either to stenosis of the cervix or to cervical incompetence. Both phenomena depend on the volume of the removed specimen and, more specifically, on its depth. For this reason, they are more frequent after cold knife conization than after LLETZ. Dysmenorrhea, pelvic pain and abnormal bleeding due to endometritis are rare (conization actually cures such symptoms by radical treatment of endocervitis, as opposed to creating them by alteration of cervical patency). Fertility problems are classically more common: infertility, miscarriage, premature delivery and uterine rupture. The careful assessment of large series of patients submitted to conization demonstrates the rarity of a clear link between surgery and fertility problems. Conization cures as much infertility as it creates. Miscarriages and premature deliveries due to cervicoisthmic incompetence can be prevented by adequate care. In cases of pregnancy failure, inserting an isthmic cerclage between pregnancies (see Chapter 10) can make a second pregnancy possible and successful (inserting such a cerclage or, at least, a Mac Donald suture is a necessity in the rare instances where conization has to be carried out during pregnancy). With regard to delivery, great attention has to be paid to monitoring as the "conization uterus" is a scar-bearing uterus.

Indications and postoperative management

The strength of the indication for conization depends on the potential of the intraepithelial lesion to transform into invasive cancer. This potential is considered to be low for low-grade SIL: low-grade SIL is not an indication for conization and can be either managed conservatively or destroyed by cryo-dessication or laser beam vaporization. The transformation potential of low-grade Glandular Intraepithelial Lesion (GIL) is low as well. However the colposcopic assessment of GIL is more difficult than the assessment of SIL. The lesions can be multifocal and errors are common (most GIL are coincidentally found during assessment of a cone biopsy specimen performed for SIL!). For this reason, low-grade GIL can be considered as an indication for conization as are the high-grade intraepithelial lesions either squamous or glandular.

Colposcopy is mandatory before any conization. The "see and treat" policy (LLETZ for every single cytologic atypia even of low grade or of undetermined signification) is not acceptable under normal conditions of medical practice. Discussions are ongoing regarding selection of patients for referral to the colposcopist. A Pap smear suggesting a high-grade intraepithelial lesion is surely an indication. For other presentations there are alternatives but we won't take a position on that here. Whatever the indication for it, colposcopy not only identifies cases for conization but also produces a map of the lesion(s) (in one out of three cases two or more types of lesions coexist in the same cervix). This map has to be sketched by the colposcopist and will help the surgeon to choose the instrument he will use for resection. Lesions confined to the ectocervix (Figure 5.23) can be managed using LLETZ while lesions involving the endocervix (Figure 5.24) have to be resected with the cold knife, for comparative studies consistently demonstrate that the average depth of the specimen is greater using the cold knife technique. All surgeons accept this

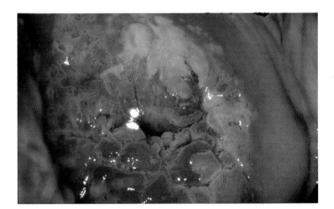

Figure 5.23 Atypical transformation zone grade 2. Squamocolumnar junction fully visible. Indication for LLETZ.

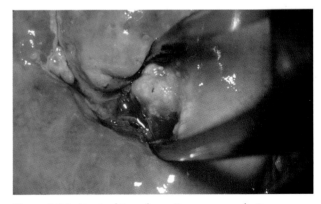

Figure 5.24 Atypical transformation zone grade 2. Squamocolumnar junction partly visible. Indication for cold knife conization.

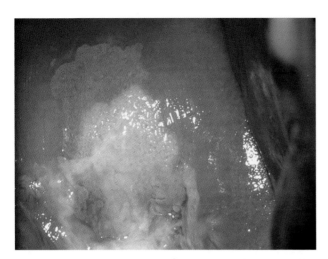

Figure 5.25 Atypical transformation zone grade 2 (centrally) associated with an atypical transformation zone grade 1 (peripherally): indication for conization plus ablation.

principle but practice differs from one to the next: the degree of endocervical involvement prohibiting the use of LLETZ is a matter for debate. It is worth mentioning that in cases where a large low-grade SIL surrounds the peripheral limit of a high-grade SIL (Figure 5.25), one option is to resect the central lesion alone and to ablate the peripheral one.

Assessment of the specimen is of crucial importance and it is the duty of the surgeon to make sure that this assessment is done properly, i.e. using semi-serial section technology (30–90 slides depending of the size of the specimen). There are two questions to answer: (1) is there invasive cancer associated with the intraepithelial lesion? (2) are the margins clear?

The rate of infiltrative cancers accompanying intraepithelial lesions varies from 5% to 10% if cases of "early stromal invasion" are included – these can escape detection if assessment is not performed by serial sectioning. The rate of unclear margins (incomplete excision) is on average 25% if the deliberate "non in sano resections" are included (see above).

In the presence of invasive cancer, management depends on the pathological stage. In early stromal invasion and stage p1A1 (tumoral diameter less than 7 mm and depth of infiltration less than 3 mm) conization may be considered adequate if the margins are clear. In stage 1A2 (tumoral diameter less than 7 mm and depth of infiltration between 3 and 5 mm) reoperation is mandatory even in cases where the margins of the specimen are clear: pelvic lymphadenectomy and radical hysterectomy (or trachelectomy). The Society of Gynecologic Oncologists recommends following the same rules for stage 1A1 when there is evidence of lympho-vascular space involvement.

When the margins of the specimen are not clear, different presentations have to be distinguished and managed accordingly. If the ectocervical margin is not clear, colposcopy performed at the first postoperative visit easily differentiates cases requiring further treatment from cases for conservative management. If the endocervical margin is not clear, colposcopy can be fully informative when the SC junction is fully visible. However, in other cases reoperation must be scheduled if the postoperative Pap smear shows cellular atypia even of low grade or undetermined significance. If the lateral limits are not clear, reoperation is mandatory whatever the results of Pap smear and colposcopy.

6 Colpotomy

Colpotomy was a major subject in the ancient textbooks of vaginal surgery and also a major part of the daily practice of yesteryear. It was thanks to colpotomy that pelvic abscesses were managed and thanks to this very simple procedure that many women's lives were saved. Colpotomy also provided access for the management of chronic adnexal disease and the performance of all types of operations on ovaries and tubes. It is still a simple, fast and low-cost approach to tubal sterilization.

The advent of laparoscopic surgery completely changed the landscape. Laparoscopy undoubtedly provides a better assessment of adnexal disease and makes ovarian and tubal surgery more precise and safe. However, colpotomy remains worthy of description and is now taught all the more as it plays a role in laparoscopic surgery itself: colpotomy is the best way to remove bulky specimens resulting from laparoscopic dissection that are impossible to remove directly through the endoscopic ancillary ports. Actually the "new colpotomy" is no longer a purely vaginal procedure but rather a laparoscopic procedure that is described herein once the purely vaginal technique has been outlined.

Technique

Laparoscopy undoubtedly facilitates performing colpotomy. Even the aperture of the vagina can be made using a purely laparoscopic approach. A purely vaginal approach can also be used and is associated with a risk of rectal injury that is lower than low.

Classical colpotomy

Access to the pelvic cavity and to the ovaries and tubes can be obtained either through the anterior vaginal fornix or through the posterior one. Clearly, posterior access is simpler. As far as posterior access is concerned, a transverse incision is also likely to be the simplest, as the peritoneum is closer to the skin at the top of the posterior fornix of the vagina than anywhere else. If a vertical incision is performed, the space located between the vagina and the rectum is entered introducing a risk of intestinal injury. This

Figure 6.1 Making the first incision with a 23-blade at the junction of the dorsal vaginal wall and the cervix.

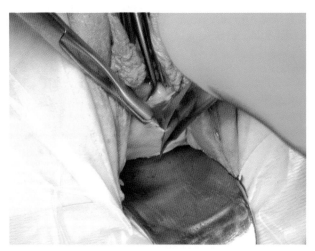

Figure 6.2 Two Gaston Cotte forceps are used to elevate the lips of the incision that is enlarged by the Mayo scissors. These are inserted half open and used to push the rectum away from the midline.

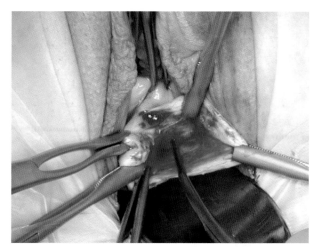

Figure 6.3 Using two Gaston Cotte forceps to retract each flap, the Douglas and the rectum are separated from the deepest aspect of the vagina.

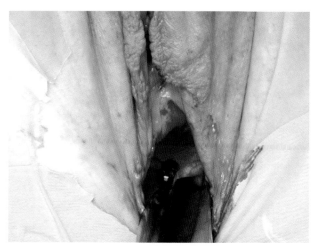

Figure 6.5 Applying the Filshie clip to the isthmus of the tube (the indication for colpotomy in this case was tubal sterilization).

Figure 6.4 Opening the Douglas.

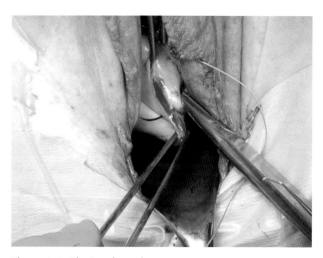

Figure 6.6 Closing the colpotomy.

risk can be eliminated by correct technique, which provides the advantage of wider access, or of an access that can be easily widened.

By pulling upward on a bullet forceps transversely applied to the posterior lip of the cervix and pressing downward on the rectum using the Mangiagalli retractor, the place where the incision is to be made is exposed. The first incision is made on the midline starting from the point where the vaginal skin joins the cervix. It is 3–4 mm deep and 10–15 mm wide (Figure 6.1).

The two lips of the incision are taken close to the inferior angle with two Gaston Cotte grasping forceps. Traction on these forceps stretches the vaginal wall upward and allows one of the blades of a Mayo scissors to be introduced behind the vaginal fascia. This moves the rectovaginal structures away as the other blade divides the full thickness of the vagina

(Figure 6.2). The same action can be repeated as required to obtain an aperture 4–5 cm wide.

Once the vaginal incision has been made, the deep surface of the vaginal flaps is freed while pulling on each of the two lateral flaps with Gaston Cotte forceps and detaching the underlying structures (the cul de sac of Douglas and the intestinal wall, which are usually easy to differentiate) with Mayo scissors (Figure 6.3).

By placing the Mangiagalli retractor in the inferior angle of the enlarged incision while maintaining traction on the cervix, the peritoneal curtain is brought into view and enters the operative field. It is taken with surgical forceps and opened transversely (Figure 6.4). The initial incision is made larger by digital dilation and the Mangiagalli retractor is introduced into the peritoneal cavity (Figure 6.5): adnexal surgery can now be performed (tubal occlusion as it happens in Figure 6.5).

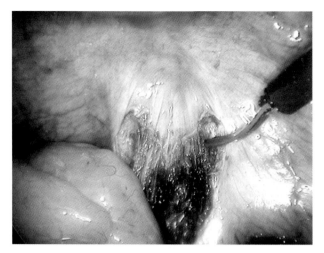

Figure 6.7 Using the monopolar coagulating scissors during laparoscopy to open the base of the Douglas in between the uterosacral ligaments.

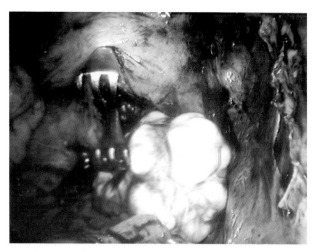

Figure 6.10 Introducing a Museux forceps into the peritoneal cavity to retrieve the specimen. Wrapping the instrument in gauze reduces loss of gas.

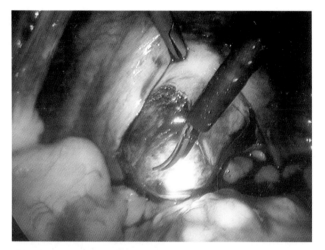

Figure 6.8 Cutting transversely through the vagina onto the illuminated Hegar dilator.

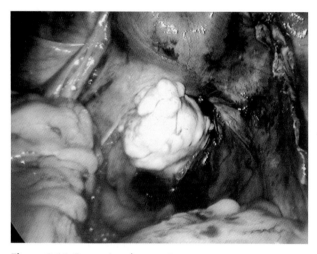

Figure 6.11 Removing the specimen.

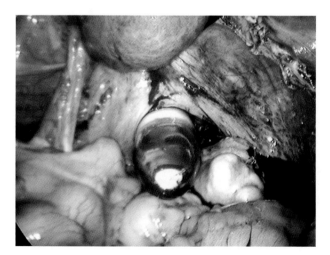

Figure 6.9 The vagina is opened.

Closure of the vertical colpotomy is performed in two layers: one purse-string suture on the peritoneum and a series of interrupted sutures on the vagina (Figure 6.6). If the peritoneum is closed a drain must be put

between it and the vaginal suture. It is best to leave the peritoneum open as this avoids the development of hematomas and obviates the requirement for drainage.

Laparoscopic vaginal colpotomy

The laparoscopic approach has the advantage of clearly demonstrating the bottom of the cul de sac of Douglas where the serosa covering the ventral aspect of the rectum reflects onto the dorsal surface of the uterus. Here the peritoneum is opened transversely while the intestinal wall is held in an appropriate forceps and moved dorsally (Figure 6.7).

As far as the colpotomy itself is concerned, it is best performed over a Hegar dilator no. 30. The end of this instrument is placed in contact with the top of the vagina in the posterior vaginal fornix. Pressure on

(a)

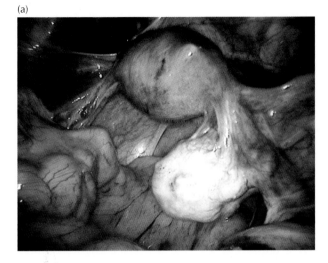

(b)

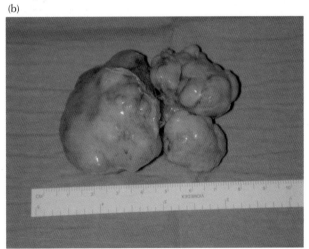

Figure 6.12 (a) The fibroma before removal (the indication for colpotomy in this case was ovarian fibroma). (b) The fibroma after transvaginal removal.

this probe unfolds the vaginal wall and moves the rectum away. The incision is made transversely using the free edge of the monopolar scissors as a cutting blade (Figure 6.8). Increasing the pressure on the dilator results in it entering the peritoneal cavity (Figure 6.9). It is then removed and replaced by a Museux forceps. The pneumoperitoneum collapses. A "gas-proof" pack is put in the vagina around the instrument and the pneumoperitoneum becomes effective once again. The Museux forceps can then be opened (Figure 6.10) ready to grasp the specimen to be removed (Figure 6.11).

Removing bulky tissues (Figure 6.12(a) and (b)) through the colpotomy is surprisingly easy even if there is a considerable discrepancy between the size of the tissue and the size of the colpotomy. Thanks to the elasticity of vaginal tissues, direct extraction is generally possible even in nulliparous patients. One rarely needs to resort to morcellation.

The laparoscopic vaginal colpotomy may be closed either transvaginally or laparoscopically. The approach taken is determined by vaginal access. If this is adequate, closure should be performed transvaginally. If not, the laparoscopic approach is the method of choice. Two or three stitches are usually adequate and closing the peritoneum is not mandatory.

Postoperative course and complications

The postoperative course following colpotomy is generally uneventful. The procedure may be performed as an outpatient procedure if the operation done through the colpotomy is a simple one. The best example is tubal sterilization, which has been done in a type of "production line" in sterilization clinics in developing countries. The procedure can even be carried out under local anesthesia. However the advantages of simplicity, rapidity and low cost of the operation are counterbalanced by a specific infectious risk.

Although postoperative infectious morbidity following pelvic surgery carried out through colpotomy is generally limited to an isolated rise in temperature, authentic infections may occur including tubal, ovarian and tubo-ovarian abscess formation and peritonitis. Leaving the peritoneum open may be a good prophylactic measure as the infection probably starts as a vaginal vault abscess resulting from infection of a vaginal vault hematoma. Giving perioperative antibiotics is an evidence-based mandatory precaution. As well as complications associated with the classical colpotomy it is worth mentioning a complication common to both the ancient technique and to the new one (the laparoscopic vaginal technique), i.e. rectal injury.

Rectal injury is the number one concern during and after posterior colpotomy. If such an injury is detected during the operation it must be repaired immediately by interrupted transverse stitches. In cases where there is no clear evidence of such an injury but there is nonetheless doubt (e.g. difficult bloody dissection), it is safest to perform a waterproof test, which may be done with the laparoscope. Actually the injuries that may occur during posterior colpotomy involve the part of the intestine that is located below the rectovaginal peritoneal fold and could therefore be assessed and managed transvaginally. However, the laparoscope offers a safer approach.

Theoretically, rectovaginal fistulas and peritonitis due to an undetected rectal injury may be observed after posterior colpotomy. This is more than exceptional and all the more so with the laparoscope, which allows better assessment of the contraindications to the operation and an even better opportunity to overcome these contraindications.

Indications and contraindications

Posterior colpotomy is theoretically indicated for all procedures involving the ovaries and tubes. Tubal sterilizations, tubal pregnancies and ovarian cysts including chocolate cysts can be managed via colpotomy and of course, pelvic abscesses may be laid open this way. The only contraindication is obliteration of the cul de sac due to deep rectovaginal endometriosis. However, the subject has evolved further since laparoscopic surgery was originally introduced (see below).

Laparoscopy undoubtedly allows management of adnexal disease under optimal conditions. Better quality assessment of lesions and of their peritoneal environment is possible. The incisions and sutures can be placed with greater accuracy and even obliteration of the cul de sac due to deep rectovaginal endometriosis can now be managed using the laparoscope (see Chapter 11). The postoperative course is generally simple and painless and the recovery is short, i.e. the same as it is after colpotomy but without the infectious risk. The continuing survival of colpotomy is only due to the contraindications to laparoscopic surgery. These contraindications are few but do nonetheless exist. Colpotomy must not be forgotten.

7 Vaginal hysterectomy

Hysterectomy forms the foundation stone of the vaginal surgeon's repertoire. There are multiple indications. It is important to have a standard technique that will stand you in good stead whatever the clinical diagnosis or variation in anatomy. Improvisation is not an option in vaginal surgery. It is vital to perform each step of the surgery in the same way and in the same order.

Technique

Since the first description of Joseph Récamier, multiple variations have been introduced. It is important to pick a technique and to stick with it. The technique that we describe here is the technique Alberto Centaro used in Padua in the 1960s. This technique is a modification (or simplification) of a technique described in 1934 in the text *Operative Gynecology* edited by Peham and Amreich. It includes five stages:

- Detaching the ventral vaginal wall and mobilizing the bladder
- Detaching the dorsal vaginal wall and entering the pouch of Douglas
- Division of the broad ligaments
- Delivery of the uterine fundus and division of the attachments to the uterine cornua
- Re-peritonealization and closure.

Detaching the ventral vaginal wall and mobilizing the bladder

The incision that enables the separation of the ventral vaginal wall from the ventral lip of the cervix must be made in the so-called bladder groove. This landmark is situated just adjacent to the step made by the lower part of the bladder floor, which is pulled downward when traction is exerted on the cervix. It is usually possible to locate this crucial landmark visually. The groove is situated at the point where the vaginal skin with its transverse ridges meets the smooth ectocervical epithelium. It may be necessary to alternately pull and push the cervix to make this border more clearly visible. Another way of locating the groove is to use the handle of the scalpel to palpate the step below the inferior border of the bladder (Figure 7.1).

The ventral incision involves three steps. An assistant positioned to the right of the surgeon (assuming the surgeon is right-handed) depresses the perineum using a posterior vaginal wall retractor (Mangiagalli retractor). The ventral vaginal wall is exposed between two sidewall retractors. A Museux forceps is applied to the ventral lip of the cervix and used to apply downward traction to the uterus. In addition to the downward traction a slight clockwise twisting motion exposes the upper right side of the vagina. It is at this level that the incision is started (Figure 7.2). Only the vaginal skin is incised. Rotating the Museux forceps in an anticlockwise direction exposes the middle part of the anterior vaginal wall. At this point a full thickness incision is made (Figure 7.3).

Figure 7.1 Searching for the sulcus of the urinary bladder with the handle of the scalpel. Strong downward traction is applied to the cervix with Museux forceps. Two retractors are better than one to demonstrate the ventral wall of the vagina.

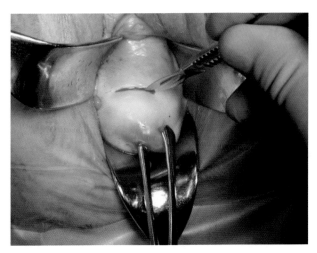

Figure 7.2 Initiating the ventral transverse colpotomy after clockwise rotation has been effected by the Museux forceps. Note that the incision is skin-deep only.

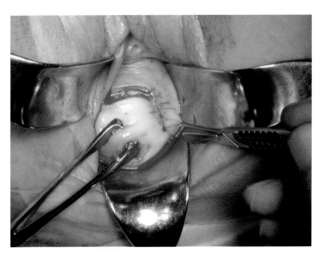

Figure 7.4 Completing the incision on the left side. Note that it is now superficial again.

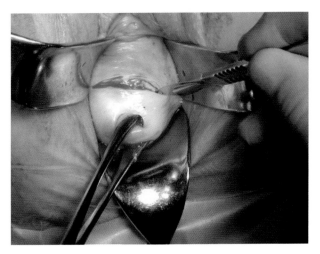

Figure 7.3 With an anticlockwise rotation the incision is deepened and extended.

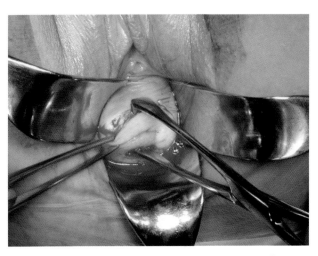

Figure 7.5 Grasping the lower lip of the incision with the Museux forceps.

The third and last part of the incision continues toward the left side of the vagina and is again superficial including only the skin (Figure 7.4).

The next step is to divide the supravaginal septum. This septum is a sort of surgical artifact created by downward traction on the uterus and upward traction on the vaginal flap. It is a pseudo-aponeurotic structure formed by the condensation of the connective tissue joining the deepest surface of the vaginal wall to the corresponding part of the bladder floor. It prevents access to the vesico-uterine space. To divide it, the Museux forceps that is holding the ventral lip of the cervix is repositioned to include the inferior leaf of the incised vaginal wall (Figure 7.5). The downward traction exerted on the instrument is exaggerated (the Mangiagalli retractor can be removed to aid this maneuver). The superior leaf of incised vaginal wall is grasped with a toothed dissecting forceps to apply countertraction. It is important to apply the dissecting forceps exactly on the midline.

For this reason, two lateral wall retractors are used instead of just one: this demonstrates the anterior vaginal wall so that the external urethral meatus that marks the midline is not obscured. The forces of traction and countertraction make the fibers of the supravaginal septum tighten and appear to fan out from the midline forceps to the ventral surface of the cervix. The supravaginal septum is divided using Mayo scissors. The scissors are held with their concavity toward the surgeon and the convexity toward the bladder, perpendicular to the cervix and therefore tangentially to the bladder (Figure 7.6). The septum is white and fibrous unlike the bladder muscle that is grayish in color and plexiform. A few cuts are sufficient to gain access to the utero-vesical space (Figure 7.7(a) and (b)) If you listen (very) carefully this movement makes a sound like the skin of a drum bursting. When you see a fine pale gray tissue you know that you are in the correct plane (Figure 7.8). If the first attempt fails, reposition the dissecting forceps to pick up the vaginal wall more firmly and

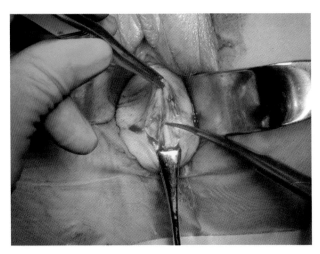

Figure 7.6 Demonstrating the so-called supravaginal septum before incising it on the midline at the appropriate point between the urinary bladder and the cervix.

(a)

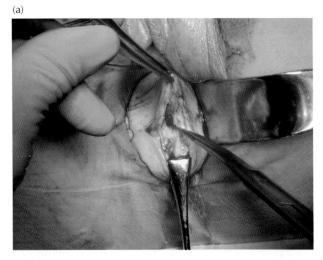

(b)

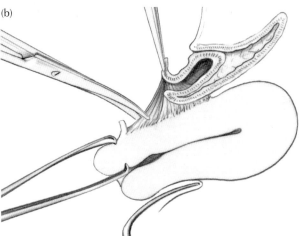

Figure 7.7 (a) and (b) Opening the supravaginal septum. The scissors are held perpendicular to the uterus.

try again to find the loose tissue of the utero-vesical space. Once this space has been identified use the Mayo scissors to widen it, which may now be used parallel to the axis of the uterus (Figure 7.9). Then

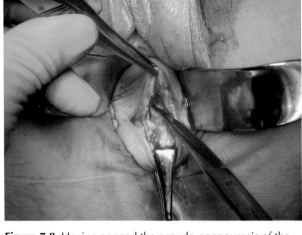

Figure 7.8 Having opened the pseudo-aponeurosis of the supravaginal septum, the scissors enter the loose areolar tissue between the floor of the urinary bladder and the ventral aspect of the cervix. The scissors may be held parallel to the uterus.

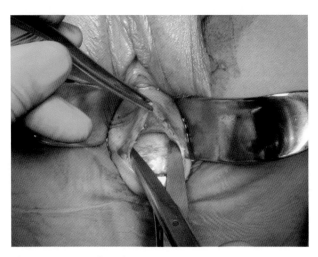

Figure 7.9 Extending the opening.

insert one of the lateral wall retractors into the utero-vesical space (Figure 7.10). Under the protection of this retractor the last fibers of the supravaginal septum can be cut (Figure 7.11(a) and (b)). If this step has been successful, palpation will show that the bladder is completely separated from the uterus. Remove the retractor. Introduce the finger (Figure 7.12). If there is any resistance, insert the retractor again and cut any remaining fibers under direct vision. Palpate again and so on until you feel that the space is completely freed up. This will only occur when your finger is situated between the anterior fold of the utero-vesical peritoneal cul de sac and the muscle of the bladder wall. The anterior leaf of the utero-vesical peritoneal fold is now visible when you reinsert the retractor (Figure 7.13(a) and (b)). We avoid opening the peritoneum at this stage.

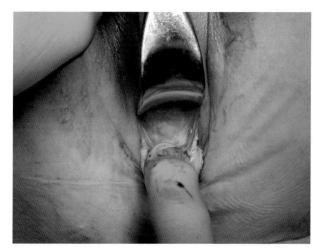

Figure 7.10 Introducing one of the Breisky retractors to elevate the bladder floor on the midline.

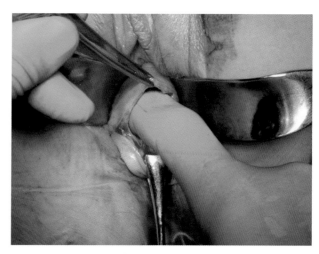

Figure 7.12 Checking the axis of dissection and proceeding with digital pressure.

(a)

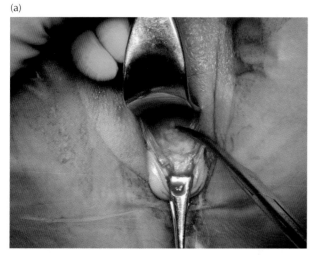

(b)

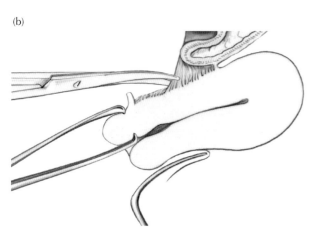

Figure 7.11 (a) and (b) Cutting the remaining fibers while protecting the urinary bladder with the retractor.

(a)

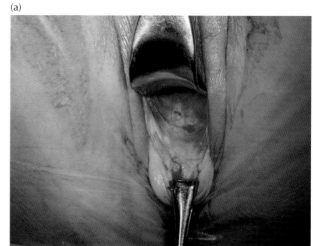

(b)

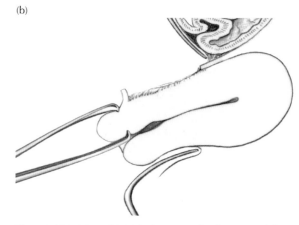

Figure 7.13 (a) and (b) Having completely opened the space the vesicouterine peritoneal plica is now visible: don't open it at this stage.

Detaching the dorsal vaginal wall and entering the pouch of Douglas

The incision separating the dorsal vaginal wall from the dorsal lip of the cervix must be made just beneath the point where the lowest part of the pouch of Douglas is attached to the deep surface of the posterior vaginal fornix. At this point, there is usually a dimple or at the very least a flattening that is visible by pressing on the perineum and pulling on the forceps attached to the dorsal lip of the cervix. If this anatomical landmark is not immediately obvious you can make it appear by alternately pulling and relaxing the traction on the dorsal lip of the cervix.

The incision is made with a scalpel and has three constituent parts. The left lateral vaginal wall is exposed and a clockwise incision is made extending the previously made anterior incision (Figure 7.14).

This incision is superficial. After adjusting the position of the lateral wall retractor, make a similar incision on the right side of the posterior fornix (Figure 7.15). The third step completes the opening of the posterior vaginal wall by joining together the two previous incisions (Figure 7.16). This part of the incision is deeper and should cut through all the layers of the posterior vaginal wall.

After making the incision grasp the superior leaf of the dorsal vaginal wall with the Museux forceps (Figure 7.17). Pull this forceps in the direction of the pubic arch. At the same time press firmly down on the perineum. The inferior leaf of the incised vaginal wall is grasped on the midline with toothed dissecting forceps and the "posterior supravaginal septum" becomes obvious. If access is limited, removing both the lateral wall retractors and Museux forceps attached to the anterior lip of the cervix can make exposure of the

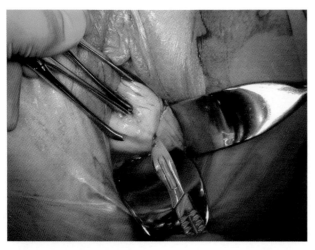

Figure 7.14 Initiating the dorsal transverse colpotomy after strong upward traction has been applied to the cervix with two Museux forceps. On the lateral sides the incision is only skin-deep.

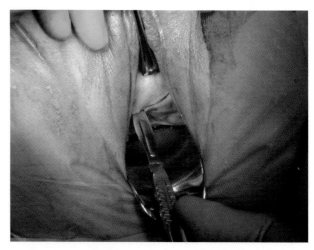

Figure 7.16 Joining the lateral incisions. Note that this part of the incision is deeper.

Figure 7.15 The skin-deep incision on the right side.

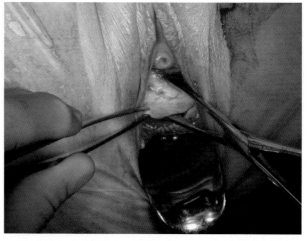

Figure 7.17 Grasping the upper lip of the incision with the Museux forceps.

"posterior supravaginal septum" easier (by facilitating the movements of traction and countertraction). The septum is opened using Mayo scissors held with the concavity toward the front and the convexity toward the back (Figure 7.18). The first cut of the scissors should generally get through both the septum, which is thin but tough, and the posterior leaf of the peritoneal pouch of Douglas. The small hole in the peritoneum of the pouch of Douglas is widened with a finger and the closed scissors. If the hole is not sufficiently wide to allow the placement of the retractor the medial fibers of the uterosacral ligaments can be divided (Figure 7.19) and then the Mangiagalli retractor is inserted into the hole (Figure 7.20).

Dividing the broad ligament

Having freed the ventral and dorsal aspects of the uterus, it is now time to tackle the structures that join

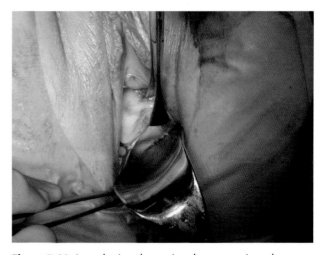

Figure 7.20 Introducing the perineal retractor into the peritoneal cavity.

Figure 7.18 Opening the pouch of Douglas. Note that the Museux forceps that was on the ventral lip of the cervix has been removed in order to optimize upward traction, which demonstrates the dorsal wall of the vagina.

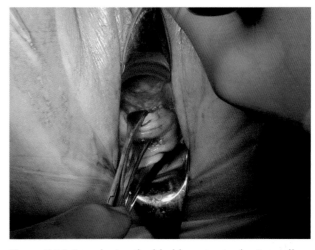

Figure 7.21 Introducing the bladder retractor horizontally.

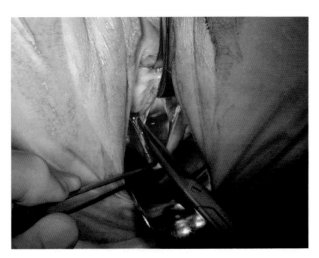

Figure 7.19 Extending the opening.

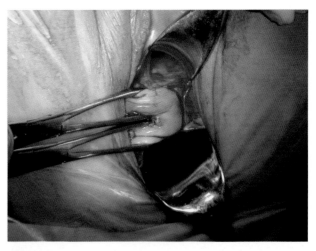

Figure 7.22 Rotating the bladder retractor clockwise: the bladder floor and left ureter are thus elevated.

(a)

(b)

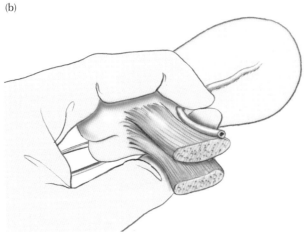

Figure 7.23 (a) and (b) Palpating the broad ligament on the left side and assessing the three parts thereof: pars flaccida, arch of the uterine artery and paracervical ligaments.

the lateral surfaces to the pelvic sidewall. These structures are the broad ligaments. The division of the superior portion is easy and risk free. The lower part is more complex and can be the source of various difficulties and complications. The management of these problems is the point that differentiates the various techniques that have been described in the history. In the technique that we recommend, the lower parts of the broad ligament are sutured before being divided. Before proceeding, the constituent parts of the lower broad ligament are located by palpation after appropriately protecting the bladder in front and the rectum behind.

To protect the bladder the surgeon inserts a retractor (Breisky) into the vesicouterine space. He initially slides the retractor in from front to back in the midline up to the hilt (Figure 7.21) and then lightly presses on the retractor to rotate it clockwise, lifting it to the left. Once positioned (Figure 7.22) the instrument is transferred to the hand of the assistant

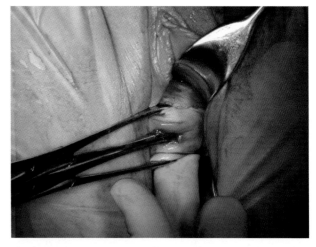

Figure 7.24 Demonstrating the ventral aspect of the broad ligament while pushing its dorsal aspect forward with the forefinger introduced in the Douglas pouch and elevating with the retractor the floor of the urinary bladder.

standing on the right of the surgeon. The same assistant pulls down on the posterior wall retractor to protect the rectum, just as the anterior retractor protects the bladder base and distal ureter.

The assistant to the left of the surgeon pulls on the forceps attached to the cervix, the direction of traction being obliquely toward the right in the horizontal plane. The surgeon is now able to palpate the broad ligament. Ideally this should be between two fingers (Figure 7.23). When space is limited, the broad ligament can be palpated against the anterior retractor (Figure 7.24). The aim is to identify the uterine artery, the "paraisthmic window" and the para cervical ligaments. Pressing ventrally wih the forefinger one opens this normally virtual space (Figure 7.24).

Needling of the paracervical ligaments
The paracervical or suspensory ligaments are identified, ligated and cut twice prior to tackling the uterine artery.

The initial pass of the needle picks up the ligament fibers only. The so-called vaginal Deschamps needle is loaded (with a synthetic slowly absorbable suture – Vicryl® 0) and passed from front to back. The assistant on the left pulls downward and laterally. The surgeon locates the paraisthmic window with the index finger of his left hand and directs the tip of the needle to this point (Figure 7.25(a) and (b)). He then pushes the needle through, while the assistant on the left side changes the direction of traction from downward to upward (Figure 7.26). Once the needle has been pushed through, the surgeon removes his finger and the tip of the needle is visible in the operating

(a)

(b)

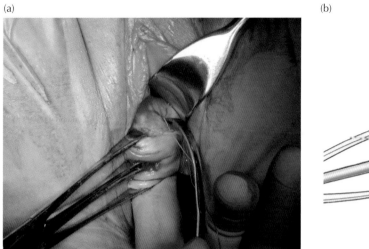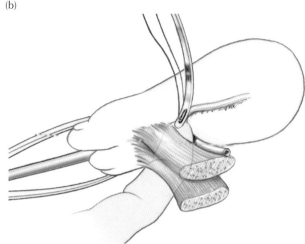

Figure 7.25 (a) and (b) Placing the tip of the vaginal Deschamps needle in contact with the entrance to the paraisthmic window whose exit is guarded by the index finger.

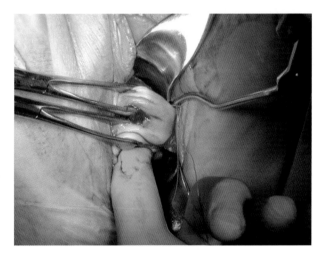

Figure 7.26 The surgeon pushes the needle through the broad ligament as the assistant changes the lateral traction from a downward to an upward direction.

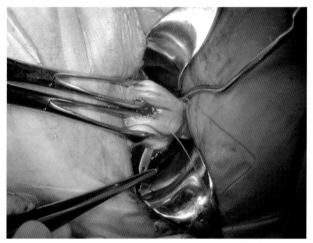

Figure 7.27 The tip of the needle appears in the pouch of Douglas and the thread is grasped before the needle is removed.

field. The tie is grasped (Figure 7.27) and the needle can be removed.

This pass of the needle includes the whole of the "suspensory ligaments": the lower part of the bladder pillar, parametrium and uterosacral ligament (the finger that guides the Deschamps needle ensures that the needle tip enters medial to the uterosacral peritoneal fold). It seems like a lot of tissue, but the techniques that advocate taking the uterosacral ligament, the parametrium and the bladder pillars separately are not ideal. This is because the fibers of the three elements are intimately connected at their insertion onto the uterus and separating them from each other is rather artificial.

Ligating and dividing the paracervical ligaments

The assistant on the left side changes the lateral traction to the horizontal plane and the surgeon is then able to ligate the first pedicle (Figure 7.28). He

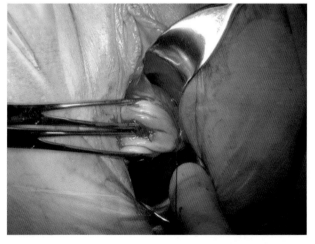

Figure 7.28 Tying the first suture using an auto-locking technique: this suture includes all the paracervical ligaments, i.e. the lower part of the urinary bladder pillar, the parametrium and the lower part of the rectal pillar (rectouterine ligament).

forms a self-locking knot by making a double throw and tightening the ligature with the two threads held 90° apart. The assistant releases the traction as the ligature is tightened. Once the knot is tight the threads are held 180° apart. The knot is secured with two further throws.

One can see from Figure 7.29 that the knot is applied immediately adjacent to the limits of the two initial colpotomies. You will recall that these colpotomies are, in their lateral parts, very superficial. This maintains the connection between the vaginal fornix and the paracervical ligaments and avoids disruption of the natural vaginal vault support. The knot applied to the pedicles of the ligaments secures the permanence of the connection.

The paracervical ligaments are divided 10 mm beyond the ligature with a scalpel (Figure 7.30).

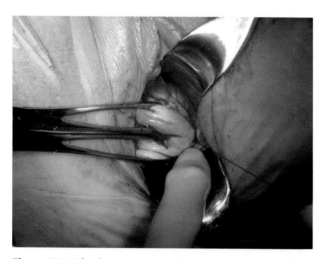

Figure 7.29 The first suture is tied.

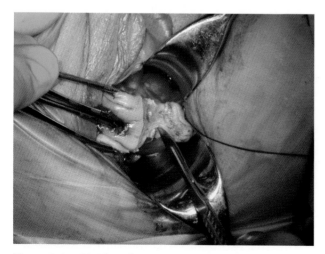

Figure 7.30 Dividing the paracervical ligaments, which must be cut perpendicular to the uterus without oblique divergence. The upper ventral fibers must be kept intact.

A small portion of vaginal skin sits on the stump of the pedicle. This reduces the risk of the ligature slipping and improves the cohesion between the stump of the ligament and the vaginal vault.

A single incision may be enough to cut all the fibers inserted laterally into the cervix. Often more than one cut is necessary. To assess the effect of each cut on the mobility of the uterus the surgeon can hold the Museux forceps and create traction himself while cutting the fibers of the ligaments. This division should be perpendicular to the axis of the uterus. The higher fibers must be spared because if they are completely transected the uterine artery will disappear moving upward and out of reach. There is also a risk of the deeper fibers slipping out of the ligature with the further risk, if this happens, of the whole pedicle slipping.

Initial ligation of the uterine artery

The second needling of the base of the broad ligament incorporates the afferent branch of the arch of the uterine artery and the paracervical ligaments. The technique used is similar to the initial needling. The surgeon uses the index finger of the left hand to open the arch of the uterine artery. The needle tip is pushed through right in the middle of this arch (Figure 7.31) between the afferent and efferent branches. The tie is held and the needle withdrawn. The knot is pressed against the ligament pedicle.

Before tying the knot two Kocher forceps are applied to the stump of the first pedicle and used to apply medial traction in the horizontal plane. These forceps hold apart the two points on the base of the small triangle of vaginal skin that has been left on purpose to maintain cohesion between the vaginal fornix and the suspensory ligaments. The knot is then placed just above the first knot using the same self-locking technique (Figure 7.32). The thread of the first ligature is cut. The second is held. The second ligature holds the afferent branch of the arch of the uterine artery against the stump of the first pedicle. With this protection it is now possible to electively prepare the uterine artery.

Dissection of the uterine artery

In order to access the arch of the uterine artery one divides the highest fibers of the paracervical ligaments. This is done with the tips of the scissors (Figure 7.33). These fibers hide the arch of the uterine artery, which is therefore prone to injury.

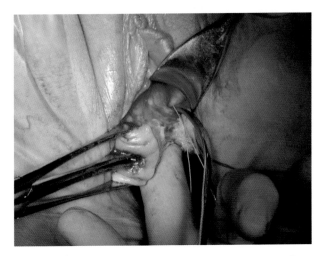

Figure 7.31 Applying the curve of the Deschamps needle around the afferent branch of the arch of the uterine artery while assessing its contour with the index finger. Note the intact upper fibers of the paracervical ligament that prevent the uterine artery escaping from the operative field.

(a)

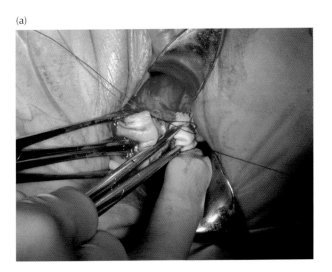

(b)

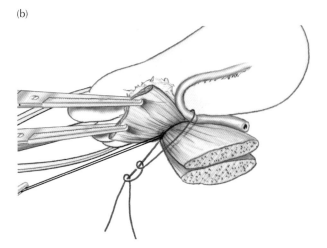

Figure 7.32 Tying the suture around the paracervical stump, which constitutes the first ligature on the uterine artery.

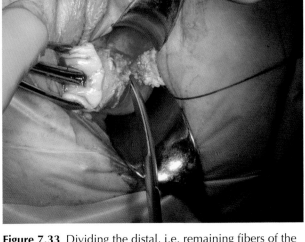

Figure 7.33 Dividing the distal, i.e. remaining fibers of the paracervical ligaments.

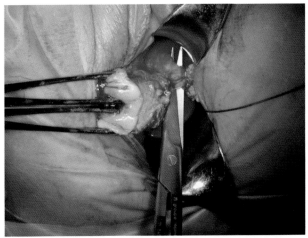

Figure 7.34 Dissecting the afferent branch of the arch of the uterine artery.

This injury should not be a problem because the artery has already been ligated once.

Once the highest fibers have been divided one can see on the lateral aspect of the uterus a triangle that corresponds to the insertion of the ligaments. The apex is located just below the paraisthmic window. The arch of the uterine artery is found just above this apex, generally in a ventral position. Once the arch has been identified the afferent branch of the artery is freed up to about 5–10 mm (Figure 7.34). Two clamps are placed on the freed vessel and the artery is then divided between the two clamps (Figures 7.35 and 7.36(a)).

The lateral arterial stump is the most important one to control. To facilitate access to this stump we recommend pushing the uterus deeply inside. This

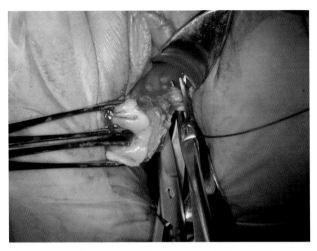

Figure 7.35 Clamping the afferent branch of the arch of the uterine artery.

Figure 7.37 Ligating the parietal stump of the uterine artery.

(a)

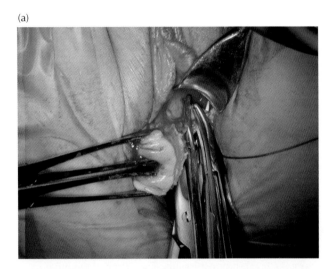

(b)

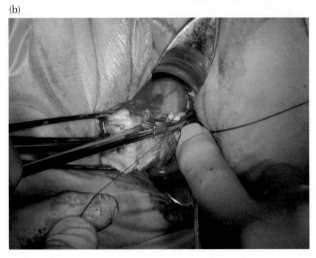

Figure 7.36 (a) Dividing the uterine artery between two clamps and then (b) ligating the visceral stump.

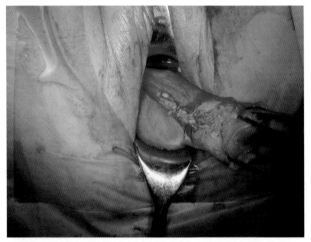

Figure 7.38 Having repeated these steps on the other side, the visceral stump of the uterine artery and the site of insertion of the paracervical ligaments are visible.
Note that this insertion is triangular with the uterine artery at its apex.

stump is not mandatory because this is part of the specimen-to-come. Nevertheless we recommend securing it with a ligature (Figure 7.36(b)) to avoid "back bleeding" in the time remaining before the specimen is removed. Following this last ligation the ties are cut together with the ties from the pedicle of the suspensory ligament that until now have been conserved.

The same is done on the other side. Figure 7.38 clearly shows the triangular insertion of the paracervical ligaments on the surface of the uterus. The medial stump of the uterine artery is above its apex. Above this point there is nothing between the uterus and the pelvic sidewall apart from the "pars flaccida" of the broad ligament. This is the great advantage of the needling technique as compared with the clamping technique. In the needling

action reveals the stump of the paracervical pedicle and the artery requiring ligation is situated on the medial surface of this stump (Figure 7.37). Ligation is with 2×0 Vicryl®. Ligation of the medial arterial

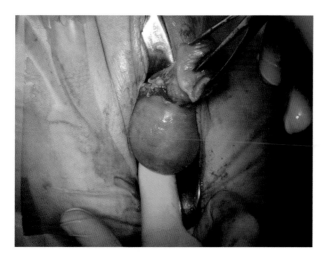

Figure 7.39 Delivering the fundus of the uterus – not always this easy! See pp. 67 and 75.

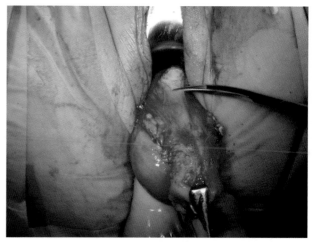

Figure 7.40 Opening the vesicouterine cul de sac.

technique one knows that after the division of the afferent segment of the arch, one is situated in a space lateral to the efferent segment. In the clamping technique the clamp used to control the arch very often clamps both the afferent and the efferent segments making it necessary to control all the horizontal medial collaterals of the efferent segment to reach the uterine cornu.

Delivery of the uterine fundus

Having completely divided the broad ligaments to the point where the adnexae insert onto the uterine fundus, the uterus now moves directly downward when simple traction is exerted on the Museux forceps in an umbilical–coccygeal axis (as long as it is not enlarged and/or deformed by fibroids). The fundus is then delivered posteriorly as the traction exerted on the Museux forceps is moved upward (Figure 7.39).

Once the fundus has been delivered the forefinger of the left hand is introduced along the dorsal surface of the corpus and then behind the fundus. It reaches around as far as the lower limit of the utero-vesical peritoneal fold. You will recall that this cul de sac has not been opened during the very first step of the surgery. This will now be done. Traction on the Museux forceps is switched from upward to downward. The fingertip in the anterior cul de sac is now visible. One cut is made just below the visible finger (Figure 7.40). The initial small opening is then widened laterally toward the insertion of the round ligaments (Figure 7.41). The incisions made after opening the peritoneal cul de sac completely free the insertion of the adnexae onto the uterine cornua. If conservation of the adnexae has been scheduled their pedicles are now clamped and divided. In the majority

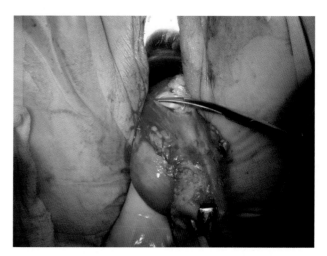

Figure 7.41 Extending the opening in the vesicouterine cul de sac.

of cases the uterine cornu is sufficiently prepared so that the three elements (round ligament, fallopian tube and utero-ovarian ligament) can be taken in the same clamp (Figure 7.42). The pedicle is divided at a sufficient distance from the clamp (Figure 7.43), and one proceeds with the same on the opposite side (Figure 7.44).

When planning to remove the adnexae at the same time as the uterus it is possible with easy cases to perform this in continuity. We suggest a two-step technique where the adnexae are not removed until after the uterus. The technique will be described later on. Whether or not the adnexae have been removed a gauze roll should be placed in the peritoneal cavity before proceeding with the next steps of the operation: this takes the place of the uterus and avoids descent of the intestinal loops. The gauze is positioned by pushing it from front to back (Figure 7.45) and from below to above (Figure 7.46). The exterior

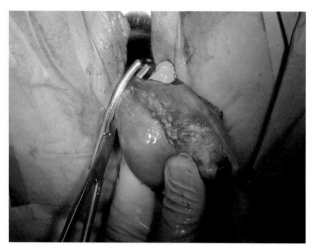

Figure 7.42 Disconnecting the uterine cornu on the right side: clamping.

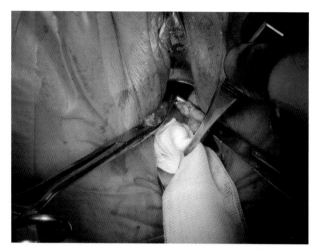

Figure 7.45 Placing a gauze roll in the peritoneal cavity: the first step is to push the gauze roll into the hollow of the sacrum.

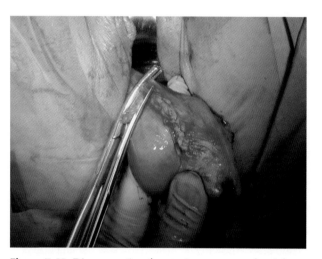

Figure 7.43 Disconnecting the uterine cornu on the right side: dividing.

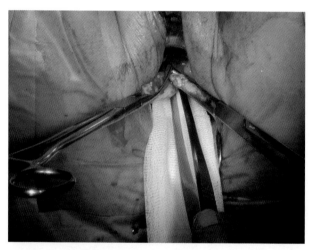

Figure 7.46 Placing a gauze roll in the peritoneal cavity: the second step is to push the gauze roll cranially to displace the ileal loops upward.

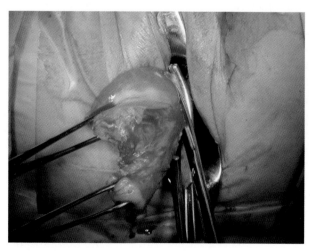

Figure 7.44 Disconnecting the uterine cornu on the left side: dividing.

portion of the gauze roll is placed on the patient's abdomen. A Breisky retractor is used to hold the gauze in place.

If the adnexae are to be conserved, hemostasis of the adnexal stumps is achieved by suturing. The round ligament is stitched a few millimeters above the clamp (Figure 7.47). A knot is tied in front of the clamp (Figure 7.48) and then a knot behind. This latter is tightened at the same time as the clamp is released. Then the clamp is closed again (Figure 7.49). A second suture is placed directly next to the clamp, using the same technique. At the moment the second knot is tightened the surgeon allows the tissues to escape a little to widen the distance between the two stitches (Figure 7.50). The first stitch may now be cut and the second is held with a small Kocher forceps.

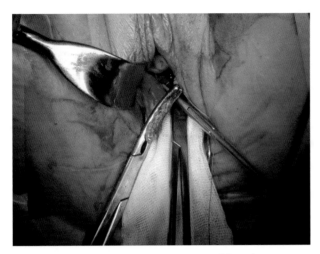

Figure 7.47 Stitching the uterine stump of the adnexa at a distance from the clamp.

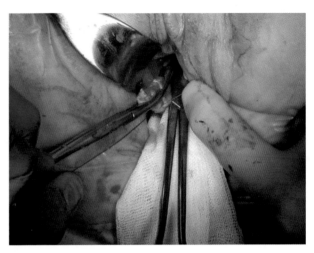

Figure 7.49 Completing the figure of 8 suture.

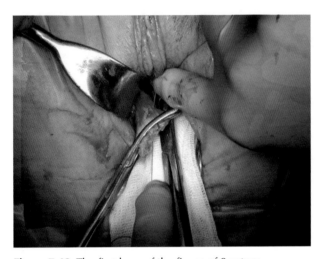

Figure 7.48 The first loop of the figure of 8 suture.

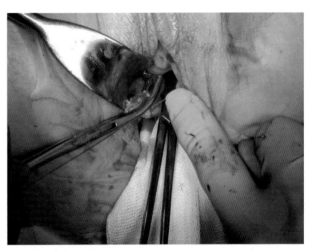

Figure 7.50 Stitching the uterine stump of the adnexa a second time – this time on the clamp. Note that the clamp is opened as the stitch is tied to ensure that there is a space between the two sutures.

Re-peritonealization and closure

In the technique that we recommend the vagina is left partially open. The peritoneum must therefore be closed. This position is open to debate and is indeed debated. The method we use dates from the time when prevention of infectious complications was the primary concern when performing vaginal hysterectomy: the best way to prevent infection is to avoid closing the vagina completely.

Gathering stitch of the dorsal vaginal flap
The first step in re-peritonealization and closure involves gathering the dorsal vaginal flap: a continuous suture using large stitches that secure hemostasis of the dorsal vaginal flap is performed, while at the same time approximating the pedicle stumps of the suspensory ligaments.

One starts by exteriorizing the stump of the suspensory ligaments on the left side. In order to do that the longest and widest Briesky retractor is placed into the pelvic cavity and pressed obliquely on the intraperitoneal gauze revealing the first stump. This stump is held with toothed dissecting forceps. The first stitch is inserted into the dorsal vaginal flap just medial to the stump (Figure 7.51). The next action is to take the stitch through the rectal peritoneum just in front of this first vaginal stitch (Figure 7.52). Then this continuous suture moves clockwise taking in succession the rectal peritoneum and then the vaginal wall; the bites are 7–8 mm apart (Figure 7.53). The last stitch is made at the point of contact with the insertion of the pedicle of the suspensory ligament on the right side (Figure 7.54). This pedicle has been exposed by rotating the anterior wall retractor clockwise. The continuous stitch is tied at this point. The thread used is Vicryl®

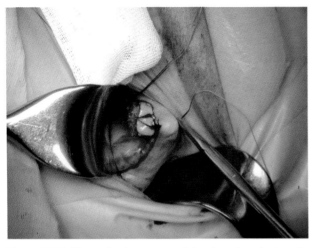

Figure 7.51 The gathering suture of the dorsal vaginal wall: the very first stitch is inserted close to the stump of the paracervical ligament on the left side.

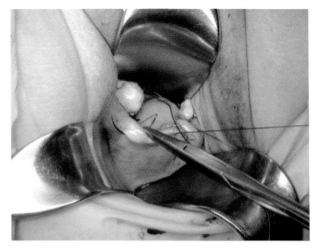

Figure 7.53 The penultimate stitch approximating the rectal peritoneum to the dorsal vaginal wall.

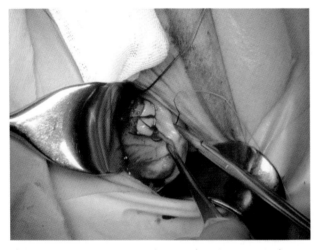

Figure 7.52 Approximating the rectal peritoneum to the dorsal vaginal wall.

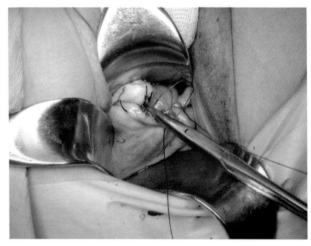

Figure 7.54 The last stitch approximating the rectal peritoneum to the dorsal vaginal wall. Note that it is adjacent to the paracervical ligament on the right side.

2-0 mounted on a semicircular 26-mm Black Laser® round-bodied needle. The threads at the beginning and at the end of the stitch are held with small Kocher forceps.

Re-peritonealization

The re-peritonealization comprises two angle stitches and one single continuous suture. Each of the angle stitches is made up of two steps: dorsal and ventral. Right-handed surgeons are better starting with the right-angle stitch. In the dorsal step a stitch is used to suture in turn the peritoneum covering the anterolateral surface of the rectum (Figure 7.55) and the uterosacral peritoneal fold (Figure 7.56). Firm handling of the anterior retractor pushes back the intestinal loops. A toothed dissecting forceps exteriorizes the stump of the pedicle of the suspensory

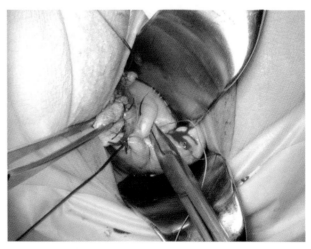

Figure 7.55 The dorsal part of the first angle stitch of the peritonealization: taking the peritoneum.

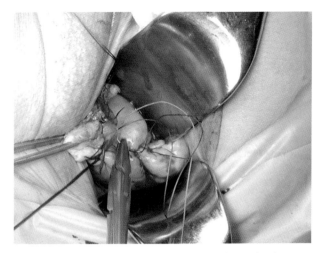

Figure 7.56 The dorsal part of the first angle stitch of re-peritonealization: taking the rectouterine fold.

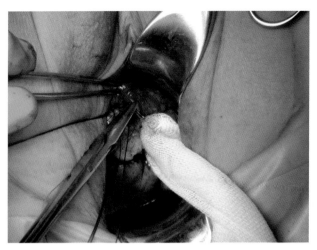

Figure 7.58 The ventral part of the first angle stitch of re-peritonealization: taking the bladder peritoneum.

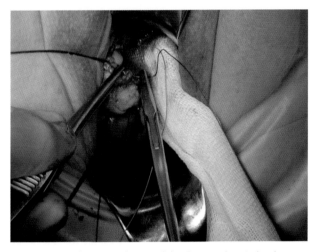

Figure 7.57 The ventral part of the first angle stitch of re-peritonealization: taking the adnexal stump between the two securing sutures (see Figure 7.50).

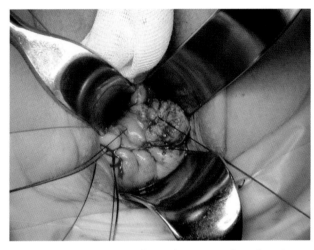

Figure 7.59 The same angle stitch is inserted on the other side. Note that all the stumps will be extraperitonealized.

ligament. The two stitches are placed either in two movements or in a single movement. The ventral step requires exteriorization of the adnexal stump by pulling on the held thread. The long and wide retractor is removed, the exterior part of the gauze roll is moved from superiorly to inferiorly and a short narrow retractor is used to reflect the bladder without entering the peritoneal cavity. The adnexal pedicle is sutured between the two stitches that were previously inserted (Figure 7.57). The bladder peritoneum is revealed by progressively lifting out the bladder retractor and is thus sutured in turn. The suturing is done first from inside to outside and then from outside to inside (Figure 7.58). The contralateral angle stitch is performed in the same way but in reverse order: bladder peritoneum, adnexal stump, uterosacral peritoneal fold and rectal peritoneum (Figure 7.59). This second angle stitch is closed first, tightening the knot to exteriorize all ligamentous and

vascular stumps. Then the other angle stitch is tied before the last step of the re-peritonealization. This step approximates the bladder peritoneum to the anterior rectal peritoneum (Figure 7.60). The assistant who is standing to the right of the surgeon pulls on the thread of the ipsilateral angle stitch and pushes on the Mangiagalli retractor. The assistant standing on the left side of the surgeon pulls on the right-angle stitch and reflects the bladder with the anterior retractor. One to three stitches are generally enough to reach the end of the continuous suture. At the end of the re-peritonealization suture all the stumps are extraperitoneal: paracervical ligaments, uterine arteries and adnexal stumps (Figure 7.61).

Gathering stitch of the ventral vaginal flap

The gathering of the ventral vaginal flap follows on from and completes the gathering of the dorsal

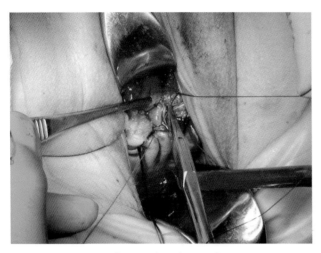

Figure 7.60 Joining the rectal and vesical peritoneum in between the two angle stitches.

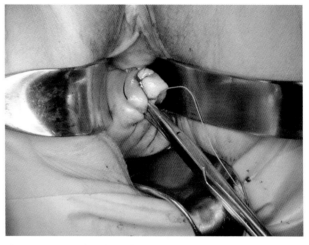

Figure 7.62 Undertaking the ventral-gathering suture: the very first stitch starts where the gathering dorsal stitch finished.

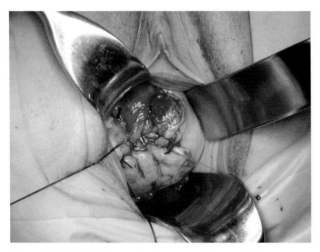

Figure 7.61 Final view after the re-peritonealization suture. Note that the vaginal-gathering suture has approximated the stumps of the paracervical ligaments towards the midline and that the stumps are extraperitoneal.

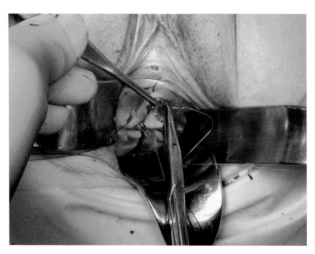

Figure 7.63 Continuing the ventral-gathering suture: the midline stitch.

vaginal flap. It is done in a clockwise direction. It starts just outside the point where the first stitch finished. The vaginal wall is stitched from inside to outside (Figure 7.62). The short end of this stitch is tied to the short end of the final stitch of the dorsal vaginal flap running suture. These threads can now be cut.

The next stitches are inserted at intervals of 5–7 mm. One needs to take the full thickness of the ventral vaginal wall, but it is also necessary to avoid damaging the bladder. In order to avoid the bladder one reflects the vaginal wall before stitching under the protection of the lateral retractor, which needs to be repositioned before each bite of the stitch (Figure 7.63). The last stitch (Figure 7.64) is made in front of the insertion of the stump of the suspensory ligament pedicle on the left side. To do this the assistant

on the right of the surgeon puts strong pressure on the perineum with his left hand and pulls on the thread obliquely using his right hand. The other assistant reflects the anterior vaginal wall with a retractor held in his left hand and pulls on the thread that was the first stitch of the dorsal-gathering suture. The ventral-gathering suture thread is then knotted with the held thread from the dorsal vaginal wall suture (Figure 7.65).

Before this ultimate knot is tied bleeding can persist. Once the knot is secured there should be no bleeding at all. If there is persistent bleeding one has to resist the temptation to insert a vaginal pack. It is necessary to take down the continuous sutures, to chase the bleeders and to secure hemostasis with transfixion sutures. This point leads us from the section devoted to the description of the

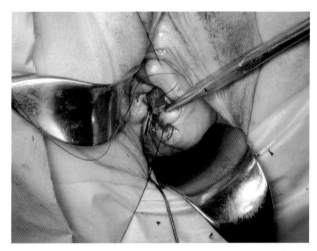

Figure 7.64 Finishing the ventral-gathering suture: the last stitch – note that it is in contact with the very first stitch of the dorsal-gathering suture.

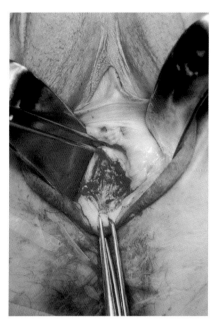

Figure 7.66 Intrafascial false passage made during the opening of the vesicouterine space.

Figure 7.65 The effect of the gathering suture is evident. It only leaves a small orifice in the apex of the vagina, which allows drainage.

technique to the section devoted to intraoperative difficulties.

Intraoperative difficulties – how to manage them and how to avoid them

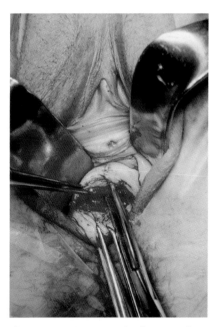

Figure 7.67 Grasping the fascia with strong Kocher forceps.

Mobilizing the bladder

The major risk in mobilizing the inferior pole of the bladder is injury to the bladder. These injuries are due to poor identification of the plane of cleavage between the uterus and the bladder (Figure 7.66). Such false passages are considered by many to be the correct route. Our opinion (even if there is no evidence to support this viewpoint) is that the risk to the bladder is higher if one uses the intra-fascial route rather than the extra-fascial one. For this reason we propose that, in the event that the very first step of the operation erroneously follows an intra-fascial plane, the error is corrected as follows.

In order to relocate the extra-fascial plane (i.e. the correct anatomically preformed separating space) grasp the already cut fascia in two Kocher forceps (Figure 7.67) and pull on them firmly in a downward direction. Then reapply the dissecting forceps to the superior leaf of the anterior vaginal wall. Traction and countertraction will re-expose the supravaginal septum that should be managed as previously described (Figure 7.68(a) and (b)). At the end of this "second chance" dissection the situation is like the one obtained when performing the ideal procedure (Figure 7.69).

(a)

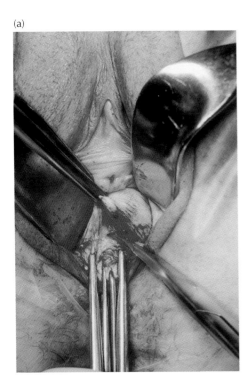

(b)

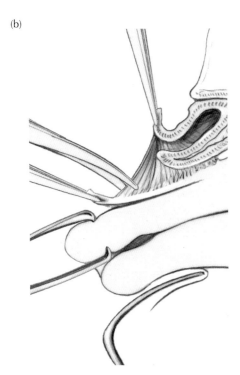

Figure 7.68 (a) and (b) Opening the supravaginal septum in front of the fascia.

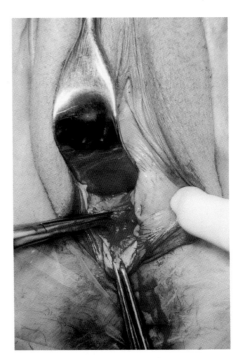

Figure 7.69 Demonstrating the vesicouterine peritoneal plica.

Despite the fact that we prefer the extra-fascial technique it still does not completely avoid bladder injury. In every single technique mobilization of the bladder remains the most difficult step of the operation. In order to facilitate this step Frank Novak proposed starting with a circular incision, then opening the pouch of Douglas and dividing the uterosacral ligaments. This facilitates greater descent of the uterus

and mobilization of the bladder becomes easier. Although this tactic deserves mention, it is not our preferred technique.

Detaching the dorsal vaginal wall

The risk encountered while detaching the posterior vaginal wall and opening the pouch of Douglas is rectal injury. This risk is statistically minimal, because the anatomical relationship between the dorsal surface of the uterus and the ventral surface of the rectum is much less close than that between the ventral surface of the uterus and the bladder. Direct injury to the rectum may be caused by a false passage formed during separation of the posterior vaginal wall from the rectum. This is exceedingly rare. Much more common is the false passage made when passing between the peri-cervical fascia and the posterior surface of the cervix itself. This is similar to the problem described in the previous section. The rules of management are the same. In cases where opening the posterior supravaginal septum does not quickly lead to opening of the pouch of Douglas, and in cases where the dissection one performs (having readjusted traction and countertraction) leads to a diffuse ooze and doesn't succeed, it is generally because one is in the intra-fascial plane. We believe that this is not the correct plane. In order to rectify the error one proceeds in the same manner as recommended anteriorly. Two Kocher forceps are positioned on the fascia at 6 o'clock. Strong upward traction is exerted on them. The dissection is resumed in a more superficial plane, i.e. closer to the rectum. This dissection opens the extra-fascial

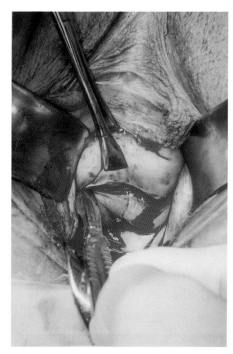

Figure 7.70 Difficulty experienced on attempting to open the dorsal fornix.

Figure 7.71 The difficulty was due to rectovaginal endometriosis (left uterosacral ligament).

plane. One soon reaches the peritoneal cul de sac, which can then be opened.

Difficulties encountered while detaching the dorsal vaginal wall and opening the cul de sac of Douglas can be due to unexpected rectovaginal endometriosis. These difficulties may cause one to give up and to use complementary laparoscopy, an alternative to laparoscopic preparation. In fact, laparoscopic preparation is undoubtedly better and must be the preferred approach in all cases where the history and clinical assessment demonstrate a high probability of rectovaginal endometriosis (see Chapter 11). However problems encountered due to unexpected rectovaginal endometriosis are not always insurmountable: Figures 7.70 and 7.71.

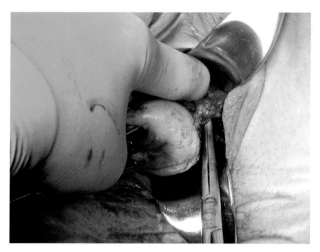

Figure 7.72 Dissecting the arch of the uterine artery in cases with no descent: use an O'Shaughnessy clamp from back to front under the guidance of a forefinger placed ventrally.

Division of the broad ligaments

The assessment of the lower broad ligament is not always easy. Exact localization of the paraisthmic window can be difficult and management of anatomical structures lying cranial and caudal to it can be a source of difficulty.

It can be difficult to include all the fibers of the paracervical or suspensory ligaments in the passage of the needle. If this happens one will observe the highest fibers escaping from the ligature when the ligament is divided. Once the first fibers escape the others follow. This escape leads to bleeding. However this bleeding is not usually heavy as long as there is traction on the uterus. Don't try to stop it before the uterus has been removed. Once it has been, one can comfortably place the stitches that will stop all oozing (Figures 7.101 and 7.102).

Management of the uterine artery may be rendered difficult when it remains in a deep position despite division of most of the paracervical ligamentous fibers. In such a situation one can use a right-angled dissecting forceps that one pushes under the control of the left forefinger and places on the ventral surface of the broad ligament (Figures 7.72 and 7.73). Once the broad ligament has been transfixed the dissecting forceps are opened and the afferent branch of the arch is freed (Figure 7.74). Two clamps can then be put on it.

Detachment of the pars flaccida of the broad ligament does not usually necessitate any suturing, clamping or cutting but this can be difficult if endometriosis or the sequelae of pelvic infection fix the tubes and/or the ovaries to the sides of the uterus. If predictable this situation represents one of the best indications for laparoscopic assistance. If such assistance has not been planned one

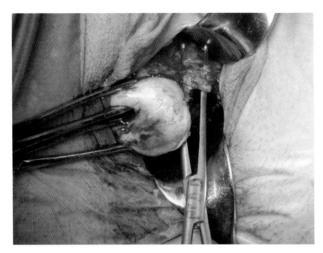

Figure 7.73 Opening the O'Shaughnessy clamp allows visualization of the arch of the uterine artery.

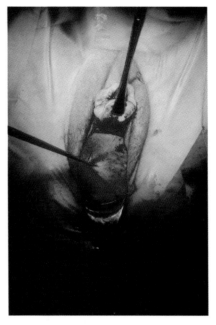

Figure 7.75 In cases where the uterus is too large to deliver, a tenaculum is placed on the midline of the dorsal uterine surface and traction is applied.

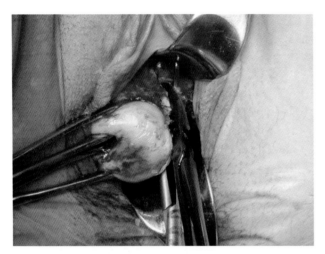

Figure 7.74 Clamping the afferent branch of the uterine artery.

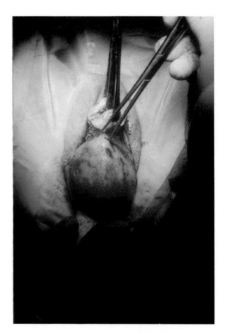

Figure 7.76 Traction is successful.

can generally overcome the difficulty using blunt digital dissection to separate the adnexae. If this proves difficult it may be necessary to proceed to immediate laparoscopy, after firmly packing the vagina to avoid loss of gas. Equally one can continue transvaginally but it is then necessary to perform a check laparoscopy once the hysterectomy is complete and the vagina closed.

Delivery of the uterine fundus

Difficulty in delivering the uterus is a common occurrence in vaginal hysterectomy. These difficulties can be overcome using various tricks to reduce the volume of the uterus. The very first trick is to apply a tenaculum to the dorsal aspect of the uterus (Figure 7.75) and to pull it forward while pulling upward on the cervix at the same time (Figure 7.76). If this fails there are different techniques to try: amputation of the cervix,

myomectomy, morcellation, hemisection and so on. Here we describe the ways in which we proceed from one approach to the next when it is not possible to deliver the uterus simply by pulling on the cervix and the fundus.

Amputation of the cervix

Amputation of the cervix is the first action to try. As the cervix meets the resistance of the symphysis

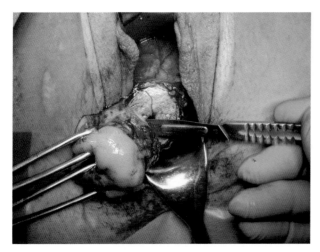

Figure 7.77 When direct delivery of the uterus is unsuccessful, the first thing to do is to amputate the cervix.

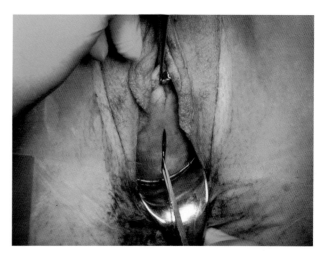

Figure 7.79 A small midline incision is made on the dorsal aspect of the uterus.

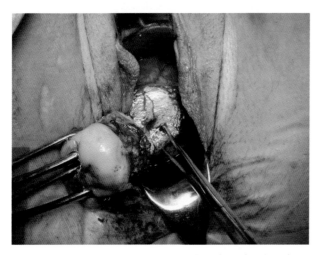

Figure 7.78 A tenaculum has been placed on the dorsal part of the uterus before completing the amputation.

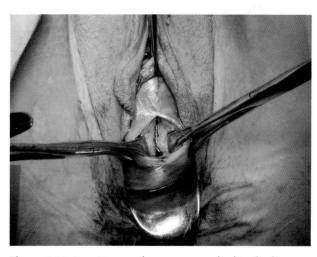

Figure 7.80 Two Museux forceps are applied to the lips of the incision.

pubis the posterior toppling movement of the uterus is prevented. Once the cervix has been amputated this movement may become easier. The amputation is done with a scalpel, perpendicular to the axis of the uterus just underneath the medial stumps of the uterine arteries (Figure 7.77). A bullet forceps is put on the isthmic stump (Figure 7.78) and then pulled directly upward.

Median posterior hysterotomy
If despite removing the cervix it is still not possible to deliver the uterus, a midline incision of 2 cm is made on the posterior surface of the uterus (Figure 7.79). A Museux forceps is placed on each leaf of this incision (Figure 7.80). Exerting traction on these two Museux is often enough to achieve delivery of the fundus. If not the incision is extended downward while maintaining strong upward traction on the Museux (Figure 7.81). A third Museux forceps is put on one of

the leaves of the extended incision and the ipsilateral Museux is placed lower down on the opposite leaf (Figure 7.82). The remaining Museux is removed (Figure 7.83) and traction that is exerted close to the dorsal extremity of the hysterotomy, i.e. closer to the fundus, often succeeds (Figure 7.84). If not the action may be repeated several times. If this fails one may consider myomectomy and/or morcellation.

Myomectomy
When a fibroid is encountered during the vertical posterior hysterotomy one can grasp it with a Museux forceps, if it is not too big, and enucleate it (Figure 7.85). If the fibroid is too big it is necessary to divide it to remove it. The most elegant way of doing it is hemisection. The visible portion of the fibroid is incised with a scalpel in an equatorial plane (Figure 7.86). Two Museux forceps are put on the edges of the incision. The divergent traction exerted

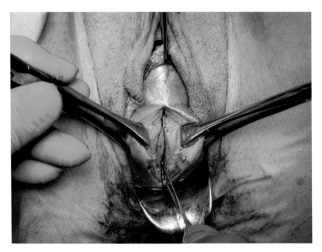

Figure 7.81 The incision is extended and deepened.

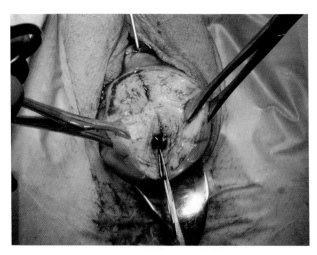

Figure 7.84 The second Museux forceps has been removed and the incision has been extended and deepened even further: delivery will now be successful.

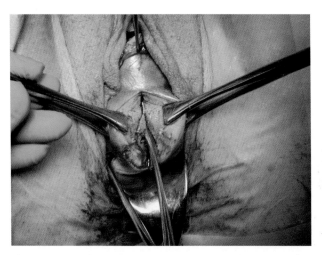

Figure 7.82 A third Museux forceps is applied on one side close to the distal angle of the hysterotomy.

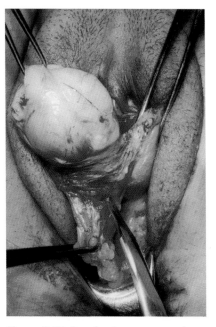

Figure 7.85 Enucleating a myoma that prevents delivery of the uterus (lysing an omental adhesion at the same time).

on the Museux makes the incision gape and it becomes possible to reach the deepest pole of the fibroid (Figure 7.87). The two halves of the fibroid are then enucleated one after the other (Figure 7.88).

Morcellation

When it is not possible to enucleate the fibroids using the hemisection procedure, it is necessary to resort to morcellation. One starts by freeing one of the visible surfaces of the fibroid. An incision made on the visible part of the surface of the fibroid enables the placement of a Museux forceps, which is used to provide traction in a medial direction. The handle of the scalpel, closed scissors and/or the fingers are introduced laterally, in between the

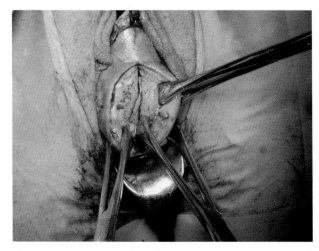

Figure 7.83 The contralateral Museux is moved and placed opposite the third one.

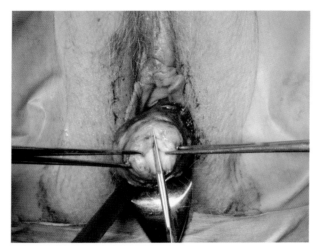

Figure 7.86 If direct enucleation of the myoma is not possible we may resort to hemisection.

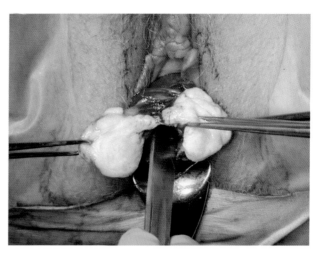

Figure 7.88 Completing the hemisection.

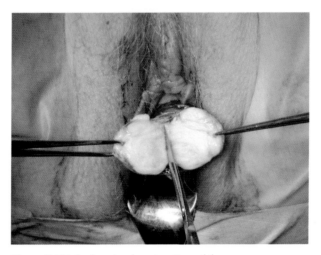

Figure 7.87 Performing hemisection of the myoma.

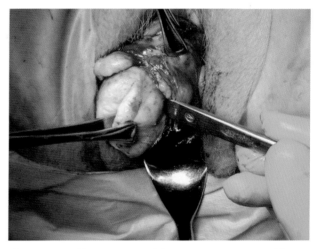

Figure 7.89 If hemisection of the myoma is not possible we may resort to morcellation: freeing up the surface of the myoma lateral to the incision.

fibroid and the myometrium so as to free as large a piece of fibroid as possible (Figure 7.89). A second incision is then made on the free part (Figure 7.90) and the piece located between the two incisions is removed (Figure 7.91). The maneuver can be repeated as often as necessary. Delivery of the uterus is generally not achieved before the fibroid is completely removed. However this latter is not always possible: there may be other fibroids to remove or it may not be possible to complete the first enucleation. In these cases it is necessary to revert to hemisection and eventually to direct morcellation of the myometrium.

Hemisection
When it is not possible to extend the posterior median hysterotomy further without danger (only cut what you can see!) it is necessary to perform a similar incision on the anterior aspect of the uterus.

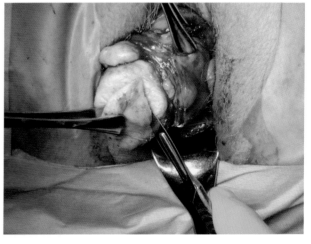

Figure 7.90 Performing the first wedge resection of the myoma.

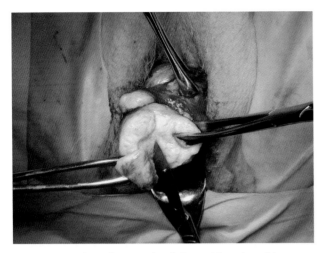

Figure 7.91 The volume to be delivered is reduced by performing these wedge resections: clearly, delivery will now be successful.

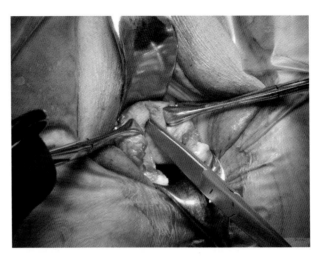

Figure 7.93 The scissors approach the summit of the fundus.

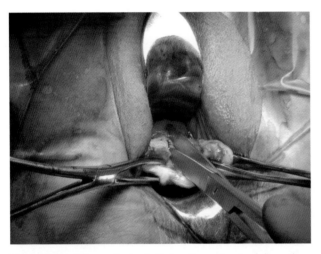

Figure 7.92 When all else fails in attempting to deliver the uterus we perform midline hysterotomy.

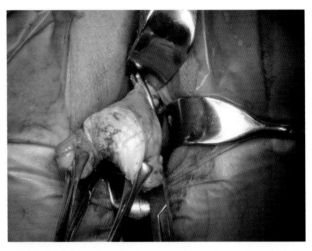

Figure 7.94 The uterus has now been completely bisected: delivering the first half of the uterus.

In order to do this, reverse the toppling movement. Find the isthmus again. Apply a bullet forceps to each of its lateral sides and cut between these two instruments (Figure 7.92). The incision should be continued as high as possible and the forceps then replaced close to the tip of the incision. Continue incising as often as necessary as far as the fundus (Figure 7.93). Once the fundus is delivered one finds oneself in a familiar situation. If the fundus can't be delivered one performs a "two-step" hysterectomy, i.e. two successive hemihysterectomies. The hemiuterus that descends the best is removed first. One or two clamps are put on the adnexa inserted on the cornu of the hemiuterus (Figure 7.94) and it is then possible to proceed to the other hemihysterectomy.

If it is completely impossible to deliver the fundus the next step is morcellation of the myometrium. The procedure is the same as fibroid morcellation. Reduction in volume generally allows delivery of the fundus and thus finally hysterectomy, or two hemihysterectomies. If after all this it is still impossible to deliver the uterus, laparotomy is the only answer. This disaster can generally be avoided with appropriate patient selection

Adnexectomy

It is unfair to include adnexectomy in the section devoted to intraoperative difficulties. In fact, adnexectomy can generally be achieved easily using the vaginal route. It can be performed in continuity with the hysterectomy. Nonetheless, we think it is preferable to perform hysterectomy first and then adnexectomy.

The clamp that has been used to take the round ligament, the Fallopian tube and the utero-ovarian ligament en bloc is pulled toward the midline. A Jean-Louis Faure forceps is put on the round ligament 10–15 mm above the clamp (Figure 7.95). The ligament is divided between the two clamps (Figure 7.96). Strong upward traction is required on the round ligament whilst pulling the other clamp downward. That has the effect of tightening the peritoneal fold situated between the round ligament and the infundibulopelvic ligament. This peritoneal fold is cut with the scissors (Figure 7.97). This allows access to the tube and ovary.

The tubes and ovaries are held in Duval forceps and pulled downward (Figure 7.98). This traction frees the infundibulopelvic ligament, which can be clamped just above the superior tip of the ovary (Figure 7.99). The stump of the round ligament and the stump of the infundibulopelvic ligaments are

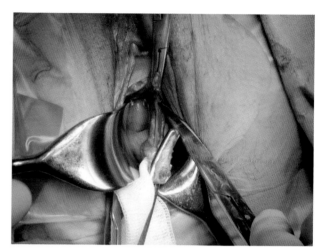

Figure 7.97 Separating the adnexa from the round ligament.

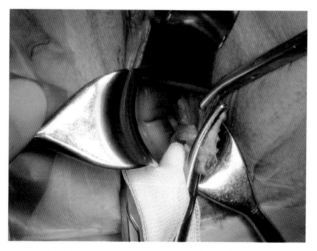

Figure 7.95 When adnexectomy is indicated it is performed after removal of the uterus. First step of left adnexectomy: clamping the round ligament adjacent to the clamp on the uterine stump of the adnexa.

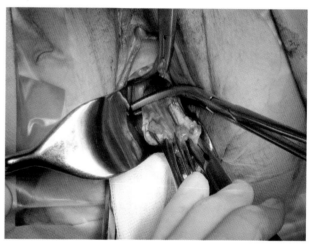

Figure 7.98 Clamping the infundibulopelvic ligament.

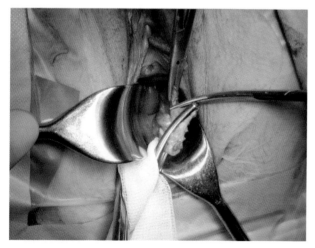

Figure 7.96 Dividing the round ligament.

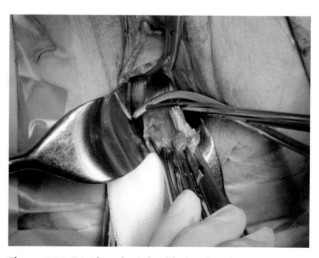

Figure 7.99 Dividing the infundibulopelvic ligament.

managed later on just as they are when taken together in an interadnexal hysterectomy.

If the stump of the infundibulopelvic ligament is in a very high position, rather than exerting traction that is too strong, we recommend use of an endoloop. This trick, originally devised for laparoscopic surgery, has found another niche here. The loop is placed around the clamp (Figure 7.100), and then the knot is sited at the same time as the clamp is released.

Approximately one in ten adnexectomies is difficult due to the adnexae being in a very high position (this becomes more common with advancing age) or, more often, because it is adherent to the posterior surface of the broad ligament. Digital mobilization is often possible. If it is not, we recommend stopping, closing the vagina and resorting to laparoscopy. There are some indications for complementary laparoscopy, but there is no indication for laparoscopic preparation in the field of adnexectomy combined with vaginal hysterectomy.

Re-peritonealization and closure

Gathering the posterior vaginal wall should not in itself pose any difficulties. During this step it may be necessary to fix the consequences of a (relatively frequent) slippage of the ligatures from the suspensory ligament pedicles. As mentioned previously the bleeding due to this slippage is modest and doesn't impair completion of the surgery. It is important to resecure the pedicle before completing the operation. The pedicle is exteriorized (Figure 7.101) with a toothed dissecting forceps and stitched once or twice (Figure 7.102).

After interadnexal hysterectomy re-peritonealization is generally very easy. The only slight difficulty

one can encounter is with the bladder peritoneum, which can remain high up. This is generally due to filling of the bladder. Emptying it with a catheter may solve the problem. If an adnexectomy has been performed at the same time as the hysterectomy one can have difficulty drawing the infundibulopelvic pedicle downward (theoretically it should be extra-peritonealized). If one encounters this difficulty it is better to leave the pedicle in an intraperitoneal position.

The last difficulty relates to the very last part of the surgery as has already been mentioned. This is the persistence of bleeding after completion of suturing. It is worth repeating that packing is not the answer. The stitches have to be removed and the bleeding vessels controlled: they are generally situated on the vaginal wall close to the insertion of the paracervical ligaments. Specific stitching of the bleeders secures hemostasis.

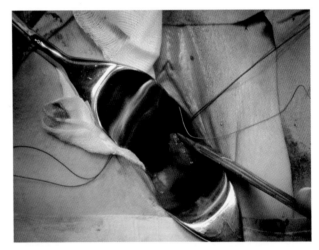

Figure 7.101 If the suture around the infundibulopelvic ligament slips, exteriorize it.

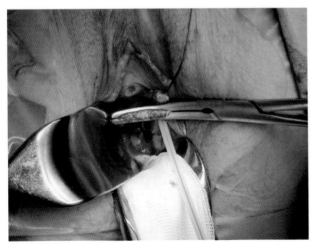

Figure 7.100 Applying an endoloop® suture around the infundibulopelvic ligament.

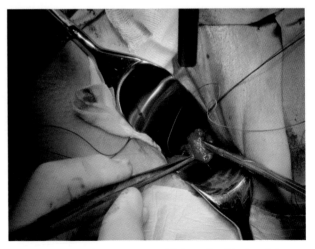

Figure 7.102 If the suture around the infundibulopelvic ligament slips, exteriorize it and suture it by hand.

Postoperative course/complications

The postoperative course after vaginal hysterectomy is usually rapid, simple and afebrile.

The patient can and should be got out of her bed on the first evening. The patient can drink as soon as she is sufficiently awake. Bowel sounds are present within 24–48 h. As soon as they appear solid food is allowed (initially a light diet and then normal diet).

Discharge may be on the second or third day and convalescence lasts 3–6 weeks, depending on the socio-professional status.

During convalescence the patient should be advised to take it easy and to avoid sports and driving. As far as personal hygiene is concerned vulval toilet should be advised several times a day with a nonirritant soap, but the use of douches and intravaginal preparations should be prohibited. Sexual intercourse and the use of tampons are to be avoided. It is preferable to shower rather than bathe.

A postoperative follow up examination should be scheduled before returning to normal activities. The vagina has to be examined digitally and the vault visualized with a speculum. In many cases there will be some granulation tissue. If it is present cauterize it with a silver nitrate stick.

In the medium to long term, vaginal hysterectomy does result in sequelae, particularly as they relate to pelvic floor stability. In our opinion there are no disorders that can be specifically attributed to vaginal hysterectomy itself.

Intraoperative complications

Intraoperative complications fall into three main categories: bleeding, visceral injury and inability to extract the specimen. They are rare if the decision to perform vaginal hysterectomy has been taken appropriately.

Intraoperative bleeding
Blood loss during vaginal hysterectomy is less than during abdominal hysterectomy performed for equivalent indications. Major hemorrhage is exceptionally rare. It can arise from the uterine artery, infundibulopelvic ligaments or parametrial blood vessels.

Section of the uterine artery (if not preceded by a controlling ligature) or slippage of the uterine ligature can cause significant bleeding. Both can occur before extraction of the uterus. Management is not easy, but it must be carried out immediately. If the accident happens (or is discovered) after exteriorization of the specimen it is quite straightforward to position retractors to reveal the bleeding vessel. This can then be grasped with toothed dissecting forceps and clamped with a right-angle forceps, which then allows the placement of a double ligature.

Tearing or slipping of the infundibulopelvic ligament gives rises to bleeding, which is generally minimal but must be controlled. The technique is the same. The bleeder is deeper. It is necessary to have the whole set of Breisky retractors at your disposal to deal with this problem. If one does not succeed do not hesitate to move to the abdominal approach (laparoscopy).

Slipping of the ligature around the suspensory ligament pedicles leads to bleeding, which is generally moderate. The diagnosis is made either during or after the exteriorization of the uterus. This is managed after extraction of the uterus – it is controlled by suturing (Figures 7.101 and 7.102).

Visceral injuries
Bladder injuries
Bladder injuries are undoubtedly more frequent during vaginal hysterectomy than during abdominal hysterectomy. They occur at the very first moment of the surgery. It is possible to detect the injury as soon as it occurs, but it is often only detected after exteriorization of the uterus.

Bladder injuries rarely consist of a neat cut. The wound is not like a surgical cystotomy, but is more often rather ragged and bruised. It occurs after the surgeon has created a false passage in the bladder wall, which then enters the bladder lumen. The bladder is generally empty at the time of injury and this explains why the injury is not always detected immediately but very often later on during the operation – a circumstance where the surgeon often falsely accuses the assistant and the retractors!

Whenever the injury is detected the repair does not have to be done immediately. The posterior vaginal wall should be gathered and the peritoneum should be closed before suturing the bladder. The bladder suture, obviously, has to be made using absorbable stitches. A single layer will suffice. We recommend using interrupted sutures rather than continuous. The stitches are inserted successively. They are knotted only after the last one has been positioned so that it is possible to have a good view of the wound. This is the best way of avoiding getting too close to the ureteric orifices while suturing.

Accidental bladder holes are generally situated at the level of the interureteric ridge and suturing risks catching or obstructing the terminal (intra-parietal) portion of the ureter(s). We therefore recommend asking for an intravenous injection of Indigo Carmine dye before undertaking suturing in order to clearly identify the ureteric ejaculations.

The integrity of the suture has to be assessed by instilling saline dyed with Methylene blue into the bladder. The Foley catheter used for this test is left in place. Retrograde cystography is ordered approximately 8–10 days later. If the pictures are reassuring the catheter may be removed.

Prevention and early detection of bladder injuries are a matter for debate. As far as prevention is concerned, it is better operating under continuous bladder drainage. As far as early detection is concerned it is better to operate after instilling the bladder with a colored liquid. Our approach falls somewhere between the two. We empty the bladder just before surgery but the catheter is not left in place. If an injury occurs during the very first step it can escape diagnosis, but as the bladder fills during surgery, the hole inevitably becomes obvious later. This is not a problem because as already mentioned treatment should be delayed until after re-peritonealization.

Intestinal injuries

Injuries to the rectum are exceptionally rare. They obviously need to be repaired immediately. The repair is done with interrupted extra-mucosal sutures aligned transversely. It is not necessary to perform a defunctioning colostomy. Leaving a Penrose drain adjacent to the suture is recommended.

Injuries to loops of bowel (sigmoid, ileal loops and cecum) are rare. They are generally the consequence of abnormal adhesions between the intestine and the uterus. They obviously have to be repaired immediately. If they are small they can be managed via the vaginal route. If however there is anything larger do not hesitate to take recourse to laparotomy.

Inability to extract the uterus

When the indication is appropriately selected, vaginal hysterectomy is in theory always possible. Selective use of preoperative laparoscopy further reduces the prevalence of this complication. Nevertheless it is impossible to totally exclude such an event and the patient must be made aware of this fact.

If one has to abandon the vaginal route don't wait too long. Surrender is not glorious, but it is less damaging for the patient than perseverance knowingly misguided.

Removing the uterus abdominally after failing to extract it by the vaginal route is fast and easy because the difficult steps of the surgery have already been completed.

Postoperative complications

The complications of vaginal hysterectomy include general complications as seen after any surgical intervention. The general complications include thromboembolism, pulmonary complications, cardiovascular complications, ileus and so on. The specific complications after vaginal hysterectomy are bleeding, infection and fistula formation.

Postoperative bleeding

Bleeding after vaginal hysterectomy is usually minimal. We have observed that this bleeding, whatever the clinical condition (bloody surgery or not), is more significant if a pack is left in place at the end of the operation and we have abandoned this practice.

First-day hemorrhage resulting in intervention is on average observed in only 1% of cases. Bleeding usually starts in the hours immediately following surgery. It is observed more frequently if the patient is premenopausal and in cases with a long history of abnormal uterine bleeding. This epidemiological particularity raises the hypothesis that postoperative bleeding could, at least in part, be related to local disorders of hemostasis. This supports the argument against an ill-considered prompt return to the theatre. If one is dealing with moderate hemorrhage, without evidence of collapse or a drop in hemoglobin concentration, a simple firm vaginal pack can be inserted on the ward after a speculum examination. A Foley catheter should also be inserted.

If the hemorrhage appears heavy or if moderate hemorrhage persists despite packing, it is necessary to take the patient back to theatre. Reoperation must be carried out under the best conditions. General anesthesia is necessary. The patient has to be set up in an adequate position. The team of staff must be complete. All the instrumentation must be available. The first action is to cut the vaginal sutures. Then one evacuates all the clot. After evacuation, the operative field may be completely dry. Alternatively, one may see active bleeding either at the level of one pedicle or at the level of the vaginal wall (generally at the point of insertion of one of the pedicles). These bleeders must be controlled. Whatever the situation, all the stumps must be prophylactically resutured.

Prevention of first-day hemorrhage is instituted during initial surgery. At the end of the operation the operative field must be completely dry. If this is not the case, one has to resist the temptation to pack the vagina but rather cut the vaginal sutures and properly reassess the operative field.

After the first day, postoperative hemorrhage is rare and it becomes less likely as time passes. This type of bleeding tends to be less heavy. It is exceptionally rare to have to reoperate after the first 24 h.

Medium- and late-term hemorrhage are usually due to an exaggeration of the healing process and granulation tissue formation. An early resumption of sexual intercourse may cause this. Management must be conservative: packing (and a Foley catheter – it is impossible to pass urine when the vagina is correctly packed).

As far as the prevention of postoperative hemorrhage is concerned many authors recommend complete closure of the vagina. This closure does not completely prevent hemorrhage and it is not without danger as far as infectious complications are concerned.

Infections

The prevalence of postoperative infection largely depends on the definition one adopts. The majority of infections following vaginal hysterectomy are benign infections that do not necessitate antibiotics or reoperation. An isolated rise in temperature is relatively frequent (5–15% of the cases). This does not necessarily indicate infection, but during the initial phase of true infection this is the only sign or symptom. For this reason one has to delay discharge until the temperature is completely normal.

Urinary tract infection

Urinary tract infections are more frequent in patients operated on transvaginally rather than transabdominally. Many so-called isolated temperatures are due to urinary tract infection. The usual symptoms of cystitis may be absent. In fact many urinary tract infections are totally asymptomatic with neither fever nor functional symptoms.

If symptomatic, antibiotic therapy is necessary. In the asymptomatic form of infection the use of antibiotics is controversial. In any case, antibiotics or not, it is important to repeat a mid-stream sample of urine culture after 10 days.

In order to prevent urinary infections one should refrain from catheterizing and draining the bladder. We always empty the bladder with an in and out catheter before commencing surgery but we don't leave a catheter *in situ* during and after surgery. Postoperative urinary retention is rare after simple vaginal hysterectomy (with the exception of operations performed under spinal anesthesia).

Vault abscess

Vault abscess is a difficult entity to define. It occurs when infection develops in the cellular pelvic tissue in contact with the vaginal vault. Clinically this is associated with a moderate fever of 38–38.5 °C, turbid offensive vaginal discharge and, at vaginal examination, infiltration of the pelvic cellular tissues in contact with the vaginal wall, which is thickened and edematous. To be honest these signs are difficult to quantify. One can try to do it by using a scoring system. Vaginal examination allows diagnosis and has a therapeutic role as well: it facilitates the drainage of pus. Antibiotics should be given and recovery is usually rapid. Antibiotic therapy can be stopped after 10 days. Prevention of pelvic cellulitis and pelvic abscess relies on the methods we have previously described. Since the systematic application of these methods these complications have become rare.

Pelvic abscess

Infected pelvic collections have become extremely rare. From the anatomical viewpoint they include Fallopian tube abscesses, ovarian (corpus luteum) abscesses and abscesses in the pouch of Douglas. Presentation is usually around day 14. The first symptom is nothing other than fever without any obvious symptoms. In such a situation one has to refrain from immediately giving antibiotics. The use of antibiotics is useless in the face of a simple inflammatory process and is dangerous if given blindly for an infection that hasn't yet been characterized. In the latter case one does not need to wait long before the temperature rises accompanied by a change in the general condition of the patient. These changes are accompanied by signs of a pelvic collection developing laterally or more often posterolaterally. Ultrasound or CT scan confirms the diagnosis and allows guided puncture, lavage and drainage, which have replaced classical blind colpotomy. This drainage generally leads to healing. If after an immediate improvement that is maintained, the symptoms and signs reappear, consider a diagnosis of ovarian abscess. This requires bilateral adnexectomy, which can most often be done with the laparoscope.

Peritonitis

Peritonitis is also very rare. It can be seen in two different contexts. Early peritonitis is a contemporary of postoperative pelvic cellulitis. Secondary peritonitis is due to medium- and late-term pelvic suppuration. In the first presentation a rapid intensive course of appropriate antibiotics can cure most patients. In the second presentation on the contrary it is necessary to reoperate. This can generally be carried out laparoscopically. A particular mention should be made of hidden peritonitis. Faced with sepsis, shock and poor response to correct antibiotic therapy, one has to think of peritonitis and consider laparoscopy even if the objective peritoneal signs are vague or absent.

Fistulae

Vesicovaginal, rectovaginal and ureterovaginal fistulae represent classical but very rare complications of vaginal hysterectomy.

Vesicovaginal fistulae

Vesicovaginal fistulae are despite their rarity the most frequent postoperative fistulae (up to 2/1,000). They are the consequence of a hole in the bladder, which has been either undiagnosed or poorly managed: no water-proof test performed at the end of the operation, or no prior radiological assessment before removing the catheter in the postoperative period. The diagnosis depends on the blue dye test (a methylene blue tablet is taken and the vaginal discharge observed) followed by an intravenous pyelogram that allows exclusion of a ureterovaginal fistula and confirmation of a vesicovaginal fistula. If the diagnosis is made immediately the vesicovaginal fistula may heal with bladder drainage alone. If after 20 days the urinary loss persists the chances of spontaneous cure are very low and reoperation has to be scheduled – this is done as soon as the edges of the fistula are well defined (6–8 weeks). To prevent fistula formation it is worth repeating that bladder dissection must be performed atraumatically in the extra-fascial plane. One must remember the rules for the detection and treatment of bladder injury and one must be vigilant during the postoperative period.

Rectovaginal fistulae

Rectovaginal fistulae are exceptionally rare. Their occurrence can lead to colostomy. Spontaneous healing can occur. If the progress of spontaneous healing is not favorable one needs to consider surgical treatment once the edges of the fistula are well defined. After complete healing the colostomy can be closed.

Ureterovaginal fistulae

Ureterovaginal fistulae are practically excluded with the technique that we recommend for managing the afferent branch of the uterine artery. The pressure that one applies with the finger, on the inside of the arch of the uterine artery before passing the needle through, reflects the ureter. In addition, the retractor reflecting the bladder does so most efficiently because the vesicouterine peritoneal cul de sac has not been opened. This prevents ureteric damage. It is nevertheless necessary to be particularly careful in cases where repeated cone biopsy and/or amputation of the cervix have completely modified the anatomical relationships

between the ureter and the uterine artery. In case of urinary loss, intravenous pyelography clinches the diagnosis. The treatment is generally made using the endoscopic approach: placing a JJ stent with the cystoscopy. Open reimplantation of the ureter or uretero-neo-cystostomy is only rarely indicated.

Indications and contraindications

Hysterectomy has diverse indications. Genital prolapse and infiltrative cancer of the cervix are not considered here. Apart from these two situations the indications for hysterectomy include: first, endometrial pathology (hyperplasia, atypical hyperplasia, cancer); second, myometrial pathology (fibroids and/or adenomyosis); and third, adnexal pathology (infection, endometriosis, benign and malignant neoplasm). Malignant ovarian pathology is the only indication for laparotomy. In all other situations the vaginal approach can be considered. For decades the vaginal approach was the only approach. At the beginning of the twentieth century operating via laparotomy became possible and the use of the vaginal approach decreased. At the end of the same century laparoscopic surgery appeared and we now have at our disposal three routes for hysterectomy. The place of these routes is hotly debated and variably implemented. What follows is our current viewpoint, which we believe to be the correct way, but of course we know that ideas change and our practice can move with the times!

The vaginal approach includes the triple advantage of simplicity, rapidity and safety. The instrumentation and the technical principles practically haven't changed since the beginning. In the comparative trials, operative time is always shorter. Large studies have shown that the postoperative course is simpler. Today, death rates due to hysterectomy are extremely low. However, mortality due to vaginal hysterectomy has always been lower than that attributable to abdominal hysterectomy and the current figures suggest a mortality rate three times lower. The drawback of the vaginal approach is that it does not allow complete assessment of the peritoneal cavity. This limitation prevents the use of the vaginal approach for the management of some pathologies and in particular adnexal pathology.

The abdominal approach has the advantage of being appropriate for all pathologies. It includes the drawback of being more traumatic. The abdominal wound, apart from esthetic sequelae and complications (wound healing problems, hernias and bowel obstruction), increases postoperative immobility. As a consequence the thromboembolic risk is increased. It is this phenomenon that explains the differences in mortality rates for abdominal and vaginal hysterectomy.

To be honest, one has to recognize that the comparative surveys are largely biased. However a prospective and randomized trial seems to be impossible to set up nowadays. No woman with the choice of either transvaginal or transabdominal surgery would accept a choice made by randomization. Furthermore, no ethical committee would agree to a study where one arm has three times the mortality of the other.

The laparoscopic approach has the advantages of both the vaginal and the abdominal routes. It leaves practically no scars. It allows complete assessment of the peritoneal cavity and the performance of the different steps of hysterectomy either partially or totally. However laparoscopic hysterectomy has the disadvantage of complexity. It requires sophisticated fragile equipment. The duration of surgery is longer and the rate of complications higher. These two facts are probably related to the learning curve and may change with time. However laparoscopic hysterectomy will always have complications of both hysterectomy and laparoscopy whereas vaginal hysterectomy simply has the complications of hysterectomy.

Faced with uterine and/or adnexal pathology (excepting prolapse and invasive cancer of the cervix) we think that the vaginal approach should be the preferred option if hysterectomy is required. The vaginal approach has to be preferred in all cases where the clinical and anatomical conditions make it possible and in all cases where the nature of the lesions to be treated does not prevent it. Laparotomy only survives because of the contraindications to vaginal hysterectomy. The laparoscopic approach may reduce the length of this survival.

Elective indications for the vaginal route

Obesity and poor general condition are two of the main indications for the less-aggressive vaginal route. The vaginal approach enables us to operate on inoperable patients!

Obesity
The prevalence of obesity in industrialized countries is constantly on the increase. It is becoming more common to be faced with a patient who requires hysterectomy and is affected by morbid obesity.

Vaginal hysterectomy in an obese patient is less easy because the overhang of the buttocks complicates the access to the vaginal vault. Nonetheless, this is minimal when compared to the problems with access either at laparotomy or laparoscopy. On the other hand, the vagina and the pelvic cellular tissue are usually softer in the obese patient.

Frailty of general condition
Conditions that compromise vital functions represent other indications where the vaginal route is preferred. The vaginal route is the preferred route for patients affected by respiratory problems (it is possible to operate with a regional block), cardiac problems, hemostatic disorders (both idiopathic and iatrogenic i.e. warfarin therapy). More generally speaking, the vaginal approach suits the patient whose status prevents surgery by laparotomy and even more so by laparoscopy, the latter being reserved for patients who are physiologically healthy.

Contraindications to the vaginal route

The vaginal route is contraindicated in certain conditions relating to the patient and her disease.

Contraindications related to the state of the patient
Disorders of the hip and spine
To perform a vaginal hysterectomy it is necessary to put the patient in the so-called lithotomy position (the position used by surgeons of the Renaissance to break up stones by opening the bladder via the perineum). Both legs must be hyperflexed at the hip. It is also necessary for the patient's buttocks to hang over the end of the table. If one cannot set the patient up in this position, it is better to abandon the vaginal approach. Actually operating on a patient who is not in the lithotomy position is uncomfortable for the surgeon, but the main issue is the risk to which the patient is exposed if one does not operate under ideal conditions. As a consequence, it is important to simulate the lithotomy position for every patient affected by hip or spinal disorders before induction of anesthesia. If this simulation does not succeed or if it results in pain, however slight, it is better to resort to another approach.

Narrow vaginal access
Vaginal access is governed by the width of the sub-pubic arch, the suppleness of the perineum and the width of the vagina. In a woman who has delivered vaginally, vaginal access is generally good. Multiparity however is no guarantee. Traumatic sequelae of a spontaneous delivery can occasionally represent an obstacle. On the contrary nulliparity does not necessarily represent a contraindication.

To operate comfortably via the vaginal route it is necessary that the sub-pubic arch is adequately wide. The criterion used in obstetrics to assess the pelvic outlet can also be used in surgery: if one can insert the fist in between the two ischial tuberosities the space is sufficient.

Suppleness of the perineum is essential for operating vaginally. One assesses this during vaginal examination. Resistance of the perineum is often due to reflex spasm of the levator muscles and this spasm can disappear under anesthesia.

The vagina must be of sufficient capacity to allow access to the cervix and the ligaments inserted on to it. Digital assessment is again used to judge this. If the index and middle fingers can only just be introduced and it is not possible to separate them once inside the vagina, hysterectomy will be difficult if not impossible. If you can only separate them slightly, the surgery will be difficult and potentially dangerous.

Sclerotic pelvic cellular tissue
Laxity of the supporting ligaments (uterosacral and cardinal ligaments) is the most important anatomical condition for performing hysterectomy vaginally. vaginally. If the ligaments are very resistant the uterus will not descend and one will be working with the instruments up to their hilts, i.e. dangerously. Lack of compliance of the ligaments can be the consequence of sclerosis due to dystrophic healing of an obstetric tear or of a parametritis that was part of a pelvic infection. It may also be constitutional: the tissue surrounding the collaterals of the iliac vessels is particularly rich in elastic and collagen tissue. In the first situation anesthesia does not make any difference to the problem. On the contrary, in the second one the situation completely changes as soon as the patient is anesthetized.

From the practical viewpoint, it is admitted that it is necessary for the cervix to reach halfway down the vagina when traction is exerted in the umbilical–coccygeal axis. Poor descent preoperatively is not uncommon but it markedly improves under anesthesia. The contraindications due to poor compliance of the ligamentous supports, just as those related to the suppleness of the perineum, should be reevaluated as soon as the patient is anesthetized. The patient must be warned about the uncertainty regarding the final evaluation of the route of her surgery.

Contraindications related to the pathology
The big uterus
There are practically no fibroids too big that they cannot be removed by the vaginal approach. The (French) pioneers of vaginal surgery amply demonstrated this by using morcellation to extract tumors of a volume we no longer see. Such exploits are no longer acceptable. Operating through the vaginal route takes longer and risks higher blood loss, so it must be preferable to operate via the abdominal route in these cases.

That said it is difficult to precisely set the limits. A generally accepted limit is a uterus larger than the normal uterus at 16 weeks gestation. This rule is rather artificial. It all depends on the size of the largest fibroids and their topography.

If the fibroid is fundal and subserous, hysterectomy is in general easy even if the fibroid reaches beyond the umbilicus. Access to the uterine cornua and the structures inserted there is not difficult. After detaching the adnexal structures it is possible to continue and extract the uterus without risk as it is now lying free of all its pelvic attachments.

When the fibroid has developed in the myometrium at the base of one of the cornua, it can often be easily accessed by dividing the adnexal attachments and pediculizing the "specimen to come" on one of the contralateral cornua. Extraction is then easy.

It is only in cases where the fibroid has developed in the myometrium underneath both cornua that access to these cornua is difficult and hysterectomy can become rather acrobatic.

Ultrasound allows measurement and topographic definition of the fibroids. Contrast sonography is the key to delineating the uterine cavity. If the dimensions and shape of the cavity are normal the cornua will be easily accessible. If one side of the cavity is elongated then in principle the other cornu will be accessible. If both sides are elongated then the vaginal approach may be very difficult.

A recent proposal has been to use chemical castration in the form of gonadotrophin releasing hormone (GnRH) analogs to reduce the volume of the fibroids. The effect starts within 10 days of the first injection. Within 6 months the fibroids will have reduced in volume by half on average. However the hysterectomy is not twice as easy because there is a corresponding reduction in the size of the vagina. To avoid this effect one can utilize "add-back" therapy without diminishing the effect on fibroid volume reduction. This strategy is complex and problematic. We tend to advise using monthly injections and reexamining the patient 15 days after the second injection. By this time the uterine volume should have reduced by about 30% on average without a reduction in vaginal capacity. If it looks as though the vaginal route is possible it is best to proceed to this without undue delay.

Suspicious or malignant adnexal pathology
Adnexal pathology in addition to uterine pathology requiring hysterectomy is a contraindication to the vaginal route. It is theoretically possible to ignore this and to perform adnexectomy in continuity with

hysterectomy using the vaginal route in cases where triple assessment by examination, sonography and tumor markers point to benign pathology. This is technically quite easy but overall not a good strategy if a lesion initially thought to be benign turns out in fact to be malignant, thereby risking contamination of the peritoneal cavity at the time of specimen delivery.

This is the area where laparoscopic assistance comes into its own. Systematic laparotomy for all patients who present with benign uterine pathology and an ovarian tumor will mean many unnecessary laparotomies as the great majority of ovarian tumors in premenopausal women with benign uterine disease will turn out to be benign. Laparoscopy with biopsies and frozen section will allow operation without recourse to laparotomy if the lesion turns out to be benign.

Relative contraindications to the vaginal route

There are certain conditions related to the general state of the patient that are not absolute contraindications but can nonetheless make vaginal hysterectomy difficult. These should be taken into account.

Contraindications related to the condition of the patient

Menopausal status

It is accepted that hysterectomy when done at the end of the reproductive phase should be completed by bilateral adnexectomy. It is fair to say that this indication gives rise to much controversy, which we are not going to touch on here. Many consider that when an adnexectomy is necessary it is better to choose laparotomy. More recently this situation has been considered an indication for laparoscopic assistance. In reality one can say that in nine out of ten cases it is easy to remove the adnexae by the vaginal route. It is only in about one in ten cases that difficulties are encountered. If the difficulties are insurmountable it is necessary to close the vagina and finish under laparoscopic control.

Previous laparotomy

It is generally considered that the vaginal route should not be used in women who have undergone a previous laparotomy. This contraindication is in reality only a relative contraindication.

The nature of the previous surgery plays an important role. Cesarean section is the commonest previous procedure that one meets in women who are candidates for vaginal hysterectomy. Cesarean can be the cause of difficulties in identifying and handling the supravaginal septum, but this is not a huge problem and it is therefore only a relative contraindication. Conservative

pelvic operations on the uterus and or adnexae can leave adhesions between the genital organs and the omentum and/or intestine (sigmoid, ileum and cecum). If the approach is cautious these adhesions can be perfectly managed by the vaginal route.

Operations for peritonitis can lead to huge difficulties subsequently, depending on the nature of the peritonitis and the route of access. This is not always an absolute contraindication. In women who present with adhesions after an operation for peritonitis, the pouch of Douglas is often free and one can reach the uterine fundus more quickly by approaching it from below rather than from above.

Finally a previous abdominal operation is never an indication either for systematic laparotomy or for laparoscopic assistance. The only exception to this rule is a history of laparotomy for hysteropexy: laparoscopic assistance is mandatory in such cases.

Poorly defined adnexal pathology

When clinical examination and/or ultrasonography do not allow differentiation of a subserous fibroid from an ovarian mass it is not a good idea to operate via the vaginal route. In reality it is possible to do this, but one must perform a diagnostic laparoscopy before proceeding vaginally.

Unexplained pelvic pain

Pelvic pain seen in the absence of any obvious adnexal pathology can be due to misplacement of the pelvic cellular tissue that is eventually associated with a varicocele (Allen and Masters's syndrome). It can also be due to hidden peritoneal endometriosis in the pouch of Douglas, the uterosacral ligament and/or the rectovaginal septum. Clinical examination and imaging are not contributory in all cases. Hysterectomy practiced in a "blind" fashion will cure the patient if she has Allen and Masters's syndrome and/or a varicocele, but occult endometriosis can be more problematic. Therefore, unexplained pelvic pain affecting a woman listed for vaginal hysterectomy is an important indication for initial laparoscopic assessment.

Future

Vaginal hysterectomy nearly fell out of favor more than once since the Recamier's première in 1829. At the turn of the twentieth and twenty-first centuries, a new threat is appearing with the development of laparoscopic hysterectomy. This minimal access operation is highly appealing for both surgeons and patients. The surgery is clearly less traumatic and intraoperative bleeding is less. Comparative trials show that the postoperative course is less painful and recovery shorter. The only drawback is that these trials reported that the operative time was greater. But this drawback is disappearing as the properly trained surgeon is now able to perform laparoscopic hysterectomy within the timeframe required for vaginal hysterectomy.

The advantages of laparoscopic hysterectomy are the paradoxical consequences of one of the weaknesses of endoscopic surgery. When operating with the laparoscope, it is not easy to clamp and tie the blood vessels one has to divide. For these reasons, surgeons and manufacturers have developed alternative solutions for laparoscopic surgery such as stapling devices and electrocauterizing instruments. Refined and easy-to-use instruments are now at our disposal. One can electively and safely control ligaments and vessels. Tissue damage is strictly limited to the area of concern. As a consequence, extended necrosis and inflammatory reactions are no longer a threat.

Atraumatic laparoscopic surgical technology is now being applied to open surgery and also to vaginal surgery. The use of stapling devices, which actually started long before laparoscopic surgery, does not afford convincing benefits to the vaginal approach. But the instruments proposed for fusing tissue buntles with heat, using electrical bipolar energy, appear to be appropriate for vaginal hysterectomy. A new "electric vaginal hysterectomy" or "ligature free vaginal hysterectomy" is on the horizon, and is apparently easier, equally safe and better tolerated. Even if evidence is lacking to show that the new technique is better than the old one, and even if we lack the experience to clearly define its potential place in the different anatomico-clinical situations one is faced with, we describe here this very appealing new technique.

The new bipolar thermofusion technology

Electrosurgery was born when Arsène d'Arsonval first demonstrated the specific effect of high frequency alternating current. The subject took a giant step forward when it became possible with the use of microprocessors to modulate the energy distributed by the machines and received by the tissues.

Contemporary electrosurgical generators, such as the ERBE VIO System® (ERBE Elektromedizin GmbH, Tubingen, Germany), are able to provide (thanks to modulation of voltage and arcing) power outputs that fit the functions one assigns to electrosurgery: cutting and coagulating and all blends of these two fundamental functions. The machine (Figure 7.103) can be used in all types of operations. In vaginal surgery, diathermy loop excision of the transformation zone is an excellent application (Chapter 5). The machine is

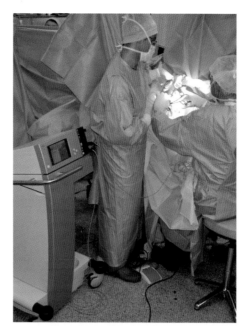

Figure 7.103 The ERBE generator.

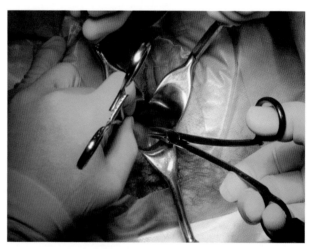

Figure 7.104 The ERBE BiClamp.

also able to provide a so-called thermofusion effect, which could make vaginal hysterectomy easier, faster and better tolerated.

The thermofusion effect is the result of two facts: the pressure exerted on the tissues thanks to a specially designed clamp, the BiClamp® (Figure 7.104), and the power distributed by the generator. The electrical power of the BiClamp mode is modulated, meaning the thermal effect is optimally adapted. At the crest of the wave the current reaches about 4 Amp. The intensity increases and decreases rapidly, which ensures the tissue fusing effect. An "autostop" digital system automatically stops the coagulation process when the optimal coagulation has been achieved, i.e. at the time the tissue impedance goes up to a defined level. This is indicated to the surgeon by a sound signal. The coagulated area develops a parchment-like appearance and can be divided without bleeding occurring (Figure 7.10 and others).

The new "ligature free" vaginal hysterectomy

Technique

The new electrocauterization technology does not exempt the surgeon and never will exempt the surgeon from identifying the anatomical spaces giving access to the ligaments, preparing these ligaments and dissecting the vessels before controlling and cutting them. The basic principles of vaginal hysterectomy remain the same. It is at the moment when one undertakes dividing the broad ligaments (third step of the operation) that things change.

Management of the paracervical ligaments

A three-step cauterization procedure replaces the two-step needling procedure we recommend for managing the paracervical ligaments. The short BiClamp takes at first the paracolpos, which means it is put perpendicular to the uterus at the level where the ventral colpotomy merges with the dorsal one. The fibers and vessels that must be controlled in this way are running to and from the small piece of vagina that one removes at the same time as the cervix. The second ones taken by the BiClamp are the true paracervical fibers (and vessels). Adequate pressure is exerted on the clamp and the power is distributed over adequate time (Figure 7.105). Having obtained sealing of the tissue, the desiccated ligament is cut (Figure 7.106). As can be seen in Figures 7.105–7.107, the convex part of the curved clamp is very close to the lateral part of the vagina and vulva. During the coagulation process the heat dramatically decreases beyond the space situated between the two jaws of the clamp but it remains 40 °C at 1 mm. This could be a source of first degree burns if the technique is used to prepare a deeply intravaginal cervix. The technique surely has to be reserved for patients offering good vaginal access.

The second step involves the uterosacral ligament that is desiccated (Figure 7.107) and divided (Figure 7.108). It is only in the third step that the paracervical ligament is, in turn, desiccated (Figure 7.109) and cut (Figure 7.110). The uterosacral and

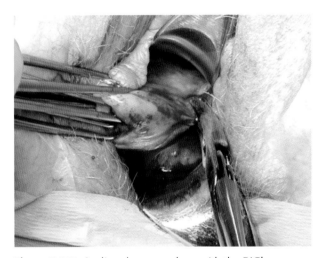

Figure 7.105 Sealing the paracolpos with the BiClamp.

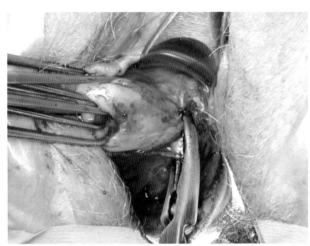

Figure 7.107 Sealing the uterosacral ligament.

Figure 7.106 Cutting the sealed paracolpos.

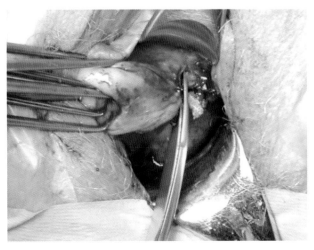

Figure 7.108 Cutting the sealed uterosacral ligament.

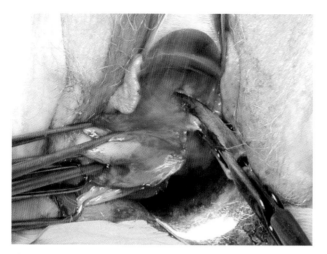

Figure 7.109 Sealing the parametrium: the arch of the uterine artery is visible cranial to the BiClamp.

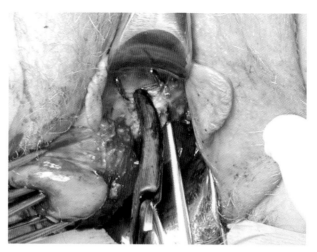

Figure 7.111 Sealing the uterine artery after it has been demonstrated with the O'Shaughnessy Clamp.

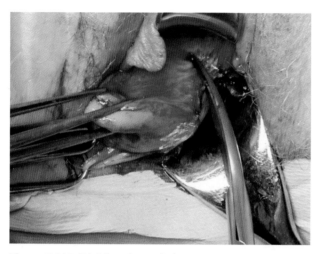

Figure 7.110 Dividing the sealed parametrium.

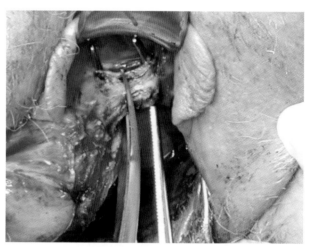

Figure 7.112 Cutting the sealed uterine artery.

paracervical ligaments are surgically managed under the permanent control of the anatomical landmarks: palpation of the paraisthmic window must be repeated before each application of the BiClamp in order to be sure one stays below and posterior (dorsal) to the arch of the uterine artery.

Management of the uterine artery
At the end of the paracervical preparation the arch of the uterine artery becomes visible. We recommend managing the vessel electively, i.e. dissecting the afferent branch of the arch at first. The arch of the artery is opened using an O'Shaughnessy dissecting forceps from back to front (see Figures 7.72 and 7.73). The dissector is opened and the afferent branch of the arch freed for 1–1.5 cm.

Desiccation of the artery should be performed in two applications (Figure 7.111). During the second application one has to take care releasing the traction

exerted on the uterus and the pressure exerted on the O'Shaughnessy forceps so as not to stretch the artery, which can escape during the second desiccation. After dividing the vessels (Figure 7.112) bleeding does not usually occur. If it does, complementary hemostasis is achieved using the standard tools of bipolar cauterization.

Management of the adnexae
Whatever the type of hysterectomy, conservative or not, the management of the adnexae can be carried out by continuing to use bipolar cauterization technology. In case of adnexal conservation, the utero-ovarian ligament, the Fallopian tube and the round ligament can either be managed separately or en bloc depending on the mode of insertion onto the uterine cornu. In case of complementary salpingo-ophorectomy the round ligament and the infundibulopelvic ligament are managed separately.

In all types of transvaginal management of Fallopian tubes and ovaries there is a risk that the lateral stumps might escape during section or stitching. This is a source of bleeding that is hard to fix and can lead to conversion to laparotomy or, better, to laparoscopy. The hazards, surely, are more if one uses bipolar cauterization technology. It seems wise to clamp and stitch (endoloop) in cases where the tension to be exerted on the ligaments is strong.

Closing the vagina

As the "ligature free" vaginal hysterectomy is a reverse copy of the laparoscopic hysterectomy, closure can be performed in the same way, i.e. without re-peritonealization and by performing a complete suture onto the vaginal vault. Before undertaking this stitch, which will be the only one of the operation, one assesses carefully the area where the stumps of the paracervical ligaments are situated. The triangular shape of the area of insertion of the paracervical ligament is fully recognizable with the stump of the uterine artery at the tip of the triangle (Figure 7.113). If bleeders are identified they are controlled by standard bipolar cauterization, then the stitch is initiated: this brings together the ventral and dorsal vaginal walls starting from the left angle (Figure 7.114) and finishing at the right angle (Figure 7.115).

Benefits of the "ligature free" vaginal hysterectomy, foreseeable pitfalls and potential place in the gynecologic surgery repertoire

Great experience is not required to appreciate the indisputable advantages of the new bipolar cauterization technology. Intraoperative bleeding is almost zero. Postoperative pain is almost nonexistent. The latter is likely to be attributed to the absence of necrotic phenomena, which occur at the level of the big stumps one leaves in place using the standard technique. These phenomena, which are the potential source of vaginal vault abscesses, oblige us, we believe, to re-peritonealize and to avoid total closure of the vaginal vault at the end of the standard vaginal hysterectomy. In the "ligature free" technique the final step of the operation is different with two advantages. The first is the absence of re-peritonealization contributing to the lowering of postoperative pain. The second advantage is the complete closure of the vagina reducing the risk of vaginal vault granulations.

As opposed to its advantages, the new bipolar cauterization technique includes an obvious drawback, which is the counterpart of its main advantage: there are situations where we need strong ligamentous stumps in order to reattach the vaginal vault to its

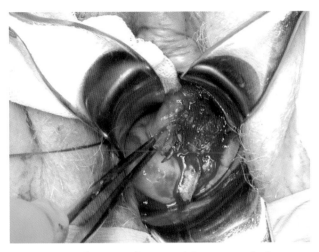

Figure 7.113 The parietal stump of the paracervical ligaments: note the uterine vessels at the apex of the triangle as seen on the visceral stump (see Figure 7.38).

Figure 7.114 The first step of the vaginal suture: note that this suture hides the stumps.

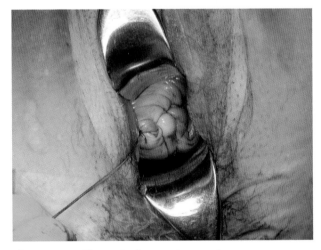

Figure 7.115 The vaginal suture is complete.

natural supports. It is theoretically possible to desiccate the ligaments with the BiClamp, to cut them and then to stitch the lateral stumps. However this sequence is neither logical nor easy and safe (stitching the ligaments after having cut them is more dangerous because anatomical relationships are no longer identifiable). Finally, the ligature free technique is only usable in cases where there is no prolapse or no potential prolapse.

On the other hand, one has to recognize that the ligature free vaginal hysterectomy can be difficult to perform and/or dangerous in some cases where a non-prolapsed uterus has to be removed transvaginally. If the cervix does not arrive flush with the vulvar orifice, putting the BiClamp in place can be a problem (Figure 7.103). If the traction one has to exert on the uterus stretches the vessels too much they escape, which is another problem. At the end of the day one can tell that the new technology is undoubtedly a great step forward. Laparoscopy is beaten in its own field of excellence: the same atraumatic technique yet much more rapid and simpler and without the hazards of the endoscopic approach. However, new technology will never be exempt from careful astute assessment. A complex problem will never be solved by a universal simplistic technique.

8 Genital prolapse

In this chapter devoted to the management of genital prolapse, we restrict ourselves (of course) to operations using the vaginal route. These operations are performed to correct so-called pelvic relaxation (prolapse), which can also be managed by laparotomy, an approach that has never really become popular. This does not apply to laparoscopic operations, which bask in the glory of minimally invasive surgery. However, laparoscopic operations are based on the same rationale as operations performed in the past by laparotomy and, in our opinion, this rationale isn't rational!

A sort of auto-blocking mechanism guarantees normal pelvic "statics" (Figure 8.1). The pelvic organs are subject to pressures that are exerted in the umbilical– coccygeal axis. These pressures are initially exerted on the uterine fundus whose ante-flexion is accentuated. The cervix, on the contrary, is maintained in its dorsal position thanks to the tone of the so-called uterosacral ligaments. As a consequence, the uterine fundus is pushed over the bladder dome under the force of these pressures. The pressure is transmitted through the bladder to the fascia of Halban (vesicovaginal septum), and then thanks to the virtual character of the vaginal cavity, transmitted to the fascia of Denonvilliers (rectovaginal septum) and to the perineal body supported by the puborectalis muscle. The tone of these muscles increases in response to this pressure making the vaginal angle more acute: the greater the pressure the more acute the angle. This is the auto-blocking mechanism, which prevents the vagina from folding back on itself. In women affected by genital prolapse, the auto-blocking system does not work anymore.

Destruction of the perineal body and alteration of the puborectalis muscles comprise the first pathophysiological events in the natural history of genital prolapse. The buffer of the core of the perineal body disappears. Once the puborectalis muscle has been destroyed or thinned and weakened, the urogenital hiatus becomes widely open. The ventral vaginal

(a)

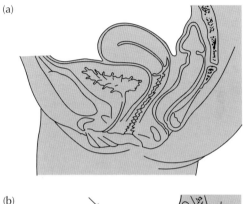

(b)

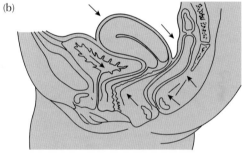

Figure 8.1 Artist's impression of the auto-blocking system. The excess pressure exerted on the pelvic organs pushes the vaginal vault dorsally and caudally producing a response from the pelviperineal muscles. The angulation of the cape of the vagina becomes more acute preventing intussusception. Reproduced from Dargent D., Mathevet P., Mellier G. (2002) Traitement chirurgical des prolapsus génitaux par la voie vaginale. EMC – Traité de Techniques chirurgicales – Gynécologie, 41: 800–824, Paris: Elsevier, by permission of Elsevier.

wall sticks out. It pulls the uterine cervix downward, reduces the physiological anteversion of the uterine body and facilitates eversion. Fascial thinning is the second event that encourages the development of pelvic relaxation. This thinning is at the same time both cause and consequence of the bulging of the vagina. The vagina will not bulge if the fascia resists. It is because it bulges that the fascia becomes thinner. The same issues are pertinent to the third factor that is implicated in the genesis of genital prolapse.

Elongation of the so-called suspensory ligaments is the third pathophysiological event. For decades, deficiency of the uterosacral ligaments has been a subject for discussion. Not so the parametria, whose orientation (oblique from back to front and from outside to inside) and constitution (elastic connective tissue surrounding blood vessels) contribute to the efficiency of the system that maintains the cervix in its cranial and dorsal position. The progressive regression of the genital blood supply observed after menopause, leads to weakening of the cardinal ligaments explaining why the incidence of genital prolapse increases at this time of life. As far as the lateral stabilizers of the vagina are concerned, one hears a lot about the so-called paravaginal defect, which is likely to be present in 30–40% of cases with genital prolapse. In actual fact, anchorage of the lateral edge of the vagina to the pelvic sidewall is debatable. The arcus tendineus fascia pelvici is not a constant structure. Neither is the pelvic fascia. At least, it is more than easy in normal cases to detach the vagina from the pelvic sidewall by means of gentle digital pressure and this disruption, which is performed during radical hysterectomy, does not result in genital prolapse.

The essential aim of operations performed abdominally for pelvic relaxation is to restore the so-called suspensory ligaments. Sacrocolpopexy aims to restore the uterosacral ligaments (mesh attaches the cervix and/or the vaginal vault to the promontory of the sacrum). The stitches one performs during the so-called paravaginal repair restore the pelvic aponeurosis and reconstitute the lateral attachments of the vagina. The meshes one attaches to the ventral and dorsal walls of the vagina to suspend from the promontory of the sacrum and/or from the arcus tendineus aim to replace the thinned fascia. At the end of the day these actions correct elongation of the suspensory ligaments and thinning of the fascia. However, rebuilding the central perineal body and reducing levator diastasis are neglected. Even if it is possible to gain access to the cranial aspect of the levator muscles to suture them to re-approximate them to each other and/or to suspend them to the sacrum, the other surface of the pelvic diaphragm cannot be reached and a true levator plasty is not possible.

The rationale of operations performed vaginally is quite different. The seminal step comprises reconstruction of the central fibrous core of the perineal body and correction of the levator diastasis. The vagina is restored to its normal bisegmental morphology (see Chapter 2) and in this way the auto-blocking system, which ensures stability of the pelvic organs, is also restored. The second objective of the vaginal operation is to restore normal tension in the distended fascia and in this way to allow normal transmission of pressures. This restoration however has its limitations. In cases where fascial thinning is very severe ("deadly thinning") it cannot be "resuscitated" and so is replaced by mesh. It is possible to introduce mesh using the vaginal route but this is a more dangerous approach and the risk increases with the size of the mesh.

Technique

Even if one deliberately excludes operations performed from above there are innumerable procedures for correction of pelvic relaxation. Faithful to the spirit of this book we only describe herein the technique we routinely use: the triple perineal operation with hysterectomy. This operation has replaced the so-called Manchester operation (Fothergill triple perineal operation) in which the cervix was amputated but the uterine body left in place. The current operation starts with a hysterectomy that is followed by reshaping of the ventral and dorsal walls of the vagina.

Hysterectomy is doubly useful in women treated for pelvic relaxation. Descent of the uterus is not the only element of prolapse, but if it exists it must be addressed. Hysterectomy is the simplest way to solve this problem! Furthermore, the uterus in these cases is generally affected by the diverse and various pathologies associated with aging: hysterectomy definitively cures these pathologies.

Reshaping of the ventral and dorsal vaginal walls plays a seminal role. It is obviously mandatory in cases where there is ventral and dorsal bulging but it must also be performed in cases where bulging is minimal or inapparent.

Hysterectomy

The technique we recommend for hysterectomy performed in the framework of surgery for pelvic relaxation is not different from the technique we recommend for managing benign disease that has developed in a non-prolapsed uterus. Many surgeons recommend making a T-shaped incision on the ventral vaginal wall, or two oblique incisions outlining a triangle with a ventral apex. This "shape-cutting" leads to bleeding, which it is best not to start in the first place. Furthermore, the identification of the space separating the vagina from the bladder is easier after hysterectomy than before.

Hysterectomy on a prolapsed uterus is apparently easier than hysterectomy on a non-prolapsed uterus. This is often a false impression. In case of the former, the position of the urinary bladder is unpredictable.

The lengthening of the supravaginal part of the cervix makes the supravaginal septum thicker and in any case more difficult to traverse. Intrafascial false passages are more frequent. It is necessary to carefully respect the rules laid out in Chapter 7. On the other hand the lengthening of the supravaginal part of the cervix is generally associated with atrophy and one can easily get lost laterally and penetrate the bladder pillars in error. To avoid mistakes it is necessary, as soon as the supravaginal septum is opened, to palpate with a finger to identify the correct path that one must follow.

Bilateral adnexectomy, taking the age of the patients affected by genital prolapse into account, is almost a medico-legal obligation. It is not invariably easy because the "scleroatrophic" ovaries are often in a high position – the older the patient the higher the ovaries. Now, the benefit of prophylactic adnexectomy lessens with age. For patients over 70 years there is no reason to take risks if the adnexectomy appears difficult. But in younger women, on the contrary, one has to insist on it even if this leads to complimentary laparoscopy.

When operating on a woman with genital prolapse, re-peritonealization is performed using a specific technique. This is a step of the so-called culdoplasty, i.e. the plasty of the upper part of the dorsal vaginal wall. This culdoplasty, which is part dorsal colporrhaphy, is described on p. 93.

Ventral colporrhaphy

The ventral colpocele or cystocele is an almost constant component of the complex of lesions defining genital prolapse. As a consequence the so-called ventral colporrhaphy is a quasi obligation during surgery for pelvic relaxation. The greater the prolapse is the easier the preparation. In contrast the restoring part of the colporrhaphy is as complicated as the tissue damage is severe. The standard colporrhaphy is described herein later. The complementary procedures to add in advanced and/or complex cases are described in the section "Indications and contraindications" on p. 105.

The so-called anterior repair involves five steps. The first is a midline ventral colpotomy. The second is mobilization of the urinary bladder. The third is splitting of the vaginal flaps that isolate the vesicovaginal septum or fascia of Halban. The fourth is a "cardigan" (overlapping) plasty of the fascia. The fifth comprises colpectomy and colporrhaphy.

In order to do a midline ventral colpotomy we take the ventral vaginal wall with two Cotte forceps placed side by side on the midline. Exerting traction

directly upward one exposes the inferior part of the urinary bladder. Having taken this inferior part with surgical forceps, one draws it down. This countertraction action exposes, between the three instruments, a triangular connective tissue structure that corresponds to the condensation of fibers separating the bladder from the deepest aspect of the vaginal wall. These fibers are cut in the midline using Mayo scissors with the tips directed forward (Figure 8.2). This first "moucheture" opens the space situated between the bladder and the deep aspect of the vaginal wall. It is an anatomical space in which one proceeds without difficulty by pushing the scissors held in a closed position (Figure 8.3) and removing them in an open position. The action is repeated until one perceives a feeling of resistance. One must then refrain from going deeper. The part of the vaginal

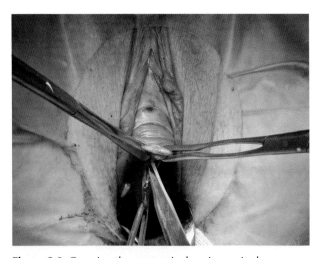

Figure 8.2 Opening the anatomical vesicovaginal space: hysterectomy has been done, the ventral vaginal flap is everted by two Gaston Cotte forceps applied to either side of the midline and the bladder is drawn downward.

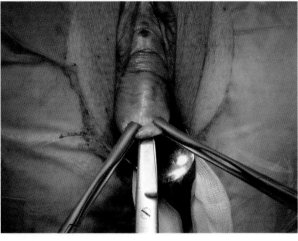

Figure 8.3 The scissors are introduced into the anatomical vesicovaginal space along the midline.

wall that has been separated from the bladder can now be cut on the midline (Figure 8.4). In order to proceed one places, at the superior angle of this incision, two new Cotte forceps on which one exerts diverging traction to perform, as before, the actions to open the space (Figure 8.5) and to then cut the vagina on the midline. It is generally necessary to do this a third time. The aim is to reach the junction of the intermediate and ventral thirds of the vaginal wall (Figure 8.6). This point corresponds to the bladder neck. For women affected by urinary stress incontinence (which has either been confessed or detected by clinical and/or paraclinical assessment) it is necessary to perform specific procedures on the bladder neck and/or on the proximal urethra. These techniques and their indications will be described later. In cases without urinary symptomatology it is at the level of the junction of the intermediate third and the ventral third that one stops the colpotomy and also the colporrhaphy.

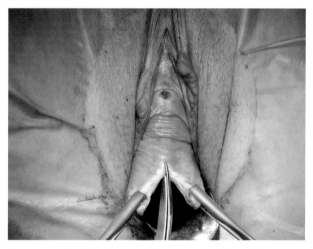

Figure 8.4 The freed vaginal flap is cut on the midline.

Bladder mobilization is performed in two steps. One starts as one wishes either on the right or on the left side. One asks for divergent traction on the three Cotte forceps that have been put on the edge of the vaginal flap (the assistant on the same side as the flap exerts, with his two hands, traction on the first and second forceps, and the other assistant exerts traction on the third forceps). This divergent traction exposes the deep surface of the vaginal flap that will be separated from the urinary bladder. It is at the most dorsal part that one has to start mobilization because this is the place where it is easiest. The bladder is taken with a surgical forceps and traction and releasing actions are alternated to identify the connective fibers one will have to cut. One cuts them with the tip of the scalpel (Figure 8.7). At the level of the intermediate third the separation of the urinary bladder becomes less easy. One has to try to follow the same plane one has identified at the beginning. One goes on working with the tip of the scalpel and continues the process with the handle (Figure 8.8). The line where one has to stop is identified through an increase in resistance to blunt dissection and, almost inevitably, to the occurrence of bleeding, which generally happens in the upper part. This bleeding signifies that one has reached the lateral limit of the vaginal mobilization. The fascia whose deepest aspect is mobilized is nothing other than the vessel holder of the vaginal wall whose blood supply is provided by the collaterals of the vaginal artery, which branches from the internal iliac artery and also gives raise to the arteries devoted to the bladder floor, i.e. the inferior vesical arteries. The vascular bundle one reaches at the end of lateral mobilization can be detached medially from the pelvic sidewall (this detachment has to be carried out in order to correct the paravaginal defect: see later). But in the standard operation the linea vasorum is the place where the lateral mobilization of the vaginal wall must stop. Bleeding, if it occurs at the lateral limit of the dissection, is

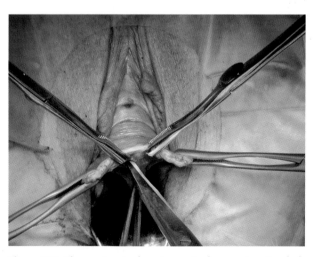

Figure 8.5 The anatomical vesicovaginal space is extended after application of two further Gaston Cotte forceps.

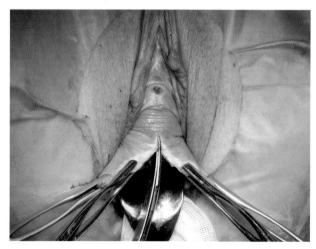

Figure 8.6 The midline colpotomy is extended.

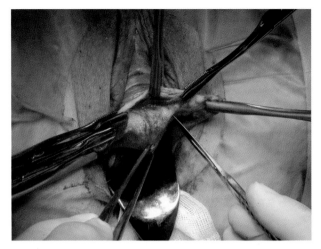

Figure 8.7 Separating the bladder from the deep surface of the vaginal flap on the left side. Note that three Gaston Cotte forceps are put on the edge of the vaginal flap and are held in separate assisting hands to spread the flap out. The bladder is drawn in the opposite direction. The fibers interposed between the flap and the bladder are cut with the tip of the scalpel.

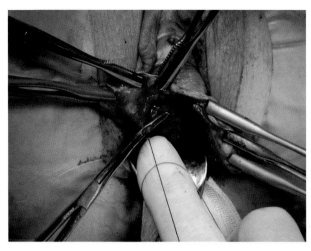

Figure 8.9 Controlling a bleeder on the deep aspect of the vaginal flap. Being behind the vesicovaginal septum, which is the vaginal vessel holder, bleeding is unavoidable when mobilizing the flap laterally.

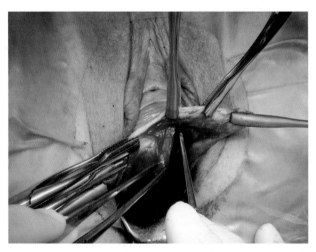

Figure 8.8 Separating the bladder from the deep surface of the vaginal flap on the left side: the job is finished using the handle of the scalpel (we are in the anatomical vesicovaginal space).

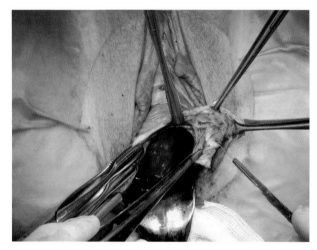

Figure 8.10 Splitting the vaginal flap. The vesicovaginal septum is separated from the vaginal wall. This is the surgical vesicovaginal space.

stopped either by bipolar cauterization or by stitching around a right-angle forceps (Figure 8.9).

Splitting the vaginal flaps reveals the fascia of Halban. If the initial dissection has been performed in the right plane and if the bladder has been correctly separated from the deep surface of the vaginal flap, the so-called pubo-urethro-vesico-uterine fascia is easily revealed. This splitting is initiated at the level of the dorsal part. An Allis forceps that takes only vaginal wall replaces the Gaston Cotte forceps. The fascia is taken with a surgical forceps and separated from the vaginal wall itself with the tip of a

scalpel (Figure 8.10). The plane thus opened is not an anatomical plane but it is rather easy to open, at least it is at the level of the dorsal part. Dissection proceeds in the same plane once the Cotte forceps have been replaced by Allis forceps. This is done with the tip and then with the handle of the scalpel (Figure 8.11). The lateral limit of the splitting of the vaginal wall is at the same level as the lateral limit of the mobilization of the vaginal wall, i.e. the linea vasorum. The same actions are repeated on the other side. Once splitting of the two vaginal flaps has been achieved, four flaps are available for covering the caudal aspect of the bladder floor (Figure 8.12).

The fascial repair is performed by overlapping the two flaps. The edge of the left fascial flap is joined to

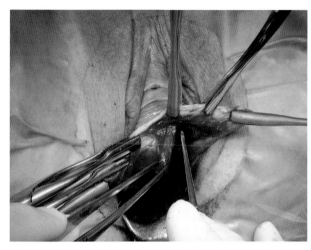

Figure 8.11 Splitting the vaginal flap on the left side: the job is finished with the handle of the scalpel.

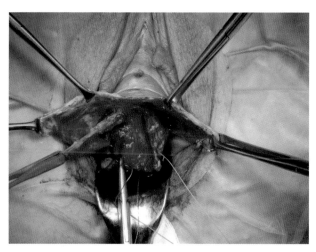

Figure 8.13 The first cardigan suture: the edge of the left fascial flap is joined to the hinge of the deep surface of the fascial shutter on the right side.

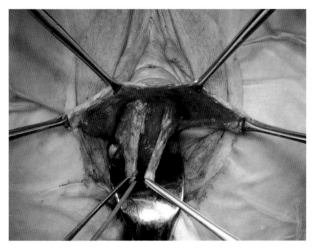

Figure 8.12 The two vaginal and two fascial flaps.

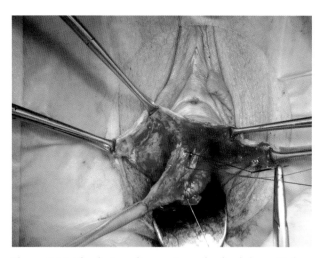

Figure 8.14 The first cardigan suture: the final deep stitch.

the hinge of the deep surface of the fascial shutter on the right (Figure 8.13) using a short continuous suture (Figure 8.14) or three to four interrupted stitches. One must take care not to transfix the vaginal flap at the same time as the fascial flap. Once the first fascial flap is in place the second one is closed over the surface of the first (Figure 8.15). The "cardigan" closure of the vesicovaginal septum approximates the hinges of the fascial shutters, which remain attached to the bladder. The objective is the same as when one performs a classical plication, placing stitches in the fascia that is left in place in contact with the bladder: the lower part of the bladder is elevated. In the "cardigan" technique the result is the same but the bladder is sustained by a double thickness of fascial tissue.

The colporrhaphy itself is carried out after two symmetrical colpectomies have been performed. These

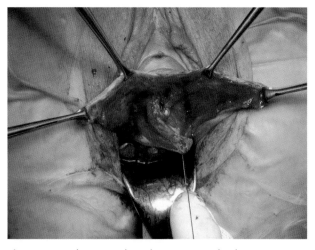

Figure 8.15 The second cardigan suture: the first step.

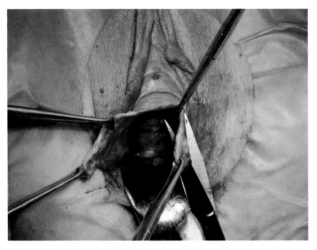

Figure 8.16 Colpectomy: only a small triangle is removed. Don't be too enthusiastic!

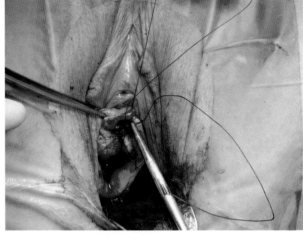

Figure 8.18 Completing the ventral vaginal suture and reaching the paracervical stumps.

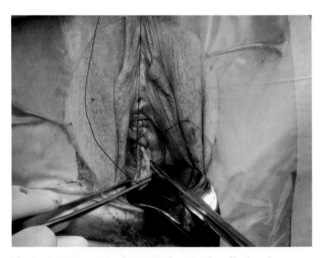

Figure 8.17 Suturing the ventral vaginal wall after the two symmetrical economical colpectomies.

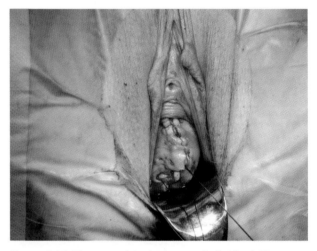

Figure 8.19 The ventral vaginal suture is finished. The McCall stitch, which was prepared just after the hysterectomy, is now ready to be tied (see Figures 8.24 and 8.25).

colpectomies have to be as economical as possible. Using curved scissors, a small triangle of vaginal wall is removed. The triangle has a dorsal base and a ventral tip. Its lateral margin must be curvilinear (Figure 8.16). Once two triangular areas of tissue have been removed, one re-approximates the two vaginal flaps on the midline with either a short continuous suture (Figure 8.17) or interrupted stitches. The advantage of interrupted stitches is that they do not shorten the vaginal wall. The suture is continued just as far as the stumps of the paracervical ligaments (Figures 8.18 and 8.19).

Dorsal colporrhaphy

Prolapse surgery is inconsequential unless the perineal body is reshaped and plasty of the levator ani muscles is performed, and there is no simpler and more anatomical way to do this than by performing

dorsal colporrhaphy. Dorsal colporrhaphy is a mandatory part of the triple perineal operation and has two main constituent parts: reshaping and suspension of the vaginal vault or culdoplasty and reshaping of the dorsal vaginal wall. The latter is combined with levator plasty and with perineal body reconstruction and these last two actions are linked in the acronym colpoperineorrhaphy.

Culdoplasty

Reshaping the vaginal vault has two main constituent parts: removing redundant distorted vagina and removing the redundant pelvic peritoneal rectouterine cul de sac (the deepening of the cul de sac is both part of the "lesional complex" and an etiological constituent of it). Strictly speaking, this culdoplasty has to be combined with re-suspension of the vault. In most cases, the shortening of the uterosacral liga- ments produced by the so-called McCall stitch is enough. It is described later. In cases of major pelvic relaxation a different technique is required and will be described in the section "Indications and con- traindications" on p. 105.

Strictly speaking, the culdoplasty is initiated as soon as the hysterectomy is finished. Re-peritonealization after hysterectomy for prolapse is achieved using two angle stitches (see Chapter 7) and one intermediate continuous suture. But unlike the technique used after removal of a non-prolapsed uterus, one per- forms angle stitches before contracting the vaginal orifice with the "godronnage" (gathering stitch). On the other hand, the continuous suture joining the

rectal peritoneum to the vesical peritoneum is performed at a different level. The line along which the stitches are inserted on the vesical peritoneum is irrelevant but the line of stitches inserted on the rec- tal peritoneum must be as high as possible. It is nec- essary to pull the ventral aspect of the rectum (held in surgical forceps) downward while inserting the stitches (Figure 8.20).

To reshape the vaginal wall, a triangular area is resected from the dorsal third of the dorsal wall. At first, two forceps are placed on the dorsal vaginal wall as close as possible to the points of insertion of the paracervical ligaments. Upward divergent trac- tion is exerted on these forceps. Next, the dorsal vagi- nal wall is taken with surgical forceps on the midline at the junction of the intermediate and dorsal thirds. Downward countertraction is applied to these for- ceps. The three instruments delineate a triangle from within which a piece of vagina will be removed. One

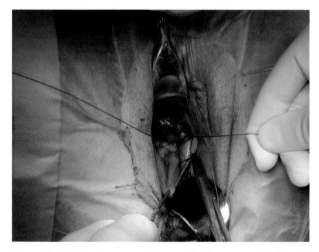

Figure 8.20 The first step of the culdoplasty or vaginal vault plasty: after hysterectomy and angle peritoneal stitches, the rectal peritoneum taken as high as possible and the bladder peritoneum are approximated.

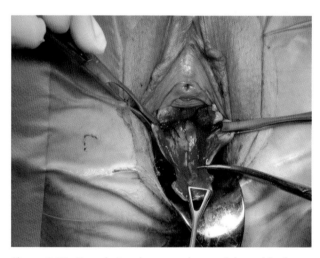

Figure 8.22 Completing the second step of the culdoplasty.

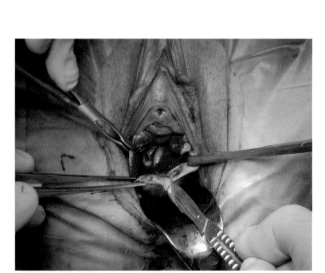

Figure 8.21 The second step of the culdoplasty: a triangle-shaped resection of the posterior vaginal wall is performed between the two paracervical stumps.

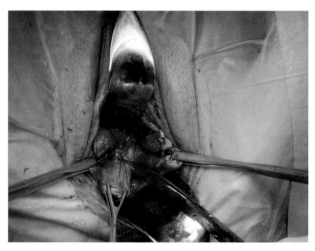

Figure 8.23 The third step of the culdoplasty: the redundant part of the rectal peritoneum is removed (low Douglasectomy).

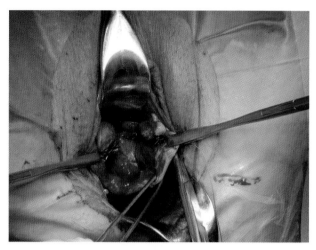

Figure 8.24 The fourth step of the culdoplasty, the McCall suture: the first stitch is inserted through the vaginal wall in contact with the paracervical stump on the left side.

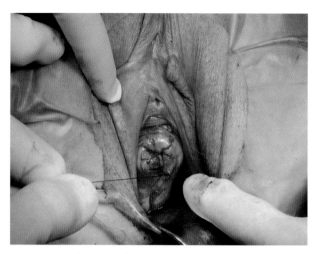

Figure 8.26 The McCall suture is tied. This suture is prepared as the last step of the culdoplasty just after hysterectomy is performed. However, it is not tied until the ventral colporrhaphy is finished.

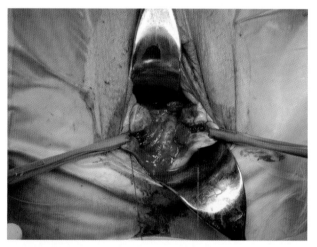

Figure 8.25 The McCall suture is finished. It takes the vaginal wall, the uterosacral ligament, the anterior surface of the rectum just below the peritonealization suture, and then the uterosacral ligament and the vaginal wall on the other side.

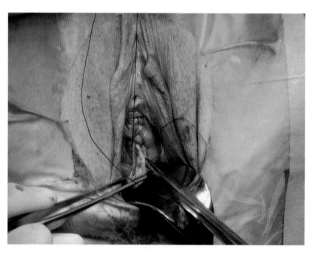

Figure 8.27 Suturing the dorsal vaginal wall with the thread used for the McCall stitch. This constitutes the very last step of the culdoplasty.

starts with the first lateral incision starting from one extremity of the base of the triangle and going to its tip (Figure 8.21). The same is done on the other side. Then the base of the triangle is grasped with two Cotte forceps and pulled downward. The forefinger of the nonoperating hand is placed behind the triangular flap and by pushing it one is able to detach the vagina from the underlying structures while closely shaving its deep surface with a scalpel (Figure 8.22). Although it generally moves out of the way, take note and take care of the rectum with each move of the scalpel.

Once the upper triangular colpectomy has been carried out the ventral surface of the rectum is exposed. It is, in its upper part, covered with a

peritoneal leaf that must be removed. In order to excise it, one detaches it from the bottom to the top with the tip of the scissors (Figure 8.23) before cutting it at the point where it is attached to the vesical peritoneum. As soon as this "Douglas-ectomy" has been performed one anchors the vaginal vault to the uterosacral ligaments following the principle of the so-called McCall stitch. This stitch is performed in five steps. First, the left vaginal flap is stitched as close as possible to the insertion of the uterosacral ligament (Figure 8.24). Then the uterosacral ligament itself is stitched. The third stitch is inserted into the ventral surface of the rectum just below the re-peritonealizing stitch. The fourth and fifth stitches are inserted into the right uterosacral ligament and through the right vaginal flap close to the ligament.

Figure 8.25 demonstrates the finished stitch. At the time this stitch is tied (Figure 8.26) the vaginal vault is anchored to the uterosacral ligaments and the reshaped cul de sac of Douglas supported by the ligamentous repair. It is with the same suture that is used to make the McCall stitch that the colporrhaphy itself will be performed. The two lateral edges of the triangle will be re-approximated thanks to a short running suture (Figure 8.27). The last stitch of this suture will form the summit of the dorsal repair.

Colpoperineorrhaphy

The lower part of the posterior repair aims to reshape the abnormal bulging of the lower part of the dorsal wall of the vagina, to correct the underlying rectocele, to restore the levator diaphragm and to rebuild the central fibrous core of the perineum. This is done in eight steps: mucocutaneous resection, opening of the pararectal spaces, management of the rectocele, stitching of the levator muscles and the central fibrous core of the perineum, closure of the colpotomy and tying the stitches previously placed in the muscles.

The colpoperineorrhaphy includes mandatory removal of the redundant part of the distorted dorsal vaginal wall. However, this resection must be strictly limited to the lower third and resections of the middle third should not be performed. These latter resections are the cause of narrowing of the vagina and dyspareunia (which is often falsely attributed to the myorrhaphy) and have contributed to unwarranted criticism of myorrhaphy, which is in fact a more than useful part of the triple operation for genital prolapse. Removal of the redundant part of the dorsal vaginal wall is performed within a triangle-shaped frame. This triangle is adjacent to another triangle drawn on the skin of the perineum and the two triangles together constitute a diamond. The two halves of this diamond are detached one after the other. The base of the two triangles is located while placing two tenacula on the dorsal extremities of the labia majora. These tenacula have to be far enough away from each other to correct gaping of the vulva. However, if placed too far from each other, stenosis of the introitus (a source of dyspareunia) will result. With divergent downward traction applied to these two tenacula, one places a strong forceps on the midline of the dorsal vaginal wall at the junction of the dorsal and intermediate thirds (Figure 8.28). Upward countertraction is applied to this forceps.

With a scalpel, two lateral incisions are made from the midline forceps to each of the two tenacula, incising all layers of the vaginal wall (Figure 8.29). The triangular vaginal flap delineated by the two lateral incisions is then elevated from top to bottom. Its top is grasped in a Cotte forceps and pulled

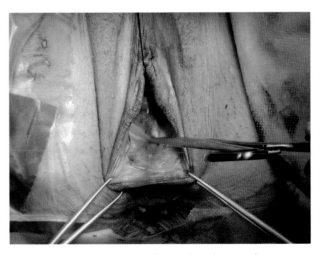

Figure 8.28 Delineating the lower dorsal triangular colpectomy.

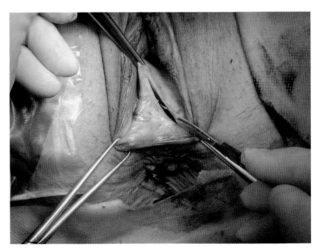

Figure 8.29 The first lateral incision. Note the traction and countertraction exerted on the Kochers placed at the apex of the triangle and the tenaculum, placed at end of the base of the triangle.

downward. Using the tip of the scalpel the deep surface of the flap is detached from the ventral surface of the rectum, which is covered by the fascia of Denonvilliers. The dissection is continued up to the base of the triangle (Figure 8.30), the forefinger of the nonoperating hand pushing onto the superficial surface of the vaginal flap to keep the deep surface in contact with the scalpel.

The inferior triangle of the mucocutaneous diamond-like resection is drawn on the skin of the perineum. The base of the triangle is the line joining the ends of the two tenacula. These are pulled upwards before the skin is incised obliquely aiming at a point on the midline equidistant from the fourchette and the anus (Figure 8.31). The skin at the summit of the triangle is grasped and pulled upward in the same way that the summit of the vaginal triangle was elevated before.

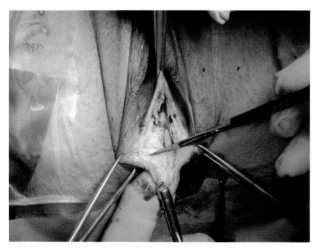

Figure 8.30 Detaching the triangular flap from the perineal body working from the apex to the base rather than the other way around – this reduces the risk of injury to the rectoanal junction because obstetric scar tissue is more common in the lower part.

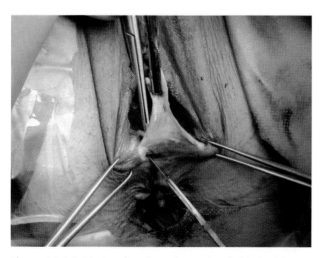

Figure 8.31 Initiating the triangular perineal skin incision.

The hinge of this fold is situated in front of the angle of the anus and it is freed with a stroke of the scalpel (Figure 8.32).

The pararectal spaces are opened one after the other. In order to open the left pararectal space a traction forceps is put on the left vaginal flap. By pulling on this forceps at the same time as on the ipsilateral tenaculum and also on the forceps at the summit of the triangle of the mucosal resection, the flap is put under tension. The rectum is grasped with the surgical forceps and pulled medially. The traction exerted on the vaginal flap and this countertraction expose the connective fibers joining the rectum to the deep surface of the vagina. They are cut with the tip of the scalpel handled perpendicularly to the vaginal flap (Figure 8.33). This action is repeated until one finds the loose cellular tissue of the paravesical space. One can move to the other side (Figure 8.34) and

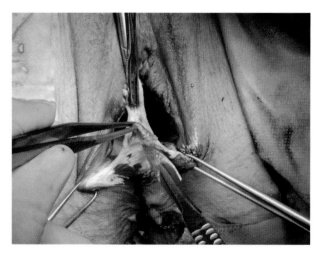

Figure 8.32 The diamond-shaped mucocutaneous flap is detached from the perineal body.

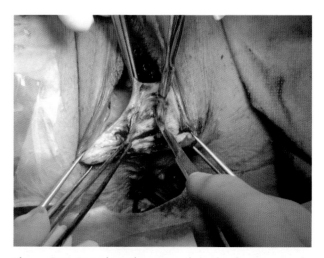

Figure 8.33 Detaching the rectum from the deep aspect of the vaginal flap on the left side. A Gaston Cotte forceps has been applied to the intermediate part of the flap. This instrument like the Kocher forceps and the tenaculum applied to the edges of the flap are held in separate assisting hands to spread it out.

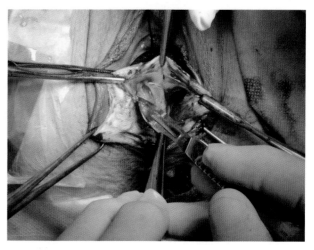

Figure 8.34 The same is done on the right side. Note the smooth arachnoid connective tissue of the pararectal space.

enlarge the opening with the handle of the scalpel (Figure 8.35).

Having opened the two pararectal spaces and exposed the lateral surfaces of the rectum, mobilization of the dorsal vaginal wall is completed while separating on the midline the adhesions that fix it to the ventral surface of the rectum. Once this mobilization is complete, one stroke of the scissors on the midline separates the dorsal vaginal wall from the summit of the lower triangle to the summit of the upper triangle (Figure 8.36). At the end of the day we have carried out an inverted Y-shaped incision that totally exposes the lateral and ventral surface of the rectum at the same time as the contour of the puborectal and iliococcygeus muscles. We are now ready to repair the rectocele and perform myorrhaphy and perineorrhaphy.

To repair the rectocele we recommend introducing the forefinger of the nonoperating hand into the rectum. One pushes from back to front and exposes the rectal mucosa that has herniated through the muscular layer of the intestine. The muscular layer, which is pushed away laterally by the hernia, is stitched at the upper angle of this hernia (Figure 8.37). We use either 00 Vicryl or PDS and we continue from top to bottom (Figure 8.38) until reaching the perineal body.

We recommend using the Emmet needle for the myorrhaphy. With this needle, the two levator muscles are taken successively. In order to stitch the left

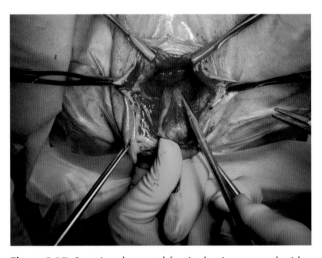

Figure 8.37 Suturing the rectal fascia: having opened wide the two pararectal spaces and exposed the ventrolateral aspects of the rectum, the forefinger of the nonoperating hand is introduced into the anal canal and hooked. The rectocele, i.e. the hernia of the rectal mucosa through the weakened rectal fascia, is demonstrated and the repairing stitch inserted.

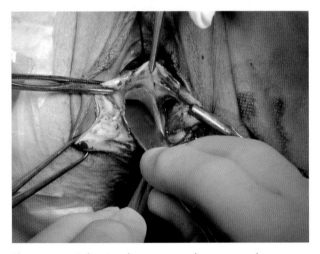

Figure 8.35 Enlarging the access to the pararectal space.

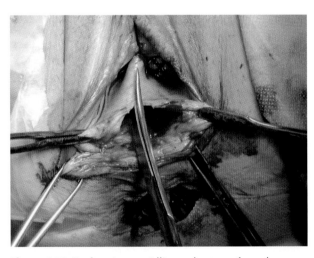

Figure 8.36 Performing a midline colpotomy from the apex of the lower triangular colpectomy to the apex of the upper dorsal colporrhaphy.

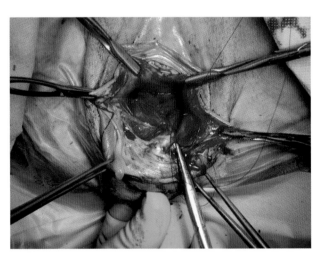

Figure 8.38 The rectorrhaphy suture is stitched to the perineal body.

muscle the forefinger of the nonoperating hand is put in the pararectal space. This finger pushes the lateral surface of the rectum away with its dorsal surface and palpates the superior brim of the muscle with its tip. The ipsilateral vaginal flap is pulled laterally and the needle transfixes the muscle from front to back (Figure 8.39). Before the needle comes in contact with the tip of the forefinger, a turning movement makes the tip of the needle visible deep in the operative field. This is lateral to the rectum, which is protected by the forefinger (Figure 8.40). Transfixion of the contralateral levator is performed using the same technique. When the tip of the needle appears in the operative field, the perineal extremity of the suture is put in the eye of the needle (Figure 8.41) and the suture is passed around the muscle. The advantage of the Emmet needle is that it allows one to stitch both

muscles in exactly the same way taking exactly the same thickness of each. If we use a standard needle, it is easy to stitch one of the muscles front to back. But in stitching the contralateral one with the same needle from back to front, one never succeeds in taking the same amount of muscle tissue. The same Emmet needle is used to make the second stitch, which is made using the same technique in a more superficial location. Traction on the first myorrhaphy stitch allows one to position the second stitch in a more superficial position (Figure 8.42). From the anatomical viewpoint the first stitch involves the puborectalis muscles and the lower fibers of the iliococcygeus muscles. The second stitch involves the perineal body and the lower part of the puborectalis muscles. The muscular stitches are not immediately approximated. One has to first close the inverted

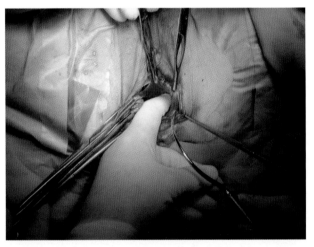

Figure 8.39 The first stitch of the levator myorrhaphy – the first movement on the left side: the Emmet needle is pushed from front to back in a lateral direction.

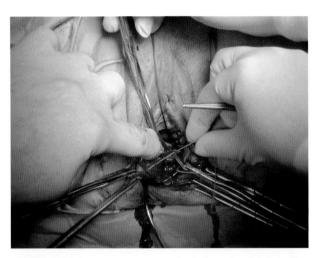

Figure 8.41 The same action on the right side. The thread is put through the eye of the needle that has been pushed through the right levator ani.

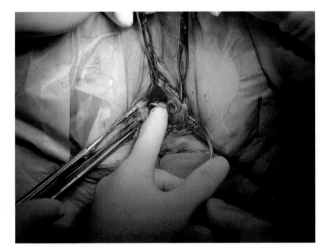

Figure 8.40 The first stitch of the levator myorrhaphy – the second movement on the left side: the Emmet needle is rotated with a spiral movement. Note the width of the piece of muscle thus taken.

Figure 8.42 The second stitch of the levator myorrhaphy: pulling on the first stitch allows placement of the second stitch closer to the vagina.

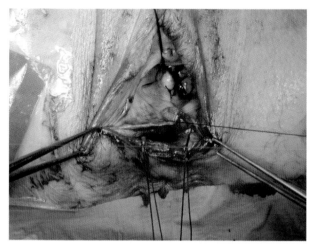

Figure 8.43 Initiating the inferior dorsal vaginal closure (colporrhaphy). This suture has to be performed before the two levator myorrhaphy sutures are tied.

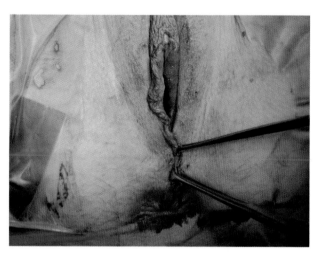

Figure 8.46 Cutaneous closure: the endogenic glue does its job if the Allis clamps are left in situ for 6 min.

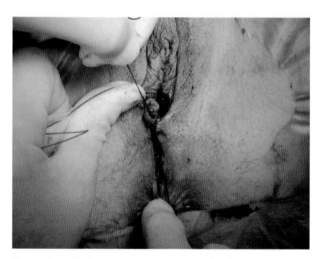

Figure 8.44 Tying the two levator myorrhaphy sutures: this is done only after the ventral colporrhaphy is finished.

Figure 8.47 The job is done.

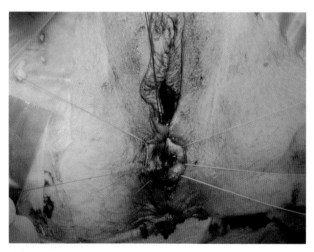

Figure 8.45 The perineorrhaphy is prepared (three separate subcutaneous colorless absorbable sutures).

Y-shaped incision, which is done with 00 Vicryl® starting from the upper angle and going (Figure 8.43) up to the vulvar fourchette. Once the colporrhaphy has been finished the myorrhaphy stitches are tied (Figure 8.44). Closure of the perineum is achieved with two or three uncolored 00 Vicryl® stitches taking large bites of the tissues but not of the skin (Figure 8.45). The skin itself is closed using either interrupted stitches of monocryl (4-0), or by applying simple pressure for 5 min with Allis forceps ("glue-ing" suture using endogenic biological glue): Figures 8.46 and 8.47.

Postoperative course and complications

The triple perineal operation enjoys the same advantages as all vaginal operations. The postoperative course is generally simple and complications few. As far as end results are concerned, failures and complications can occur but are no more common after this operation than after any other. Furthermore, they may be prevented if the cases are carefully assessed and appropriate adjuvant procedures eventually added to the basic operation.

Postoperative course

The triple operation lasts on average twice as long as simple vaginal hysterectomy. Mobilization of the vaginal flaps leads to increased bleeding although this generally remains clinically insignificant (blood transfusions are exceptionally rare during surgery and rarely considered during the immediate postoperative period). Many surgeons recommend using preoperative infiltration of diluted catecholamines to limit bleeding. We believe that this makes identification of the anatomical spaces more difficult and suggest that the technique is not indispensable. At the same time we do not recommend vaginal packing. A triple operation involving standard ventral colporrhaphy alone is not an indication for an indwelling urethral catheter, this being of course mandatory if a specific corrective procedure of the bladder neck or urethra (see later) is performed.

The postoperative course is generally the same as after simple vaginal hysterectomy and the only issue specific to this operation is the pain experienced by some patients in the area of the colpoperineorrhaphy. Anti-inflammatory drugs provide the answer to this problem. Some surgeons recommend preventing these pains by infiltrating the perineum with appropriate anti-inflammatory drugs. We agree with this policy for patients that do not present contraindications to this approach. Apart from this, there are no differences in management of the postoperative inpatient course and after discharge, which can be scheduled for the third postoperative day. We recommend a period of convalescence lasting 6 weeks.

The end result can be assessed as early as 6 weeks following surgery. Prolapse of the vagina is no longer visible either in the supine or in the standing position and the vagina is normal (it must be assessed by digital examination, which, in some instances, breaks weak intracavitary adhesions). Failures seen at the first postoperative visit are more than few. They are the testimony of either a worthy indication or an incorrect execution of the surgery. It is the same for some failures occurring in the following months, but late failures are generally due to aging of the tissues. The use of estrogen therapy either general or local and either strong (estradiol or premarin) or weak (estriol) can obviate this problem but it is not the panacea. Nevertheless one recommends prescribing it largely during the preoperative period and during the postoperative period too.

Intraoperative and postoperative complications

Intraoperative complications

Even if intraoperative oozing is greater, the risk of true intraoperative hemorrhage is not greater during the triple operation than it is during simple vaginal hysterectomy.

Intraoperative injuries to the bladder and intestine are more common, because ventral and dorsal colporrhaphy are both associated with this risk and together they produce a risk equivalent to that of hysterectomy itself. The recognition and management of these complications is the same irrespective of the primary procedure causing them and their consequence is generally minimal.

Injury of the ureter, paradoxically, is not more common during the triple operation than during simple vaginal hysterectomy. Yet the knee of the ureter is lower and comes down lower still during transvaginal surgery for pelvic relaxation. But the arch of the uterine artery, due to lengthening of the uterine isthmus, comes down even lower, which reduces the risk during preparation and division of the arteries. The bigger the cystocele, the lower the risk: the greatest part of the prolapse is made up of the part of the bladder lying under the interureteric ridge, which generally remains in the normal position.

Postoperative complications

Postoperative bleeding and infection are no more common after the triple operation than they are after simple vaginal hysterectomy. The rules governing management are the same.

The only specific complication is that of hematoma formation in the spaces opened in the triple operation but left intact in simple vaginal hysterectomy. As far as ventral colporrhaphy is concerned, plication of the vesicovaginal fascia provides perfect prophylaxis. However, in the dorsal area collections can develop in the pararectal spaces that are opened to gain access to the levator muscles. Pain, moderate hyperthermia and perception of a retrovaginal mass on digital examination are the symptoms and signs of a collection. Ultrasound confirms the diagnosis before some of the stitches are cut to allow the collection to drain.

Complications and failure

The triple perineal operation generally results in satisfactory restoration of the pelvic architecture, which in itself restores the auto-blocking mechanism that guarantees normal functioning of both the lower urinary and lower intestinal tracts. Complications and failures that are not always related can occur: urinary or other functional complications coexisting with good anatomical results or anatomical failures without functional problems.

Complications

Many patients affected by genital prolapse do not ask for surgery because they are frightened of subsequently developing urinary incontinence. This widespread belief is not pure fantasy: prolapse surgery can cause problems in patients who previously had none, or cure some problems while creating new problems of a different nature.

Urinary problems

Urinary problems are the most common complications of prolapse surgery. Stress incontinence is the main preoccupation, but it is neither the most common nor the most embarrassing.

Urinary stress incontinence is part of the symptomatologic complex in two out of three patients affected by genital prolapse. The triple perineal operation can cure or alleviate this type of symptom but fails to do so in 30–60% of the cases. On the other hand the standard operation can cause genuine stress incontinence in patients who were perfectly continent before having surgery. There is no correlation at all between the anatomical result of the surgery and the functional outcome. On the contrary, the better the anatomical result, the more common the de novo urinary stress incontinence. This is due to suppression of the so-called "ball effect" of the cystocele.

Postoperative stress incontinence can largely be anticipated before surgery by detecting so-called "potential stress incontinence." This is done by taking a good history, performing a careful clinical examination and, to a large extent, by performing urodynamics. In cases where the preoperative work-up detects potential stress incontinence, specific procedures must be added to the standard ventral colporrhaphy. This point will be developed in a forthcoming section but we only mention it here to stress that the routine addition of other procedures can be more detrimental than abstaining from their use altogether. Be careful in your choice of complementary operations.

Urinary voiding difficulties are uncommon after the triple perineal operation unless an extra procedure aiming to correct or avoid urinary stress incontinence has been added. The first symptom is urinary retention, which occurs after removal of the urinary catheter. Care must be taken in interpreting the symptoms observed after removal of the catheter: micturition may be incomplete (leaving a residual of more than 100 ml) or may be symptomatic of complete retention (overflow incontinence). Quantification of the post-micturition residual must be routinely performed either by re-catheterization or by ultrasound assessment.

The incidence of postoperative urinary bladder voiding difficulties depends on the details of the operative technique. To a certain extent they can be predicted by urodynamics. If the "stop-test" does not show clear detrusor systolic activity, postoperative urinary retention has to be anticipated. The patient must be aware of this potential complication, which can, in extreme cases, lead to the requirement for long-term self-catheterization (teaching self-catheterization before surgery is a good prophylactic technique as it reduces anxiety related to this complication).

Too often, urinary urgency spoils the well-being of patients undergoing prolapse surgery. In most cases, the history is purely one of frequency, either diurnal or nocturnal as well (nocturia). More embarrassing is true urgency, which forces the patient to limit or modify her daily lifestyle for fear of the dreaded urge incontinence, which is the worst of handicaps. Such symptoms can exist before surgery. The triple operation can make them disappear but improvement may be only partial and the opposite can also be seen: postoperative urinary urgency in a patient whose urinary bladder function was normal before surgery. There is no correlation between anatomy and the functional syndrome: postoperative urinary urgency can occur whatever the initial lesional complex and whatever the quality of surgical correction. There is no predictive tool: urodynamics (cystomanometry), which is often silent even in cases of characteristic clinical history, cannot preclude the syndrome appearing after surgery. In cases of postoperative urgency, biofeedback and drugs are generally effective. Nonetheless, before proceeding with the triple operation, the patient must be clearly informed that postoperative urgency can occur and that its management is not always completely successful.

Total urinary incontinence due to urethral sphincter incompetence may be revealed by the triple operation. The mechanism is the same as that of stress incontinence "unmasked" by surgery, i.e. suppression of the "ball effect" due to the cystocele. The Bonney test can predict this event. But urodynamics alone is able to determine whether sphincter incompetence exists or not. This is another reason for the regular, if not routine, request for this investigation before prolapse surgery. It is the best way to avoid many problems for the patient and for her surgeon.

Dyspareunia

Transvaginal surgery for genital prolapse is a well-known cause of dyspareunia. As a consequence most surgeons reserve the vaginal approach for older patients, the younger ones being managed by the abdominal route. This dichotomy is illogical as older patients generally have older sexual partners who require a more easily accessible vagina. However, in reality the problem does not exist as long as the operation is carried out properly.

Postoperative dyspareunia is due to shortening and shrinkage of the vaginal cavity in any of its constituent segments. Alteration of the lower third is a source of so-called superficial dyspareunia. Alteration of the middle third is the most embarrassing and can lead to complete apareunia. Alteration of the upper third is less likely to produce consequences. All these alterations are due to excessive removal of vaginal skin and are avoidable.

During ventral colporrhaphy, we recommend that procedures using strips of ventral vaginal wall for repair are avoided (autoplastic strips or autoplastic flaps for bladder neck suspension). Furthermore, we strongly advise that resection of the redundant vaginal wall is kept to an absolute minimum: a moderate persisting excess of tissue is of no consequence because the vaginal skin is elastic and models itself on the underlying structures – the only goal of surgery is to reshape these structures.

During dorsal colporrhaphy we recommend avoiding all resections of the middle third of the vagina completely. As far as the cranial third is concerned no adverse consequences are anticipated. With regards to the caudal third, narrowing of the introitus is easy to avoid as long as care is taken to ensure that the two tenacula, which limit the base of the triangular skin resection, are not placed too far from each other.

Constipation
Constipation is a functional problem that is too often neglected in genital prolapse patients. It can apparently arise as a consequence of the triple operation but it generally predates surgery and can be one of the factors leading to pelvic relaxation and to failure after surgery for pelvic relaxation.

Abdominoperineal dysynergy is the most common mechanism resulting in constipation. The absence of relaxation of the anal sphincters in response to increasing abdominal pressure causes the problem and results in the patient exerting abnormally strong straining efforts in order to empty her intestine. These excessive efforts put the pelvic support system to the test and play a part in the etiologic–pathogenic complex. They can also be a cause of failure following surgery. It is also known that straining can cause lengthening of the pudendal nerve and consequently functional incompetence of this nerve. This

results in atony of the anal sphincter and thus the final consequence of the pathogenic process: fecal incontinence.

Excessive tightening of the so-called dorsal levator plasty can partially obstruct correct physiological voiding of the intestine, even if it acts on the anorectal junction in a manner that favors evacuation – flattening of the anorectal angle can paradoxically, in the long term, play a role in fecal incontinence.

Management of intestinal problems that coexist with genital prolapse must start before surgery. The initial assessment includes precise questions about defecation and paraclinical investigations such as anorectal manometry and/or defecography. In cases with evidence of abdominoperineal dysynergy (abdominoanal asynchronism) rehabilitation exercises using biofeedback processes are indicated: their results determine the postoperative prognosis. In cases where imaging reveals morphological abnormalities specific correction should be scheduled (see later). In any case, dorsal levator plasty, which is in our opinion mandatory in all cases, must be graduated and never overtightened.

Failure
The failures observed after the triple operation for genital prolapse can be early or late. Early failures are attributed to strategic or technical mistakes and late failures to aging of the pelvic and perineal supports. They can produce two anatomicoclinical presentations: vaginal vault prolapse and recurrent cystocele and/or rectocele. This dichotomy is not absolute but is the one we adopt for describing the facts.

Vaginal vault prolapse
Vaginal vault prolapse consists of an inversion of the vaginal vault into the vaginal cavity. The vaginal vault becomes convex rather than concave: "inversio vaginalis." The prolapsed vault can remain intracavitary with no bulging at all of the ventral and dorsal walls of the vagina – this is generally asymptomatic. Once the prolapsed vaginal vault presents at the vulvar introitus and prolapses through it, total eversion of the vagina occurs and significant discomfort results. One can generally see two lateral dimples at the tip of the everted cylinder, which mark the insertion of the paracervical ligaments on the deep aspect of the vault.

In spite of the clinical appearance, vaginal vault prolapse in certain cases does not include cystocele and/or rectocele: even in the everted form (stage IV), when the dorsal and ventral vaginal walls are completely exteriorized, the bladder floor and the rectal ampulla can be in the normal place – but this may only seem so. Concomitant cystocele and/or rectocele may nonetheless be present – a fact that is important to consider in the management of postoperative vaginal vault prolapse. However as far as the mechanism and prevention of this very peculiar entity are concerned, it must be emphasized that the only constant phenomena are enterocele and atrophic lengthening of the paracervical ligaments.

Prevention of postoperative vaginal vault prolapse relies on appropriate preoperative and intraoperative assessment of the paracervical supports of the genital organs. Complete failure of this support should be considered in all cases where the prolapse exceeds grade II, but the information one gets at preoperative clinical examination may be challenged by the *assessment* made during surgery or, to be more precise, just after removal of the uterus. The depth of the Douglas pouch should be assessed while pushing downward with a finger on the anterior aspect of the peritonealized part of the rectum (Figure 8.48). Lengthening of the paracervical ligaments can be evaluated by pulling on the stumps after removal of the uterus (Figure 8.49(a)). If the posterior leaf of the Douglas pouch sinks behind the dorsal vaginal wall and/or the stumps of the paracervical ligaments come up to the level of the vulvar introitus or deeper (Figure 8.49(b)), simple culdoplasty (McCall stitch) is not adequate. Under these circumstances, sacrospinous fixation is indicated. This technique is described later. It is both a treatment for postoperative vaginal vault prolapse and a preventative procedure that should be used prophylactically in cases at high risk of postoperative vaginal vault prolapse.

Recurrent cystocele and/or rectocele

Recurrent cystocele and rectocele are the true failures of the triple operation. From the patient's perspective, the situation reverts back to the problem that motivated the initial surgery. However, the truth of the matter is that recurrent cystocele and/or rectocele are never exactly the same as they were initially.

Recurrent cystocele can develop in a patient who was initially free or almost free of ventral vaginal wall descent. As the uterus has been removed and dorsal colporrhaphy has been performed but nothing has been done to the ventral vaginal wall, it will develop a secondary bulge: the stronger the dorsocaudal

(a)

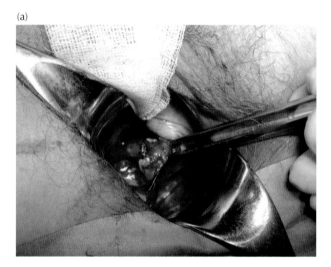

(b)

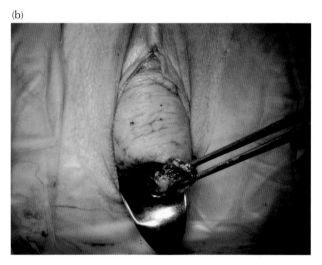

Figure 8.49 (a) Assessing the situation in a post-hysterectomy prolapse. The stump of the paracervical ligaments is drawn downward: it does not descend to the introitus: the indication for the McCall suture. (b) Assessing the situation in a post-hysterectomy prolapse. The stump of the paracervical ligaments is drawn downward: it descends beyond the introitus: the indication for sacrospinous fixation (Richter procedure).

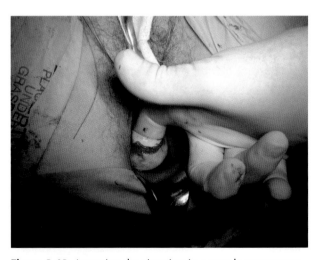

Figure 8.48 Assessing the situation in a post-hysterectomy prolapse. The forefinger is introduced behind the dorsal vaginal fornix and hooked to demonstrate an enterocele.

reattachment of the vaginal vault, the greater the bulge. The opposite can also occur particularly if a procedure to stabilize the bladder neck has been added to ventral colporrhaphy. This favors descent of the dorsal vaginal wall pushed down either by an enterocele or by a rectocele or by a combination of both.

The name "recurrent" cystocele and/or rectocele is not appropriate for disorders that were initially absent and appeared after correction of a different type of disorder. However, the patient experiences the phenomenon as a true recurrence. This "recurrence" is in fact the consequence of a mistake that is not technical but rather strategic in nature: whatever the appearance, one has to remember that genital prolapse is a consequence of weakening of the common supporting structures of the pelvic organs and that the triple operation must in all cases include at least three steps.

"True true" recurrent cystoceles and/or rectoceles occur after a correctly executed ventral and/or dorsal colporrhaphy. Weakening of the repaired fascia is the main cause of recurrence. One can blame incorrect technique for identification, mobilization and/or tightening of the fascia whereas the main issue in fact relates to the quality of the fascia itself, which of course does not improve with time. This raises the issue of using synthetic mesh that aims to replace destroyed natural fascia. Ignorance or incomplete management of a paravaginal defect is another mechanism of failure. In this situation too the use of mesh stitched on both sides to the arcus tendineus fascia pelvici and supporting the bladder floor can be the answer either as a curative treatment or as a preventive tool.

The use of synthetic mesh fixed to the pelvic walls is a technique specific to transabdominal surgery for prolapse. Mentioning its use to prevent failure of vaginal surgery for prolapse brings us back to the seminal question of the preference to give to one approach over and above the other. Among the prospective and randomized trials studying the two approaches, the most convincing is the one published in 1993 by Fatton et al. (Fatton B, Grunberg P, Ohana M, et al. Cure de prolapsus chez la femme: la voie abdominale n'a pas d'avantage sur la voie vaginale. A propos d'une étude rétrospective randomisée. Résultats anatomiques et sexuels. Job Gyn 1993; 1: 66–72 and 133–4). The number of cases was low (16 in the "vaginal approach" arm and 14 in the "abdominal approach" arm) but all the patients were operated on in a short space of time (January 1990 to July 1991) by the same surgeon who had mastered the two approaches with equal skill. On the other hand, all the patients were less than 55 years old and sexually active. The result of the cystorrhaphy was considered imperfect in six patients in the first group and four patients in the second group. This means that colposuspension is not superior to repair of the vesicovaginal fascia in preventing secondary bulging of the ventral vaginal wall. On the other hand, no difference was observed in terms of Quality Of Life and particularly so in the field of sexuality. According to this trial, the abdominal approach is clearly not superior to the vaginal one. For these reasons, we continue to believe that preference should be given to the vaginal approach, even though certain failures of the vaginal approach force us to use techniques that are specific to the abdominal approach such as colposuspension and the interposition of mesh. But this recourse is not frequently indicated and the procedures can be implemented while continuing to use the vaginal approach.

Indications and contraindications

Prolapse surgery belongs to the peculiar realm of medicine where the patient is the only judge of the indications and contraindications. One of our teachers used to say: "one never dies from genital prolapse but one can die from prolapse surgery." This axiom is no longer pertinent today in so far as the risk of intra- and postoperative death is now zero or close to zero. However, the patient must be fully informed about the risks and benefits of surgery. She is the only one who knows the extent of the symptoms she endures due to pelvic relaxation and she is the only one in the position to decide whether surgery is indicated or not. The times when the physician has to impose his viewpoint are rare. It is only with advanced age (80 years? 90 years? 100 years? more?) and generally poor condition that the surgeon has to warn patients against curative surgery and eventually recommend a palliative surgical approach. In all other cases the patient who asks for relief of symptoms due to pelvic relaxation must be accepted for the triple operation once certain criteria have been met: the symptoms she suffers must be clearly related to the lesions identified and accessory procedures should be added to the standard operation as indicated to prevent sequelae/failure.

Palliative surgery

The high-risk surgical patient is not the only one to dissuade from having surgery. At the other end of the spectrum is the very young patient affected by slight or moderate relaxation who should be persuaded at least to avoid immediate surgery. Her fate will be discussed later on. Here we only consider patients whose general condition makes standard surgery excessively dangerous. One may consider colpocleisis and/or masculinization of the perineum for these patients. Among the numerous variants of this historical surgical approach, the Labhardt operation has our preference because it can be performed under local anesthesia and leads to very good end results in spite of its unbelievable simplicity.

The operation described by Labhardt in 1923 as "colpoperineocleisis subtotalis" is a modification of the standard colpoperineorrhaphy. It can be performed under local anesthesia, which, apart from avoiding the hazards of general anesthesia, facilitates dissection of the flaps. The first two incisions delineate a triangle whose base is at the fourchette. The tip of the triangle is on the midline at the junction of the lower and intermediate thirds of the dorsal wall of the vagina. Starting from the middle of these two oblique incisions, two more incisions are made on each side. These complementary incisions delineate another triangle on each side lateral to the first (once made, the incision looks like a ghost with two large wings) (Figure 8.50). It is important that the tip of each of the lateral triangles is at the level of the urethral meatus: not higher but not lower. It is also important that the medial edges of the lateral triangles are as close as possible to the midline so that the remaining part of the ventral wall of the vagina does not exceed 4 cm in width: the channel that will replace the vagina underneath the urethra must have a diameter that does not exceed 1–1.5 cm.

The second step of the Labhart's operation involves removal of the vulvovaginal skin lying within the "ghost-like" incision. In the original Labhardt's technique this removal was purely superficial. If one operates under local anesthesia this has to be the rule. If not the central part can be managed just as it is for standard perineorrhaphy, i.e. the pararectal spaces are opened and then the colpotomy extended in an inverted Y shape (Figures 8.28–8.34) to enlarge the opening of the lateral spaces and gain wide access to the levator muscles, which allows a true dorsal levator plasty (Figures 8.39–8.42). Whatever the anesthetic modality used, the lateral vulvovaginal dissections must be purely superficial: skin alone is detached at the level of the two wings flanking the lateral aspects of the ghost's body.

The deep levator plasty stitches are placed before colporraphy is undertaken. This colporrhaphy starts at the extremity of the central triangle. Once one arrives at the origin of the lateral wings, the other plasty stitches are put in place. They take the bulbocavernosus muscles and the underlying structures (Figure 8.51) in two to four successive stitches (Figure 8.52). It is only after the stitches have been placed and the colporrhaphy completed (Figure 8.53) that the plasty stitches are tied (Figure 8.54).

The postoperative course after Labhardt colpocleisis is incredibly simple. Thanks to this operation there is

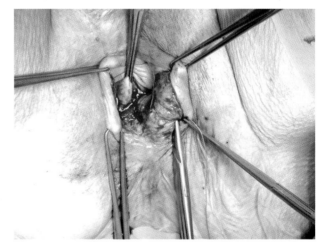

Figure 8.51 Stitching the bulbo-cavernous muscle.

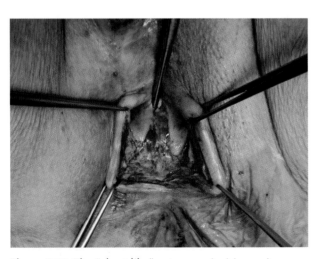

Figure 8.50 The "ghost-like" cutaneous incision as it appears after the desepidermization has been carried out.

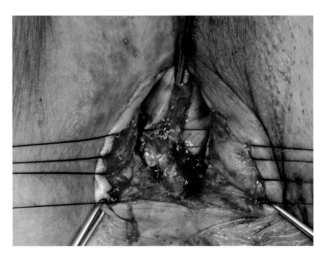

Figure 8.52 Four stitches have been put on the lateral wings and central body of the "ghost-like" desepidermized area.

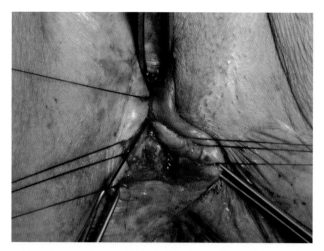

Figure 8.53 The vaginal part of the incision has been closed (note that the vaginal sheath remaining open after the last stitch is only a small suburethral channel); the first deep stitch is already in place.

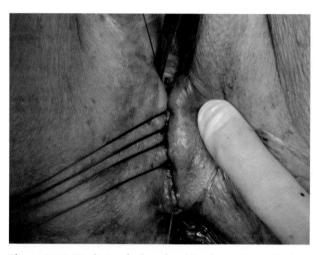

Figure 8.54 Final view before the skin closure (so-called masculinization of the perineum).

no patient affected by prolapse who cannot benefit from surgery whatever the degree of relaxation. The midterm results are generally excellent. However, if the life expectancy of the patient has been underestimated and if physiological activity remains more or less tremendous, recurrences can occur in spite of the very efficient closure offered by the final arrangement due to the Labhardt's operation.

Additions to the triple operation

The triple perineal operation is the gold standard of vaginal surgery for genital prolapse. However additional procedures must be frequently implemented to avoid the sequelae and failures that have been mentioned in the preceding section of this chapter. These procedures will be described following the same outline. The procedures preventing functional sequelae are considered first and then the procedures preventing failure.

Cure of concomitant urinary stress incontinence and prevention of postoperative urinary stress incontinence

The ventral colporrhaphy described in the first section of this chapter is not enough to cure urinary stress incontinence, which is associated with genital prolapse in two out of three cases. On the same theme, ventral colporrhaphy cannot in itself prevent postoperative unmasking of so-called potential stress incontinence. A specific "anti-urinary stress incontinence" procedure must be added to the standard ventral colporrhaphy both in patients suffering from genuine urinary stress incontinence before surgery and in patients who are at risk of developing it after surgery. A correct history is adequate for selection of the former. Selection of the latter is based on clinical examination and urodynamics.

The first step of clinical assessment is the cough test in lithotomy position with a full urinary bladder. If a loss of urine occurs the Bonney test must be performed. The extremities of a large half-opened anatomical forceps are applied on each side of the midline on the vaginal wall at the level of its intermediate third (i.e. roughly at the level of the vesicourethral junction). This elevates the bladder floor without compressing the urethra (Figure 8.55(a) and (b)). If the urine loss observed in the cough test disappears it means that an antistress incontinence procedure should be added to the ventral colporrhaphy and has a good chance of success.

If no urine loss is observed in the cough test, one has to rule out the possibility of the so-called "ball effect." Such a phenomenon should be suspected in patients who were affected by incontinence in the past, the incontinence progressively disappearing or being replaced by voiding difficulties at the same time as bulging of the vaginal wall appeared and increased. In fact, the ball effect should be suspected in all patients with cystocele but no incontinence. To exclude this possibility a test elevating the ventral vaginal wall should be done. It is not the intermediate third of the ventral vaginal wall that has to be elevated but rather the dorsal third using either the fingers or a Breisky retractor in order to completely reduce the cystocele. The cough test is repeated. If it is not productive the same should be done in a standing position. Such interventions may reveal stress incontinence. If they do, an antistress incontinence procedure should be scheduled.

The so-called Q-tip test is a very simple and very useful test to add to clinical examination. It is done by introducing a short smooth stick into the urethra

(a)

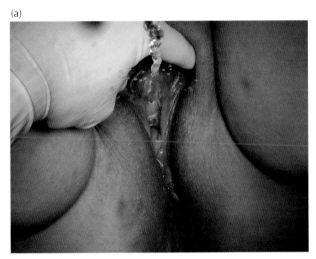

(b)

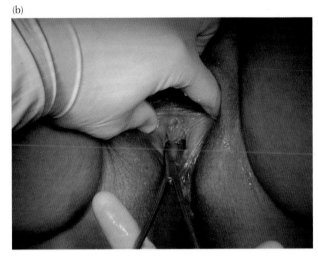

Figure 8.55 (a) The Bonney test: coughing provokes loss of urine. (b) The Bonney test: by maintaining the urethrovescial junction in the correct position loss of urine during coughing is prevented.

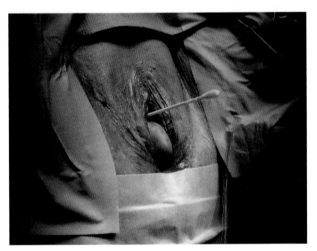

Figure 8.56 Q-tip test: in a patient in the lithotomy position and in the absence of urethrovesical hypermobility, the Q-tip is in the horizontal position and remains so even during coughing.

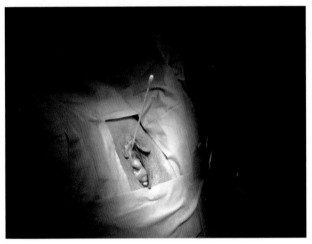

Figure 8.57 Q-tip test: in a patient in the lithotomy position and in the presence of urethrovesical hypermobility, the Q-tip is in the vertical position or becomes vertical during coughing.

(Q-tip). In the normal woman lying in the lithotomy position the stick takes up a horizontal orientation because of the strength of the ligaments attaching the dorsal part of the urethra to the pubic arch (Figure 8.56). In the patient whose urethra is unfastened and hypermobile the axis of the stick is oblique and becomes even more oblique as the patient pushes and coughs (Figure 8.57). This phenomenon is constant in cases of urinary stress incontinence. It can be seen in patients who are not complaining of incontinence. If so, it is a marker of significant risk of postoperative urinary incontinence and constitutes an indication for an additional antistress incontinence procedure.

The place of urodynamics is a matter for debate. Its usefulness in relation to potential urinary stress incontinence is questioned. The hypothesis that the main cause of stress incontinence is due to a defect in transmission of excess pressure in the bladder to the urethra (Einhorn hypothesis) is no longer accepted. This so-called defect of transmission (as calculated from the graphs demonstrating variation in urethral and bladder pressures) is neither constant in genuine stress incontinence nor really indicative of potential stress incontinence in patients not suffering from such a symptom. An increase in the rate of postoperative voiding difficulties occurs when urodynamics is the only indication for an antistress incontinence procedure. This is not the indication for urodynamics. The true goal of urodynamics is detection of detrusor instability and sphincter incompetence. It is reliable enough to be regularly if not systematically used for this indication.

Once preoperative assessment has been completed, two situations must be distinguished. In the absence of stress incontinence, either self-confessed or potential, the triple operation alone without additional procedures should be scheduled. When this is not the case, the Q-tip test will determine the outcome. The first situation is where obvious urethrovesical unfastening and hypermobility exist: a procedure for urethrovesical stabilization should be added to ventral colporrhaphy. In the second situation such a procedure is not mandatory and a more simple procedure may be chosen. The first situation will be considered first.

The procedures for vesicourethral stabilization are of two types. The choice depends on the state of the urogenital and pelvic diaphragms. If these diaphragms are not too badly damaged they can be restored and used as supports. If they are, a colposuspension procedure should be selected. Our choice for the former situation is ventral levator plasty, and for the latter the inverted Burch procedure. Before describing these operations an important point should be made: if a stabilization procedure is added, the midline ventral colpotomy (which is the prelude to ventral colporrhaphy in the triple perineal operation) must be extended up to its ventral extremity, i.e. 5–10 mm from the urethral meatus.

Ventral levator plasty
Suburethral plication (Kelly stitches) has a poor reputation. It is performed by juxtaposing the paraurethral structures belonging to the urogenital diaphragm (bulbocavernosus muscles) on the midline. These procedures have been improved by Richter and Nichols who went further laterally to try to take the posterior pubourethral ligaments, and to perform a more sophisticated plasty (figure-of-eight stitches). The results of such plication are good if the surgeon is good. In contrast the ventral levator plasty is less surgeon-dependent because the anatomical material used is easier to identify. But, success depends on the quality of this material (i.e. the puborectalis muscles).

Ingelmann Sundberg has devised a procedure using the puborectalis muscles to stabilize the bladder neck and the urethra. It involves separating a bundle from each of the puborectal muscles, the bundle being separated from the medial aspect of the muscular body but not detached from its superior insertion. The free extremity of this bundle is joined to the extremity of the bundle made from the contralateral muscle. Lahodny proposed a modification wherein the two muscles are only juxtaposed on the midline. For either procedure the puborectalis muscles have to have a normal or almost normal morphology. However, alterations in these muscles are frequent in women affected by genital prolapse.

The muscles are assessed by first requesting a voluntary contraction of the puborectalis muscles (standard perineal testing) and by then palpating the medial aspect of the ischiopubic bone with the forefinger used as a hook. Alterations in the muscles are not always symmetrical. If one scores the muscles on a 5-point scale, the total of the two scores must be five or more for ventral levator plasty to be considered.

If a decision is made to perform ventral levator plasty, one searches for the puborectalis muscle at the point where the fascial flap is detached from the vaginal flap (Figure 8.11). Pushing against the resistance one feels at the hinge of the two flaps, the paravesical space at the ventrocaudal extremity of this hinge is entered (Figure 8.58). The lateral surface of the bladder is separated from the pelvic sidewall. In this way the paravesical space is entered and the cranial surface of the puborectalis muscle palpated with the finger. To free the caudal surface of this muscle, it has to be separated from the deep surface of the vagina to which it is adherent at the junction of the ventral and intermediate thirds. To get to this point, the Cotte forceps that was sitting on the free border of the vaginal flap is moved to be placed as lateral as possible and closed. The forefinger of the nonoperating hand is introduced behind the vaginal flap (Figure 8.59). By pulling on the forceps and pushing with the forefinger the deep surface of the vaginal flap is exposed. A narrow retractor is placed in front of the exposed area and pushes the bladder medially. An incision is made with the scalpel just behind the nail of the forefinger of the nonoperating hand (Figure 8.59). This incision disconnects the vaginal wall from the caudal surface of the puborectalis muscle and opens the "sheet" of the muscle.

Once the sheet of the puborectalis muscle has been opened, the Mayo scissors are introduced into this

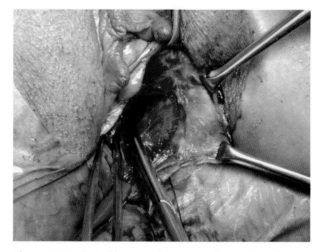

Figure 8.58 Ventral levator plasty according to Lahodny: opening the paravesical space having mobilized the lateral vaginal flap (see Figure 8.8).

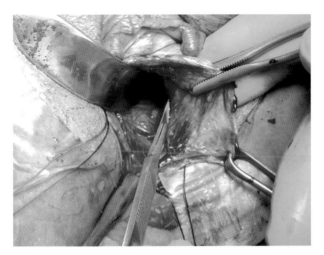

Figure 8.59 Ventral levator plasty according to Lahodny: incising the sheath of the puborectalis muscle on the left side. A retractor is pushing the urethrovesical junction medially. The forefinger has been introduced behind the everted vaginal flap and exposes the point where it crosses the puborectal muscle.

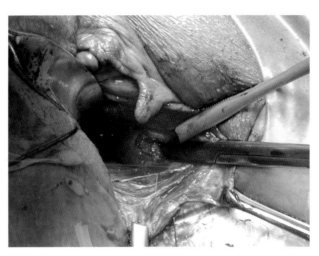

Figure 8.61 Ventral levator plasty according to Lahodny: the scissors are used as a lever. The puborectal levator muscle bundles separated from the dorsal surface of the bone are elevated.

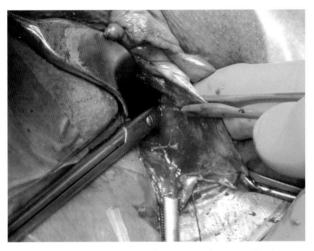

Figure 8.60 Ventral levator plasty according to Lahodny: a pair of scissors is introduced through the scalpel incision and pushed laterally until it is in contact with the ischiopubic bone. Then the forefinger pushes the instrument dorsally so that it slides to the dorsal surface of the bone.

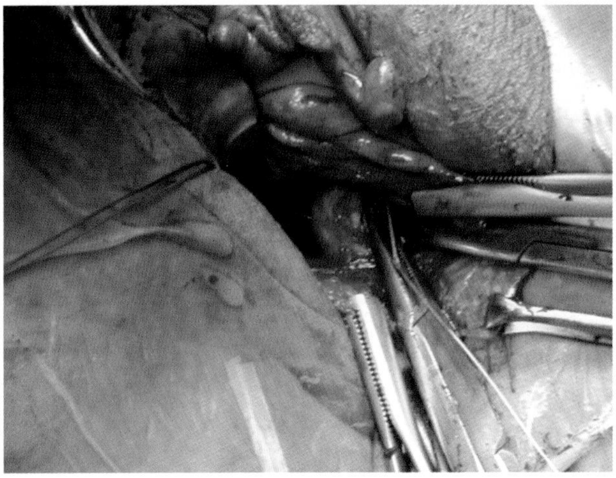

Figure 8.62 Ventral levator plasty according to Lahodny: the puborectal levator muscle bundles are stitched firmly.

small wound and pushed laterally until the tip touches the ischiopubic bone. Once this contact has been made, the lateral pressure exerted by the operating hand is maintained and pressure from front to back is exerted with the forefinger of the nonoperating hand. This makes the tip of the scissors move behind the ischiopubic bone (Figure 8.60).

As soon as the scissors have been inserted between the puborectal muscle and the ischiopubic bone to a depth of approximately 1 cm, the handle of the instrument is rotated laterally. The instrument works as a lever with the ischiopubic bone as the fulcrum.

This action detaches the medial part of the muscle, which becomes apparent in the paravesical space (Figure 8.61). The muscular bundle revealed by the action is 1–1.5 cm wide. It is stitched (Figure 8.62) with a so-called urological needle (5/8 needle) and the suture used for traction. The same is done on the other side (Figure 8.63).

The two traction sutures in the puborectalis muscles are pulled medially. This action approximates the two muscles on the midline. This allows, using a third urological needle, placement of the first myorrhaphy stitch (Figure 8.64). Once the first stitch has been placed the traction sutures are removed. By pulling on the first myorrhaphy stitch the spot where the second myorrhaphy stitch will be placed is chosen. By assessing the two orifices

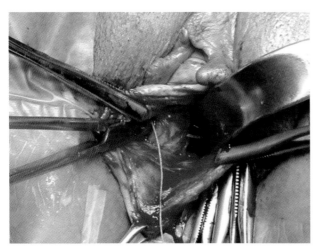

Figure 8.63 Ventral levator plasty according to Lahodny: the same is done on the other side.

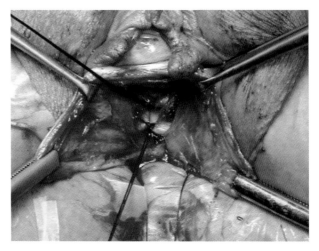

Figure 8.65 Ventral levator plasty according to Lahodny: a second stitch has been placed on the puborectal levator muscles.

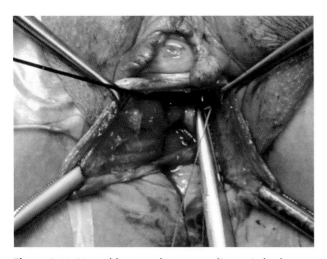

Figure 8.64 Ventral levator plasty according to Lahodny: the two puborectal levator muscles are joined together on the midline.

situated in front of and behind the first stitch the choice is made. If the orifice situated in front of the stitch (the orifice through which the urethra leaves the pelvis) remains too wide, then the second stitch is placed in front of the first (Figure 8.65). The opposite is done in the opposite situation: the second stitch is placed behind the first if the "urethral" orifice is narrow.

In the course of the standard triple operation, the ventral levator plasty procedure is done between the steps of "cardigan" plasty of Halban fascia and colpectomy-colporrhaphy. The puborectalis muscles are revealed at the end of the vaginal flap-splitting procedure. After the ventral levator plasty has been prepared the two fascial flaps are overlapped and it is only after this overlapping action that the myorrhaphy is secured. Then the colpectomy-colporrhaphy is performed.

The retropubic colpopexy or inverted Burch procedure

The fixing of the ventral vaginal wall to the dorsal surface of the abdominal wall and/or to the bones (onto which the abdominal muscles insert) indirectly produces stabilization of the bladder neck and urethra. This is a hammock effect. Fixation to the abdominal wall is not robust whereas fixation to the pubic bone is difficult and hazardous (Marshall Marchetti Krantz procedure). Fixation to the pectineal line (Burch procedure) is the current gold standard. This operation is readily performed laparoscopically and can be completed by suturing the vaginal fascia to the arcus tendineus fasciae pelvis (paravaginal repair).

Abdominal (or laparoscopic) ventrofixation can be adapted to the vaginal approach. Fixation to the abdominal wall can be achieved by percutaneous transfixion from the suprapubic area to the vagina or from the vagina to the suprapubic area (Pereyra and derived procedures). The results are poor. Fixation to the pectineal line can also be performed using the vaginal approach. This operation may be called an inverted Burch procedure.

The inverted Burch procedure requires access to the aperture of the Retzius space. This aperture is made during ventral colporrhaphy as one separates the bladder from the deep surface of the vaginal flap (Figure 8.8). By pushing ventrally against the resistance felt at the end of this separation, the paravesical space is penetrated (Figure 8.66). This space is developed. The dissection, which is done with the finger (Figure 8.67), is extended to the Retzius space just until the superior edge of the iliopubic bone is seen. The pubic tubercle, which is situated approximately 2 cm lateral to the midline, becomes apparent.

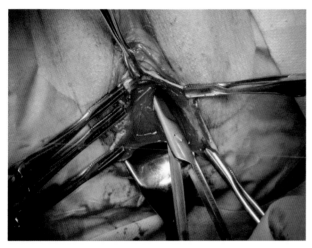

Figure 8.66 The inverted Burch procedure: entering the paravesical space having mobilized the lateral vaginal flap (see Figure 8.8).

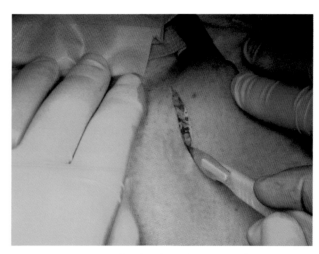

Figure 8.68 Incising the skin from the inguinofemoral fold to the genitofemoral fold (2–3 cm long).

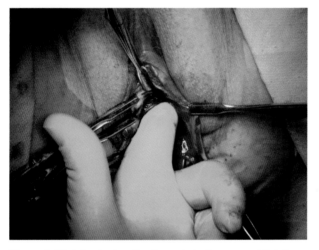

Figure 8.67 Introducing the finger into the cave of Retzius.

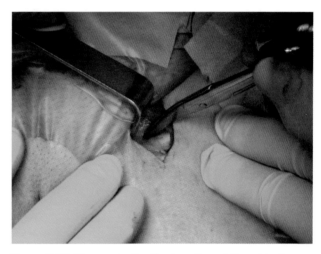

Figure 8.69 Demonstrating the insertion of the adductor magnus muscle onto the iliopubic bone.

This is where Copper's ligament is inserted and where the fixation should be done.

The approach to the pubic spine is made using a 2 cm oblique incision astride the contour of the pubic insertion of the middle adductor muscle. This insertion is onto the ventral aspect of the pubic bone. The projection of the muscle contour under the skin marks the boundary between the cutaneous inguinofemoral and genitofemoral folds. The incision is started in the inguinofemoral fold and extended into the genitofemoral fold (Figure 8.68). Once the skin has been incised one proceeds using blunt scissor dissection so that injury to the genital branches of the genitofemoral nerve (Figure 8.69) can be avoided.

After preparing the part of the pubic bone where the fixation will be placed, the fixation suture is placed

in the deep surface of the vaginal flap. Some surgeons are happy with just one stitch, which is inserted *vis-à-vis* the vesicourethral junction. Others perform two or three stitches using two or three sutures respectively. Mellier proposed using a single suture but taking the deep aspect of the vaginal flap at three points in succession. This is the procedure we recommend. The first stitch is placed in a position facing the vesicourethral junction (Figure 8.70). The two subsequent stitches are placed on a line following the linea vasorum, the last one being placed at the dorsocaudal extremity of this linea (Figure 8.71(a) and (b)). Thanks to this artefact, tying the suture will elevate both the vesicourethral junction and the bladder floor, and the paravaginal defect will be indirectly corrected.

Once the fixation suture has been placed in the deep surface of the vaginal flap, it is carried upward into the retropubic space using a vaginal Deschamps needle or a Stamey needle. This needle is pushed from tip to bottom starting at the small inguinal incision (Figure 8.72). As the tip of this needle arrives in the

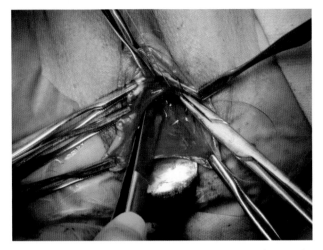

Figure 8.70 Stitching the deep aspect of the lateral vaginal flap: the first stitch facing the vesicourethral junction.

(a)

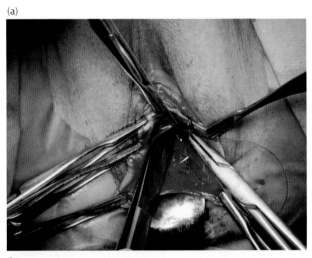

(b)

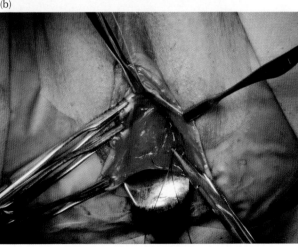

Figure 8.71 (a) Stitching the deep aspect of the lateral vaginal flap: the second stitch. (b) Stitching the deep aspect of the lateral vaginal flap: the third and last stitch.

paravesical area, the suture and the needle on which it is set are placed in the eye of the Deschamps needle.

Before stitching the pectineal line, the vaginal flap is split (Figure 8.73). Then by withdrawing the Deschamps (or Stamey) needle, the suspension suture is brought into the small inguinal incision (Figure 8.74). The following steps are the same as in the standard ventral colporrhaphy: cardigan plication, colpectomies and colporrhaphy.

The pectineal line is stitched at a point lateral to the pubic tubercle. This stitching runs from inside to outside (Figure 8.75) and once completed on both sides secures the retropubic ventral colpopexy. A Q-tip is placed in the urethral canal (Figure 8.76(a)). On tying the sutures it forms an angle of 90° or less (Figure 8.76(b)).

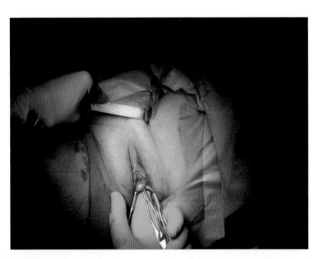

Figure 8.72 Preparing to introduce the Stamey needle into the cave of Retzius through the incision.

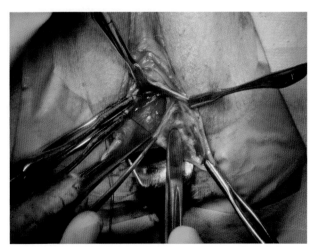

Figure 8.73 The suspending suture has been drawn upward.

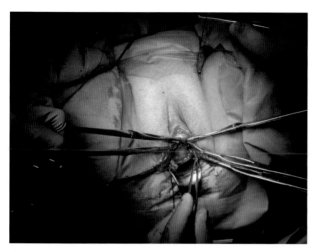

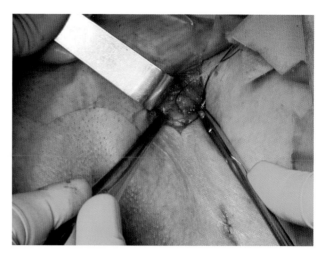

Figure 8.74 Splitting the vaginal flap in order to prepare the cardigan suture. This has to be done before the ventral vaginal wall is suspended.

Figure 8.75 Stitching to the pubic tubercle.

(a)

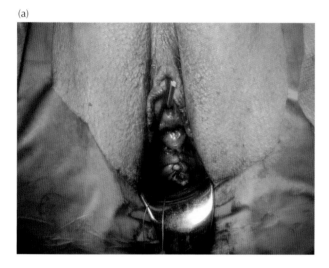

(b)

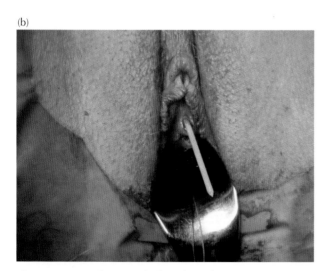

Figure 8.76 (a) The Q-tip before the colposuspension. (b) The Q-tip after the colposuspension.

Transobturator tape

In patients with stress incontinence (either self-confessed or potential, i.e. unmasked by the preoperative workup) but without obvious vesicourethral unfastening and hypermobility, procedures for vesicourethral stabilization appear excessive and can also be a source of sequelae (voiding difficulties) rather than prophylactic against failure. There is today an exceedingly simple and efficient solution for these cases since the introduction of the so-called urethral tension-free tapes. The indications and contraindications to this procedure are easy to assess thanks to a modified Bonney test that may be called the Ulmstem test in reference to the Swedish urogynecologist who first proposed this new type of procedure: the test is the same as the Bonney test, except that the two extremities of the elevating anatomical forceps are placed at the very end of the ventral vaginal wall, just 1 cm above the urethral meatus (Figure 8.77(a) and (b)). If the test is conclusive, the risk of failure after positioning the tape is almost zero. One can go even further and consider the Ulmstem test to be the ultimate step of the preoperative workup before requesting urodynamics: stress incontinence that is not corrected by either the Bonney or the Ulmstem test is probably due to either detrusor hypertony or to sphincter incompetence and urodynamic assessment is mandatory.

The rationale for prosthetic urethral suspension is very different from the rationale for the other operations aiming to cure urinary stress incontinence. The goal is no longer repositioning and suspension of the bladder neck but rather placement of a prosthetic hammock underneath the distal urethra, which will be compressed the moment an excessive increase in intra-abdominal pressure lowers the vesicourethral

(a)

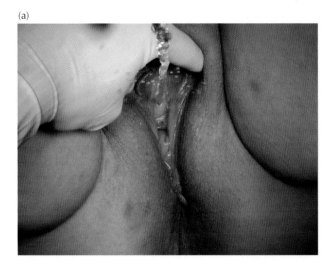

(b)

Figure 8.77 The Ulmstem test. (a) Coughing provokes loss of urine. (b) By maintaining the distal part of the urethra loss of urine during coughing is prevented.

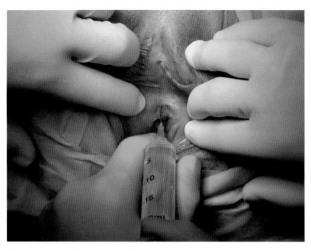

Figure 8.78 The first infiltration of local anesthesia performed with an intradermal needle on the lower edge of the urethral meatus before the TOT procedure.

complex to provoke a loss of urine. The most popular procedure is the TVT in which the tape is placed by making a small vaginal vertical midline incision. Two needles inserted through this incision are pushed from bottom to top to transfix the abdominal muscles. They exit on the surface of the abdominal wall on either side just above the pubis. The two ends of the tape are stuck to the blunt extremities of the needles and pulling on the needles positions the tape around the urethra. The structure of the tape allows it to stay in the position in which it was initially put without suturing or fixation. One merely cuts the pieces of tape where they protrude through the skin: the "Velcro effect" maintains the tape in the tissues of the abdominal wall through which it crosses.

The technique we prefer is inspired by the TVT technique but the two extremities of the tape are introduced through the obturator foramina. As a consequence, the tape sits in an oblique axis. The name TOT is doubly appropriate for this technique: tension-free obturator tape or tension-free oblique tape. The main advantage of the transobturator technique is that it reduces to zero, or almost zero, the risk of bladder injury, which is due to the needle used to position the tape. In fact, the TVT needles are pushed blindly into the Retzius space risking perforation-transfixion of the ventrolateral aspects of the bladder (as well as risking injury to the retropubic vessels and even, if one strays laterally, to the pelvic sidewall vessels, essentially the iliac veins). With the transobturator technique the needles are introduced from the outside to the inside under the guidance of a finger. The chance of bladder or vascular perforation is obliterated.

Placing the TOT can be integrated with complete management of genital prolapse. If such a decision is taken, the ventral colporrhaphy is limited to the dorsal two-thirds of the vaginal wall and then a separate incision is made on the ventral third to place the TOT. The TOT is not placed until after the triple perineal operation is completely finished. One can also use the TOT as an isolated operation to cure pure (not associated with prolapse) urinary stress incontinence. For this second indication, the procedure can be done under local anesthesia and it is this example that we describe hereafter.

Anesthetic infiltration starts as a bleb on the circumference of the urethra at 6 o'clock. A needle for intradermal injection is used (Figure 8.78). Next, an Allis forceps is placed on the dorsal edge of the meatus. This is pulled upward while a series of subcutaneous injections into the vaginal wall are made on the midline with the same needle (Figure 8.79). After that, midline colpotomy can be performed. It starts

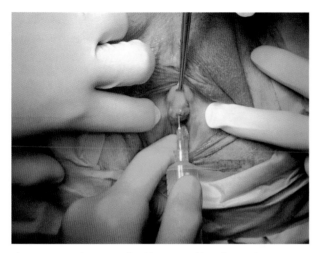

Figure 8.79 The second infiltration of local anesthesia on the lower edge of the urethral meatus: an Allis forceps retracts the vagina upward while the assistant's fingers separate the labia.

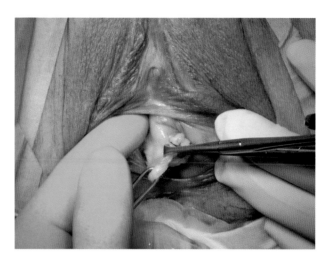

Figure 8.81 Two Allis forceps are applied to the edge of the lateral flap (2 cm wide).

Figure 8.80 The first incision.

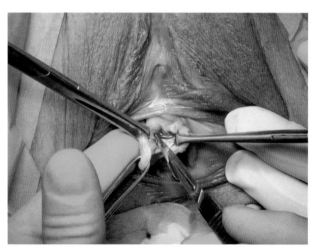

Figure 8.82 Mobilization of the flap: the forefinger is introduced behind this narrow flap and everts it. The dissection is performed under the control of this finger.

5 mm from the meatus (Figure 8.80) and extends to approximately 15 mm.

The midline colpotomy must be shallow and the urethral fascia must be spared – the two mini vaginal flaps are mobilized in front of it. Each of the flaps is mobilized in the same way. The nonoperating hand takes the two Allis forceps holding the edge of the flap (Figure 8.81). The forefinger of this hand exerts pressure on the vaginal flap from outside to inside and presents the deep aspect of this flap to the scalpel, which works from inside to outside at the appropriate depth (Figure 8.82). One works with the tip of the scalpel and pushes the urethra adorned with its fascia medially.

Once the midway point is reached, further anesthetic infiltration is required. A needle for intramuscular injection is used and introduced in the direction of

the posterior surface of the ischiopubic bone (Figure 8.83). Once the running injection (performed as the needle is withdrawn) is done, the handle of the scalpel (Figure 8.84) is introduced into the cleavage plane and then the tip of the scissors pushes from inside to outside until the bone is touched (Figure 8.85). Arriving in contact with the bone, one pushes the tip of the instrument from front to back with the finger of the nonoperating hand in the same way one does during ventral levator plasty (Figure 8.61) but without pushing the dissection quite that far. The aim is to get the tip of the finger in contact with the bone where it will await the Emmet needle, which will be introduced from outside to inside.

The point of introduction of the tip of the Emmet needle is chosen while palpating the anterior surface of the obturator area. It is situated in the cranial and medial angle of the foramen, i.e. on the horizontal

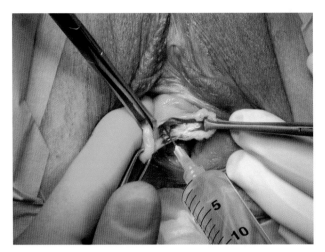

Figure 8.83 Local anesthesia is extended laterally using an intramuscular needle until it is in contact with the ischiopubic bone.

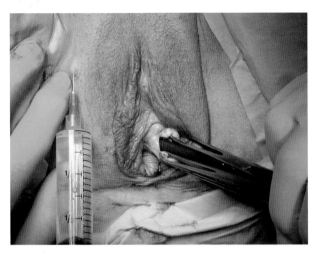

Figure 8.86 The local anesthetic is injected into the genitofemoral fold at the same horizontal level as the clitoris.

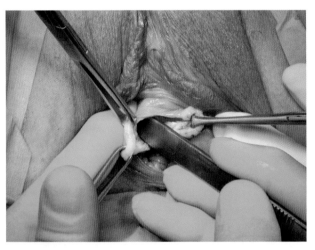

Figure 8.84 Mobilization of the flap is extended with the handle of the scalpel.

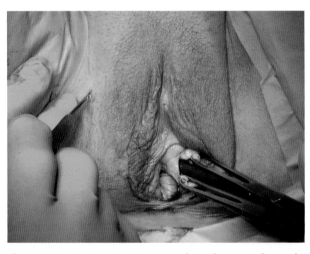

Figure 8.87 A micro-incision is made in the genitofemoral fold.

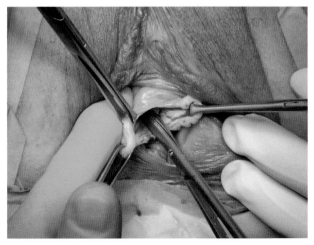

Figure 8.85 Mobilization of the flap is completed with the scissors.

line running roughly at the level of the clitoris. Once the point of introduction of the needle has been chosen one makes an anesthetic bleb (Figure 8.86) and a vertical 2–3 mm incision (Figure 8.87). Starting from this micro-incision one uses the intramuscular needle again to perform a second running injection from outside to inside up to the ischiopubic bone (Figure 8.88).

The Emmet needle (used for getting around the ischiopubic bone and for placing the two lateral ends of the suburethral tape) is introduced through the micro-incision made in the genitofemoral fold. It is at first pushed directly from front to back (Figure 8.89). One then performs a rotating movement directing the needle obliquely toward the tip of the finger, which is waiting for it behind the ischiopubic bone (Figure 8.90).

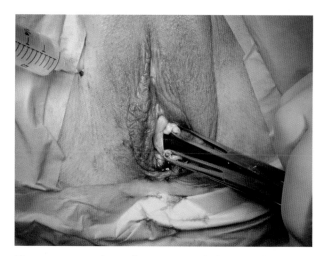

Figure 8.88 Local anesthesia is extended to the other side of the ischiopubic bone by means of an intramuscular needle.

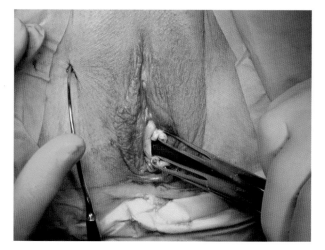

Figure 8.89 The Emmet needle is introduced directly from front to back.

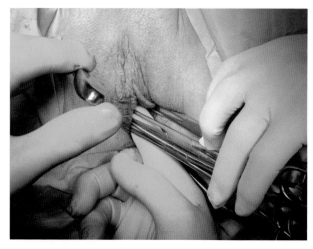

Figure 8.90 The Emmet needle is rotated under control of the forefinger placed in the paraurethral space.

Once the tip of the needle is felt in the depths of the paraurethral space, the finger is withdrawn and the instrument is pushed to free the tip. This tip contains the eye of the needle to which the lateral extremity of the tape is fixed (Figure 8.91). The tape we use is a polypropylene tape 1.5 cm (Figure 8.92) and 30 cm long. It is attached to the Emmet needle using an O polypropylene suture (Figure 8.93). Once attached in this way, the Emmet needle is removed by reversing the rotational movement used to push it through the tissues. The lateral extremity of the tape is exteriorized (Figure 8.94) and the same is done on the other side. Before removing the redundant parts of the tape one makes sure that there is no tension at all. The tip of the scissors should be able to slide between the tape and the urethra with ease (Figure 8.95). This assessment can result in an increase or reduction in traction. We refrain from using the cough test and from cystoscopic assessment. Once the tape has been put in place the redundant pieces are cut and removed (Figure 8.96) and the ends are buried under

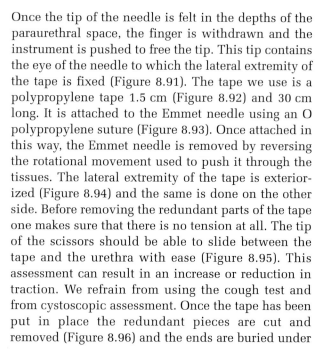

Figure 8.91 The tip of the Emmet needle appears lateral to the urethra.

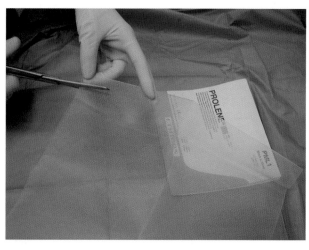

Figure 8.92 Tailoring the polypropylene mesh.

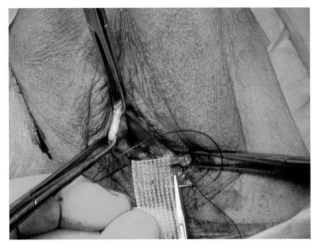

Figure 8.93 Fixing the end of the mesh to the eye of the Emmet needle.

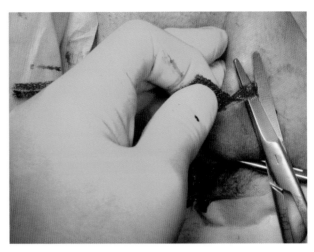

Figure 8.96 Cutting the redundant end of the mesh.

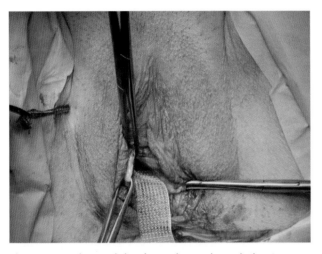

Figure 8.94 The mesh has been drawn through the tissues.

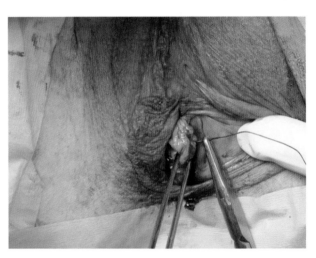

Figure 8.97 Closing the mini-colpotomy.

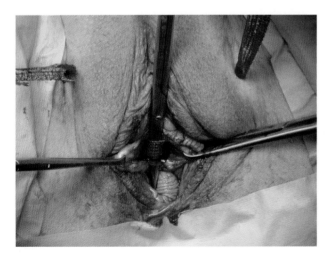

Figure 8.95 Assessing the tension of the mesh.

the skin. The micro genitofemoral incisions are closed with a 4-0 Monocryl stitch. Then the colpotomy is closed using a series of 4–5 interrupted stitches of 00 Vicryl® (Figure 8.97).

As this book is published, new instruments aiming to facilitate needling of the obturator foramen are being developed. The needle designed by Mellier looks particularly promising. This instrument is like the classical Deschamps needle in the sense that the needling part of the instrument is perpendicular to the handle. The dimensions of the device and the angle between the needle and its handle are specifically designed to match the contour of the ischiopubic bone. Handling this instrument is easier than handling the Emmet needle (Figures 8.98 and 8.99).

Prevention of postoperative vaginal vault prolapse and recurrent cystocele and rectocele

Postoperative vaginal vault prolapse and recurrent cystocele and/or rectocele can be the consequence of poor technical performance in the successive steps of the triple perineal operation. They are more frequently the result of very significant alterations in the fascia and ligaments – restoration of this fascia and these ligaments is the basis of the triple perineal

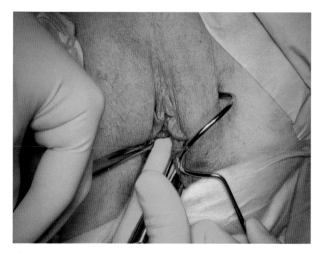

Figure 8.98 The new corkscrew needle: the first position.

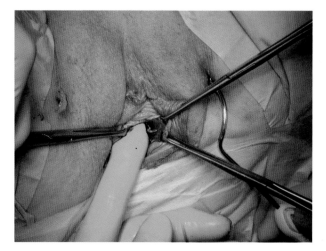

Figure 8.99 The new corkscrew needle: the second position.

operation. These recurrences can be prevented by the addition of specific procedures: sacrospinous fixation for vaginal wall prolapse and the use of prostheses for recurrent cystocele and/or rectocele.

Sacrospinous fixation

The idea of fixing the vaginal vault to the most caudal part of the pelvic dorsal wall belongs to the Austrian surgeon Amreich who in 1942 described the "vaginae fixura sacrotuberalis vaginalis." Amreich fixed the vagina to the sacrotuberous ligament. His pupil Richter chose to use the sacrospinous ligament. The operation was initially reserved for post-hysterectomy vaginal vault prolapse. The operation can and must equally be used at any time one is clear, either before or during the triple perineal operation, that there is a risk of postoperative vault prolapse (see section "vaginal vault prolapse" in this chapter on p. 103).

The aim of sacrospinous fixation is to reposition the vaginal vault, placing it back into the location it

would hold in a woman with normal pelvic statics, i.e. being pulled close to the most caudal part of the sacral concavity by the uterosacral ligaments and parametria, which are not transverse structures but oblique structures pulling obliquely from inside to outside and from front to back. The sacrospinous muscle-ligament extends in a fan shape from the ischial spine to the lateral border of the sacral bone and sacrococcygeal joint. This is the ideal point for fixing the vaginal vault. Theoretically, fixation should be onto each of the two sacrospinous ligaments and should be made with the interposition of a mesh or autoplastic vaginal flap to avoid a stricture of the rectal ampulla. By fixing the vaginal vault directly onto one of the two sacrospinous ligaments one achieves a set-up that is theoretically less satisfying but which is, from a practical perspective, excellent, while being much easier and faster to perform.

In cases with post-hysterectomy prolapse, the incision in the bulging vaginal wall is made at the level of the "internavicular line." This line is situated between the two dimples that mark the initial insertion of the paracervical ligaments onto the prolapsed vaginal vault. The vaginal wall is grasped dorsally astride the internavicular line with two tenacula placed on the midline. One pulls divergently on these tenacula and incises the fold this traction produces. In cases where sacrospinous fixation is carried out to complement the triple operation for grade 4 genital prolapse, the vaginal incision is made perpendicularly to the dorsal edge of the circular colpotomy that allowed the inaugural hysterectomy to be performed (Figure 8.100). The incision involves the three layers of the vaginal wall. Once the incision has been made two Cotte forceps are placed, one on each lip of the wound. Pulling on these forceps slightly, one continues the incision on the midline up to the junction of the most dorsal and intermediate thirds. Having reached this point, the incision is extended obliquely toward the tip of a tenaculum placed on the fourchette. This tenaculum is one of the two positioned opposite each other to delineate the base of the triangle of the low dorsal vaginal colpoplasty (Figure 8.101). The same is done on the other side. Once the colpotomy has been completed, the edge of the left vaginal flap is grasped with three Cotte forceps. The assistants pull on these forceps to expose the deep surface of the flap. The ventral surface of the rectum is grasped with surgical forceps. By using traction and releasing maneuvers the fibers joining the two organs are located. These fibers are commonly called "rectovaginal ligament" or "rectal pillar." They are divided with scissors (Figure 8.102). This is easily done and is often unnecessary as simple digital pressure is adequate in many cases. The pararectal space is opened over its entire length.

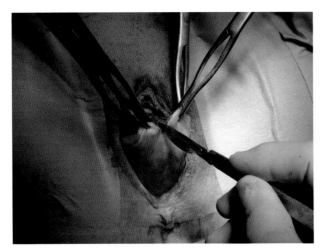

Figure 8.100 The first step of the Richter procedure: incision on the midline of the dorsal vaginal wall. The uterus has been removed and a ventral colporrhaphy performed; the stumps of the paracervical ligaments are pulled upward and outward.

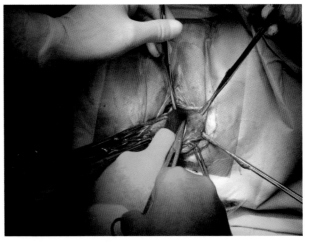

Figure 8.102 The "huge" left vaginal flap is drawn laterally, the fibers joining it to the rectal ampulla are divided and the left pararectal space opened.

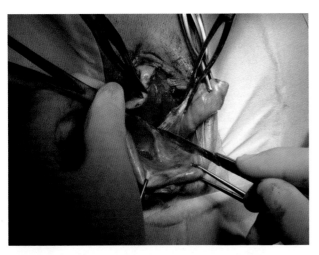

Figure 8.101 At the junction of the middle and lower thirds of the dorsal vaginal wall, the incision diverges obliquely to one of the tenacula marking the base of the colpoperineorrhaphy triangle. This is repeated on the other side.

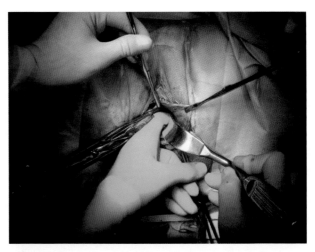

Figure 8.103 The ischial spine is located with the finger and a Richter speculum is placed in the pararectal space, slipping onto the puborectal muscle. This speculum will be rotated counterclockwise to retract the paracervical ligaments upward.

The finger that separated the rectovaginal ligament assesses the pelvic sidewall and locates the ischial spine. As soon as the spine is identified, the finger is used to guide the placement of retractors that are introduced to allow dissection of the sacrospinous muscle-ligament. The first one is placed in an oblique plane where it slips onto the puborectal muscle (Figure 8.103). With 90° axial torsion, the instrument moves in a horizontal direction. It pushes the parametrium upward and frees the lateral aspect of the pararectal space where the sacrospinous muscle-ligament is situated.

Under the protection of the "parametrial" retractor, and with a Mangiagalli retractor pushing on the

perineal body, preparation of the pararectal space with forceps and scissors used as blunt dissectors continues until the pelvic sidewall is completely free (Figure 8.104). Once the ischial spine is completely free, the Mangiagalli retractor is replaced by a Richter retractor, which is rotated counterclockwise at the same time as the parametrial retractor is rotated axially through a further 90° counterclockwise, i.e. placed facing the first one. The medial retractor pushes the rectum and the lateral retractor pushes the muscles covering the pelvic sidewall. Everything is ready for suturing of the sacrospinous ligament (Figure 8.105).

The sacrospinous muscle-ligament that is to be stitched is hidden by the outline of the dorsal edge of the iliococcygeal muscle. It is important to locate the

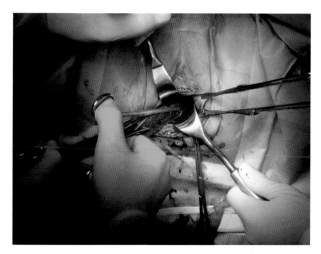

Figure 8.104 Under the protection of the Breisky speculum and a Mangiagelli speculum retracting the puborectal muscle, the preparation of the pararectal space is extended to completely clear the pelvic sidewall dorsal to the ischial spine.

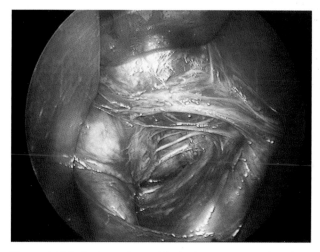

Figure 8.106 A view taken with the laparoscope (placed at the entrance to the operative field) showing the pelvic sidewall dorsal to the ischial spine: the first bundle is the dorsal edge of the iliococcygeus muscle and the sacrospinous muscle/ligament is set back dorsally. This latter is the structure to stitch.

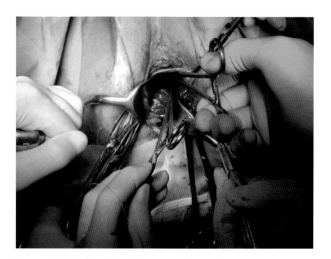

Figure 8.105 Stitching the sacrospinous ligament – demonstration of the position of the instruments. One Breisky retractor pushes the rectum medially. A second Breisky retractor placed opposite the first pushes the iliococcygeus muscle laterally.

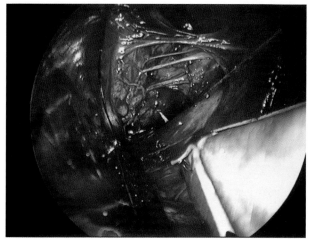

Figure 8.107 A view taken with the laparoscope: the needle is oblique in the first needle holder.

former precisely. This goal is achieved by sliding the lateral retractor along the muscles of the pelvic sidewall. The stitches must be placed in the sacrospinous muscle-ligament and not in the iliococcygeal muscle (Figure 8.106).

To place the sacrospinous fixation sutures, we use 1/3 needles 30 mm long, which are held obliquely in the needle holder (Figure 8.107) and pushed from front to back through the sacrospinous muscle-ligament (Figure 8.108). Because it is easier for a right-handed surgeon to do this on the left pelvic sidewall, we perform sacrospinous fixation on that side. A left-handed surgeon can do it on the right side, which is also the side chosen by all surgeons

using modified Deschamps needles, staples or other gadgets instead of stitches. Once the tip of the sacrospinous fixation needle has passed through the muscle-ligament, it is taken in the depths with a second needle holder (Figure 8.105).

The sutures used are of two different types: one absorbable and one nonabsorbable suture. They are placed at a distance of 5–10 mm from each other on the sacrospinous muscle-ligament (Figure 8.109). The two threads are destined to pass through the vaginal wall, which they will apply and fix to the sacrospinous muscle-ligament. The absorbable suture is passed through the vaginal wall and arrives in the vaginal cavity equidistant from the midline and from each of the dimples previously described (Figure 8.110). The nonabsorbable suture is passed

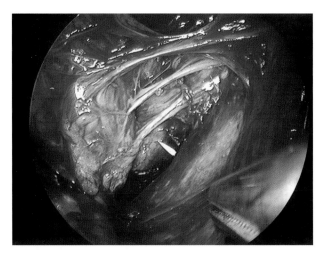

Figure 8.108 A view taken with the laparoscope: the two sutures placed in the sacrospinous muscle/ligament.

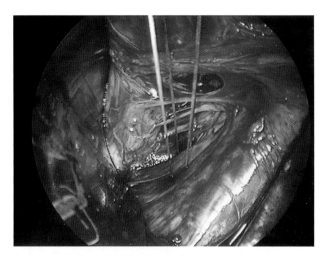

Figure 8.109 A view taken with the laparoscope: the needle is pushed through the sacrospinous muscle/ligament – its tip will be taken with the second needle holder (see Figure 8.105).

at the same level but without going through the skin: it arrives in the perineum and not in the vaginal cavity (Figure 8.111). For both sutures, insertion of the needle is made on one side with the needle itself and on the other side with a free needle.

Before tying the sacrospinous fixation sutures the colpotomy that allowed access to the pararectal spaces must be closed. If one ties the sacrospinous fixation sutures before performing colporrhaphy, the superior angle of the colpotomy disappears into the depths making the colporrhaphy impossible to perform. The colpotomy is sutured from the depths to the surface using 00 Vicryl®. Closure is stopped approximately 2–3 cm before the ventral extremity of the colpotomy is reached to leave a space through which the deep sacrospinous fixation stitch will be tied. As a matter of fact the first stitch (i.e. the absorbable one) is tied inside the vaginal cavity

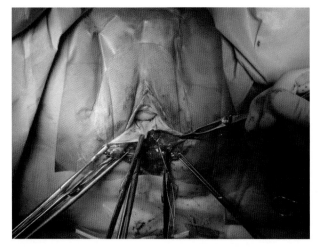

Figure 8.110 The absorbable stitch is passed through the vaginal wall 1 cm from the edge of the midline colpotomy. Note that this case is one of vaginal vault prolapse as opposed to the previously presented case which was a case of standard stage IV prolapse (see Figures 8.100–8.104). The same is done on the other side.

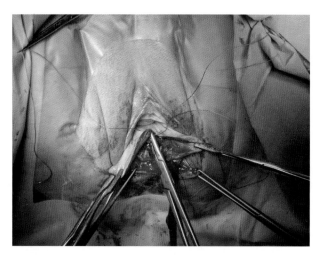

Figure 8.111 The nonabsorbable stitch is passed through the vaginal wall staying deep to the skin and close to the midline. The same is done on the other side.

(Figure 8.112) whereas the second one (i.e. the nonabsorbable one) is tied inside the perineal area behind the closed vaginal wall (Figure 8.113). An important detail in relation to tying the sacrospinous stitches should be noted: take care when first stitching the sacrospinous ligament to avoid crossing the two ends of each stitch, so that on tying, the stitches come into frank contact with the pelvic wall.

The last step of the procedure is the same as in the standard dorsal colpoperineorrhaphy. The dorsal levator myorrhaphy is an important part of the definitive anatomical arrangement that is illustrated in Figure 8.114. In this figure, one can see the vaginal vault fixed to the posterior pelvic wall. One can also see the angle of the vagina restored thanks to the

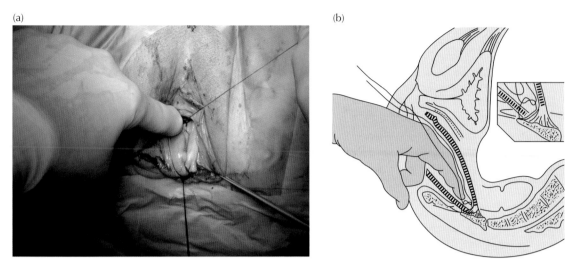

Figure 8.112 (a) and (b) The absorbable stitch is tied on the skin surface (after the midline colpotomy has been almost completely closed). The knot is inside the cavity of the vagina. Reproduced from Dargent D., Mathevet P., Mellier G. (2002) Traitement chirurgical des prolapsus génitaux par la voie vaginale. EMC – Traité de Techniques chirurgicales – Gynécologie, 41: 800–824, Paris: Elsevier, by permission of Elsevier.

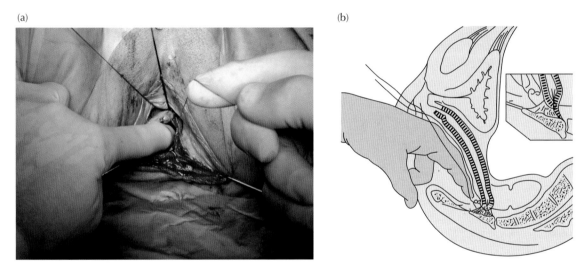

Figure 8.113 (a) and (b) The next knot is tied deep to the skin of the perineum. The knot is inside the perineum. Reproduced from Dargent D., Mathevet P., Mellier G. (2002) Traitement chirurgical des prolapsus génitaux par la voie vaginale. EMC – Traité de Techniques chirurgicales – Gynécologie, 41: 800–824, Paris: Elsevier, by permission of Elsevier.

myorrhaphy stitches: This arrangement restores the bisegmental anatomy of the vagina and thus the auto-blocking mechanism, which ensures stability of the pelvic organs. This is the point that Figure 8.114 illustrates. This last figure also illustrates that after the Richter procedure the ventral vaginal wall is at risk of bulging: cystocele can occur as a consequence of sacrospinous fixation.

Prosthetic reinforcement of the pelvic fascia
Abdominal prolapse surgery (either by laparotomy or laparoscopy) relies on the use of prosthetic mesh that produces both reinforcement of thinned fascia and replacement of stretched ligaments. The mesh is placed in the vesicovaginal and rectovaginal spaces and is anchored onto the pelvic walls where the

ligaments are normally inserted. The tolerance of the materials used continues to improve: polypropylene, which is most commonly used, seems to be the most reliable. However, tolerance does not depend solely on the nature of the material as the surgical approach also plays an important role. If the mesh is placed at laparotomy or laparoscopy, tolerance is generally excellent except in those cases where the vagina is opened: if hysterectomy is done with pelvic reconstruction, expulsion and exposure of the foreign body (mesh) and erosion may occur. Most experts recommend avoiding hysterectomy or performing subtotal hysterectomy rather than total hysterectomy when using laparotomy or laparoscopy for prolapse surgery. One might conclude that using the vaginal approach will increase the risk. However, thanks to the TVT experience, we know that polypropylene

(a)

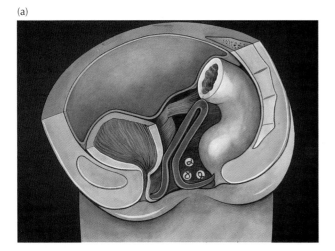

(b)

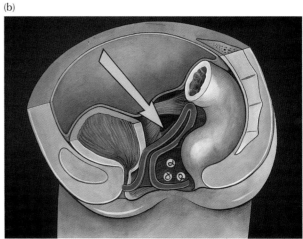

Figure 8.114 (a) and (b) Artist's impression of the pelvic sidewall following sacrospinous fixation and levator myorrhaphy: effect of excessive pressure on the combined repair. Note that the vault and posterior vaginal walls continue to be protected while the anterior vaginal wall is vulnerable and at risk of future cystocele formation – an unavoidable weakness of the Richter operation.

mesh placed transvaginally is tolerated perfectly well for many years. In spite of this reassuring fact, one must remember another factor in the tolerance/nontolerance equation – the size of the mesh: the smaller the prosthesis the better the tolerance. The prosthetic mesh used for fascial reinforcement in prolapse surgery is much larger than that used for TVT. For this reason we recommend that prosthetic mesh is reserved specifically for selected indications.

Recurrent cystocele and/or rectocele are clearly indications for the use of prosthetic mesh. With few exceptions, a second fascial restoration is doomed to failure if performed after a first attempt has already failed. A paravaginal defect identified at preoperative assessment is also an indication for its use as the main cause of recurrent cystocele is omission of the paravaginal repair. Extreme thinning of the fascia is the other indication for the primary use of prosthetic mesh. In cases of giant cystocele and/or rectocele, extreme thinning can be suspected on principal. It can also be discovered during surgery itself either at the point when the vaginal wall is opened or when the fascial plasty is undertaken.

The technique used in "mesh surgery" is a matter for debate. Some surgeons advocate placing the mesh without any sutures. We are afraid that, due to a rolling-up effect, such a technique results in failure or even more commonly in unexpected anatomical distortions and/or functional disorders. For this reason we might recommend stitching the mesh to the anatomical surfaces being reinforced or replaced. On the other hand, it is logical to anchor the mesh to those structures that are normally attached to the organs the mesh intends to maintain in a normal position. For this reason we recommend anchoring the mesh but we recommend anchoring it to the pelvic walls rather than other structures like uterosacral and/or paracervical stumps which are, in the situations where mesh surgery is indicated, weakened and inefficient. And last but not least, mesh surgery, as far as we are concerned, does not obviate the requirement for fascial surgery, particularly in managing the cystocele where "cardigan plasty" has the advantage of interposing a thick double protective layer between the mesh and the vaginal cavity.

Placing a mesh to reinforce the ventral colporrhaphy is done after the two vaginal flaps have been separated from the bladder (Figure 8.8). This involves passing beyond the lateral limit of the standard mobilization and almost always leads to some bleeding due to tearing of one of the vessels belonging to the linea vasorum. Once the bleeder is fixed (Figure 8.9) the paravesical space is entered at first with scissors and then with the finger (Figures 8.115 and 8.116), which identifies the arcus tendineus running from the dorsal aspect of the pubis to the ischial spine. The tendon appears vertical because the patient is in the lithotomy position (but feels horizontal in the standing position). It is usually clearly identified but not always. Two Breisky retractors are put in place to allow placement of a polypropylene stitch (Figure 8.117) in the dorsal end of the insertion (or alleged insertion) of the arcus tendineus. The same is done on the other side and the dorsal edge of the mesh can be applied.

The mesh is tailored by cutting a trapezium shape from a sheet of polypropylene. The base of the trapezium shape is 12 cm wide (the average distance between the two ischial spines) and its summit is

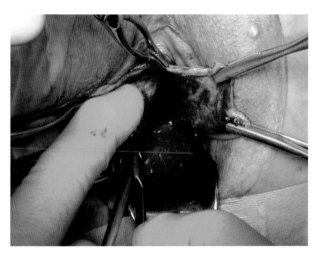

Figure 8.115 The first step of cystocele-mesh surgery: opening the paravesical space with scissors before introducing the finger.

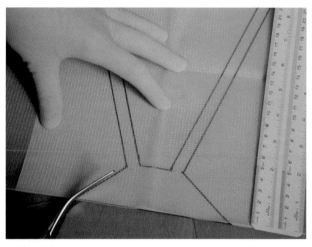

Figure 8.118 Tailoring the "Dirndl" mesh – the shape is a truncated triangle with two braces. The corners at the base of the truncated triangle will be placed in contact with the ischial spines.

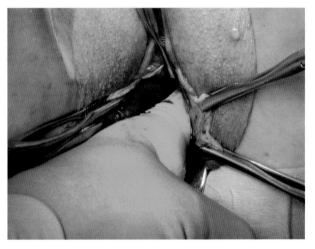

Figure 8.116 The finger is introduced and locates the ischial spine where the arcus tendineus inserts.

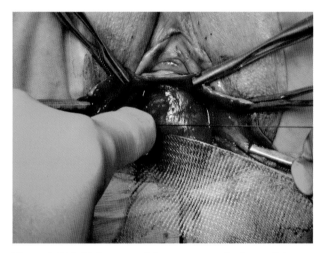

Figure 8.119 Fixing one of the corners at the base of the mesh to the right ischial spine. This is repeated on the left side.

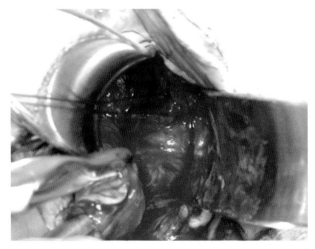

Figure 8.117 A stitch has been placed in the arcus tendineus at its insertion onto the ischial spine.

4 cm wide and lies 4 cm above the base – it is a truncated triangle. It is extended by two braces approximately 10 cm long and approximately 1.5 cm wide. The whole piece (Figure 8.118) looks like the apron worn by waitresses in a German "Gasthaus": the Dirndl. Ideally the lateral edges of the mesh are stitched over the entire length of the arcus tendineus on each side to reinforce the fascia of Halban. This stitching is ergonomically difficult and is the rationale for the Dirndl shape of the mesh.

The extremities of the base are fixed in front of the ischial spines (Figure 8.119). The two extremities of the summit are fixed to the bone thanks to the braces that prolong it upward. These braces are drawn ventrally using the Emmet needles in the same way as they are used for placing the TOT (Figures 8.120 and 8.121). Once the Dirndl mesh is in place its

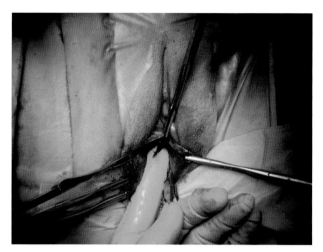

Figure 8.120 Passing the Emmet needle around the ischiopubic bone on the left side, starting from a micro-incision made in the genitofemoral fold.

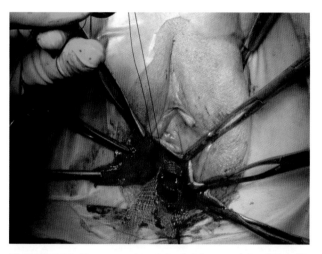

Figure 8.121 The extremity of the left brace of the "Dirndl" mesh is stitched to the eye in the tip of the Emmet needle – it will be pulled through the obturator foramen. The same will be done on the other side.

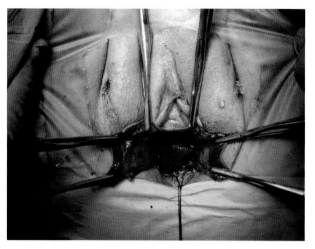

Figure 8.122 Final view showing the position of the mesh in place underneath the bladder floor. The corners at the base of the truncated triangle are stitched to the ischial spines and the corners at the top are secured to the dorsal surface of the pubic bone thanks to the Velcro effect exerted by the two braces. Note the lack of tension.

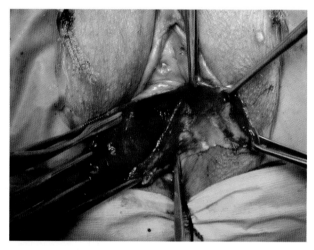

Figure 8.123 Splitting the vaginal flap on the left.

dorsal edge is stitched to the most dorsal part of the bladder floor (Figure 8.122). The ventral edge is fixed to the bladder neck in the same way. There must not be any tension: just as a seat belt prevents protrusion of the body when a crash submits it to an unexpected increase in pressure, the mesh prevents descent of the organ rather than elevating it. A fascial "cardigan plasty" is a mandatory addition to insertion of the mesh (Figures 8.123 and 8.124).

Stitching the arcus tendineus at its dorsocaudal extremity is not easy. The same trick used to get around the "insurmountable" difficulty encountered at the ventrocephalic extremity is implemented at the dorsocaudal extremity. The Dirndl mesh is tailored in a different way: two braces extend the base of the truncated triangle horizontally for placement under the bladder floor: Figure 8.125. These two braces are

placed using an Emmet needle or similar instrument. Under the control of the finger that is in contact with the ischial spine (Figures 8.116 and 8.117) an Emmet needle is introduced alongside the pelvic sidewall starting from a point situated between the anus and the ischial tuberosity (Figure 8.126). Once the tip of the needle is identified by the waiting finger, a rotating movement makes this tip leave the plane it was running in (the muscles covering the medial surface of the obturator foramen) to move around the dorsal edge of the iliococcygeus muscle and thus appear in the paravesical space close to the ischial spine, i.e. close to the extremity of the arcus tendineus. The extremity of the horizontal brace of the mesh is secured in the eye of the needle and drawn outside. The same is done on the other side. The final arrangement, in spite of the external appearance (Figure 8.127) is no different from that obtained by direct stitching (Figure 8.128).

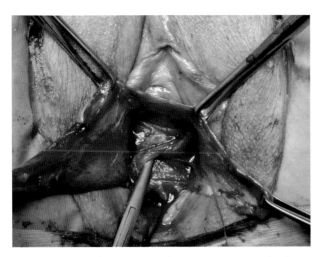

Figure 8.124 Performing a cardigan repair to completely cover the mesh.

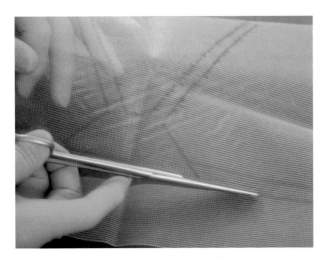

Figure 8.125 Modification of the "Dirndl" mesh as an alternative approach to securing the corners at the base of the truncated triangle to the ischial spines. Two horizontal braces are added to extend the base.

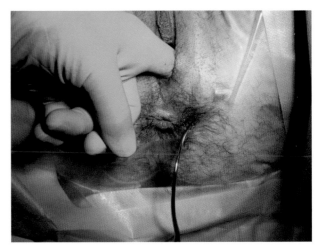

Figure 8.126 The Emmet needle is introduced at a point midway between the anus and the ischial tuberosity. It is pushed at a slightly oblique direction along the pelvic sidewall going through the muscles that cover it (the obturator internus muscle and the iliococcygeal muscle). The finger introduced into the paravesical space controls the movement. Once the tip of the needle is identified, the needle is rotated horizontally to emerge in the paravesical space. The end of the horizontal brace will be attached to the eye of the needle and drawn back to the skin incision.

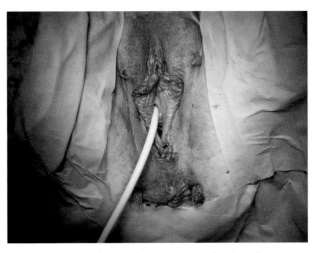

Figure 8.127 Final view showing the ends of the four braces in place. It may appear that the mesh is in a coronal plane. However, this is not the case as the posterior braces form a type of pulley system around the dorsal edge of the iliococcygeus muscles (see Figure 8.129).

Prosthetic reinforcement can be used for the dorsal colporrhaphy as it can be used for the ventral colporrhaphy. Instead of opening the pararectal space on one side only it is now opened on both. Two nonabsorbable stitches destined to anchor the craniodorsal extremity of the mesh (Figures 8.129 and 8.130) are placed in each sacrospinous ligament. Depending on the pathology to be cured or prevented, one or two mesh are used. Defecography is the key to this decision. In cases of giant rectocele just one mesh is used. It is applied to the front of the rectorrhaphy suture on the ventral surface of the rectal ampulla and its ventrocaudal extremity is fixed to the perineal body to prevent its descent while reinforcing the rectorrhaphy. In cases of internal rectal prolapse two mesh are used, their ventrocaudal extremities being fixed to the ventrolateral aspects of the rectum itself. One is placed in an almost vertical position and the other in an almost horizontal position so that their ventrocaudal extremities remain at a sufficient distance from each other to allow free filling and emptying of the rectal ampulla (Figure 8.131). Whatever the indications and techniques the mesh must be positioned without any tension and the vaginal suture must be placed with the greatest care.

The future of vaginal prolapse surgery is difficult to predict. The use of prosthetic material was introduced at the end of the 1990s, i.e. when polypropylene

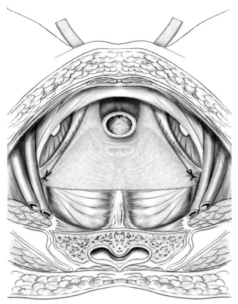

Figure 8.128 Artist's impression of the position of the four corners of the "Dirndl" mesh secured in place.

Figure 8.129 The first step of the prosthetic reinforcement of the dorsal colporrhaphy: placing stitches in the sacrospinous muscle/ligament.

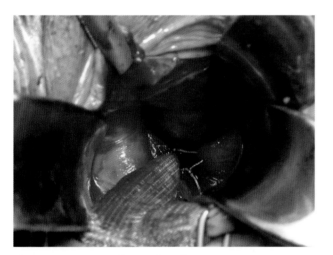

Figure 8.130 Fixing the mesh to the sacrospinous muscle/ligament. The same can be done on the other side.

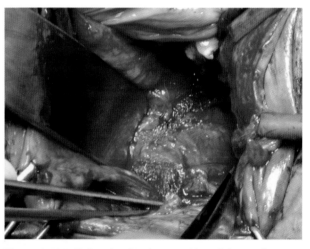

Figure 8.131 Fixing the distal extremities of the meshes. Note that they are not immediately adjacent to each other to allow the rectum to expand.

mesh became available. Perhaps tolerance of this material won't stand the test of long-term surveillance. Perhaps it will. If the latter holds true, one predicts a great and successful future for prosthetic surgery, which can be used as described in the preceding paragraph as a complement to classical surgery or alternatively as the original ultra-simplified surgery. One can use staplers instead of stitches to anchor mesh to the pelvic wall. The percutaneous technique described just above for placement of mesh in the region of the ischial spine can be used without any prior preparation of the paravesical and/or pararectal spaces. One may restrict one's self to applying mesh over deficient fascia without anchoring it to the pelvic wall and so on.

Chi vivrà vedrà!

9 Vesico- and rectovaginal fistulas

Vesico- and rectovaginal fistulas represent one of the fields where human pathology completely changed during the twentieth century. The large urogenital fistula due to protracted deliveries has disappeared. The large rectovaginal fistula due to traumatic instrumental extraction of the fetus has also disappeared. Fistulas occurring after hysterectomy are more than rare. Even fistulas due to extended cancer operations and/or radiotherapy are infrequent. These last, like the fistulas associated with Crohn's disease and sigmoiditis, are the only ones that mandate an abdominal approach.

The rare small vesicovaginal fistulas and the very rare rectovaginal fistulas currently observed after hysterectomy can be cured by upper colpocleisis as described by Latzko. The even more rare small vesico- and/or urethrovaginal fistulas observed after traumatic delivery can be managed using a simple vaginal flap technique. Rectovaginal fistulas caused by obstetric laceration of the perineum can be successfully treated using a purely perineal approach. These are the procedures we describe hereafter omitting as usual the abdominal operations and the vaginal operations we don't perform on a regular basis.

Upper colpocleisis described by Latzko

The operation devised by the Austrian gynecologist Latzko in 1911 is perfectly suited to the post hysterectomy vesico- and rectovaginal fistulas as most of those that we have to manage today are small and simple. The operation is much less aggressive than the abdominal one and offers the same chance of cure.

Technique

The operation consists of removing the epidermis of the upper part of the vagina and then stitching together the stripped-out surfaces. A Foley catheter of appropriate size is introduced into the bladder through the orifice of the fistula (Figure 9.1). The balloon is inflated. The catheter is held under traction. The surface can now unfold due to this traction. Subcutaneous infiltration of a mixture of saline and adrenaline is performed (Figure 9.2). Then a circular incision 4 cm in diameter is made around the vaginal orifice of the fistula. The incision is made with a no. 11 blade. It is shallow and incises the skin only. The circular incision includes the piece of epithelium and subepithelial tissue that is to be removed.

The removal of the perifistular vaginal skin is performed using the same cold knife after four counter incisions have been made in each of the four cardinal radii of the circle. One starts at the level of the

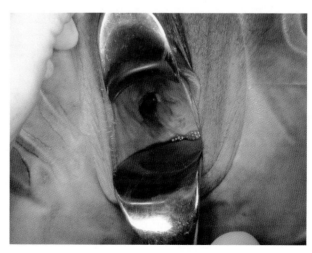

Figure 9.1 Demonstrating the fistula (a rectovaginal fistula in this case).

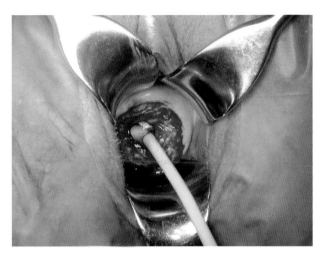

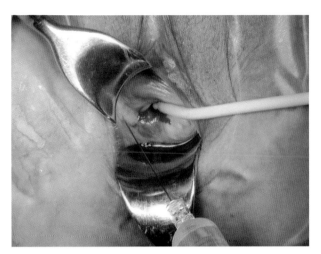

Figure 9.2 Subcutaneous infiltration of saline into the vagina surrounding the fistula. The vagina is spread out by traction on the Foley catheter.

Figure 9.4 After removal of four skin quadrants the vaginal wall around the fistula is completely naked.

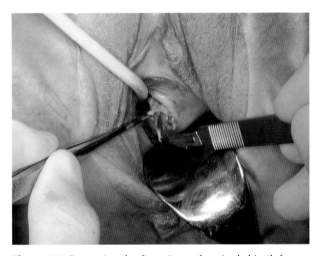

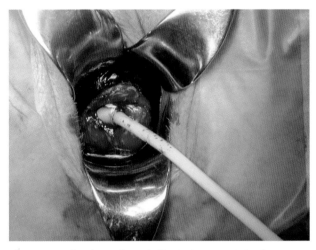

Figure 9.3 Removing the first piece of vaginal skin (left dorsal quadrant) with a no. 11 blade.

Figure 9.5 Thanks to the Schiller iodine test, it is clear that no vaginal epithelium remains in the prepared area.

posterior flaps detaching the subepithelial connective tissue from the underlying fascia (Figure 9.3). The plane one works in is not an anatomical dissecting plane. The previous subcutaneous infiltration assists the dissection, but one has to take care to work in a plane that is neither too deep nor too shallow. If too deep, there is a risk of bladder injury and exacerbation of pathology. If too shallow, some pieces of epithelium may persist and impair the healing process. To be sure that no epithelial fragments persist, which is frequent because of the irregular shape of the vaginal surface around the orifice of the fistula, the Schiller test may be used and is very helpful – if iodine positive islands persist they must be resected.

Once the epidermis around the orifice has been completely removed (Figures 9.4 and 9.5), the anterior and posterior surfaces are stitched together using interrupted stitches. We recommend using a semi-circular 26 mm needle of 00 Monocryl. The first stitch involves the anterior surface. The vaginal fascia is stitched in a sagittal plane taking the full thickness of the tissue. Care is taken to avoid placing the needle so deep that injury of the underlying organ occurs (Figure 9.6). The second stitch involves the posterior surface (Figure 9.7). Four anteroposterior stitches are placed. The traction catheter is removed and the stitches are tied.

The second closing suture is placed in the peripheral skin. 00 Monocryl is used again for a continuous suture which stitches the anterior and posterior lips of the initial circular incision together in a frontal line (Figure 9.8).

At the end of the operation a waterproof test of the suture is performed by injecting 300 ml of saline colored with methylene blue into the organ that previously communicated with the vagina. If dealing with a vesicovaginal fistula, a Foley catheter is

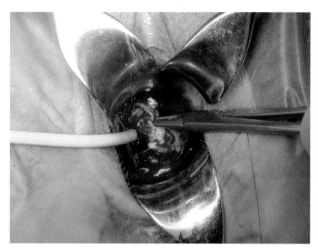

Figure 9.6 The ventral part of the first deep stitch takes the tissues in full thickness but is not too deep to avoid injury to the underlying bladder. Monofilament is the suture of choice to reduce risk of infection.

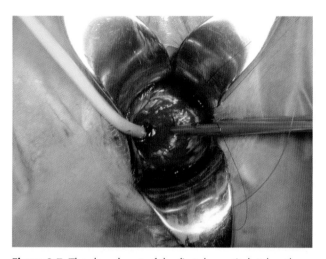

Figure 9.7 The dorsal part of the first deep stitch takes the tissues in full thickness but is not too deep to avoid injury to the underlying rectum.

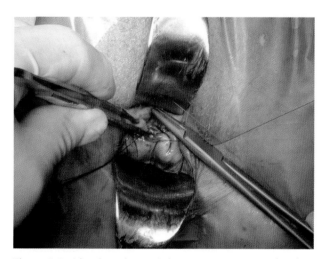

Figure 9.8 After four deep stitches, a covering superficial running stitch is performed.

inserted to perform the waterproof test, and could theoretically be removed if the test is satisfactory. We prefer to leave it *in situ* for a number of days.

Postoperative course and complications

The Latzko operation is carried out in 20–30 min. The postoperative course is usually uneventful and the patient could be discharged the following day. The only problem, if one is dealing with a vesicovaginal fistula, is bladder drainage. This drainage is theoretically pointless. No suturing is performed on the bladder itself and as the bladder fills up, the pressure on the fasciofascial suture is increased, i.e. the healing process is promoted. In spite of this argument, we prefer to drain the bladder for 10 days after which we perform a retrograde cystogram. The catheter is only removed in cases where absolutely no leakage is identified after injecting 300 ml of contrast fluid. Another precaution is to prohibit sexual intercourse for 6 weeks.

The only complication of the Latzko operation is failure. The failure rate is less than 10%. If the length of the vagina allows it, a second attempt can be suggested after complete healing. If not the abdominal approach is mandatory.

Indications and contraindications

The only drawback of the Latzko operation is that it requires optimal vaginal anatomy. If the lower third of the vagina is narrow an episiotomy can solve the problem but if the upper part is narrow and short the operation is not feasible. There is one exception when colpocleisis is appropriate even when the vagina is short: this is in the palliative treatment of large vesicovaginal fistulas in relapsing cancer patients (obliterating vaginal patency, in such cases, can be acceptable).

As far as "other" aspects of the pathology are concerned, there are practically no contraindications to the Latzko procedure either for vesicovaginal or rectovaginal fistulas. As far as the vesicovaginal fistulas are concerned, the ideal indication is the case where the vesical orifice of the fistula is small and located on the midline at a distance from the ureteric orifices. But even if the fistula is large and located close to ureteric orifices, upper colpocleisis can be considered on condition that there is no ureteric stenosis. If such a stenosis is present, a uretero-neo-cystotomy should be performed. In the past, some urogynecologists were able to do this using the vaginal approach. We prefer to recommend the abdominal approach. These considerations lead to the conclusion that one never undertakes the Latzko operation without having previously assessed the patient with cystoscopy and intravenous pyelography. The same is true for rectovaginal fistulas: we recommend assessing the rectal aspect with rectosigmoidoscopy in every case.

Another condition for proceeding with upper colpocleisis is that the lesions are stabilized, i.e. that both orifices of the fistula are surrounded by a smooth whitish circular ring of sclerosis. Operating before this has developed results in failure. This is very important for patients who present with incontinence some days after hysterectomy. One must never try to close the fistula immediately. A delay of 2 months is necessary although it is not easy to convince patients to wait for such a long time. It is particularly difficult for patients with vesicovaginal fistulas because continuous drainage does not completely prevent the loss of urine. For those with rectovaginal fistulas, colostomy totally prevents the loss of feces. However, it is never easy to persuade a patient to accept a colostomy even when it is temporary.

Vaginal flaps for lower fistulas

Small vesico- or rectovaginal fistulas that have developed in the middle third of the anterior or posterior wall of the vagina can be cured in a very simple and safe way using short vaginal flaps.

Technique

The principle of the operation is the same as the principle of the Latzko operation in so far as the first goal is to close the vaginal orifice of the fistula. However, it differs in that the fistular orifice itself is (economically) resected and the vaginal suture is placed after elevation and mobilization of a full thickness vaginal flap.

The incision is made drawing a double "J". The two Js have the same vertical stem on which two parallel curves are separated by a distance of approximately 20 mm. The space located between the two curves includes the vaginal orifice of the fistula. The incision is made with a no. 11 blade and is a full thickness incision. The piece of vaginal wall that is located between the two curves is removed first. This removal reveals the bladder wall and makes the hole look larger. Actually it is not.

The vaginal flap is elevated while separating the piece of vaginal wall included inside the drawing of the smallest J. This dissection must be done in the right plane: not too deep to avoid making the vesical defect larger and not too shallow so as to maintain the blood supply of the flap which comes from the side

opposite to the vertical stem of the J. The mobilization of the flap must be large enough to extend to the point where its convexity joins the concavity of its extremity inside the curve of the longest J.

Closure is performed in two layers. The first layer consists of two separate Monocryl 00 stitches made transversely across the bladder orifice. The second layer is made by a series of interrupted stitches joining the convexity of the smallest J to the concavity of the longest one.

Postoperative course and complications

There is no difference between "mini-flap" surgery and upper colpocleisis as far as the postoperative course and complications are concerned. The bladder is drained for 10 days. A cystogram is performed at the end of this period requesting a micturating image to exclude a persistent ureterovaginal communication. This is more than rare. The rate of failure is very low.

Indications and contraindications

Vesico- and ureterovaginal fistulas are the elective indications for "mini-flap" surgery (with the exception of those occurring after hysterectomy and located at the tip of the vaginal vault). The conditions under which this surgery may be considered or refused are the same as the ones listed for upper colpocleisis. Rectovaginal fistulas can also be managed using "mini-flap" surgery. However, the rectovaginal fistula is generally only the tip of an iceberg of perineal destruction that requires specific complementary reconstruction. That is the rationale for the perineal bipartition and reconstruction as described by Musset.

Perineal bipartition and reconstruction described by Musset

The operation launched by Musset in 1950 is not only a technique, but also a strategy. As a matter of fact, the Musset operation is a two-step operation. The first step consists of opening the perineum completely, placing a "sonde cannelée" (grooved probe) into the fistula and cutting all the tissues located in front of the instrument with a cold knife (Figure 9.9). After electrocautery hemostasis the wound is left open. The healing process leads to the clinical appearance found in cases of postobstetrical complete (grade 3) laceration of the perineum which has either not been treated or where treatment has failed completely (Figure 9.10). Nothing but a fibromucous fold is interposed between the vaginal cavity and the orifice of the anus. The circle of radial wrinkles, which corresponds to the connection between the skin and the external sphincter of the anus, is interrupted on its ventral aspect making this circle a ventrally opened crescent. Two dimples located at the extremities of the crescent mark the extremities of the interrupted anal sphincter. The healing process proceeds relatively fast. However, one has to allow at least 6–8 weeks before undertaking reconstruction. During this period of time the patient lives at home and her situation is generally better than it was before the perineotomy, because fecal continence is generally improved: the anal sphincter whose ventral part is replaced by a fibrous string has got a certain efficiency, whereas the orifice of the fistula did not offer any resistance to feces before the perineotomy was performed.

Technique

The first step of the operation consists of separating the vaginal wall from the intestinal wall. The operative field is opened thanks to four forceps. The first two forceps (Allis forceps) are put at the level of the dimples marking the extremities of the external anal sphincter. The two other forceps are put at the dorsal extremities of the vulvar labia (Babcock forceps). The first incision is made with a no. 11 blade and is a transverse incision from one extremity of the anal sphincter to the other (Figure 9.11). The vaginal flap, having been taken with a stronger grasping forceps (Gaston Cotte forceps), is elevated. The cold knife is first used on the lateral side (Figure 9.12), followed by

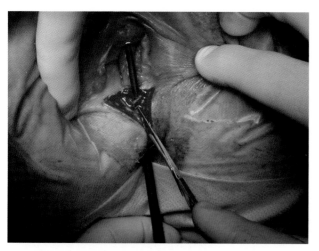

Figure 9.9 Incision of the perineum over a "sonde cannelée" (grooved probe) introduced through the anus into the vagina via the fistula.

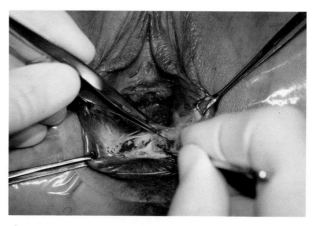

Figure 9.11 Separation of the vaginal and rectal walls using a no. 11 blade.

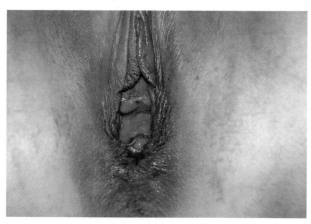

Figure 9.10 Anatomy of perineum some weeks after the fistula has been laid open: the vaginal mucosa is in direct continuity with the rectal mucosa.

Figure 9.12 Elevation of the vaginal wall with a no. 11 blade.

Metzenbaum scissors (Figure 9.13). The dissection allows rather an easy opening of the lower part of the pararectal spaces. Once the same has been done on the opposite side, two retractors are placed in the opened spaces and the fibrous tracts joining the vaginal wall and the rectal wall on the midline are stretched and can be cut with scissors with a lower risk of injuring either one or the other of the two organs that one is holding apart (Figure 9.14). The dissection has not extended too high: 1.5–2 cm is enough.

The second step of the operation is to reconstruct the wall of the intestine. One has first to remove the fibrous tissue surrounding the former fistular orifice. This is done with scissors that separate the strip of tissue between the two forceps put at the extremities of the anal sphincter (Figure 9.15). The strip has to be broad enough to get sound tissues but narrow enough to avoid making the tissue defect, which is part of the pathology, larger. The intestinal wall is sutured with interrupted sutures of 00 PDS, each of the stitches taking, as is usual in gastrointestinal tract surgery, all the layers except the mucosa (Figure 9.16). The stitches are tied inside the perineum (outside the intestinal cavity).

The third step of the reconstruction deals with the muscles: the levator ani and the external anal sphincter. The levator ani represents the lateral boundary of the pararectal space, which was opened during the very first step of the operation. It is stitched transversely using a 0 Vicryl® on a semicircular 26 mm needle which provides a large enough hold (Figure 9.17). The first stitch is made close to the

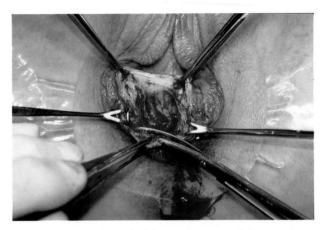

Figure 9.15 Resecting the fibrous ring around the rectal orifice of the fistula.

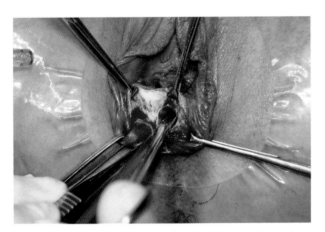

Figure 9.13 Proceeding in elevating the vaginal flap with the Metzenbaum scissors.

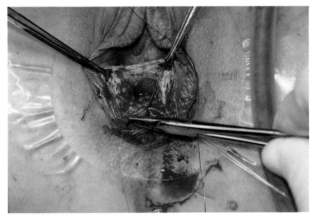

Figure 9.16 Performing the first stitch on the sound part of the ventral rectal wall using a 4 × 0 monofilament suture.

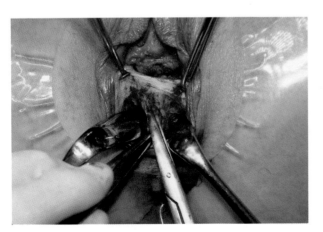

Figure 9.14 Elevating the midline area of the vaginal flap after its two lateral parts have been elevated.

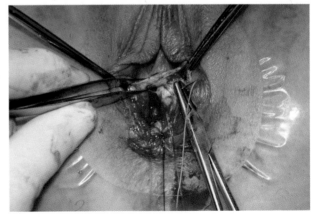

Figure 9.17 Performing the first movement of the first ventral myorrhaphy stitch using 0 Vicryl®.

vagina. A second stitch is performed the same way at an intermediate level (Figure 9.18). Then one moves to the third stitch, which is made on the horns of the sphincter. These horns must not be separated from either the skin attached to them or the levator muscle fibers connected to them. They are "harpooned" blindly using a semicircular 26 mm needle that is introduced under the wrinkled skin covering the sphincter and parallel to the direction of its fibers. Then the needle is pushed in a 180° circular motion (Figure 9.19). The same is done on the other side. The threads are used as retractors and the sphincteroplasty stitch can be carried out using the same technique and the same material that were used for the two levator plasty stitches (Figure 9.20).

The final steps of the operation involve the vaginal wall and the perineal skin. A strip of vaginal wall is removed from between the dorsal extremities of both vulvar labia (Figure 9.21) so that the fibrous environment of the former vaginal orifice of the fistula is excised. Then the vaginal wall is reconstructed with a series of interrupted stitches (Figure 9.22) until the boundary between vaginal and

(a)

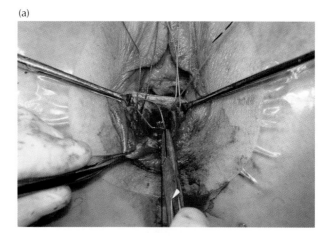

(b)

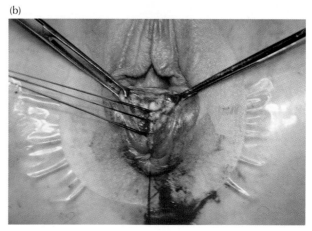

Figure 9.20 (a) Performing the sphincteroplasty stitch while suturing the two horns of the sphincter which have been harpooned and approximated by convergent traction exerted on the harpooning threads. (b) Final view after tying the sphincteroplasty and myorrhaphy stitches.

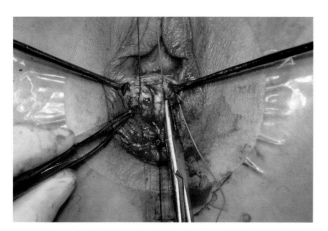

Figure 9.18 Performing the second movement of the second ventral myorrhaphy stitch using 0 Vicryl®.

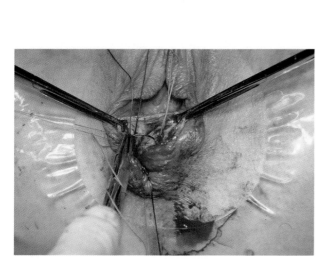

Figure 9.19 Subcutaneous harpooning of the left horn of the external anal sphincter.

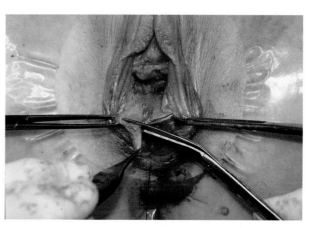

Figure 9.21 Resecting the fibrous ring around the vaginal orifice of the fistula.

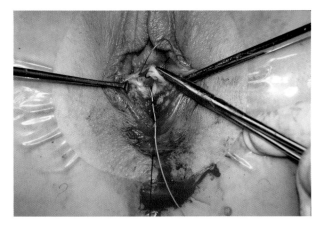

Figure 9.22 Performing the last stitch on the dorsal vaginal wall using 2 × 0 Vicryl®.

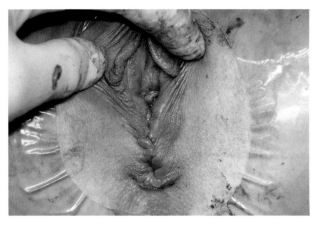

Figure 9.24 The final view.

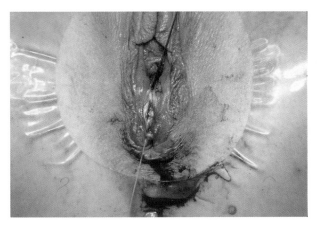

Figure 9.23 The superficial perineum is stitched using 2 × 0 colorless Vicryl®.

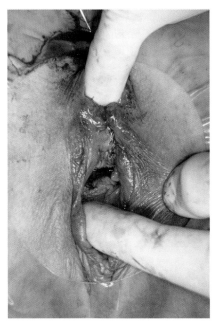

Figure 9.25 Careful digital dilation of the anus and assessment of the perineal body and rectovaginal septum.

perineal skins is reached. The very last step of the operation involves closing the perineal skin using subcutaneous 00 Monocryl stitches (Figure 9.23). At the end of the operation, the anal wrinkled circular line is restored and also the perineal body (Figure 9.24). A digital dilation of the reconstructed anal canal is performed carefully (Figure 9.25) to confirm that the abnormal communication between vagina and intestine has disappeared and to facilitate future bowel movements.

Postoperative course and complications

The postoperative course after perineal reconstruction is uneventful. The only point to watch is the return to normal defecation. This event is often delayed as the intestine will have been washed out before surgery thanks to lactulose. If it does not occur before day 3 a laxative should be given.

Healing generally follows in the normal course of events. If not, wound leakage is purely superficial and the definitive result still adequate. Actually, the most important issue is not the cosmetic result but the functional one. The latter is usually excellent and depends on the preoperative function of the sphincter. In most cases this sphincter, whatever its appearance, has more or less deteriorated. The sphincteroplasty (and the levator plasty), which is in the perineal approach an unavoidable step of the procedure, can only have a favorable effect.

Indications and contraindications

The elective indication for the Musset procedure is a rectovaginal fistula occurring after a complete obstetric perineal laceration, grade 3. Nowadays, most of these severe injuries are managed immediately and correctly. In some instances, the repair fails either completely or partially: persistence of a communication between the vagina and the intestine above an apparently normal perineal body. Whatever the clinical presentation, the second being much more frequent than the first, one has to refrain from undertaking a corrective procedure immediately and the problem is: when is it done? What type of procedure should be used?

As far as timing is concerned, this depends on the course of the healing process. It takes on average 6–8 weeks before conditions are ideal. Once they are, another question arises if the Musset procedure is chosen: two-step surgery or one-step surgery? The first solution is safer but in cases where the appearance of the scarred area is impeccable, perineotomy and reconstruction can be carried out in the same session. It saves 6–8 weeks of discomfort for the patient and does not affect the cure rate. The same applies if the issue arises some time after the initial event.

The choice of the type of procedure depends on the state of the perineal body and above all on the state of the anal sphincter. The assessment of the first is made clinically (with some exceptions, imaging – Magnetic Resonance Imaging (MRI) – is not mandatory). Assessment of the state of the sphincter is better by manometry and imaging (endoscopic ultrasound). In cases where the perineal body and the anal sphincter are completely normal a flap procedure may be appropriate but in most instances the existence of mild to severe alterations makes the perineal approach better.

Low rectal fistulas are not only due to obstetrical trauma. Some are due to surgery (extirpation of a Bartholin's cyst, perineoplasty, etc.): the vaginal flap procedure and the perineal approach are appropriate here. Fistulas due to Crohn's disease, fistulas occurring after radiotherapy and fistulas recurring after a first attempt at repair can also be managed using the simple procedure. However, operating under the protection of a temporary colostomy and/or adding the interposition of either the content of the labia majora (Martius procedure) or the gracilis muscle to the perineal reconstruction may be indicated in these cases.

10 Vaginal surgery in obstetrics

Obstetrics is the last realm where laparoscopic surgery has not had an impact. Laparoscopic surgery can be very helpful during pregnancy and in the postpartum period, but as far as operations aiming to maintain or interrupt pregnancy are concerned, it has no place. Curettage is the most commonly performed surgical procedure of all: there is no question about the technique. Cesarean section (C-section) is the second most common: here there is a role for vaginal surgery but no place for laparoscopy! Cerclage has only rare indications: here there is no place for laparotomy (or laparoscopy) even for so-called isthmic cerclage.

Curettage and its variants (vacuum extraction) won't be described here. Neither will the standard Mac Donald cerclage. This chapter includes a description of three operations: vaginal Cesarean section, vaginal isthmic cerclage and cervical closure according to Saling.

Vaginal Cesarean section

Vaginal C-section has a very limited place in contemporary obstetrics but its lack of credibility may be harmful. In any case, an awareness of the technique is important, even if one limits the indications to rare circumstances.

Technique

Anterior colpotomy is the first step of vaginal C-section. It is made transversely in the "bladder fold" over approximately 4 cm. The incision is a full thickness incision. The inferior lip of this incision will be grasped by two bullet forceps juxtaposed on the midline.

Opening the vesicouterine space and mobilizing the bladder constitute the second step. This is done in the same way as at the beginning of vaginal hysterectomy: incision of the supravaginal septum,

introduction of the finger along the anterior surface of the uterus, introduction of a Breisky retractor, sectioning of the remaining vesicouterine fibers with the scissors, further blunt digital dissection etc. until the vesicouterine peritoneal cul de sac becomes apparent.

The hysterotomy itself is performed on the midline between the two bullet forceps using straight scissors. The incision is continued up to the bottom of the peritoneal vesicouterine cul de sac: 5–6 cm if the C-section is carried out during the second trimester and 7–8 cm in the third trimester. Extraction is performed manually by taking one foot of the fetus and following the rules of podalic extraction.

After removal of the placenta and membranes, the hysterotomy is sutured using 0 Vicryl® for either interrupted or continuous stitches. The first stitch is made at the superior angle of the incision. The stitches are single-layer stitches and care is taken to avoid stitching the mucosa. Suturing the initial colpotomy constitutes the very last step of the operation.

Postoperative course and complications

As far as the maternal postoperative course is concerned, vaginal C-section is undoubtedly the most simple and least painful technique of surgical evacuation of the pregnant uterus. Common complications of C-section can occur such as endometritis, pelvic infection, thrombophlebitis, and so on, but they are less frequent and there are no wound healing problems such as hematoma, abscess, dehiscence, incisional hernia, etc. The uterine scar does not differ from the one left by abdominal C-section.

Indications and contraindications

Vaginal C-section has no place at all in the surgical repertoire of most obstetricians who are likely to think that laparotomy is the only possible approach etc. because the founder of the Julian Dynasty (i.e. Julius Cesar) was born this way! A few obstetricians have a more balanced opinion and believe that the vaginal approach is a superior option when the indication for C-section arises before viability of the fetus or when the fetus is dead.

In cases of late abortion, either spontaneous or legally induced (fetal malformation), vaginal C-section is an option when medical induction fails. The same applies if a complication occurs during induced labour. Vaginal C-section is particularly interesting in the case of hemorrhage (for it takes less time) and in the case of infection (performed without opening the peritoneal cavity).

When the indication for C-section arises when the fetus is viable, vaginal C-section is almost unanimously rejected because of the requirement for podalic extraction. There is no first-level evidence that podalic extraction is in itself dangerous. Neonatal deaths and fetal distress affect babies born after abdominal C-section less commonly than after podalic extraction. However, these statistics are biased and do not take into account the conditions in which the decision is taken. Actually the classical abdominal C-section delivery is often made by "open podalic extraction" and the "traumatism" (the word being understood in its original form) is no less (probably more) than it is after podalic extraction carried out transvaginally at transvaginal hysterotomy. This applies on condition, of course, that there is no disproportion between the volume of the fetus and the width of the pelvis.

Over many decades, the main indication for C-section was the problem of cephalopelvic disproportion. In these cases, the abdominal approach was the only feasible one. That is no longer the case. Most C-sections are now performed on women harboring a pelvis of normal size and holding a fetus whose weight is normal or low and who is at risk of chronic or acute distress. In this context, vaginal C-section could theoretically be the operation of the future!

Vaginal isthmic cerclage

Cervicoisthmic incompetence is rare and can usually be managed using the classical Mac Donald cerclage, which is performed at the end of the first trimester of pregnancy. It is only in cases where this simple tool doesn't work that one has to consider doing more, e.g. Benson proposed putting the cerclage around the isthmus. In the technique described by Benson the cerclage is placed at laparotomy. It can be placed at the same level using the vaginal approach. This has obvious benefits.

Technique

Access to the isthmus of the uterus is easily obtained by mobilizing the bladder on the ventral aspect and opening the pouch of Douglas on the dorsal aspect. The ventral and dorsal colpotomies are performed in the same way as they are in vaginal hysterectomy (see Chapter 7). The only difference involves the two lateral skin incisions, which must not be made. The forefinger of the nonoperating hand is placed in the peritoneal cavity alongside the dorsal aspect of the uterus. The shrinking isthmus is felt and, moving away laterally the paraisthmic window is found above the superior edge of the paracervical ligament and below the arch of the uterine artery. This is where the cerclage must be put. The vaginal Deschamps needle is used to bring the thread around the uterus. One starts on the right side of the patient. The unloaded needle is pushed from front to back across the paraisthmic window and the free end of the suture is introduced into the eye located at the extremity of the needle, which is now visible in the pouch of Douglas (Figure 10.1). The needle is then withdrawn before being pushed from front to back again but into the paraisthmic window on the left side (Figure 10.2). The free end of the suture is grasped before the Deschamps needle is withdrawn. The suture we use is a no. 5 flexidene thread on a semi circular needle. This needle is used to stitch the dorsal surface of the isthmus (Figure 10.3) and to fix the cerclage at this level (Figure 10.4). The very last step of the operation consists of closing the anterior and posterior colpotomies.

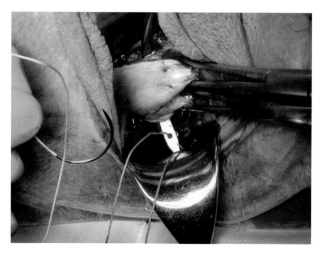

Figure 10.1 First step of the isthmic cerclage. In order to put the cerclage around the isthmus the paraisthmic window is transfixed with the vaginal Deschamps needle. The free end of the suture is placed in the eye at the tip of the Deschamps needle and will be drawn ventrally.

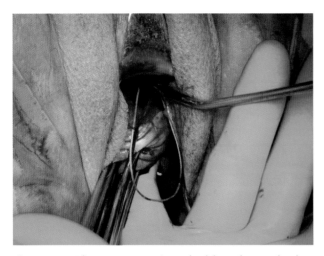

Figure 10.2 The same suture is pushed from front to back through the other paraisthmic window with the same Deschamps needle.

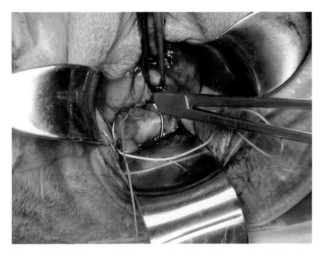

Figure 10.3 The posterior aspect of the isthmus is stitched with the cerclage needle.

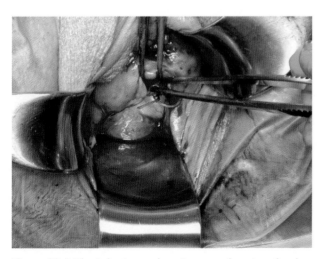

Figure 10.4 The isthmic cerclage is secured against the dorsal aspect of the isthmus. The operation is finished with closure of the two colpotomies.

Postoperative course and complications

The isthmic cerclage is in itself a very simple procedure. The only danger is of injuring the vessels running in the paracervical ligament, i.e. collaterals of the uterine arteries and veins. Holding the cerclage tight stops the bleeding. The danger is obviously greater if the operation is carried out during pregnancy. Even though operating in pregnancy is theoretically possible, we do not recommend it.

The value of the operation in preventing late miscarriage and premature delivery is illustrated by surveys demonstrating that the average length of the pregnancy after isthmic cerclage is significantly greater than the length of the pregnancy experienced by the same patient before cerclage was used. However, the isthmic cerclage does not succeed in 100% of cases. Premature rupture of membranes can occur in spite of mechanical reinforcement of the isthmic sphincter. When this occurs it usually leads to contraction of the uterus. However, unlike the Mac Donald cerclage, this one cannot be cut to allow vaginal delivery and the uterus can only be emptied by C-section. The patient must be fully informed of this drawback when the risk of failure is discussed.

Indications and contraindications

When faced with the problem of cervicoisthmic incompetence, the first choice is clearly not isthmic cerclage. First, one has to be reasonably sure of the diagnosis: all data obtained from the history in particular, and then from clinical assessment and imaging are collected and assessed before concluding that this diagnosis is highly probable, and so on, but never certain. Overall, the Mac Donald cerclage must be favored. It should be performed at the start of the pregnancy that follows on from the accident that led to the hypothesis of cervicoisthmic incompetence in the first place. In cases where this cerclage does not work and a further miscarriage occurs, the indications for isthmic cerclage may be considered. This cerclage is best performed before pregnancy rather than in the first trimester.

There are no contraindications to isthmic cerclage. Some anatomical situations make it more difficult to perform. The isthmus is less accessible in patients with a C-section scar. It is the same in cases where the cervix has been drastically reduced by conization or trachelectomy. That is why we always recommend an isthmic cerclage for patients who have reconization of the cervix after a previous cone. Prophylactic isthmic cerclage could be a step of "reconization." The same applies to patients undergoing radical trachelectomy (see Chapter 13).

Cervical closure as described by Saling

The rationale for cervical closure is based on our understanding of the mechanism of late miscarriage. Chorioamnionitis is regarded as the most common cause. Infection results in the release of endotoxins, cytotoxins, tumor necrosis factor, etc. producing fragile membranes and provoking rupture. At the same time, it induces synthesis of prostaglandins, which in turn induce uterine contractions. Ascending infection from the vagina and cervix is considered to be responsible for contamination of the membranes. Forming a barrier between the vagina and the uterine cavity could provide the ultimate answer for patients who have had multiple miscarriages in spite of the traditional prophylactic measures.

Technique

The technique described by the German gynecologist Saling involves suturing three layers. The layers are the uterine orifice, the naked endocervix and the de-epidermized ectocervix.

The first step is de-epidermization of the cervical surface around the external os. This is achieved by performing a sort of "superficial conization." We recommend first a subepithelial infiltration of saline (without adrenaline). This infiltration is done using a very fine needle (21 Gauges) at a depth of a few millimeters (mm). The aim is to create a dissection plane between the mucosa and the underlying substance that does not normally exist. If the epithelium around the os is native squamous epithelium, a depth of 1–2 mm is enough. If not (ectropion or transformation zone) the connective tissue being colonized by endocervical glands must be infiltrated to a greater depth (3–6 mm). In any case, the de-epidermization must be as superficial as possible. The aim is to strip connective tissue only so that there is no residual squamous or glandular epithelium at the end of the procedure. One can use either a fine (blade no. 11) cold knife or a rectangular diathermy loop. If the latter is chosen, adequate connection of the return electrode must be confirmed to avoid an electric arc endangering the fetus. Whatever the instrument used, the surface to be de-epidermized must be circular and approximately 2 cm in diameter. Once the area has been stripped and the absence of any epithelial residue verified by acetic acid and an iodine test, the first suture is placed. It approximates the ventral and dorsal halves of the de-epidermized circle. We recommend using an absorbable monofilament such as 4-0 Monocryl. The needle is semicircular and 26 mm long, which allows it to take connective tissue at a depth that is neither too great nor too small.

The suture is performed in the sagittal plane starting from the ventral side (Figure 10.5) and running to the dorsal side. Four stitches are placed.

Once the first stitches are in place, a second suture is performed using the same material on the mucosal circumference of the de-epidermized area. It is a continuous suture starting from one angle (Figure 10.6) and finishing at the opposite angle (Figure 10.7).

Postoperative course and complications

Cervical closure is easy to perform (less than 20 min is adequate) and the postoperative course is generally uneventful. Antibiotic prophylaxis (one dose 1 h before surgery) is recommended but neither preoperative

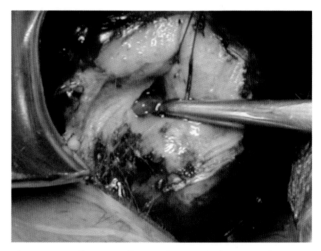

Figure 10.5 The second step of cervical closure (Saling procedure). The cervix has been de-epidermized with a superficial diathermy loop. The second part of the first deep closure stitch is underway using a monofilament 3-0 suture.

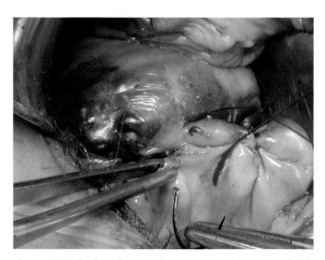

Figure 10.6 The four deep stitches are covered by a superficial transverse running suture (monofilament 3-0 suture).

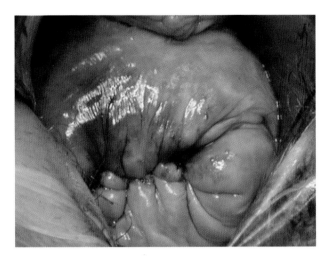

Figure 10.7 The cervix is closed.

nor postoperative antiseptics (except the preoperative dose mentioned above), nor protracted antibiotic therapy are indicated. Tocolytic treatment is also recommended but only on the day of surgery: One dose of NSAID on commencing surgery and one further dose 6 h later. Long-term tocolysis is not recommended. Follow-up should be based on ultrasound rather than intravaginal assessment. If the internal cervical os starts to open, bed rest is advised but tocolytic drugs should not be given as standard. After the C-section, which is obviously mandatory at the end of the pregnancy, patency of the cervix is restored using simple digital pressure. At the 6-week postnatal visit, the orifice is generally fully visible.

Manipulating the cervix during pregnancy carries a risk of miscarriage. To minimize the risk, one must operate at the right time and using the correct technique. The appropriate time is the 15th week: waiting until the period for miscarriage due to genetic defects has passed, but operating before the uterine isthmus starts to get higher and thinner, which increases the risk of direct trauma to the membranes. Be careful not to drive the needle too deep while placing the deep stitches.

The presence of foreign material in the vagina induces infection that can endanger the membranes: do not use nonabsorbable sutures and choose a monofilament suture rather than a braided one.

Indications and contraindications

Most late miscarriages due to cervicoisthmic incompetence can be prevented either by a Mac Donald cerclage put in place at the end of the first trimester or, in cases where this has failed, by isthmic cerclage put in place between pregnancies. It is only in a case where such a strategy fails that cervical closure should be considered. Waiting for at least three accidents (the inaugural accident, one after Mac Donald's cerclage and one in spite of an isthmic cerclage) may appear inhumane. However, cervical closure performed during pregnancy may be simple to perform and generally successful, but it is not without risk. It is really the final solution. Trachelectomy provides the only circumstance when its use is mandatory (see Chapter 13).

11 Laparoscopic assistance for vaginal surgery

The advent of laparoscopic pelvic surgery, which happened in the middle of the 1980s, changed somehow the everyday practice of gynecological surgery. At the very beginning, many surgeons saw laparoscopic surgery as a tool allowing them to extend the place of vaginal hysterectomy, which was, in their practice, very small. They thought that dividing the connections of the womb from above should make it easier to remove it from below. They quickly discovered that managing the lower connections, which is the most difficult and the most dangerous part of the operation, was generally easier from below. As a paradoxical consequence, the practice of pure vaginal surgery increased, as shown by many surveys gathered in different parts of the world.

Parallel to this movement, some specialists went on to develop a purely laparoscopic approach. They even extended it to radical hysterectomy. This option has obvious advantages and drawbacks. The main advantage is that tissue damage is less due to the use of bipolar electrosurgery which minimizes bleeding, tissue necrosis and, consequently, postoperative pain. The major drawback is that more time is spent in the OR; this increase involves increased costs and, more importantly, increased risk. The purely laparoscopic approach has to be reserved for relatively young and fit patients etc., in order to perform operations that in the majority of the cases, could have been performed transvaginally in a simpler manner!

This book does not include descriptions of pure laparoscopic gynecological operations, even if all these operations, except the ones involving the adnexae alone, finish with transvaginal extraction of the specimen (however, a place has been made for laparoscopic colpotomy in Chapter 6). On the other hand, a significant amount of room is devoted to operations for which the vaginal approach cannot be accepted without laparoscopic preparation and/or complementation: laparoscopic vaginal radical

hysterectomy and laparoscopic vaginal radical trachelectomy are described in full detail in Chapters 12 and 13. In this chapter we only consider the (few) cases in which laparoscopic assistance and/or complementation really contribute to make the vaginal hysterectomy easier and, finally, increase its range of applications.

Definitions and concepts

The concept of laparoscopic assistance for vaginal hysterectomy (LAVH) must not be confused with the concept of laparoscopic hysterectomy. The LAVH concept is based on the complementarity of laparoscopic and vaginal approaches, the former facilitating the latter. However, all laparoscopic total hysterectomies are finished vaginally. For this reason, the denomination LAVH has been widely accepted. Unfortunately, this denomination is less than precise, as it encompasses all kinds of combinations of laparoscopic and vaginal routes, using different combinations of the two approaches. In our understanding, LAVH is primarily a vaginal hysterectomy facilitated by a minimum of laparoscopic steps.

In the hands of a gynecological surgeon trained in vaginal surgery, approximately 80% of hysterectomies can be completed vaginally. In addition, 10% of hysterectomies are amenable to the vaginal approach using laparoscopic assistance. The need for laparoscopic assistance is quite infrequent when the ovaries are spared. When bilateral oophorectomy is indicated, most (but not all) of cases can be managed vaginally. In this context, the major indication for laparoscopic assistance is suspicion or evidence of adnexal disease.

The LAVH, as defined before, is not a laparoscopic imitation of an abdominal operation. It is a strategy

147

that consists of starting the operation laparoscopically, and finishing vaginally as early as possible in the course of the procedure. The point when the shift from one route to the other occurs is purely defined by the surgeon's appreciation that the operation will be concluded faster and more safely vaginally than laparoscopically. This may be dependent on the positioning of the patient and the quality of the instrumentation for laparoscopic or vaginal surgery, and on the surgeon's training or preference. This generally concerns the lysis of adhesions and optionally the control of the upper pedicles, generally leaving the management of uterine pedicles and cardinal ligaments and finally suturing of the vaginal incision to the vaginal technique.

The classification designed by the Clermont–Ferrand team can be used to clarify the definition of the operation actually completed.

- type 0: laparoscopy is only used to check the absence of obstacle or contraindication to vaginal surgery; if no cancer, or dense adhesions, are found, the operation is fully performed vaginally – this type is not an LAVH, and can be defined as a *laparoscopic first look*;
- type 1: laparoscopic management of adhesions or adnexal disease, control of the ovarian pedicles in the case of oophorectomy, division of the round ligaments;
- type 2: additional laparoscopic management of the uterine arteries – this type is quite rarely used by experienced vaginal surgeons, who feel that they are able to control almost all uterine arteries;
- type 3: laparoscopic management of the cardinal ligaments;
- type 4: full laparoscopic hysterectomy, including closure of the vaginal incision; actually, type 3 and 4 are not 'LAVH' as defined above.

However, this classification has several drawbacks. First, type 1 is not a homogeneous group, irrespective of whether it includes laparoscopic management of the upper pedicles or not; however, it is generally better to control the ovarian ligaments and to divide the round ligaments when a laparoscopic approach has been indicated to divide pelvic adhesions. Two, any type 1 can be associated with laparoscopic division of the posterior leaf of the broad ligament and/or division of the uterosacral ligaments. The goal of this additional procedure is to facilitate descent during vaginal hysterectomy. It has several drawbacks. Another indication for the combination of the laparoscopic and vaginal approaches is laparoscopic control of the ovarian ligaments and laparoscopic oophorectomy after a vaginal hysterectomy, when the ovaries are not accessible from below. In such cases, the vagina is closed, a pneumoperitoneum is created, and then the ovarian ligaments are controlled using bipolar cautery or loops.

In addition, the Clermont–Ferrand classification does not mention the management of the vesicouterine fold. Our advice, in type 1 and even in type 2, is to avoid laparoscopic incision of the fold and separation of the bladder, which is invariably easier and safer from below. Moreover, the cleavage plane created from above is almost always slightly different from the cleavage plane started from the vaginal incision, which means that the laparoscopic preparation does not help the vaginal step of the operation. Last, early opening of the anterior fold modifies the anatomical relationship between the bladder, the bladder pillars (including the ureters) and the uterus. The rules to protect the ureter during vaginal hysterectomy are not totally respected, which means that the ureter can be injured.

Place of laparoscopic assistance in different situations

Pelvic adhesions

Pelvic adhesions can be managed vaginally as long as they do not densely attach the pelvic organs and the bowel. It must be remembered that a bowel segment can be attracted by the combined effect of adhesions and traction on the uterine fundus. The vaginal surgeon must be aware of this possibility, and be prepared to divide bowel adhesions vaginally. In the case of incidental bowel injury, a vaginal repair can be performed as long as the rules of bowel suturing are respected. However, a number of post-inflammatory adhesions or of adhesions associated with pelvic endometriosis cannot be safely managed vaginally. They are the major and most logical indication for laparoscopic assistance – or laparoscopic preparation – for vaginal surgery.

Laparoscopic adhesiolysis is better performed using a standard succession of steps: (1) divide the adhesions between the bowel and the genital tract; (2) identify the ureters at the pelvic brim in the case of dense lateropelvic adhesions; (3) identify and divide the ovarian pedicles if an oophorectomy is planned (which is usually the case when dense adhesions are present); (4) free the ovaries from the posterior leaf of the broad ligament – taking care not to injure the ureter.

Each of these steps deserves a more precise description.

(1) As far as bowel adhesions are concerned, only those adhesions directly fixing the genital tract or impairing the view have to be freed. If adhesions only impair the view, LAVH is not a good tool as compared to vaginal surgery: as a matter of fact, an abusive "laparoscopic assistance" results in freeing many more adhesions than necessary for

the sole purpose of establishing laparoscopic vision. The resulting complication rate and additional operative time are absolutely useless and unwanted. As a consequence, a history of previous abdominal surgery is not a routine indication for laparoscopic assistance.

(2) The ureter is at risk whenever dense lateropelvic adhesions are found. The solution to avoid injuring the ureter is to invariably perform incision of the lateropelvic peritoneum, lateral to the iliac vessels, generally parallel to the axis of the vessels. After this incision, the psoas muscle, the iliac vessels, and then the ureter crossing the vessels are found. The paravesical space is developed, which permits separation of the adherent adnexa from the pelvic wall. This step can be preceded or completed by division of the round ligament, far from the uterus, which provides access to open the subperitoneal space and completes separation of the genital tract from the pelvic wall.

(3) The individualization of the ovarian vessels naturally follows the identification of the ureter at the pelvic brim. In difficult cases, it is advised not to coagulate and divide the ovarian ligament without prior identification of the ureter. The best approach is to create a peritoneal window between the ovarian vessels and the ureter, keeping the ureter attached to the inferior brim of the window. The ovarian pedicle can then be safely cauterized and divided.

(4) When the ovaries are attached to the posterior leaf of the broad ligament by filmy adhesions, they are easily freed. When dense adhesions are present, the best tool for freeing the adnexae is an atraumatic forceps, used in a closed position, which mimics the tip of the fingers of the abdominal surgeon. The tip of the instrument follows the classical direction used to free such adhesions (from below to above, medial to lateral and posterior to anterior). If the cleavage plane is followed in this manner, without any section with scissors, lasers or cautery, the ureter cannot be injured.

Leiomyoma of the broad ligament

Any tumor fixed in the broad ligament can modify the anatomy of the ureter, which is potentially exposed to surgical injury. The solution to this problem is quite simple. Knowing that there is always a cleavage plane around myomas, removal of the myoma using the cleavage plane and avoiding the risk of vascular and/or ureteral injury, creates the conditions of a simple vaginal hysterectomy. Considering that laparoscopic dissection of a leiomyoma is possible, the concept of LAVH fully applies to myomas of the broad ligament. The only rule is to follow the cleavage plane that can be reached after an incision of the peritoneum of the broad ligament, or after laparoscopic division of the round ligament. The myoma is stored in the pouch of Douglas, or left loosely attached to the uterus before removal through the vaginal route.

Rectovaginal endometriosis

The difficulty is in this case located in the pouch of Douglas, or in the uterosacral ligaments, infrequently laterally in the cardinal ligaments as lateral as the level of the uterine arteries or even of the pelvic sidewall. The difficulty can be anticipated preoperatively by clinical examination completed by MRI imaging. MRI clearly detects involvement of the rectal wall. It is generally accepted that oophorectomy alone is not sufficient. Removal of the symptomatic rectovaginal nodule is thus necessary. It requires a long, difficult and highly specialized operation. Bowel preparation is mandatory, as bowel injuries or rectal resections may occur. In addition, laparoscopic repair of bowel injuries is possible whenever the local conditions are favorable. The laparoscopic vaginal technique can be used with or without concomitant hysterectomy.

The solution to overcome the difficulty is the laparoscopic use of the pelvic cleavage planes as defined in oncological operations: the rectovaginal septum, the paravesical and pararectal fossae. Generally, primary opening and development of the pararectal spaces is the best solution to separate the ureters from the uterosacral ligaments, to divide and resect the uterosacral ligaments, than to cleave the endometriotic nodule or the retraction of the cul de sac. The final goal is to gain access to the rectovaginal septum.

There are two ways to reach the rectovaginal septum: anteriorly or posteriorly to the endometriotic nodule. The most experienced laparoscopic surgeons, who generally use the CO_2 laser, first separate the rectum from the nodule, which is logical when a hysterectomy is planned. Another solution is to separate the nodule from the uterus, than to manage the nodule still attached to the rectum. A majority of laparoscopic surgeons perform a full laparoscopic operation to accomplish removal of the endometriotic nodule.

The vaginal surgeon is able to start – or sometimes to finish or totally complete – the operation vaginally. The guide is the rectovaginal septum that is first easily opened and developed by this approach. Separation becomes difficult precisely at the level of the endometriotic nodule. However, even when the operation cannot be fully performed vaginally, the vaginal incision that precisely removes the vaginal part of the nodule is a good preparation for the laparoscopic operation.

Endometrial carcinoma

Endometrial carcinomas can be managed vaginally in two circumstances:

- the case of stage IA grade 1 disease, in which the risk of nodal involvement is extremely low, and the risk of tumor spillage during the operation is negligible
- the case of the patient in poor medical condition, in whom both laparotomy and laparoscopy are contraindicated.

The combination of laparoscopic and vaginal techniques has been more recently developed, following the description and worldwide spread of the technique of laparoscopic lymphadenectomy. Laparoscopic lymphadenectomy is no longer an investigational procedure. Experimental randomized studies have consistently found that the number of nodes and complication rate do not differ whether lymph node dissection is performed laparoscopically or by laparotomy. This opens the way for another application of the LAVH concept, in which laparoscopic techniques allow one to perform what vaginal surgery obviously cannot do: lymph node dissection.

Another application of the combination of techniques stems from the drawbacks of the vaginal route.

The first is that removal of the ovaries cannot always be accomplished vaginally. This can be easily overcome by laparoscopic management of the ovarian ligaments at the beginning of the operation.

The second is that uterine morcellation, which may be detrimental to the outcome, occurs when maneuvers are required to remove a large uterus. This results in a totally original use of laparoscopic preparation for vaginal hysterectomy: the concept of 'atraumatic' vaginal hysterectomy. When the ovarian and round ligaments are divided at the beginning of the operation, and when in addition the posterior leaves of both broad ligaments are divided, with or without division of the uterosacral ligaments, vaginal hysterectomy can usually be performed without any maneuver and as a consequence without risk of spillage of tumor tissue. After such laparoscopic preparation, the management of the uterine arteries and cardinal ligaments is straightforward. The uterus can then be simply pulled downward after a final incision of the vesicouterine fold.

It must be remembered that laparoscopic surgery has been accused of inducing a reflux of tumor cells through the tube, creating a high incidence of positive peritoneal cytology. This is probably due to the use of uterine cannulas and can be prevented by avoiding such instruments and by coagulating the isthmic part of the Fallopian tubes at the very beginning of the operation.

Conclusion

The combination of laparoscopic and vaginal technique is probably the most modern use of laparoscopic and vaginal techniques, combining the elegance and universality of laparoscopic techniques with the safety and efficacy of vaginal techniques. The routine use of this combination requires the full training of the surgeon in both the approaches, and patient positioning that favors easy and quick shifts from one position to the other, which is essential to allow a practical use of the concept of laparoscopic assistance for vaginal surgery.

12 Laparoscopic vaginal radical hysterectomy

The radical vaginal hysterectomy or Schauta operation is enjoying a revival since the emergence of laparoscopic surgery. We first describe in brief the history of this operation from its origin to the present restricting ourselves to the episodes that clarify the rationale of contemporary surgical strategy and technique. Then we describe the different steps of the surgery and we finish with the indications and contraindications. As far as surgical strategy and technique are concerned we limit ourselves to that which we currently practice.

The extended hysterectomy or radical hysterectomy was described at the end of the nineteenth century. The aim was to prevent the numerous pelvic recurrences observed after simple hysterectomy was performed on women affected by cervical cancer. It is possible for the most part to prevent these recurrences if one removes not only the uterus but also the upper part of the vagina and the proximal part of the parauterine tissues. The first surgeon who performed such an extended hysterectomy was the Czech surgeon, Pavlik (1889). He used the vaginal approach. The German Schuchardt (1893) and the Austrian Schauta (1901) did the same. The vaginal approach included the crucial advantage of being much less dangerous than the abdominal approach. This latter approach was first used by the American Clark (1895) and then by the Austrian Wertheim (1898). Of the first 33 patients operated on by Wertheim, 11 died during surgery or during the next few days (i.e. 33%) but the rate of casualties was only (!) 19% in the first series published by Schauta. Nowadays the operative mortality is at least 30 times lower but the difference between the two surgical approaches remains the same. This is the primary reason for preferring this approach.

After Marie Curie discovered radium (1898) and after the first clinical application of this discovery (Cleaves 1903), surgery for the management of cervical cancer was rapidly abandoned. But, it very soon became apparent that the new technique, while providing good control of central pelvic disease, did not prevent failure, especially pelvic sidewall recurrences. The idea of adding lymphadenectomy to "curietherapy" as was done for head and neck cancers emerged at this time. Leveuf (1931) in France and Taussig (1935) in USA proposed combining pelvic lymphadenectomy and intracavitary radium therapy. Surgery, reintroduced as a method of controlling the regional nodes, rapidly regained its place as a global treatment (Meigs 1945). But there was no longer a place for vaginal surgery, as it did not allow lymphadenectomy.

The renaissance of the Schauta operation was initiated by the Indian surgeon Suboth Mitra (1959), taking the idea of the Austrian gynecologist Navratil, who proposed combining the Schauta operation with pelvic lymphadenectomy performed through bilateral extraperitoneal incisions. Massi[1] (1996) proposed a new version of this operation: "the new Suboth Mitra." This operation has got the same advantage as all vaginal operations even when combined with the extraperitoneal operation: lower operative mortality. It conforms to the new standard of treatment that includes "systematic" lymphadenectomy. But it leaves three scars instead of one. Therefore, it cannot be recommended as a routine procedure.

The combination of the Schauta operation with laparoscopic lymphadenectomy seems to be more acceptable. In 1987, Dargent[2] proposed this combination. In the beginning, many surgeons expressed reservations about the thoroughness of the laparoscopic lymphadenectomy. This argument is no longer relevant today. The laparoscopic vaginal radical hysterectomy, in its various organizational and technical approaches, now enjoys its rightful place in the gynecological surgeon's armamentarium.

Act 1 and Act 2 of the laparoscopic vaginal operation can be played in the same session or in two separate sessions. It depends on the way in which the nodes are assessed. If we decree that surgery has to be reserved for patients with negative nodes one has to choose the most accurate method for assessment of the nodes. The false negative rate of frozen section is not negligible. Standard assessment after paraffin embedding is more accurate especially if it is combined with immunohistochemistry and/or molecular biology. As a consequence, in theory it is better to operate in two separate sessions with a few days' interval between them.

Technological advances could obviate the need for two separate sessions, the latter having notable disadvantages: two admissions and two anesthetics. The use of the sentinel node concept is one of these advances. If the absence of metastases in the sentinel node removed at laparoscopy is really predictive of the absence of metastases in the other regional nodes it might be possible to limit discriminative assessment to this sentinel node only. The other anticipated advance concerns immunostaining and molecular biology that can be performed with ever-decreasing delay. By combining these two techniques it may be possible to develop a tool that would be both fast (two nodes only) and infallible. The operation could offer all safety guarantees. The surgical strategy has moved on and is likely to do so again.

From the technical point of view the laparoscopic vaginal radical hysterectomy has moved on as well, but the operative procedure is now established. During our first period, laparoscopy was only used for the pelvic dissection. In cases where the pelvic nodes were uninvolved the patient was submitted to the Schauta operation either at the same sitting or after an interval. For tumors 2–4 cm in diameter the rule was to use the technique described by Peham and Amreich who were followers of Schauta in Vienna. This operation started with a Schuchardt's paravaginal incision. For tumors less than 2 cm in diameter one omitted the paravaginal incision, and the removal of the parauterine tissues was less radical than in the variant described by the German, Stoeckel. In our second period, the laparoscope while conserving its role in the selection of node negative patients was also used as a tool of preparation for the Schauta operation. The concept of the "Coelio-Schauta" was born, an operation in which the laparoscopic approach and the transvaginal approach are intimately combined to perform the radical hysterectomy.

In order to obtain maximal radicality, we at first used the endostapler with which the parametria were divided right on the pelvic sidewall. The operative specimen was the same as the one obtained by the Schauta-Amreich operation but the paravaginal incision was not required. Conversely, the complications and sequelae were the same as the ones reported after the Schauta-Amreich operation. This is the reason why we developed a new variant where the lateral part of the parametria are laparoscopically totally cleared of the cellular lymphatic tissue contained within before a so-called modified type radical hysterectomy is performed using the vaginal approach, i.e. the Schauta-Stoeckel.

Technique

The LVRH involves two steps: laparoscopic and vaginal. These two steps can be performed at one sitting or at two separate sittings. It depends on the method used for assessing the lymph nodes. These points have already been developed in the introduction and will be discussed again in the section on surgical strategy. Suffice it to say at this time that if one operates in two separate sessions the delay must be limited to less than 10 days to avoid great difficulty due to obliteration of the so-called dry pelvic spaces.

Since 1998, we routinely inject the cervix with radiolabeled marker, the day before surgery and with dye at the start of surgery, in order to activate the sentinel node. In the current state of knowledge it is not possible to limit the dissection to removal of the sentinel node alone. It is necessary to go on to perform systematic lymphadenectomy. However, we recommend attempting to identify the sentinel node in all cases with the first objective of increasing the data and the practical aim of indicating to the pathologists the node, which must be assessed with greatest care. Another advantage is facilitation of the Schauta operation itself. Actually, the lymphatic channels draining the cervix run in the adventitial sheath of the uterine artery. The blue staining allows easier identification of the arterial vessel.

The injection of colloidal technetium is carried out in the afternoon preceding surgery. A lymphoscintigram is performed immediately. It enables visualization lateral and cranial to the large spot representing the midline injection site in the cervix, smaller spots representing the sentinel nodes (Figure 12.1).

The injection of blue dye (Figure 12.2) is performed using the same technique, i.e. puncturing the cervix in each of the four quadrants with a 21-gauge needle at a depth of a few millimeters. A quantity of 1 ml is injected into each quadrant (Patent Blue Violet diluted to 50% in normal saline). Then the patient is draped and one can proceed to laparoscopy.

The laparoscopic operation

The laparoscopic part of the LVRH (Dargent[2] 1987) was initially performed with a direct extraperitoneal

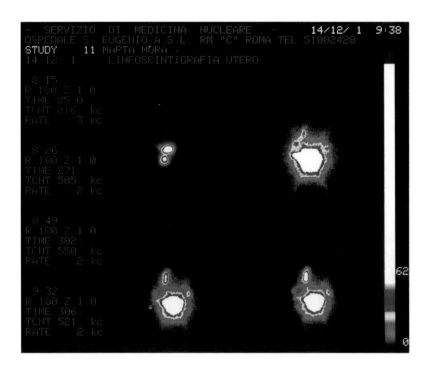

Figure 12.1 Lymphoscintigram of patient with cancer of the cervix showing four consecutive images demonstrating large hot spot corresponding to the injection site in the cervix. Cranio-lateral to this are seen two spots on one side and one spot on the other side that represent the position of the sentinel nodes.

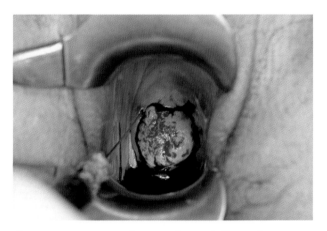

Figure 12.2 Injection of Patent Blue Violet® into the cervix around the tumor.

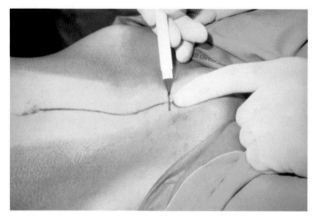

Figure 12.3 First step of the panoramic retroperitoneal pelviscopy: drawing the suprapubic incision.

approach. One remembers that the LVRH was originally conceived as a minimally aggressive variant of the Suboth Mitra operation, during which the lymph nodes are removed through bilateral abdominal extraperitoneal incisions. At the time transumbilical laparoscopic pelvic lymphadenectomy was described (Querleu[3] 1991) the direct extraperitoneal approach was progressively sidelined.

Suprapubic direct extraperitoneal approach
In order to perform pelvic lymphadenectomy using the suprapubic direct extraperitoneal approach one uses a transverse incision centered on the midline and 2 cm above the pubis (Figure 12.3). In order to penetrate the space extending cranially from the

retropubic space of Retzius, one uses a forefinger and then introduces a pneumostatic trochar such as Blunt-tip®. Such a technique requires an incision large enough to admit the forefinger of the surgeon. If one uses a trochar with a transparent cutting tip (Visiport®, Optiview®, etc.) one can make a 10 mm incision through which the tip of the instrument is introduced and followed under direct vision up to the instant the superior edge of the pubis is identified (Figures 12.4 and 12.5).

The surgeon who is standing on the side opposite to the pelvic sidewall that he intends to assess, introduces the ancillary trochars along a vertical line extending from the pubic tubercle. The first trochar is introduced just above the pubis (Figure 12.6).

(a)

(b)

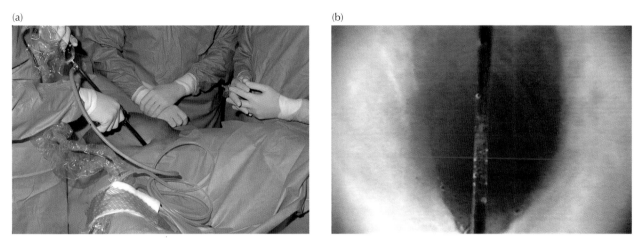

Figure 12.4 (a) and (b) Going through the successive layers of the abdominal wall with the Visiport trochar®.

(a)

(b)

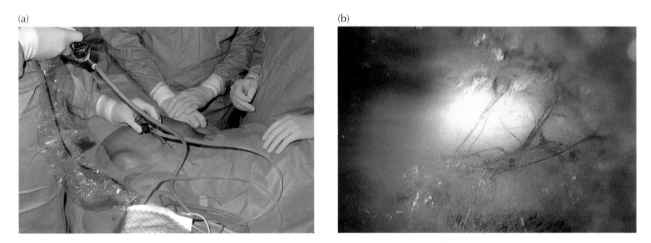

Figure 12.5 (a) and (b) Locating Cooper's ligament after the cutting part of the Visiport® has been removed, the retroperitoneal space has been insufflated and the laparoscope has been put in place.

(a)

(b)

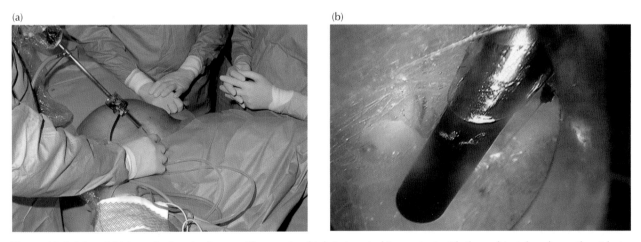

Figure 12.6 (a) and (b) Introducing the first ancillary port, which is inserted in contact with the pubic tubercle on the side to be assessed.

(a)

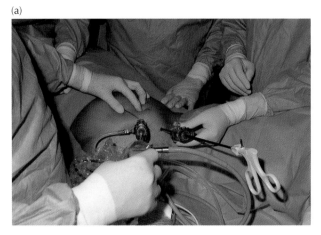

(b)

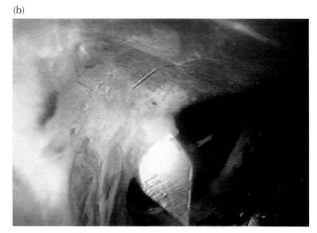

Figure 12.7 (a) and (b) Introducing the second ancillary port, which is inserted on the same paramedian line as the first one but 6 cm cranial to it. This is done after the peritoneum has been mobilized by an instrument introduced cranially through the first port.

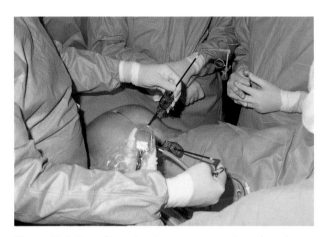

Figure 12.8 Two dissecting instruments are introduced through the ancillary ports. The cranial instrument moves the peritoneum cranially and medially; the caudal one dissects the pelvic inlet.

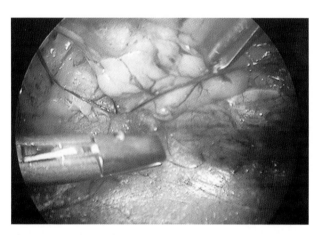

Figure 12.9 The ends of the two dissecting instruments are seen working as indicated in Figure 12.8.

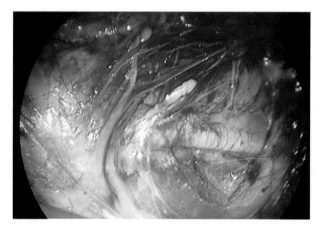

Figure 12.10 The vascular axis becomes apparent.

The second trochar is introduced 4–5 cms higher (Figure 12.7).

The ancillary trochars allow us to introduce the instruments for the dissection, i.e. a so-called crocodile grasping forceps and a fine dissecting forceps (Figure 12.8). Peritoneal mobilization is performed using a blunt technique along the axis of the external iliac vessels. The forceps introduced through the upper trochar reflects the round ligament and the umbilical ligament at the same time (Figure 12.9) as the forceps introduced through the lower trochar continues with the dissection right up to the bifurcation of the common iliac artery (Figure 12.10).

Once the level of the bifurcation of the common iliac artery has been reached the lymph node dissection

starts. This dissection is a blunt dissection. The crocodile forceps grasps the nodes. The dissecting forceps tears the connections between the nodes and neighboring structures (Figure 12.11). When

Figure 12.11 Tearing the connections between the nodes and the vessels.

Figure 12.13 The last connections (mainly lymphatic channels) are torn.

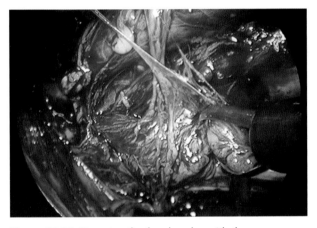

Figure 12.12 Grasping the freed nodes with the Coelioextractor®.

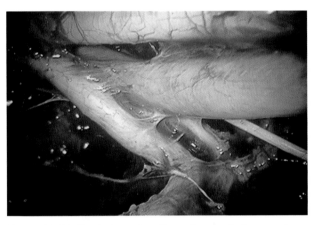

Figure 12.14 Final view after dissection carried out under panoramic retroperitoneal pelviscopy.

the nodes are free enough they are grasped with the Coelioextractor forceps® (Figure 12.12). The last connections are torn with the tip of the dissecting forceps (Figure 12.13). The nodes are retrieved without a risk of contamination of the abdominal wall.

At the end of the dissection (Figure 12.14) the obturator fossa and the external iliac area are completely devoid of all lymph node bearing tissues. The oblique approach to the pelvic sidewall allows us to retrieve the most dorsal of the obturator nodes. However, the common iliac nodes cannot be removed and surgical preparation of the parametrium is not possible.

The suprapubic direct extraperitoneal approach is no longer the preferred choice today for performing pelvic lymphadenectomy. Nonetheless, we have described it because it is still useful in certain circumstances as in the rare but not exceptional case when a woman presents with cervical cancer during the second trimester of pregnancy.

The transumbilical approach

The umbilical approach allows complete pelvic dissection, common iliac nodes included, and surgical preparation of the parametria. One can use the extraperitoneal route. This is possible using transparent cutting tip trochars (Visiport®, Optiview®, etc.) introduced through a subumbilical incision. However, the development of the retroperitoneal space in this way is time consuming. Moreover, it gives the surgeon an odd feeling, as it is the transumbilical intraperitoneal approach that is completely familiar to him. This latter approach is the one we describe.

The position of the patient and the team is the same as for standard laparoscopic surgery. It is not necessary to use a uterine manipulator for either complete inspection or for the operative procedures that will follow. Furthermore, the use of this manipulator can result in the spread of cancer cells.

The main trochar can be introduced through the umbilicus using various techniques. The technique we favor is "The Very Small Vertical Transumbilical Laparotomy" (VSV-TUL). The base of the umbilicus is perforated with the tip of a size no. 11 blade held with the cutting edge up (Figure 12.15). Starting from this perforation, a skin incision is made on a vertical line through the 6 o'clock position (Figure 12.16). The two lips of the skin incision are taken with strong Kocher forceps and forcefully elevated. Then, the incision is extended upward through the 12 o'clock position (Figure 12.17). Using a third Kocher forceps the base of the umbilicus is completely exteriorized. It once again takes on the neonatal shape (Figure 12.18). The umbilicus being "disumbilicated," a deeper incision is made on its tip, which allows direct penetration into the peritoneal cavity (Figure 12.19): there is no point where the peritoneal serosa is so close

to the skin. The small initial incision is opened by introducing closed scissors that are removed once it has been widened. Then one introduces a 10–12 mm pneumostatic trochar, e.g. Blunt-Tip® (Figure 12.20). Next, one injects 18 ml of normal saline through the channel manufactured with this intention to inflate the balloon (Figure 12.21). The sliding mobile ring is then pushed down into contact with the skin and fixed in position (Figure 12.22). The intraperitoneal insufflation of CO_2 can then begin.

Dissection of the sentinel node

The laparoscopic operation starts with inspection. Ancillary ports are opened: two of them 2–3 cm medial to the iliac spines and the third on the midline

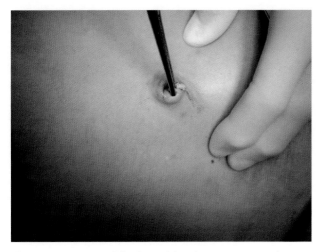

Figure 12.15 The first step of the VSV-TUL: the skin is punctured at the bottom of the umbilicus with a no. 11 blade, which is drawn upward cutting edge first.

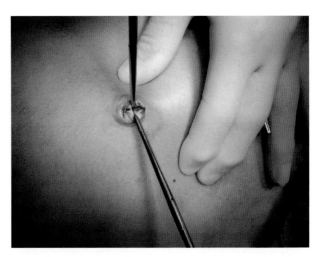

Figure 12.17 The two forceps applied opposite each other are pulled strongly upward. This action "disumbilicates" the umbilicus.

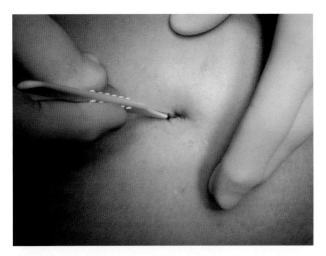

Figure 12.16 One of the lips of the skin incision is taken with forceps as close as possible to the deep end of this incision.

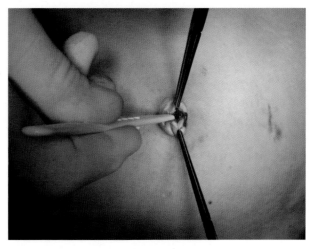

Figure 12.18 The vertical transumbilical laparotomy is extended cranially.

Figure 12.19 The deepest of each of the two skin flaps is taken and drawn upward which completes the "disumbilication."

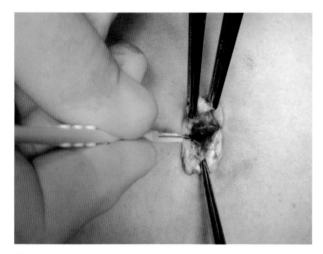

Figure 12.20 Incising between the forceps results in direct entry into the peritoneal cavity.

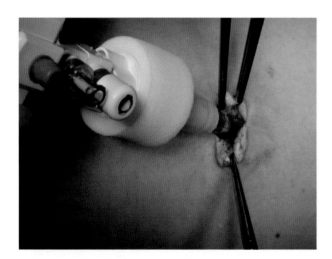

Figure 12.21 Introducing the Blunt-Tip® trochar.

(a)

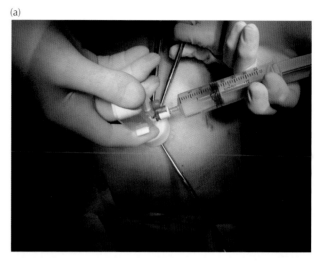

(b)

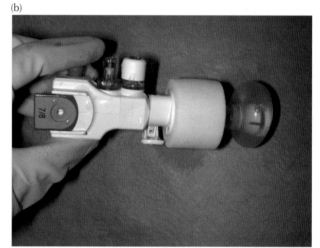

(c)

Figure 12.22 (a) Inflating the Blunt-Tip® balloon. (b) Effect of this inflation on the balloon. (c) Lowering the pneumostatic mobile ring.

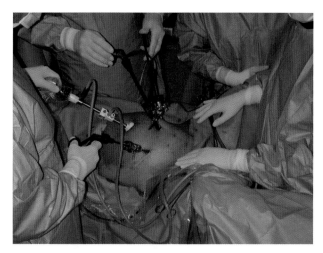

Figure 12.23 Panoramic view of the operating set up: the surgeon stays on the left side of the patient and operates with the midline and left-sided instruments. The first assistant stays on the right side and operates the laparoscope and the right-sided instruments.

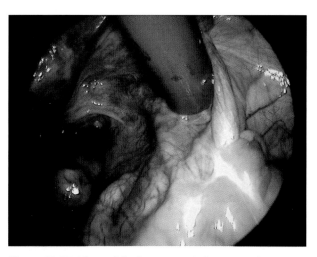

Figure 12.25 View of the laparoscopic intraoperative isotopic detection probe scanning the right side of the fifth lumbar vertebra.

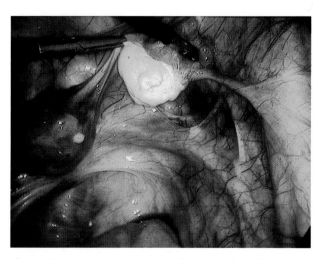

Figure 12.24 Laparoscopic view demonstrating blue channels running across the broad ligament from the uterus to the pelvic sidewall.

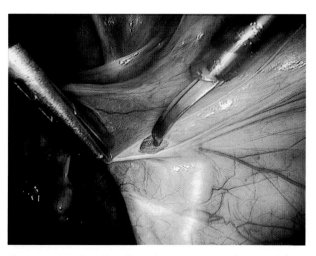

Figure 12.26 Opening the pelvic peritoneum between the round ligament (above) and the infundibulopelvic ligament (below).

at the same horizontal level (Figure 12.23). The two lateral trochars are 5 mm trochars. The midline trochar is a 10–12 mm trochar. This trochar accommodates the forceps used to reflect the intestinal loops in the upper abdominal cavity. First, the pelvic cavity is inspected, then the abdominal cavity including the domes of the diaphragm. Then one returns to the pelvic cavity. Particular attention is paid to the dorsal surface of the broad ligaments. One or more blue channels are generally visible at the base of the broad ligaments (Figure 12.24). The laparoscopic isotopic detection probe is introduced through the 10–12 mm trochar and is applied to the pelvic sidewall. The end of the probe systematically assesses the sidewall with a sweeping movement stopping at the point where a peak of radioactivity is detected. Then, the same is done along the anterior surface

of the fifth lumbar vertebra (Figure 12.25) and the cranial surface of the wings of the sacrum.

The pelvic peritoneum is opened with scissors along the axis of the external iliac vessels. In order to make the initial cut, the pelvic peritoneum is held under tension while applying a grasping forceps to the round ligament close to the uterus. This is introduced through the lateral trochar situated on the side opposite the pelvic sidewall that one intends to assess. The peritoneum situated between the round ligament and the infundibulopelvic ligament is taken at the base of the triangle with a grasping forceps introduced through the midline trochar. The initial cut is performed using the coagulating scissors introduced through the other lateral port (Figure 12.26). As soon as this initial cut is made (Figure 12.27) one

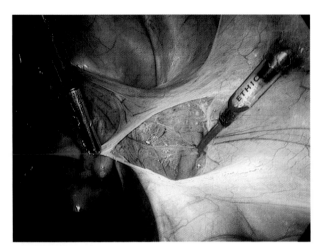

Figure 12.27 Extending the initial incision demonstrates the iliac vessels.

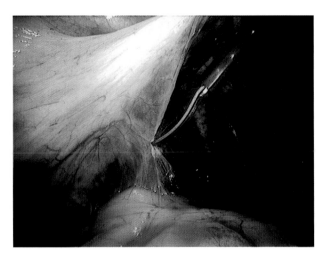

Figure 12.29 Doing the same on the patient's left side: dissecting along the contour of the sigmoid and the last part of the descending colon.

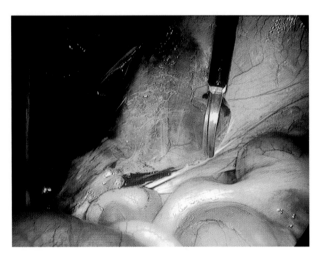

Figure 12.28 Extending the incision laterally around the contour of the ilio-cecal junction – the appendix is visible.

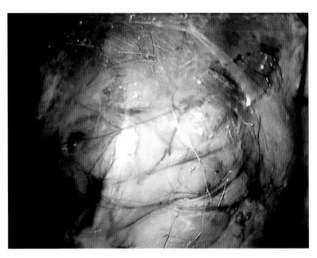

Figure 12.30 Parallel blue channels running from left to right arrive at a node seen on the right side of the image.

sees the retroperitoneal space opening up – it looks like a spider's web. The incision is extended from the round ligament to the infundibulopelvic ligament and one adds to this anteroposterior incision a lateral extension going around the lower edge of the cecum on the right side (Figure 12.28) and the fixed sigmoid on the left side (Figure 12.29), the aim being to reflect the colon and to make access to the dorsal part of the pelvic sidewall and to the area of the sacrolumbar joint better.

The opening of the retroperitoneum is performed with grasping forceps and monopolar scissors manipulated in the coronal plane. The pelvic cellular tissue is torn. The (few and small) vessels identified during this opening have to be cauterized in order to avoid any bleeding which can be a source of difficulty in

the identification of the blue lymphatic channels. The dorsal sheet of the broad ligament must be left intact during this dissection. One generally reaches the base of the broad ligament quite quickly. One or more blue channels are identified (Figure 12.30). Once the channel(s) have been identified, one has to bring the instruments into contact with them, following the channel(s) like Ariadne's thread from inside to outside up to the level of the blue nodes to which they lead (Figure 12.31).

In 85% of cases, the lymphatic channel(s) draining the cervix follow a standard path. They run parallel to the uterine artery. This artery has two segments in its parametrial part. The first is oblique from back to front and from outside to inside, almost parallel to the superior vesical artery with which the uterine

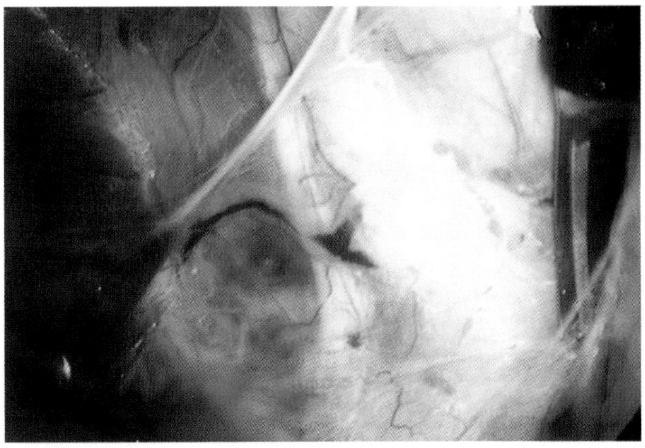

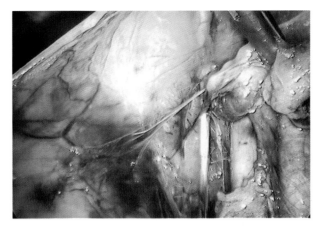

Figure 12.31 One blue channel splitting into two before joining the sentinel node.

Figure 12.34 The sentinel node has been detached and will be grasped by the Coelio-extractor® and removed.

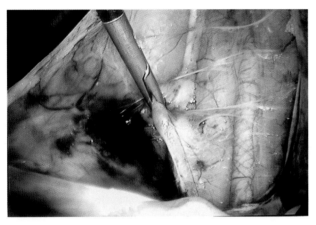

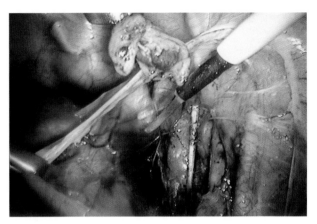

Figure 12.32 Grasping the sentinel node.

Figure 12.35 Cutting the lymphatic channel.

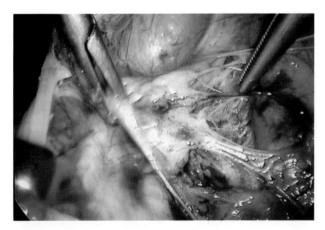

Figure 12.33 Detaching the sentinel node.

artery shares the same origin as first collaterals of the internal iliac artery. After this oblique course it takes an inward turn and becomes directly transverse. It is at the point where the two segments join that the lymphatic channel(s) leaves the artery to continue their transverse course towards the sentinel node.

Along this course they cross the umbilical ligament (which ventrally prolongs the superior vesical artery) before finishing in the sentinel node (Figure 12.32). The sentinel node is always situated adjacent to the external iliac vein either in contact with its caudal aspect (between it and the obturator nerve), or with its medial aspect or with its cranial aspect (between it and the external iliac artery). The caudal position is the most frequent one. Once located, the sentinel node is taken with the grasping forceps (Figure 12.33) then separated (Figure 12.34) and finally delivered while cutting the channel (Figure 12.35).

If opening the retroperitoneal space did not allow identification of the blue channels, we recommend exerting ventral traction on the umbilical ligament using the grasping forceps, and then following this ligament from front to back using the dissecting forceps. This action leads to the point where the ligament is crossed by the channel(s). Once the channel(s) are identified one can follow them up to the sentinel node (Figure 12.36). This is an advantage of laparoscopic assessment. The magnification due to the optical system allows identification of the channel(s) even if they are weakly stained or indeed even if not stained at all.

In 15% of cases the lymphatic channel(s) do not follow the classical pathway. As described in 1923 by the French anatomists Leveuf and Godard, the main route of lymphatic drainage of the uterus may end in the hypogastric area or in the common iliac area (Figure 12.37). With this pattern, access to the sentinel node requires a complete systematic dissection. From a practical perspective, one can no longer consider the sentinel node to be the sentinel node.

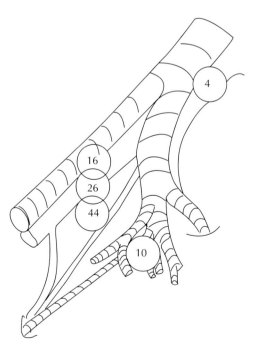

Figure 12.36 The blue channel crosses the umbilical artery.

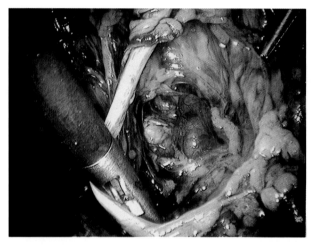

Figure 12.37 Topography of the sentinel node in the first 100 cases where it was found using the technique described herein.

As a matter of fact, the sentinel node is for the surgeon the node whose dissection obviates the requirement for systematic dissection, which nonetheless continues to be mandatory at the moment.

Systematic pelvic nodal dissection

The aim of systematic pelvic dissection is to remove all the lymph node bearing tissues surrounding the external iliac and common iliac vessels. One starts with the external iliac vessels. In order to demonstrate the surgical field one has to identify two landmarks: the umbilical ligament and Cooper's ligament.

The umbilical ligament, which is the extension of the superior vesical artery, is generally easy to find. In case of difficulty, e.g. in the obese woman, we recommend pulling on its abdominal part in order to identify the pelvic part of the ligament. This abdominal part is identified thanks to the peritoneal fold it makes on the posterior surface of the abdominal wall. It is pulled medially (Figure 12.38). Back in the retroperitoneal space the pelvic part of the ligament is identified and pushed medially. It is between this landmark and the pelvic wall that the lymph node dissection will be performed.

Cooper's ligament, which covers the cranial aspect of the iliopubic bone, is usually easy to identify (Figure 12.39). In case of difficulty, as in the obese woman, we recommend following the posterior aspect of the abdominal wall inside the axis of the iliac vessel with closed forceps. One presses on the instruments just as a blind man does when looking for the edge of the sidewalk with his white stick. The iliopubic ramus, at the point it is crossed

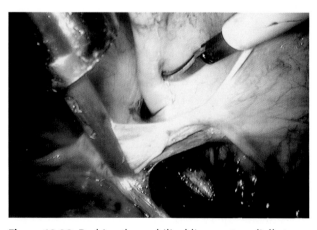

Figure 12.38 Pushing the umbilical ligament medially to demonstrate the superior vesical artery inside the opened broad ligament. The patient is obese and blue has obscured the landmarks: this trick facilitates identification in such cases.

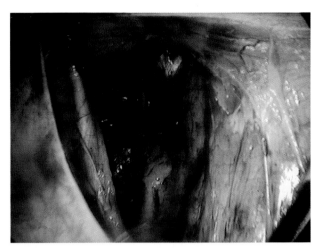

Figure 12.39 The superior vesical artery is pushed medially to demonstrate Cooper's ligament.

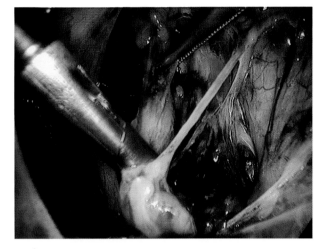

Figure 12.41 Proceeding to separate the ventral edge of the most ventral subvenous node. By avoiding the use of scissors or any cutting instrument and using only dissecting forceps one ensures that the only structures one tears are connective fibers and/or lymphatic channels: as a result there is no bleeding.

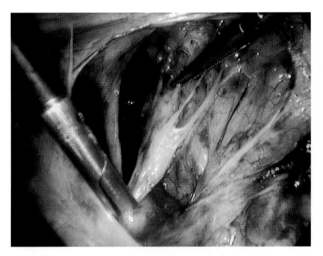

Figure 12.40 Starting to dissect the ventral edge of the most ventral subvenous node.

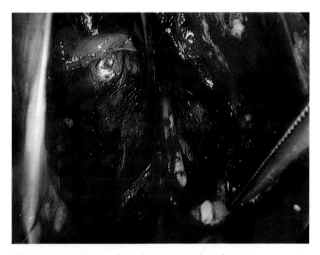

Figure 12.42 View after clearing out the obturator fossa: the obturator nerve is visible in the depths.

by the iliac vessels, has an outline that is easy to identify by palpation. The crossing-point between the iliac vessels and Cooper's ligament represents the ventral limit of the subvenous lymph node dissection.

The external iliac lymph node dissection starts by taking the celluloadipose tissue situated under the external iliac vein with crocodile forceps. Before doing so, it is necessary to initiate separation of the caudal aspect of the vein in order to identify the inferior obturator vein or accessory obturator vein coming from the obturator foramen and running vertically toward the external iliac vein, which it reaches after crossing the dorsal surface of the iliopubic ramus. Tearing this vein can cause hemorrhage that is difficult to control. If such a vein is identified, the subvenous lymph nodes are grasped ventral to it. We pull on them dorsally, and free up with the dissecting

forceps the ventral edge of the node that is within the femoral ring (Figures 12.40 and 12.41). Once the most ventral subvenous node is free (and eventually mobilized lateral to the inferior obturator vein) one proceeds from front to back. Mobilization of the lymph node chain frees the obturator nerve that represents the deepest limit of the "obturator" dissection (Figure 12.42). The same is done to the nodes situated alongside the medial surface of the vein and then to the nodes situated on its cranial surface, between it and the artery. If the subvenous nodes are numerous and big, the external iliac nodes situated alongside the vein and between the vein and the artery are few and small (and vice versa). The external iliac dissection made from front to back leads to the apex of the bifurcation of the common iliac artery. The "paravesical space" is completely opened.

Opening the pararectal space is the next step of the pelvic dissection. To do this one seeks the ureter, which runs in contact with the dorsal sheet of the broad ligament underneath the infundibulopelvic ligament. One follows it from back to front until identifying its crossing-point with the uterine artery. Starting from this landmark one reflects the posterior sheet of the broad ligament medially (Figure 12.43) and then the lateral surface of the rectum until one reaches the pelvic floor, i.e. the concavity of the sacrum and the sacrospinous muscle and ligament. This action frees the bifurcation of the common iliac artery. The most important dorsal iliac nodes are situated between the iliac vessels and the psoas muscle. The space situated between the iliac vessels and the muscle (Figure 12.44) has to be opened to gain access to them. The "retrovascular" nodes are mobilized from back to front alongside the obturator nerve and removed before returning to the "prevascular" approach (Figures 12.45 and 12.46). While proceeding dorsally one arrives at the area bounded medially by the common iliac vessels, laterally by the psoas muscle and caudally by the wing of the sacrum. The common iliac nodes lying in this space (the sacrolumbar space) are removed. At the end of the dissection the obturator nerve and the sacrolumbar nerve, which is the first root of the sciatic plexus, are fully visible (Figure 12.47).

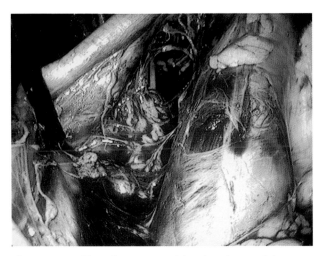

Figure 12.44 The other aspect of the dorsal part of the external iliac vessels is demonstrated while pushing them medially thus opening the space between them and the psoas muscle: note the abundant lymphoadipose tissue.

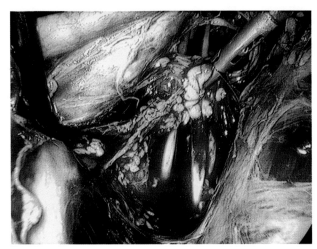

Figure 12.45 The tissue situated in the sacrolumbar space is torn and pushed ventrally.

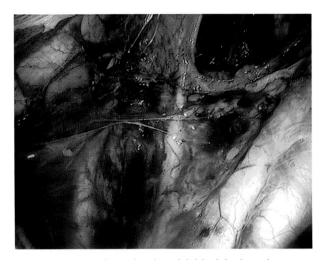

Figure 12.43 Pushing the dorsal fold of the broad ligament medially with the ureter, which is adherent to it, the aperture of the pararectal space becomes apparent. The anterior branch of the internal iliac artery is drawn medially and the area located between it and the external iliac artery, i.e. inside the bifurcation of the common iliac artery is demonstrated.

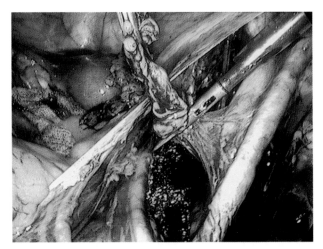

Figure 12.46 The retrovascular tissues that were pushed ventrally are now taken in the ventral part of the subvenous space.

Figure 12.47 Final view of the sacrolumbar space after node dissection: the most dorsal part of the obturator nerve is visible at the same time as the lumbosacral trunk that is crossed superiorly by the superior gluteal veins, which are collaterals of the internal iliac vein.

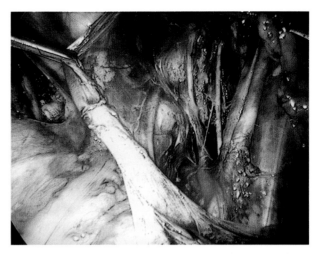

Figure 12.48 View of the pelvic sidewall after completion of the pelvic lymphadenectomy: the obturator nerve is visible but celluloadipose tissues remain below it around the cardinal ligament.

Systematic parametrial nodal dissection

Parametrial lymphadenectomy follows pelvic lymphadenectomy. It is a surgical step of radical hysterectomy rather than a step of lymphadenectomy. As a matter of fact, the aim is to remove all the lymph node bearing tissues situated in the lateral root of the parametrium. The existence of occult metastases situated in this part of the parametrium is responsible for pelvic sidewall recurrences presenting after radical hysterectomy. Conscious of this problem, gynecologists during the last century tried to extend removal of the parametrial tissue, dividing the parametrium closer and closer to its pelvic insertion. The maximal version of this supraradical surgery is where the internal iliac artery and vein are divided at the level of their origin and retracted medially cutting the lateral collaterals one after another. Such an extension undoubtedly increases the radicality but there is a price to pay: intraoperative bleeding is heavy and urinary sequelae are frequent – the branches of the inferior hypogastric plexus carrying the autonomic nervous supply of the urinary bladder running in the deepest part of the parametrium are unavoidably interrupted. The same very radical oncological clearance can be obtained while respecting vessels and nerves.

The lymph nodes to remove are the lymph nodes designated by anatomists as "deep obturator nodes," i.e. the nodes situated in the paravesical space under the obturator nerve. They are also the superior and inferior gluteal lymph nodes situated in the pararectal space in contact with the origin of the vessels bearing the same name. To these anatomically named lymph nodes one must add innominate nodes imprisoned in the vascular and nervous network that makes up the skeleton of the

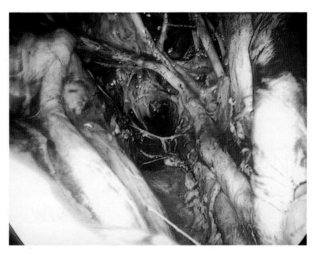

Figure 12.49 View of the pelvic sidewall after parametrial lymphadenectomy: all the celluloadipose tissue has been removed down to the level of the pelvic floor. The vascular skeleton of the root of the parametrium is now naked.

lateral route of the parametrium. In order to remove these nodes one does as before when removing the pelvic lymph nodes (two-forceps technique) starting with the ventral surface of the parametrium and continuing with the dorsal surface. At the end of the dissection, the vascular network of the parametrium appears completely free (Figures 12.48 and 12.49).

The lymph nodes dissected during the pelvic and parametrial lymphadenectomies can be retrieved one after another and sent to the laboratory with a precise topographical designation. The use of the Coelio-extractor makes this selective retrieval easy. Another solution is to collect the nodes in the vesicouterine peritoneal cul de sac and to remove them *en bloc* at the end at the procedure using a laparoscopic bag. From a practical perspective, the important issues in relation to lymph node involvement are to know whether one or more lymph nodes are affected and whether the involvement is uni- or bilateral. For this reason it is perfectly reasonable to retrieve the right-sided lymph nodes together and then the left-sided nodes. The product of the parametrial lymphadenec-tomy (which is not mandatory – see the paragraph devoted to surgical strategy) should be retrieved separately.

Division of the uterine arteries

The last step of the laparoscopic step of the LVRH is also preparation for the Schauta operation. The uterine artery whose origin has been located at the beginning of the surgery is prepared over 1–2 cm (Figure 12.50). Clips are put on it (two clips close to the origin and a third at some distance) and the artery is divided between the clips (Figure 12.51). The medial stump of the divided artery is hinged back medially up to the crossing-point of the ureter which is dissected free a little – this will later facilitate de-roofing, which will be performed vaginally. During this action one can sometimes find a uterine vein crossing over the ureter (Figure 12.52). The uterine veins, in the majority of cases are under the ureter. These veins will be managed during the transvaginal step of the operation. If one or more uterine veins cross the ureter on its upper side one must manage them at the same time as the artery. They are managed in the same way as the artery (Figure 12.53).

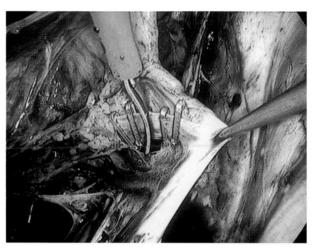

Figure 12.51 The uterine artery is divided between clips. Note the underlying uterine vein in this case and the previously seen vaginal artery.

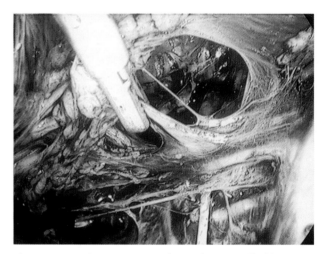

Figure 12.52 The uterine vein has to be controlled because it crosses over the ureter (as does the uterine artery).

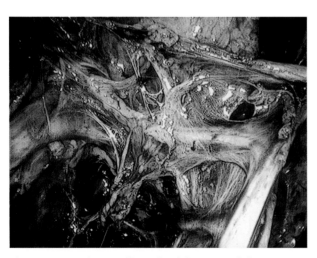

Figure 12.50 Three collaterals of the internal iliac artery: from front to back these are the vesical branch of the superior vesical artery, the uterine artery and the vaginal artery. The uterine artery crosses above the ureter whose course is drawn a little laterally due to traction on it.

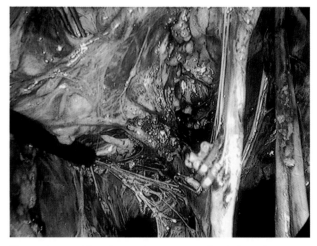

Figure 12.53 After the uterine artery and vein have been divided, and having initiated de-roofing of the ureter, its lateral and cranial aspects become apparent and the vaginal artery, which has not yet been cut is seen crossing under the ureter. It will be divided at the same time as the other vessels of the parametrium during the vaginal step of the surgery.

The vaginal operation

The vaginal step of the laparoscopic vaginal hysterectomy can be broken down into four constituent steps: (1) making the vaginal cuff; (2) preparation of the ventral surface of the specimen-to-come; (3) preparation of the dorsal surface of the specimen-to-come and division of the parametria; and (4) removal of the specimen and closure. It also involves an introduction, the episiotomy, that can be ignored in women whose vulval introitus is widely open and whose vagina is wide and compliant.

The technique we recommend (if useful) is the simple midline episiotomy. Unlike the Schuchardt incision, it is not paravaginal. The aim is to avoid opening the spaces separating the organs from the pelvic walls and to enlarge the vulval orifice: it is better to make a frank clean incision in an area where repair is easy than to observe lacerations provoked by retractors. The vulval fourchette is stretched between two fingers and incised with electrocautery (Figure 12.54), which is also used to control hemostasis.

Making the vaginal cuff

Extended hysterectomy includes removal of vaginal tissue, which in cervical cancer stage 1B1 (i.e. when appropriately indicated) has to be limited to 1 cm ventrally and 2.5 cm dorsally. In order to separate this so-called vaginal cuff, one pulls on a series of Kocher forceps positioned on the vaginal wall at appropriate distances. By pulling on the forceps one creates "internal prolapse" of the vagina. The incision is made along the periphery of the head of this prolapse. When placing the pulling forceps one has to take care to avoid putting them too far from the cervix as this would produce an excessively large

colpectomy. The first forceps is placed at the 12 o'clock position (Figure 12.55). The following forceps are placed on the left and then the right of the first one, the number used depending on the amplitude of the vagina. The forceps located at the 3 and 9 o'clock positions respectively, represent the limits of the forthcoming transverse ventral incision. As far as the transverse dorsal incision is concerned two forceps are inserted on each side of the midline. Generally, seven forceps are enough to create the internal prolapse, which in favorable cases can be pulled right up to the vulvar orifice (Figure 12.56): laparoscopic preparation facilitates this exteriorization.

Before performing the incision one infiltrates the head of the prolapse segment by segment. Divergent traction is exerted on the first couple of forceps. A fold is created and the first injection is performed at the summit of this fold (Figure 12.57). The aim

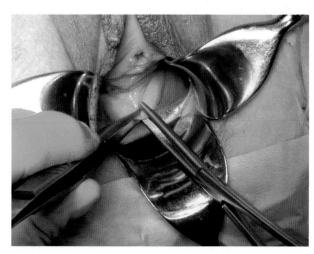

Figure 12.55 Placing the first Kochers clamp at 12 o'clock to start to delineate the edge of the vaginal cuff-to-come.

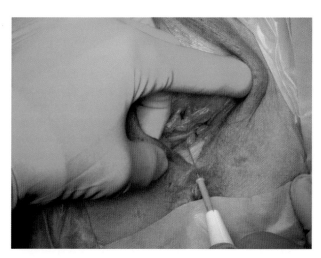

Figure 12.54 Performing a short midline episiotomy with electrocautery: this is preferable to lacerations caused by the speculum.

Figure 12.56 The Kochers clamps delineating the edge of the cuff-to-come are now in place. Placing the lateral clamps accurately is critical: a little more dorsal than 3 o'clock and 9 o'clock.

Figure 12.57 Infiltrating the folds created by pulling on the Kochers forceps: the infiltration separates the two layers of each fold.

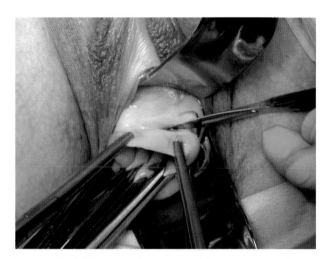

Figure 12.59 The second ventral incision to separate the cuff of the vagina.

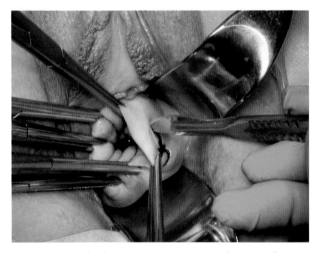

Figure 12.58 The first incision to separate the vaginal cuff-to-come. This is a full thickness incision.

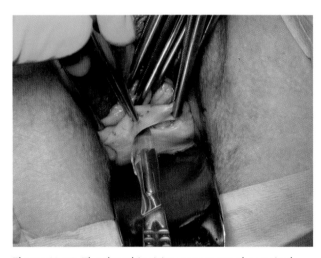

Figure 12.60 The dorsal incision to separate the vaginal cuff.

is to ensure hemostasis (one uses saline with the addition of adrenaline or vasopressin). More importantly, the injection separates the two sheets of each fold.

The circular incision, which will separate the vaginal cuff from the body of the vagina, is made at the points of contact with the Kocher forceps. It is performed segment by segment. Each segment is exposed while divergent traction is applied to the Kocher forceps. The first incision starts at the 3 o'clock position and is made counterclockwise (Figure 12.58). The second incision is made clockwise starting at the 12 o'clock position (Figure 12.59). All the layers of the vaginal vault have to be incised: skin, muscle and fascia. However, one has to take care to avoid incising too deeply, especially in the center where the bladder is drawn into the vaginal fold. From a practical perspective, one must stop as

soon as one reaches the "slick" of saline with one caveat: the injection must have been performed properly and exactly between the two sheets of the fold. Once the first half of the ventral part of the vaginal cuff has been separated one continues on with the second half (Figure 12.60). Then one does the same on the dorsal part of the vagina taking care to allow a 5–10 mm interval between the lateral extremities of the ventral and dorsal incisions. The last incisions are made between the extremities of the ventral and dorsal incisions. At this lateral level the skin alone is incised (Figure 12.61). The aim is to maintain continuity between the vaginal cuff and the parametria to which the cuff is joined thanks to the paracolpos. Once the incision has been made the vaginal cuff is closed and grasped in a series of Chrobak forceps placed transversely in a line extending from 3 to 9 o'clock (Figure 12.62).

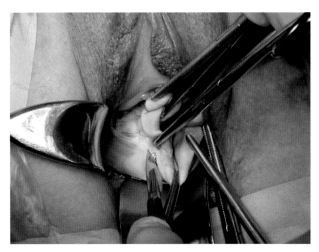

Figure 12.61 The right-sided lateral incision to separate the vaginal cuff. This incision is only a superficial skin incision. The same is done on the other side.

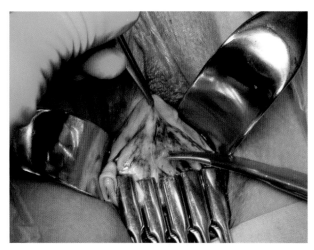

Figure 12.63 Once the vaginal cuff has been closed by the Chrobak forceps, the supravaginal septum is demonstrated and incised on the midline with the Mayo scissors.

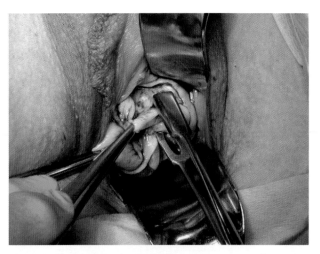

Figure 12.62 Putting the first Chrobak forceps in place. The forceps are applied in a horizontal row

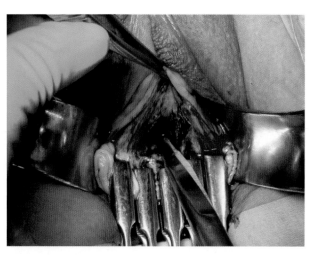

Figure 12.64 The vesicouterine space is opened horizontally on the midline with the Mayo scissors.

Preparation of the ventral aspect of the specimen to come

The preparation of the ventral aspect of the specimen to come includes opening the so-called dry spaces and dividing the ligaments interposed between the bladder floor and the future specimen. Maneuvers of traction and countertraction make this possible. Traction is exerted by pulling downward on the Chrobak forceps aligned transversely on the vaginal cuff. Then the brim of the vagina (from here on the word "vagina" refers to the part of the vagina which will not be removed) is grasped at the appropriate level and opening of the spaces is undertaken. The midline space, the vesicovaginal space, is opened first.

In order to open the vesicovaginal space one takes the vagina with a surgical forceps at the 12 o'clock position and exerts an upward countertraction opposing

the downward traction on the Chrobak forceps. One sees the "supravaginal septum" being stretched. This pseudo-aponeurotic septum has a triangular shape. It is incised on the middle, equidistant from the base and the summit, and equidistant from the two lateral edges. This is done with the Mayo scissors handled with the curve down (Figure 12.63). The opened space is bounded laterally by the two bladder pillars (Figure 12.64). The forefinger of the nonoperating hand (Figure 12.65) is introduced into this space and pushes gently toward the vesicouterine peritoneal cul de sac while always keeping the axis of the cervix straight. Having widened this space with the finger, a Breisky retractor is placed into the space and elevates the bladder floor. Under the protection of this instrument one divides the last fibers attaching the base of the bladder to the ventral surface of the uterus (Figure 12.66). One palpates another time and so on, until the free space situated between the bladder and

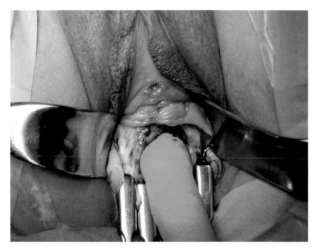

Figure 12.65 The vesicouterine space is widened by the finger, which assesses the depth of the dissection.

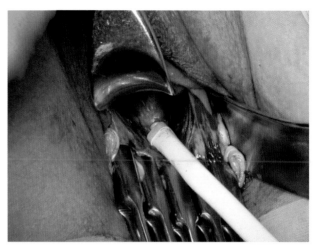

Figure 12.67 The dissection is now complete. The vesicouterine plica is now visible.

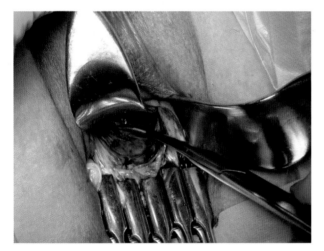

Figure 12.66 As digital assessment showed that dissection was incomplete, a Breisky retractor is placed under the bladder and the remaining fibers divided.

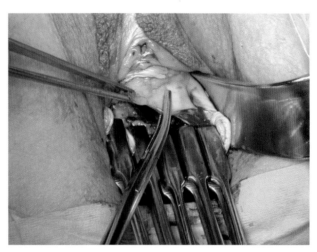

Figure 12.68 A Jean Louis Faure forceps is placed on the edge of the vaginal flap at the 1 o'clock position.

the ventral aspect of the vesicouterine peritoneal cul de sac is entered (Figure 12.67).

Opening the first (left if right-handed) paravesical space constitutes the next step of the preparation of the ventral surface. In order to locate the entrance to this space, one first positions a forceps on the vagina at 1 o'clock (Figure 12.68). Another forceps is applied at 3 o'clock. Divergent traction on both forceps defines a triangle filled by an aponeurosis. A small depression is visible at the point of contact with the second forceps (Figure 12.69). This is where one searches for the aperture of the space. The opening is made with the Metzenbaum scissors that are pushed toward the depths along a lateral and ventral axis (Figure 12.70). By opening and closing the scissors, it is generally easy to penetrate the

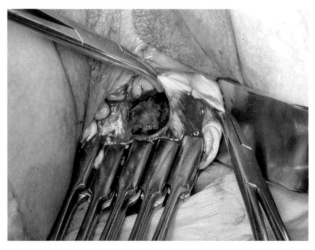

Figure 12.69 A second Jean Louis Faure forceps is placed on the edge of the vaginal flap at 3 o'clock.

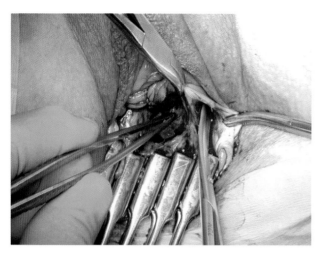

Figure 12.70 Divergent traction is exerted on both Jean Louis Faure forceps. The aperture of the left paravesical space becomes apparent. The dimple marking its entry is deepened with the tip of the scissors introduced gently in a lateral and ventral direction.

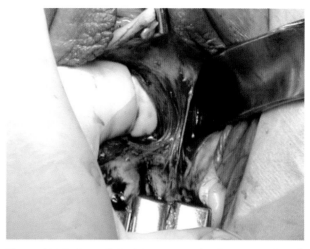

Figure 12.72 A small Breisky retractor has been introduced into the space opened with the scissors and the bladder pillar is assessed while palpating it against the retractor: the "plop" of the ureter is perceived.

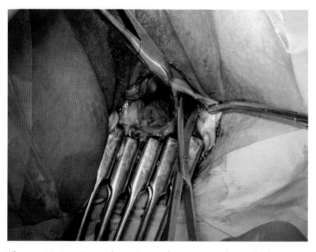

Figure 12.71 Once the scissors have gone through the pelvic aponeurosis and entered the paravesical space, they are removed in an open position.

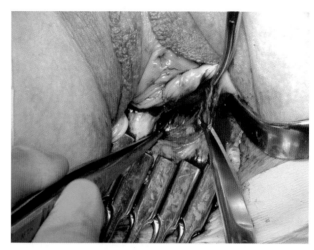

Figure 12.73 The bladder pillar is exposed by traction on the Chrobak forceps, countertraction on the forceps at 1 o'clock, lateral traction on the Breisky retractor and medial traction exerted by a surgical forceps placed on the midline. It is incised right in its middle.

pelvic aponeurosis that is blocking access to the paravesical space. As soon as the scissors sink into the space they are removed open (Figure 12.71): this widens the entrance to the paravesical space. The smallest Breisky retractor (Figure 12.72) is placed in the space.

In between the paravesical space one has just opened and the vesicouterine space one had opened before, is situated the bladder pillar one must divide in order to complete mobilization of the bladder floor and freeing of the ventral aspect of the specimen to come. In this bladder pillar runs the terminal part of the ureter. In order to locate it one palpates the pillar against the Breisky retractor (Figure 12.73). The firm consistency of the urinary "duct" (ureter) allows

its easy identification. The "plop" one perceives indicates how deep the knee of the ureter is. However, it is impossible to locate it transversely (somewhere adjacent to the paravesical space or somewhere adjacent to the vesicouterine space).

Division of the pillar is performed in two steps. One must first separate the lateral fibers from the medial fibers. The pillar is spread out by combining traction on the Chrobak forceps with countertraction on the forceps placed at 1 o'clock. This is combined with lateral traction on the Breisky retractor situated in the paravesical space and medial countertraction on the ventral surface of the cervix thanks to a surgical forceps (Figure 12.72). The opening of the pillar is performed equidistant from all these landmarks using the tip of the Mayo scissors (Figure 12.73). Once the first microincision has been made at the inferior border of the bladder pillar one introduces the scissors into it while pushing them from front to back in a lateral and ventral axis (Figure 12.74). In order to be sure that the fibers that one has isolated are really lateral to the ureter, one palpates the pillar again against the scissors as we did before against the Breisky retractor (Figure 12.75). If the "plop" of the ureter is felt against the medial aspect of the instrument, one can clamp, cut and stitch the fibers situated lateral to it without any fear of injuring the ureter. It is possible to coagulate these fibers with bipolar diathermy and to then cut them. It is also possible to directly cut them with bipolar scissors (Figure 12.76). Division is continued until the moment when the knee of the ureter becomes just visible (Figure 12.77). During this action one must

carefully control the traction and countertraction efforts. The more stretched the fibers are while being cut, the lower the risk of injuring the bladder or the uterine vessels.

The uterine artery arrives in the operative field inside the knee of the ureter. It draws an arch in the paraisthmic window. The afferent branch of the arch must be taken and pulled downward to perform the so-called de-roofing. This afferent branch is sometimes immediately visible. If not, it must be sought by sounding the tissues in the paraisthmic window using the tip of an O'Shaughnessy dissector. The instrument is pushed from top to bottom. The moment a weakness is detected a rotational movement is performed and the vessel is elevated. Visualization of the main lymphatic channel, which is a satellite of the afferent branch of the uterine

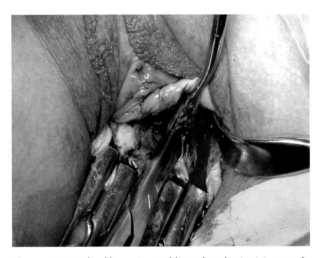

Figure 12.74 The fibers situated lateral to the incision made in the bladder pillar are separated from the rest of the pillar.

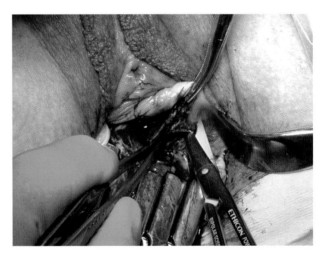

Figure 12.76 The lateral fibers of the pillar are cut using the bipolar scissors. The BiClamp® may also be used.

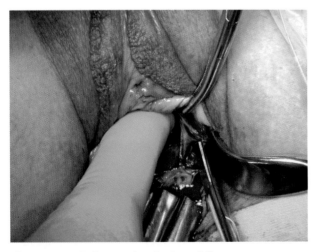

Figure 12.75 Before cutting the lateral fibers, one assesses the medial part of the pillar to ensure that the knee of the ureter is situated medial to the fibers one is about to divide.

Figure 12.77 Having cut the lateral fibers the position of the ureter is defined and the medial fibers can be divided.

artery, facilitates identification (Figure 12.78). Once the afferent branch of the arch has been isolated, it is placed under traction (Figure 12.79) that is maintained during the next action which consists of freeing the vessel from bottom to top using the tip of a second right-angled dissector. This action allows the totality of the uterine artery arch to be drawn into the operative field (whose origin has already been cut at the end of the laparoscopic step of the operation – Figure 12.80). The same is done on the other side. At the end, the ventral surface of the specimen-to-come is completely free.

Preparation of the dorsal surface of the specimen-to-come and division of the parametria

The opening of the cul de sac of Douglas is the prelude to the preparation of the dorsal surface of the specimen-to-come. It is opened the same way as in simple vaginal hysterectomy. The distance between the vaginal incision and the peritoneal cul de sac is greater. False passages are more common but the rectal risk is almost zero. Pulling on the vagina in a 6 o'clock direction, one individualizes the so-called dorsal supravaginal septum, which is the homolog of the ventral supravaginal septum. It has the same shape and must be opened in the same way (Figure 12.80). The initial peritoneal microincision is widened and the Mangiagalli retractor introduced into the peritoneal cavity (Figure 12.81). The uterosacral ligaments limit the rectouterine space that has been opened while opening the pouch of Douglas, laterally. The medial fibers in the thickness of these ligaments (the rectouterine fibers) are individualized. Separating these medial fibers opens the pararectal space and makes elective division of the rectouterine fibers possible.

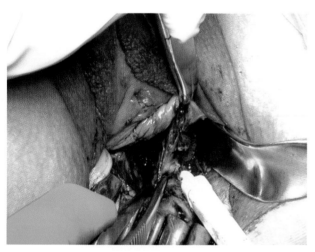

Figure 12.78 Pulling on the arch of the uterine artery. Note that the blue lymphatic channel is adjacent.

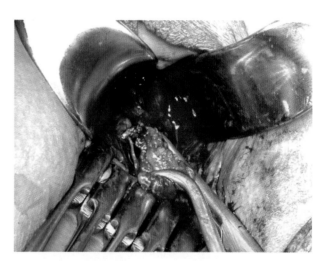

Figure 12.80 The uterine artery has been completely drawn down into the operative field and the clip previously placed on its origin is visible as is the lymphovascular tissue surrounding the artery. The so-called Lucas Champonniere lymph node may be included in this material.

Figure 12.79 Pulling on the afferent branch of the arch of the uterine artery using an O'Shaughnessy forceps. The knee of the ureter is drawn downward and is now fully visible.

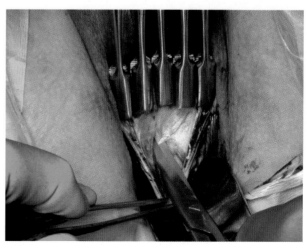

Figure 12.81 The dorsal supravaginal septum is opened.

Although there are generally no blood vessels within them, we recommend using the bipolar scissors (Figure 12.82).

Once the dorsal surface of the parametrium has been freed, the same must be done with the cranial edge. One remembers that this cranial edge corresponds to the caudal limit of the paraisthmic window, i.e. the space where the uterine artery draws its arch. The paraisthmic window will be approached from behind while introducing the tip of an O'Shaughnessy retractor pushed from back to front through the paraisthmic window. The tip of the instrument is applied against the ligament, traction on the vagina being orientated frankly toward the ceiling of the operating room (Figure 12.83). Then one inverts the direction of traction while maintaining pressure on the dissector. The tip of the dissector appears at the ventral surface of the specimen-to-come,

medial to the superior edge of the paracervical ligament and close to the bottom of the arch of the uterine artery (Figure 12.84).

The ultimate step of preparation of the parametrium involves freeing its caudal edge. To achieve this the paracolpos, which had been kept intact at the time of the initial incision, is divided. It is enough to make the lateral incision performed at the very beginning deeper. You will remember that the incision was voluntarily superficial then. As the fibers of the paracolpos are nothing other than connective or elastic fibers surrounding the vessels of the pseudo-ligament, bipolar scissors (Figure 12.85) are used to make the incision deeper.

Once the paracolpos has been divided and the caudal edge of the parametrium freed, just as the ventral and dorsal surfaces had previously been, the Rogers

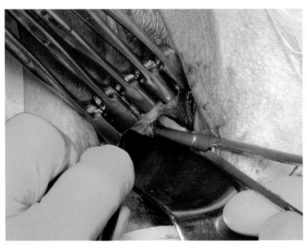

Figure 12.82 Having opened the Pouch of Douglas the rectouterine ligament is prepared.

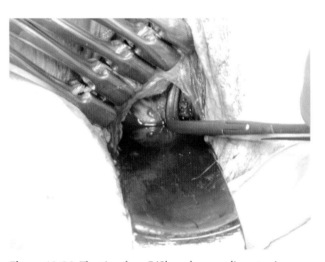

Figure 12.84 The tip of an O'Shaughnessy dissector is placed in contact with the dorsal opening of the paraisthmic window.

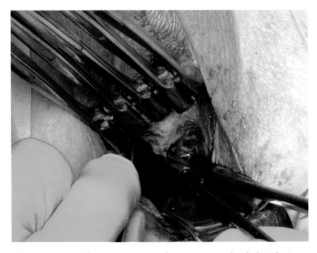

Figure 12.83 The rectouterine ligament on the left side is divided.

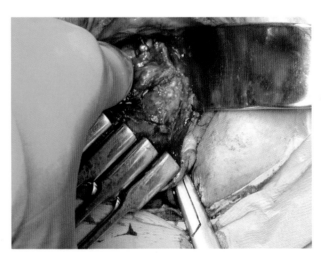

Figure 12.85 Having inverted the traction on the Chrobak forceps, the tip of the O'Shaughnessy dissector appears at the ventral opening of the paraisthmic window.

clamps may be placed. The first clamp is put roughly 15 mm from the insertion of the parametrium onto the vaginal cuff. The convexity of the clamp is just in contact with the knee of the ureter. Its tip is close to the border of the uterus but does not grasp it (Figure 12.86). This first clamp is drawn medially and the second clamp is placed while exaggerating traction on the first at exactly the same time as one progressively closes the second (Figure 12.87): the aim is to take as large a section of tissue as possible. By closing the second clamp, the ureter is pushed further out of the way. Its tip, like the tip of the first, does not touch the uterus. The ligament is divided between the two clamps (Figure 12.88). Once the parametrium has been divided a rotation is applied to the visceral clamp to free the parietal

stump (Figure 12.89). This parietal stump is stitched inserting the suture level with the convexity of the clamp, i.e. level with the knee of the ureter (Figure 12.90). This same is done on the other side. The specimen-to-come, at this point, is only attached to the pelvic walls through the adnexae and through the flaccid parts of the broad ligaments.

The use of bipolar cauterization technology greatly improves the process of dividing the paracervical ligaments. Putting two clamps on the structures to be divided, cutting between the two clamps and stitching the stumps is time-consuming. The proportion of the ligaments one removes with the specimen is less than planned after the initial preparation. Leaving part of the ligaments in place is less than desirable

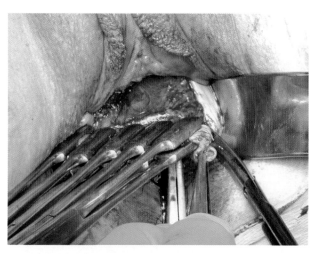

Figure 12.86 The fibers of the paracolpos are divided using the bipolar scissors. The BiClamp® may also be used. The fibers being cut are the ones left *in situ* at the time the vaginal cuff was separated (Figure 12.61).

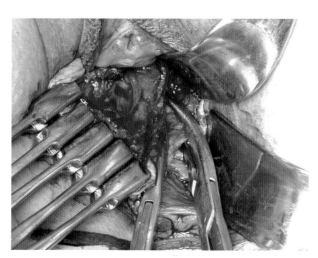

Figure 12.88 A second clamp is put on the parametrium. It is inserted 1.5–2.0 cm lateral to the vaginal cuff/cervix.

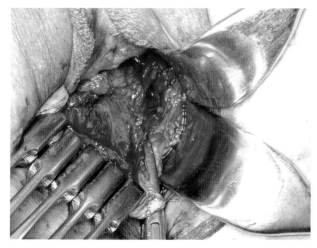

Figure 12.87 Having pushed the vaginal flap freed by division of the paracolpos into the depths, a first clamp may be placed on the parametrium.

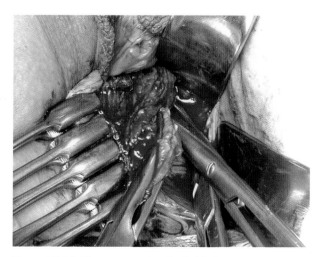

Figure 12.89 The parametrium is divided.

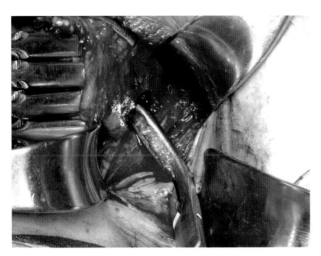

Figure 12.90 The lateral stump of the parametrium ready to be stitched.

Figure 12.91 The remaining fibers of the rectouterine ligament are divided with the bipolar scissors. The knee of the ureter is very close: take care!

with the risk this carries of necrosis, pain and bacterial proliferation. For thin structures such as the lateral and medial fibers of the bladder pillar, rectouterine fibers of the uterosacral ligaments and fibers of the paracolpos, the coagulating scissors are appropriate. The BiClamp® (see Chapter 7) can also be used and can replace the Rogers clamps used on the parametrium with the great benefit of increasing surgical simplicity, radicality and postoperative comfort.

Removal of the specimen, peritonealization and closing

There is no fundamental difference between the ultimate steps of simple and extended vaginal hysterectomy. If the uterus is of normal size it is removed by toppling backward. If this maneuver appears impossible, hemisection is forbidden (however, it is not forbidden to perform trachelectomy first before proceeding with hemisection, myomectomy, morcellation etc.). The vesicouterine peritoneal cul de sac is stretched and opened. The elements inserting onto the uterine cornu are clamped and cut and the specimen is delivered (Figures 12.91 and 12.92).

In cases where bilateral salpingoophorectomy is planned for one reason or another, it is performed as a second step. If the infundibulopelvic ligaments have been divided during the laparoscopic step of the operation, this obviously facilitates bilateral salpingoophorectomy. However, we do not recommend routinely dividing these ligaments before the very end of the operation and in fact believe that it is better to keep them intact up to the very end. Furthermore, if difficulty is experienced during transvaginal adnexectomy, this ultimate part of the operation can be postponed until the third and last step, i.e. the final laparoscopic check up. Moreover, these ligaments are the threads to which the dorsal sheets of the broad

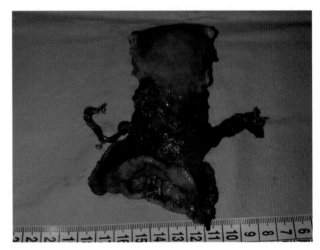

Figure 12.92 The specimen. The uterine arteries and tissues surrounding them have been completely removed. The parametria are 1.5 cm wide. The lateral parametria have been treated laparoscopically.

ligaments are suspended and the ureters are adherent to them. If the sheets are preserved one is able to locate the position of the ureters from beginning to end thanks to preservation of normal anatomy.

Peritonealization is carried out using two angle stitches and one intermediate running suture. One starts with the right-angle stitch and first sutures the right ventrolateral aspect of the rectum, then the right uterosacral peritoneal fold. One then moves on to the peritoneal leaves suspended by the infundibulopelvic ligament, then to the round ligament before finishing with the bladder dome. In the gap between the uterosacral fold and the infundibulopelvic ligament one has to take care to avoid stitching the ureter, which is attached to the peritoneum that one is stitching. The peritonealization is finished by approximating the rectal and the bladder peritoneum (Figure 12.93) transversely.

The vagina is closed once hemostasis has been achieved. Particular attention should be paid to the lateral surfaces of the stumps of the paracervical ligaments. They are separated from the edge of the vagina by a bare area corresponding to the insertion of the paravaginal ligaments (paracolpia) that have been divided using coagulating scissors. It may be necessary to stitch the stumps of these ligaments just as it may be necessary to later stitch the stumps of the bladder pillars that have been managed in the same way as the paravaginal ligaments. This is done while performing the purse-string suture on the vaginal edge (Figure 12.94).

The episiotomy, in cases where it has been done is closed very simply using a single continuous fine absorbable stitch (Figure 12.95).

The ultimate check after LVRH is done with the laparoscope. The patient is put in the appropriate position and as the trochars have been left in place, insufflation is promptly achieved and the laparoscope and ancillary instruments are introduced. Irrespective of the level of care taken in peritonealization, two windows persist at the lateral extremities (Figure 12.96). They must not be closed as they form a conduit for the lymphatic fluid to flow into the peritoneal cavity preventing the formation of lymphocysts. It is in the depths of these two windows that one has to look for potential bleeders, which must be controlled by bipolar, coagulation or clips

Closure of the trochar orifices should not be forgotten. For the suprapubic 10–12 mm orifice we use the Phipps needle which incorporates all three layers of the abdominal wall in the closure (Figures 12.97–12.100). The VSV-TUL must also be closed using a so-called urological needle. The suture used is

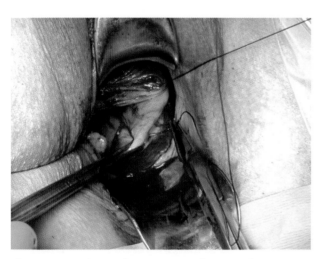

Figure 12.93 Closing the peritoneum between the two angle stitches.

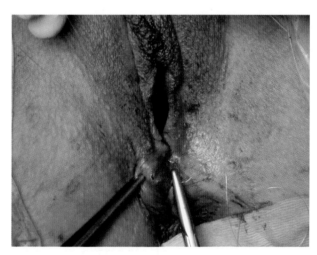

Figure 12.95 Closing the small midline episiotomy.

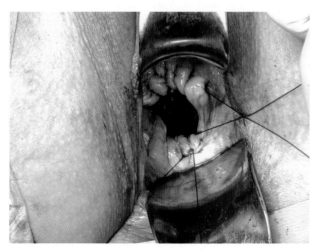

Figure 12.94 Finishing the purse-string suture around the edge of the vaginal flap.

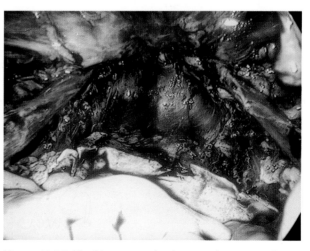

Figure 12.96 Final laparoscopic view: no tissues remain around the vaginal vault (except the ureters!).

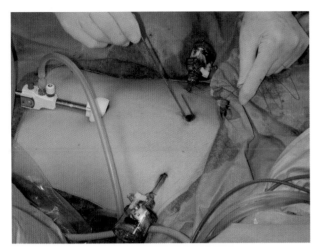

Figure 12.97 Closing the suprapubic 10–12 mm incision. A J-shaped needle has been introduced and its tip passed up through the inferior lip of the wound. A Vicryl® suture has thus been placed.

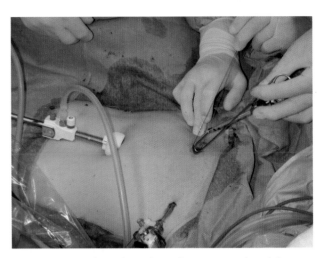

Figure 12.100 The J-shaped needle is removed and the suture may now be tied.

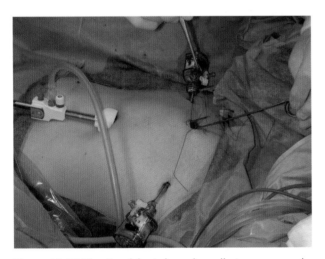

Figure 12.98 The tip of the J-shaped needle is now passed up through the superior lip of the incision – the Vicryl® can be extracted from the needle before the latter is removed.

(a)

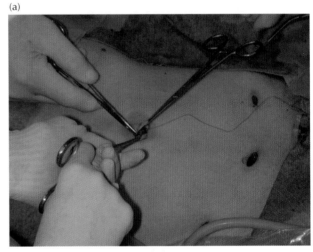

(b)

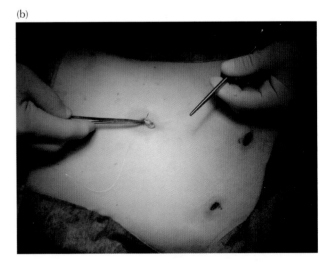

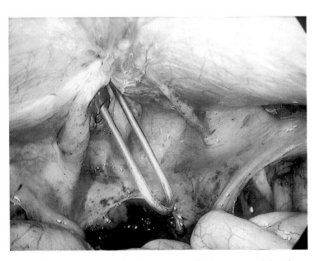

Figure 12.99 The freed J-shaped needle is removed thanks to a 5-mm trochar introduced parallel to the long arm of the needle – this protects the tip of the needle during removal.

Figure 12.101 (a) Stitching the aponeurosis of the VSV-TUL. (b) Stitching the skin of the umbilicus with interrupted 4-0 Monocril.

1 Vicryl® as it is for closure of the suprapubic wound (Figure 12.101).

Operative difficulties: how to manage them? How to avoid them?

Difficulties can occur during both steps of the operation. Most of them are due to the surgeon and to an error in the way in which actions are undertaken. These errors are mainly due to poor identification of the anatomical spaces. Other difficulties are due to the state of the patient (obesity, poor vaginal access), to the spread of the disease (undetected infiltration of the vaginal vault, of the parametria, or of the so-called dry spaces), or to the presence of associated lesions (fibroids, adhesions). In any case, insurmountable difficulties are exceptional. There is almost no contraindication (see later) and conversion to laparotomy for intraoperative complications is very rare (less than 1% of cases) with the exception of conversions that are mandatory due to lymph node involvement (see later).

Laparoscopic step

The laparoscopic approach is associated with specific complications that are well described in textbooks devoted specifically to laparoscopic surgery. We shall not describe them here particularly as the open technique (VSV-TUL) allows us, in a large proportion of cases, to prevent them. We limit our purpose here to the complications of laparoscopic dissections. These complications are not specific to this approach but their management and prevention are peculiar to it.

The dissection of bulky and adherent metastatic lymph nodes can be performed with the laparoscope just as it can at open laparotomy. The surgical hazards are neither increased nor decreased. Removal of the specimen can be achieved with the protection of an endoscopic bag. However, during dissection one cannot completely avoid the risk of opening the capsule, which favors the seeding of tumor cells. Although such a risk exists at open laparotomy, it is increased if one operates with the laparoscope because of the physicochemical modifications of the peritoneal milieu induced by insufflation of CO_2. Therefore, it is better to convert to laparotomy if one discovers bulky adherent adenopathy.

The dissection of pelvic nodes and even more so parametrial nodes result in bleeding. This bleeding in most cases is just simply oozing which stops spontaneously and does not require positive action. Wasting time to control micro-bleeders prolongs surgery and increases the bleeding. More serious bleeding may occur due to tearing of the collaterals of the iliac veins and more rarely of the iliac arteries. The inferior obturator vein, which is a collateral of the external iliac vein, can be injured during pelvic lymphadenectomy. The ventral collaterals of the internal iliac vein and artery are at great risk during preparation of the ventral aspect of the parametrium. The lateral collaterals of the common iliac vessels (psoas vessels and superior gluteal vessels) can be injured during the so-called retrovascular dissection. All these vessels are of small caliber, but if they are torn close to their origin one is left dealing with a lateral injury of the iliac vessels.

When managing intraoperative bleeding, the first choice is compression. We recommend putting a swab of 15×4 cm into the peritoneal cavity at the very beginning of the dissection. This swab is placed close to the area where one works. If bleeding occurs one pushes the swab into the area of concern. One washes. One aspirates. One washes. One aspirates and so on. The bleeding usually stops (after a certain number of maneuvers, the aspirated fluid has the same color as the injected fluid). If the bleeding does not stop the maneuvers of compression, washing and aspiration allow us to clean the operative field and to locate the bleeder, which will be controlled either with bipolar coagulation or with clips. In cases where the bleeding comes from the collaterals of the internal iliac vessels, i.e. in the most difficult cases, the use of the endo-GIA stapler often leads to miraculous results as long as the torn collaterals are medial collaterals of these big vessels. Albeit rare, it can happen that the abdomen has to be opened. The difficulty is in timing it correctly: not too late but not too early either. On the other hand, the patient has to be fully informed of that possibility.

The prevention of bleeding during lymph node dissection lies with an appropriate choice of dissecting instruments. One must avoid all cutting instruments (scissors, including monopolar scissors, laser, ultrasound, etc.) and blunt dissection is favored. This is done using the dissecting forceps with or without bipolar coagulation, at the same time as the washing/aspiration cannula, which provides a hydrodissection effect.

Transvaginal step

Most of the difficulties met during the vaginal part of the LVRH are due to incorrect identification of the anatomical spaces. It is imperative to use the extra fascial spaces. It is imperative not just from a surgical point of view but also from an oncological perspective.

Opening the vesicouterine space

Identification of the vesicouterine space is more difficult in extended vaginal hysterectomy than it is in simple vaginal hysterectomy because the so-called supravaginal septum is thicker. Now it is more important in the extended hysterectomy to make the opening in the right plane. As a matter of fact if one does not succeed in opening the anatomically preformed space the following steps of the operation will be very difficult (especially management of the bladder pillars). If progressing from the surface to the depths one does not succeed in identifying the loose cellular pelvic tissue that indicates one is in the right space, then one is proceeding erroneously inside the fascia. Traction on the fascia must be adapted so that one proceeds in front of it instead (see Chapter 7).

Opening the paravesical spaces
False passages made while opening the paravesical spaces have the same drawbacks as false passages occurring during the first step. Furthermore, they give rise to bleeding, which is due to trauma to one or other of the ligaments that bound the paravesical space, i.e. the bladder pillar ventrally and the parametria laterally and dorsally. If such bleeding occurs one has to widen the space even if this increases bleeding. In fact, a retractor must be placed in the space before bleeding can be controlled. Coagulation is not appropriate or possible because of the direction of the blood vessels. Stitches are usually required.

Prevention of these difficulties lies in the correct identification of landmarks. Traction forceps must be applied at 1 and 3 o'clock on one side and 11 and 9 o'clock on the other. Application of the second forceps is problematic. If inserted too ventrally, the bladder pillar is injured. If inserted too dorsally the parametrium is damaged. Placing the forceps is easy if the vaginal cuff is wide open. If the vaginal cuff is narrow and/or distorted by retraction due to an obstetric scar or, more rarely, to unpredicted spread of cancer, things can be much more difficult. Now, the small dimple that marks the entrance to the paravesical space is in contact with this forceps. Whether one locates the entrance well or not, it is important when opening the space to take care to progress in the correct axis, which is oblique from front to back, from inside to outside and from bottom to top.

De-roofing the ureter
Management of the bladder pillar is the most difficult step of vaginal radical hysterectomy. One has to identify the ureter and the arch of the uterine artery, and then dissect the afferent branch of this arch.

Identification of the ureter is not always easy. Difficulty is generally due to an error made during the preceding steps (see above). It can also be due to anatomical variations, which can in theory be anticipated thanks to cystoscopy: the further the ureteric

orifices are from each other, the more difficult identification of the knee of the ureter on each side is. The length of the vaginal cuff is another significant factor: the longer the cuff the thicker the pillar. If one does not succeed in cutting the lateral fibers of the pillar or, having divided these fibers, if one does not succeed in identifying the knee of the ureter, one recommends proceeding to the medial aspect of the pillar to search in the paraisthmic window (one can feel it by palpation). The arch of the uterine artery is situated inside this window (surrounded by the blue lymphatic channel if blue was injected before starting). Pulling on the afferent branch of the arch will draw the knee of the ureter into the operative field, and it is at this moment and this moment only that the lateral fibers are cut.

Identification of the uterine artery can be a problem. The problem is generally due to the errors already mentioned. They can also be due to anatomical variations (long cervix, high isthmus). The length of the vaginal cuff also plays a role: the longer it is the more difficult location of the uterine artery is. To locate it one has to first locate the paraisthmic window. It has already been said that palpation is the first identification technique. The finger slips alongside the lateral surface of the uterus and assesses the resistance of the parametrium. Going from bottom to top, this resistance stops abruptly at a certain point: this is the paraisthmic window. If development of the vesicouterine space has been properly executed, the paraisthmic window is "empty" containing loose and often adipose cellular tissue only. In cases where the initial dissection has been erroneously performed in the intrafascial space, fascia hides the paraisthmic window and so one must first return to the correct (anatomically preformed) dissection plane.

Dissection of the afferent branch of the arch of the uterine artery is not always easy. The first difficulty is in distinguishing the afferent and efferent branches. One has gone around the vessels with the O'Shaughnessy dissector and pulled the potential afferent branch but pulling becomes more and more difficult because one is pulling on the efferent branch. One must then stop and start again. However, even if the vessel being pulled is the afferent branch of the arch, difficulties can occur, e.g. the artery has not been divided properly at the level of its origin, or a second uterine artery and/or a supraureteric uterine vein exists which has not been divided. In such circumstances, one has to clip these supernumerary vessels before cutting them (remembering to carefully assess hemostasis during the final laparoscopic check). Measures can be taken at the end of the laparoscopic step of the operation to prevent these problems. Once the uterine artery has been divided, preparations for de-roofing can be made: if vessels are found crossing over the ureter (normally, the uterine artery alone runs here), they can be controlled and cut at the same time as the uterine artery.

Controlling the parametria

Clamping and dividing the parametria is never perfectly simple in the Stoeckel technique of vaginal extended hysterectomy. The absence of a wide opening into the pararectal space makes the job ergonomically difficult. One has to be aware of this but one must also know how to avoid errors that make this action even more difficult.

False passages made in the approach to and opening of the Douglas cul de sac make preparation of the dorsal surface of the parametria difficult. These false passages are managed and prevented as explained in Chapter 7 in relation to simple vaginal hysterectomy.

Preparation of the caudal edge of the parametrium and of its ventral surface have to be continued far enough but without being excessive as the latter is a source of vesicourethral sequelae. It is impossible to divide the parametrium at an appropriate level unless the vagina on the one hand and the knee of the ureter on the other are pushed away a sufficient distance (1.5–2.0 cm). It is recommended that the first clamp is placed as high as possible. By pulling on it, the fibers of the paracolpos and the remaining lateral fibers of the bladder pillar can be progressively divided. Afterwards, one can put the second clamp a little higher. If it becomes insurmountably difficult, a paravaginal incision is the key to the problem.

Postoperative course and complications

The postoperative course after LVRH is generally uneventful. The patient can and must get up the day after surgery. The return to normal diet is rapid, but resuming normal urinary bladder function is not as simple after extended hysterectomy as it is after simple hysterectomy. This is just as true for the laparoscopic vaginal approach as it is for the abdominal approach. We recommend leaving the bladder catheter in place for 5 days and removing it on the 6th day. If at the end of the first day without a catheter the post micturition residual (assessed by ultrasound or by post micturition catheterization) is more than 100 ml, which occurs in roughly one in three cases, we recommend teaching the patient self-catheterization. This is generally easy and, if patients are warned of this possibility at the very first pre-operative interview, psychological difficulty is rare.

Discharge home is possible as soon as the catheter has been removed and irrespective of the residual. As soon as the patient arrives home she generally urinates spontaneously. Convalescence lasts 6 weeks. The rules are the same as after simple vaginal hysterectomy (see Chapter 7).

The first postoperative clinical assessment is performed the day of discharge and the second 6 weeks later. An intravenous pyelography is done some days prior to the second visit to assess the urinary tract, including voiding (post-micturition film). If dilation of the upper-urinary tract is present imaging must be repeated after 1 month, by which time the ureters are usually normal again. If not, a urological opinion is sought. With regard to voiding difficulties, it must be remembered that they generally progressively disappear and that less than 5% of patients are affected by these problems after 6 months.

Intraoperative complications

Some of the complications occurring during the two steps of LVRH have already been described in the section devoted to technique. Here we restrict ourselves to ureteric complications that are linked to radical hysterectomy just as original sin is linked to human nature (Novak).

Ureteric injuries can happen at any time during LVRH. It can occur during the laparoscopic step but this is more than rare if one does not divide the IP ligament (see above). It can happen during management of the bladder pillar and, finally, it can happen during peritonealization.

Diagnosis of ureteric damage is generally easy because of urine leakage. However, leakage can be discrete or absent depending on the extent of the damage and on renal secretory function.

Ureteric injuries occurring during the laparoscopic step can be repaired laparoscopically. A ureteric catheter is placed under cystoscopic guidance and its progression to the upper-urinary tract followed laparoscopically. Repair is then performed using one or more absorbable 5-0 stitches.

Ureteric injuries occurring during the vaginal step of the operation can usually be repaired using the same approach. A ureteric catheter is put in place using either the injury itself or with cystoscopic guidance and the injury is closed with one or more stitches. However, if the injury is both very large and very close to the ureteric orifice, reimplantation may be necessary (uretero-neo-cystostomy). It can sometimes be performed without abandoning the vaginal approach.

If the uretero-neo-cystostomy cannot be performed using the vaginal approach or, more generally speaking, if repair of the injury looks difficult either using the laparoscope or the vaginal approach, one must not hesitate to make a small suprapubic transverse extraperitoneal incision on the injured side to repair the damage properly.

Some unrecognized injuries will declare themselves by forming a fistula or stenosis. Detection relies on the IVP, which must be done routinely around the sixth postoperative week.

Postoperative complications

Postoperative complications of LVRH are infrequent. When they occur it may be clear whether they are attributable to the laparoscopic part of the surgery or to the vaginal part, but it is often difficult to determine this. These complications may lead to reoperation. The approach for reoperation has to be chosen depending on the potential pathophysiology of the complication. Complications due to laparoscopy have to be managed with the laparoscope; complications due to vaginal surgery have to be managed using the vaginal approach although laparotomy is sometimes required.

Postoperative hemorrhage

Postoperative hemorrhage is rare. Most of the time it occurs in the first 48 h postop. It is generally revealed and so easily identified and evaluated. It can however, be concealed (collected in the peritoneal cavity) and present as collapse and shock associated with abdominal tenderness and dullness in the flanks. A blood count easily makes the diagnosis and ultrasound confirms it and quantifies it as well.

Postoperative hemorrhage with a major drop in hemoglobin mandates reoperation. This reoperation will be performed laparoscopically if one thinks that the bleeding comes from the collaterals of the iliac vessels. If one thinks that it comes from the stumps of the parametria and/or the stumps of the bladder pillars and paracolpos, reoperation should be performed vaginally. One can also be forced to use a mixed approach. For example, emptying the hemoperitoneum laparoscopically after dealing with hemorrhage due to a slipped parametrial stitch, or using the vaginal approach when bleeding persists after controlling the pelvic walls laparoscopically. In extreme cases laparotomy is advised. The alternative of arterial embolization must not be forgotten.

Postoperative pelvic collection
A pelvic collection may develop during the postoperative period. It may be a hematoma, an abscess secondary to hematoma formation or a so-called lymphocyst presenting as a late consequence of hematoma formation. If the collection develops above the vaginal vault it should be managed by colpotomy. If the collection develops on the pelvic sidewall and especially if straddling two areas at once (pelvic and iliac areas), it must be managed laparoscopically. In the specific case of lymphocyst formation, one must perform true marsupialization rather than simple laparoscopically guided puncture. Ultrasound-directed drainage is an alternative to reoperation. It must be reserved for small lymphocysts and must be replaced by laparoscopic marsupialization in cases of recurrence.

Fistulas
Vesicovaginal, ureterovaginal and rectovaginal fistulas may occur after LVRH. They are exceptional (many big series report no fistulas). The vesicovaginal and rectovaginal fistulas must be managed in the same way as fistulas observed (even more rarely) after simple vaginal hysterectomy (see Chapter 7). The problem of ureterovaginal fistula (and stenosis) is more specific to the LVRH.

Ureterovaginal fistulas and stenosis have to be managed as soon as the diagnosis is made. It is generally possible to site a JJ-stent, which in most cases renders the patient dry and allows the injury to heal – this should be confirmed 3 months later by intravenous pyelography. If endoscopic treatment is not possible, one has to turn to open surgery: uretero-cystoneocystostomy performed through an abdominal transverse suprapubic extraperitoneal ipsilateral incision.

Sequelae

The sequelae of LVRH cannot be ignored even if they are now more rare and transient than in the past thanks to the already mentioned strategy. These sequelae relate to bladder emptying, rectal voiding and sexual function.

Urethrovesical sequelae
Urinary bladder voiding difficulties are observed in the immediate postoperative period. They rarely persist after 6 months and very rarely persist indefinitely. This assertion concerns urinary retention alone. In contrast we must recognize that many patients have sensory loss (loss of the feeling of the need to urinate) and at the same time a reduction in flow thus taking longer to void. Stress incontinence may also present, which was almost always preexistent but increased progressively (due to the surgery? due to age?).

Urinary retention is due to spasm of the posterior urethra and to atony of the detrusor muscle. These are both due to interruption of the autonomic nervous supply, which can be demonstrated by urodynamics. Infections due to repeated catheterization could increase and prolong both types of dysfunction.

The management of postoperative urinary retention relies on postoperative self-catheterization. One can also suggest suprapubic percutaneous drainage. This may be less of a risk as far as bacterial contamination is concerned. However, repeated urinary catheterization is not really dangerous once performed by the patient herself thus simplifying management of this problem. As far as the feeling of needing to urinate goes it is recommended that the patient keep a micturition calendar.

Postoperative urinary bladder retention is prevented during the surgery itself. During pelvic lymph node dissection one must preserve the presacral or superior hypogastric nerve. During parametrial lymph node dissection one must preserve the nerves running on the dorsal surface of the parametrium, i.e. Frankenhauser or inferior hypogastric plexus. During the Schauta procedure one must preserve the nerves running lateral to the knee of the ureter: limit division of the lateral tracts of the bladder pillar to the minimum required, and even more importantly, do not completely dissect the ureter free.

Coloproctological sequelae

Coloproctological sequelae are less known and less correctly assessed than vesicourethral sequelae. One does not usually ask the patient questions about defecation and patients' modesty prevents them spontaneously speaking about it. However, "terminal constipation" often presents or increases after radical hysterectomy including LVRH. The patient does not feel the need to defecate. This feeling is replaced by a painful sensation of heaviness. Rectal voiding takes a long time and is often incomplete necessitating digital maneuvers either transvaginal or even intrarectal (obstipation).

Atony of the rectal ampulla is responsible for this problem. It only emerges if "anism" is present (failure of anal sphincter to relax). In theory, anism cannot occur as a consequence of pelvic dissection. But it is a very common abnormality in women more so than in men.

Management of constipation presenting as a result of radical hysterectomy is the same as management of all terminal constipation. The regular use of nonirritant laxatives and biofeedback are the two pillars of this management. It is important to deal with the problem because, in the absence of treatment, it can lead to atony of the anal sphincter and fecal incontinence, due to elongation of the pudendal nerve.

Sexual sequelae

Patients who have had LVRH sometimes complain of dyspareunia. This dyspareunia is obviously due to shortening of the vagina, as its upper third has been removed. It is more than rare that lengthening plasty is required. If it is, our preference is sigmoid lengthening plasty, which is the only approach that provides satisfying and durable results. Prevention of dyspareunia is best achieved by tailoring the colpectomy. Care must be taken when placing the Kocher forceps around the uterine cervix to avoid putting them too far from the cervix. This is not always easy particularly in patients with a narrow vagina.

Inferior limb lymphedema and neuralgia

The greatest advantage of laparoscopic lymph node dissection, even when followed by radiotherapy, is avoiding sequelae affecting the lower limbs. The risk of developing a "swollen painful leg" is practically zero.

Recurrences

The most serious complication of an operation performed for cancer is of course recurrence of cancer. The most common recurrence after treatment for cervical cancer is pelvic recurrence. It represents two out of every three treatment failures and is associated with distant metastases in half the cases. In this circumstance as in the first, one can, apart from tumor aggression, blame inadequacy of loco-regional treatment. Statistics demonstrate that recurrence is not more common if the radical hysterectomy is performed using the laparoscopic vaginal approach rather than the classical abdominal approach. Parametrial lymph node dissection, which is part of the laparoscopic vaginal technique, is likely to be a good technique to prevent pelvic recurrence and particularly pelvic sidewall recurrence, which is the most formidable.

Indications and contraindications

The place of radical surgery in the management of uterine cancer has been disputed since the beginning of the twentieth century and continues to be so. This is the first point we discuss in this section before defining, among the indications for radical surgery, those compatible with the laparoscopic vaginal technique.

Indications and contraindications to radical surgery in the management of uterine cancers

As indicated in the introduction to this chapter, surgery and radiotherapy are, since the beginning of the twentieth century, corunners in the management of early stage cancer of the cervix (Marie Curie discovered radium the same year as Wertheim performed his first radical hysterectomy). It has been agreed since the 1940s that surgery, renovated in its techniques and strategy, equals radiotherapy as far as chances of cure are concerned. The iatrogenic complications of the two treatment modalities are different and for this reason difficult to compare. Nonetheless, both methods are considered to be equivalent.

The prospective, randomized trial published in *The Lancet*[4] in 1997 by the team from San Gerardo Hospital in Monza, Italy, confirmed the equivalence of these two approaches. The eligible population included 343 patients affected by stage 1 and early stage 2 cervical cancer. The number of patients that were randomized to radical surgery was 172 and those to radiotherapy was 171. After exclusions for protocol violation, there were 170 patients in the "radical surgery arm" and 167 in the "radiotherapy arm". Finally, 169 patients had radical surgery and 158 were treated with radiotherapy.

The 5-year survival rate was exactly the same in the two arms: 83% for overall survival and 74% for disease-free survival. The rates of failure were not statistically different: 25% in the "radical surgery" arm versus 26% in the "radiotherapy" arm. Risk factors were the same in both arms. For tumors 4 cm or less in diameter, the recurrence rate was 20% in the radical surgery arm versus 18% in the radiotherapy arm. For tumors more than 4 cm in diameter, the recurrence rate was 34% in the surgical arm versus 42% in the radiotherapy arm.

The rate of severe iatrogenic complications was significantly higher in the radical surgery arm: 28% versus 12% in the radiotherapy arm. This difference is partly due to the increased morbidity observed among patients in the radical surgery arm submitted, after surgery, to adjuvant radiotherapy. The rate of short-term complications was 7% in the radiotherapy arm versus 19% in the surgery arm of which 16% were in patients submitted to surgery alone and 20% in patients submitted to radiotherapy after surgery. The rate of long-term complications was 16% in the radiotherapy arm versus 27% in the radical surgery arm: 24% in patients submitted to surgery only

and 29% in patients submitted to radiotherapy after surgery. However, the comparison between surgery and radiotherapy is biased by the use of a glossary specifically designed for registration of radiotherapy complications. As far as complications observed after radiotherapy are concerned, they are twice as common in patients irradiated after surgery.

Iatrogenic complications directly due to surgery are apparently more numerous. However, these complications are easier to manage. On the other hand, surgery has got the advantage of preserving ovarian function in young women and its consequences on sexual function are less numerous. Furthermore, recurrences (which are not more numerous) can, to a certain extent, be salvaged whereas recurrences observed after radiotherapy are less curable requiring more aggressive treatment with less chance of success. And last but not least, surgery, in comparison with radiotherapy, is a single-step treatment: "instant treatment" with "complete response" obtained in a few hours.

For most specialists today, radical surgery represents the ideal solution to small cancers of the uterine cervix. Today's challenge is to limit as far as possible the requirement for postoperative radiotherapy. In the current context, radiotherapy is given to patients affected by regional lymph node metastases and to those whose tumors penetrate deeply into the cervix, infiltrate the parametrium and/or involve lymphovascular spaces. This information is acquired during and after radical surgery. An advantage of the laparoscopic vaginal strategy is to allow selection under better conditions. In fact, surgery starts with laparoscopic lymphadenectomy and the removed regional lymph nodes are assessed extemporaneously after frozen section. If they are involved, surgery can be stopped and patients referred directly to the radiation oncologist. If lymph nodes are uninvolved, one proceeds to vaginal radical hysterectomy. The assessment of the vaginal radical hysterectomy specimen can in some cases demonstrate the presence of "risk factors" which result in adjuvant radiotherapy. Although there is no first-level evidence, we have a foundation for believing that radiotherapy given after laparoscopic vaginal surgery does not expose the patient to the same morbidity as radiotherapy given after open surgery.

Indications and contraindications to the laparoscopic vaginal approach in the surgical management of uterine cancers

The laparoscopic vaginal approach to the surgical management of uterine cancer recognizes specific indications and contraindications. Some of them have an anatomical basis and some an oncological basis.

Anatomicosurgical indications and contraindications

Vaginal radical hysterectomy has the same advantages as simple vaginal hysterectomy. In the first place, there is a statistically significant reduction in postoperative mortality. The immediate postoperative course appears to be more comfortable and less painful. In any case, the total absence of visible scars is greatly appreciated by most patients.

In contrast, vaginal radical hysterectomy has the same drawbacks as simple vaginal hysterectomy. The most important drawback is that assessment of the peritoneal cavity is not made. As far as assessment of the retroperitoneal pelvic cellular tissue is concerned, the vaginal approach is always a very limited approach. Laparoscopy completely changes the game enabling us to assess spaces that were completely inaccessible using the vaginal approach without reducing safety during surgery and comfort after surgery.

Elective indications

Vaginal radical surgery is an operation "allowing surgery on inoperable patients": obesity, advanced age, associated serious co-morbidity are generally not stringent contraindications. Adding laparoscopy restricts the universality of the procedure a little. Very advanced age, extreme obesity and very heavy co-morbidity are not compatible with performing so-called "advanced laparoscopic surgery."

The loss of suitable cases for vaginal radical surgery due to addition of laparoscopy is, on the other hand, counterbalanced by the cases gained. Before laparoscopy was available, it was possible to tell that the more aged and sick the patient the greater the indication for vaginal radical hysterectomy. Since laparoscopy came on the scene it is exactly the opposite. The indications for vaginal radical hysterectomy are as numerous as the patients are young and preoccupied by preservation of body image. It is even possible to propose a conservative variant of LVRH, the laparoscopic vaginal radical trachelectomy (see Chapter 13) for those patients desiring preservation of childbearing capacity.

Contraindications

Contraindications to radical vaginal hysterectomy are less numerous than contraindications to simple vaginal hysterectomy. Disorders of the hip and spine remain a preoccupation. However, poor vaginal access is not a contraindication for two reasons. First, laparoscopic preparation loosens the suspensory ligaments of the genital organs, which facilitates performing the vaginal operation. The other reason is that the Schuchardt incision completely solves the problem in extremely difficult cases (although one must avoid using it as far as is possible).

Associated lesions (pelvic masses), which were in the past a contraindication to the vaginal approach, no longer are in that laparoscopy is the first step of the operation and solves the problem at that stage.

Oncological indications and contraindications

Patients are offered the laparoscopic vaginal approach when it is clear that it offers them the same chance of cure as the alternative method.

Elective indications

The ideal candidate for laparoscopic vaginal hysterectomy is the patient with cervical cancer, with a squamous, glandular or squamoglandular histotype, a tumor with a diameter less than 2 cm and no lymphovascular space involvement. In these patients the chance of recurrence is almost zero. Operating "without opening" can only offer advantages making LVRH the ideal solution. Performing parametrial lymphadenectomy is not, in this context, mandatory.

For cancers 2–4 cm in diameter without lymphovascular space involvement, the risk of recurrence is around 15% if the nodes are not involved. It is between 30% and 50% if the nodes are involved and is even higher if the histo-type is more aggressive (small cell cancer, neuroendocrine cancer, papillary serous cancer, etc.). In the first situation, chemoradiotherapy is not indicated but in the latter it is. In these cases, it is not clear that performing LVRH before chemoradiotherapy actually increases morbidity. However, we believe that it is best to give chemoradiotherapy without performing pelvic dissection up front. This opinion becomes a certainty for cancers more that 4 cm in diameter.

Contraindications

Unfavorable histo-types (small cell cancer etc.) should be excluded straight away, as should bulky cancer. It is accepted that clinical assessment of tumor volume is fraught with inaccuracy. One must routinely request MRI. As soon as maximum tumor diameter exceeds 4 cm (the resolution of the method is approx 1 mm) the Coelio-Schauta is contraindicated.

The presence of regional lymph node metastasis is another contraindication. Imaging has certain value in identifying them. If imaging demonstrates bulky nodes one must follow this up with fine needle aspiration and if cytology is positive, surgery is contraindicated. If negative, the indication for laparoscopy is confirmed. If bulky lymph node metastases are detected at the start of the laparoscopic assessment, the laparoscopic vaginal strategy must be dismissed although fine needle aspiration may be performed and metallic clips put around the metastatic node to guide the radiation oncologist. Debulking of lymph nodes may also be indicated before referring the patient to the radiation oncologist, but this must be done at laparotomy.

If the nodes are normal in volume and appearance, laparoscopic dissection is possible. The question of how to best assess these nodes remains open to debate. We spoke about that in the introduction to this chapter: frozen section or paraffin embedding, one- or two-session surgery. The next question is a strategic one: if lymph node metastasis is found one may capitulate and refer the patient to the radiation oncologist before performing hysterectomy (the uterus will be useful for brachytherapy). Alternatively, one may perform radical hysterectomy postulating that removal of metastatic lymph nodes increases the chance of success of radiotherapy. But there is no evidence for this. If one decides to perform radical hysterectomy, one is best doing it at laparotomy.

Future

Cervical cancer is a disappearing disease in the western world. Screening has already reduced its incidence and vaccination may cause it to disappear. However, in parallel with reducing incidence, the "surgical forms" of cervical cancer paradoxically become more frequent. The cancers that present are smaller and affect younger women. The laparoscopic vaginal strategy, which allows preservation of body image, ovarian function and, for some patients, fertility (Chapter 13) could eventually become the method of choice in the near future.

Applying the concepts of the sentinel node and of supramorphological staging, the therapeutic strategy could be modified. The laparoscope allows sentinel node biopsy, this node being submitted to immunohistochemical and/or molecular biological assessment. If micrometastases are identified the patient could be referred immediately for chemoradiotherapy (presence of micrometastases in the sentinel node is likely to be a very sensitive, maybe too sensitive, risk factor). If not, surgery would be indicated, but simple vaginal hysterectomy would be adequate for this very low risk patient. At the end of the day, if the indications for therapy are based on the search for micrometastases, the Coelio-Schauta would be either too little or too much.

Other technical and conceptual advances could eventually make the statements expressed in this chapter completely obsolete: there is nothing more difficult than futurology, and even more so if the question is predicting the future!

References

1 Massi G., Savino L., Susini T. Three classes of radical vaginal hysterectomy for treatment of endometrial and cervical cancer. *Am J Obstet Gynecol* 1996; 175:1576–85.

2 Dargent D. A new future for Schauta's operation through pre-surgical retroperitoneal pelviscopy. *Eur J Gynecol Oncol* 1987;8:292.

3 Querleu D., Leblanc E., Castelain B. Laparoscopic pelvic lymphadenectomy in the staging of early carcinoma of the cervix. *Am J Obstet Gynecol* 1991;164:579.

4 Landoni F., Maneo A., Colombo A., *et al.* Randomised study of radical surgery versus radiotherapy for stage Ib–IIa cervical cancer. *Lancet* 1997;350:535–40.

13 Laparoscopic vaginal radical trachelectomy

The survival of patients with early-stage cervical cancer with negative lymph nodes is excellent, ranging between 95% and 98%. Cervical cancer frequently affects young women in their reproductive years. Consequently, particularly in western countries where women often delay childbearing to their mid- or late-thirties, fertility preservation has become a prime concern in the management of early-stage disease, since the cure rate is excellent.

Cervical cancer is known to metastasize preferentially to regional lymph nodes. For patients with FIGO stage IA2 and IB1 lesions, the risk of lymph node metastasis is in the range of 5% and 15% respectively. So, with today's knowledge, complete lymph node dissection as part of the surgical management of early-stage cervical cancer is still recommended. Cervical cancer is also known to spread laterally to the adjacent parametrium justifying bilateral parametrectomy to remove all node-bearing parametrial tissue. However, extension of the cancer vertically toward the uterine body is a rare occurrence. Consequently, Dargent proposed in 1987 a modification of the Schauta-Amreich radical vaginal hysterectomy to preserve the body of the uterus and thus reproductive function. This new procedure, called radical trachelectomy, implies removal of the cervix along with the proximal portion of the parametrium and is preceded by a complete laparoscopic pelvic lymph node dissection. This procedure thus respects the oncological principles underlying the surgical treatment of cervical cancer while preserving childbearing potential. It is also a direct extension of the evolution of surgery in the treatment of cervical cancer in the last decade: the development of laparoscopic skills and the revival of vaginal surgery.

In the present chapter we will review step by step the surgical technique of the radical trachelectomy procedure. The initial steps of the procedure are identical to those described for vaginal radical hysterectomy in the previous chapter. Emphasis will thus be placed on the specific aspects of the trachelectomy itself. The trachelectomy procedure is also preceded by laparoscopic lymph node dissection already described in Chapter 12 and this part of the procedure will not be repeated in this section. The issue of sentinel node mapping also described in the previous chapter is particularly interesting in the context of early-stage disease as the rate of lymph node metastasis is low. If this technique proves to be representative of the regional lymph node status, complete lymphadenectomy could perhaps be omitted in the future. The morbidity and length of the procedure could be substantially reduced. However, at the present time, sentinel node mapping remains experimental and complete lymph node dissection should still be performed.

Technique

With regard to the vaginal part of the surgery, the procedure can be divided into five steps: (1) vaginal cuff preparation; (2) ventral phase preparation (opening of the vesicovaginal space, paravesical spaces and mobilization of the ureters); (3) dorsal phase preparation (opening of the cul de sac and pararectal space); (4) lateral phase preparation (excision of the parametrium and descending collaterals of the uterine artery); and (5) excision of the specimen and closure. The first three steps are essentially identical to those for radical vaginal hysterectomy but will still be outlined here to facilitate reading.

Vaginal cuff preparation

Since the radical trachelectomy procedure is primarily offered to women with small cervical lesions, it is rarely necessary to remove more than 1 cm of vaginal mucosa. Thus, a rim of vaginal tissue is delineated circumferentially clockwise around the cervix using 6–8 straight Kocher clamps placed at regular intervals, about 1 cm above the cervix (Figure 13.1).

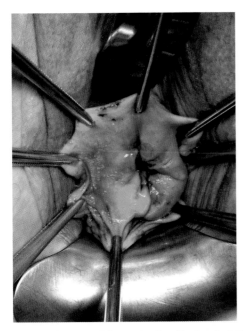

Figure 13.1 Definition of the vaginal cuff using 6–8 Kocher clamps placed approximately 1 cm above the cervix. (The cervix is blue because it was injected with vital blue dye for localization of the sentinel node.)

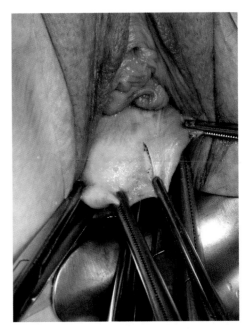

Figure 13.3 Vertical incision at 12 o'clock as a landmark for later reference.

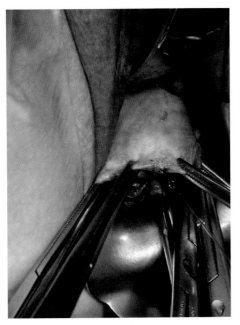

Figure 13.2 Injection of the vaginal mucosa in between each Kocher clamp with 10–20 cc of either saline or xylocaine 1% mixed with epinephrine 1 : 100,000.

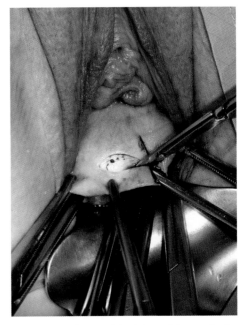

Figure 13.4 Circumferential incision of the vaginal mucosa *just* above the Kocher clamps.

In order to reduce bleeding from the edges of the vaginal flaps, 10–20 cc solution of saline or xylocaine 1% mixed with epinephrine 1 : 100,000 is injected between each Kocher clamp (Figure 13.2). It also helps to separate the two leaves of each of the folds created by pulling on the Kocher forceps. A small vertical incision is then made with the scalpel at 12 o'clock as a landmark for later reference (Figure 13.3). While pulling out the Kocher clamps, a circumferential incision is made with the scalpel just above the clamps (Figure 13.4). The mucosa and submucosa layers are incised but care is taken not to go too deep to avoid entering the opposite leaf of the fold. At the level of the 3 and 9 o'clock clamps, it is preferable to incise the skin alone to prevent tearing of the vaginal flap. It also maintains the relationship between the vaginal cuff and the parametrium as well as the integrity of the paracolpos. Once the circumferential incision is completed, the ventral and dorsal edges of the so-called vaginal cuff are grasped with Chrobak

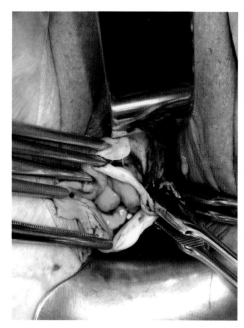

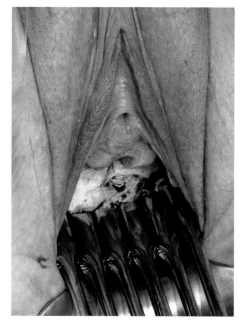

Figure 13.5 Closure of the vaginal cuff by re-approximating the anterior and posterior vaginal mucosa with Chrobak clamps.

Figure 13.6 Closure of the vaginal cuff completed.

(a)

(b)

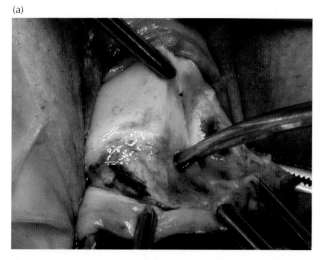

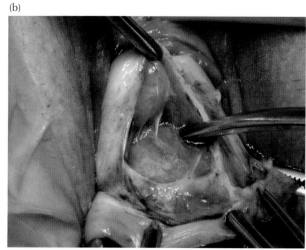

Figure 13.7 (a) Opening of the vesicovaginal space with Metzenbaum scissors. Note the triangular fold created by holding the ventral vaginal wall. (b) Further opening of the vesicovaginal space. Note that the dissection with the scissors remains in the midline to avoid bleeding from the bladder pillars laterally.

clamps in order to completely cover the cervix (Figure 13.5). The cuff thus created allows good traction on the specimen while potentially avoiding tumor spillage in the case of an exophytic lesion on the cervix. The vaginal cuff preparation is now completed using 4–6 Chrobak clamps (Figure 13.6).

Ventral phase preparation (described for the patient's left side)

Vesicovaginal space

While pulling the specimen downward, a single tooth forceps is used to hold and retract the ventral

vaginal wall, which usually creates a triangular fold indicating where to cut (Figure 13.7(a)). The vesicovaginal space is defined by using Metzenbaum scissors perpendicular to the cervix in the midline. Avoid erring laterally because of bleeding from the bladder pillars (Figure 13.7(b)). The space is further defined and stretched by gentle dissection with the index finger. Care is taken not to enter the anterior peritoneum as in a simple vaginal hysterectomy. If entered correctly, the space should be avascular and one should easily palpate the ventral surface of the supravaginal cervix and isthmus and see the whitish uterine isthmus. One should also be able to locate the bladder base (Figure 13.8). Once clearly

Figure 13.8 Opening of the vesicovaginal space completed. Note the bulge of the bladder base anteriorly.

identified, the space is stretched upward with a narrow retractor.

In patients who have had a diagnostic conization, particularly those who have had a cold knife cone, there may be substantial fibrosis and scarring between the cervix and the bladder base. Opening of the vesicovaginal space may be particularly difficult and challenging in those cases. In such situations, it may be useful to use a metal bladder catheter introduced in the urethra to try to locate the bladder base by gently probing it down.

Paravesical space

To open the left paravesical space, the Chrobak clamps are pulled toward the patient's right side. Straight Kocher clamps are placed onto the vaginal mucosa at 1 and 3 o'clock and stretched out (this is where the 12 o'clock mark made earlier is useful) (Figure 13.9(a)). This maneuver defines a triangle formed by the bladder pillars, the vaginal mucosa and the Chrobak clamps. An areolar opening is seen just medial and slightly anterior to the 3 o'clock clamp indicating where to enter to define the paravesical space. The space is blindly entered by opening and closing Metzenbaum scissors, with the tips pointing upward and outward, moving the scissors in and out following an oblique axis (Figure 13.9(b)). When entering the space, one should aim laterally with the scissors to avoid bleeding from the lateral aspect of the bladder. If entered correctly, the space should be avascular and the scissors should slide inside easily (Figure 13.9(c)). Once entered, the space is widened by rotating the scissors under the pubic bone in a semicircular rotating motion to the patient's right side.

(a)

(b)

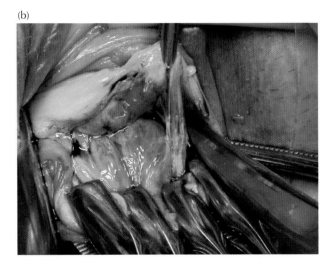

(c)

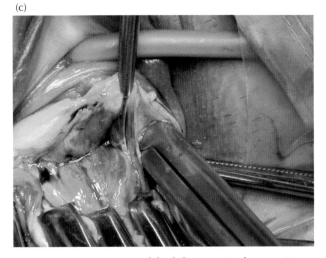

Figure 13.9 (a) Opening of the left paravesical space. Note the triangle formed by the 1 o'clock clamp, the 3 o'clock clamp and the bladder pillars. Note also the *small* opening just medial to the 3 o'clock clamp.
(b) Blind opening of the left paravesical space with Metzenbaum scissors pointing upward and outward.
(c) Opening of the left paravesical space completed. The scissors should slide in easily and the space should be avascular.

Identification and mobilization of the ureter

To palpate the ureter, the Chrobak clamps are pulled to the right of the patient; the surgeon's left index finger is placed in the vesicovaginal space while a Breisky retractor (or the back of the scissors) is placed in the left paravesical space (Figure 13.10). By pulling down and pressing the finger and instrument together, the surgeon should hear the "plop" of the ureter rolling under the finger. This maneuver orients the surgeon as to the location of the ureter in relation to the bladder pillars. Next, with the Breisky retractor placed in the left paravesical space and the narrow retractor placed in the vesicovaginal space, one should clearly identify the bladder pillars. The knee of the ureter is situated just in the middle of the bladder pillar (Figure 13.11).

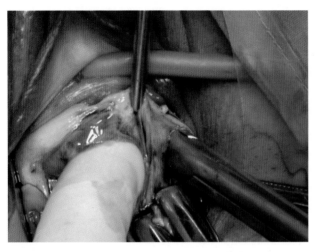

Figure 13.10 Palpation of the left ureter with the surgeon's left index finger in the vesicovaginal space and the back of an instrument (or the blade of the Breisky retractor) in the left paravesical space.

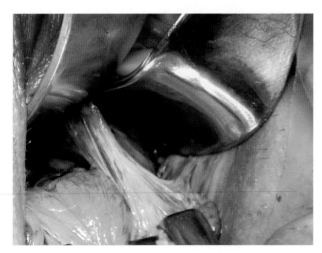

Figure 13.11 Identification of the ureter with a narrow Deaver in the vesicovaginal space and a Breisky retractor in the left paravesical space. Note the stretching of the bladder pillars and the bulge of the ureter on the lateral fold of the pillars.

Once the ureter has been precisely located by palpation, the bladder pillars are excised midway between the bladder base and the ventral aspect of the specimen. (Bipolar scissors can be used to decrease bleeding or standard Metzenbaum scissors.) It is recommended that scissors are used to stretch open the bladder pillars before cutting to separate the lateral and medial fibers of the pillar which are often designated as lateral and medial pillars (Figure 13.12(a)). Then the most distal lateral fibers of the pillar can be excised and the knee of the ureter appears in the operative field (Figure 13.12(b)). If the ureter is not unequivocally seen, it should be palpated again to relocate its position before cutting the pillars. A Babcock clamp can then be used to hold the ureter to facilitate excision of the remaining fibers (Figure 13.12(c)). The Babcock clamp is actually very useful for this step of the procedure as it allows good traction on the ureter during excision of the lateral pillar (Figure 13.12(d)) and during medial dissection of the ureter (Figure 13.12(e)) which should be done very carefully because of the risk of injury to the bladder base.

The same procedure is performed on the patient's right side. The ventral phase preparation is now completed.

Dorsal phase preparation (described for the patient's left side)

Opening of the cul de sac
Chrobak clamps are sharply angulated ventrally and the posterior cul de sac is opened using Metzenbaum scissors as for simple vaginal hysterectomy (Figure 13.13(a)). Care is taken to avoid trauma to the rectum, which can usually be avoided by offering good traction on the dorsal vaginal wall thus creating a fold indicating where to cut. Once entered, the space is stretched laterally to allow placement of a retractor. (A speculum longer and narrower than the regular speculum can be particularly useful.) The cul de sac is bordered by the uterosacral ligaments on both sides (Figure 13.13(b)).

Opening of the pararectal space and excision of the uterosacral ligaments
Using Metzenbaum scissors, the pararectal space is defined by opening a space just lateral to the peritoneal folds of the uterosacral ligaments (Figure 13.14(a)).

The medial or rectouterine fibers of the uterosacral ligaments are separated and excised (Figure 13.14(b)). This can also be done using bipolar scissors.

Excision of the paracolpos
To complete the dorsal phase preparation, the paracolpos is excised. The paracolpos is in fact the inferior border of the parametrium. It is easier to complete this step of the procedure if the vaginal wall has

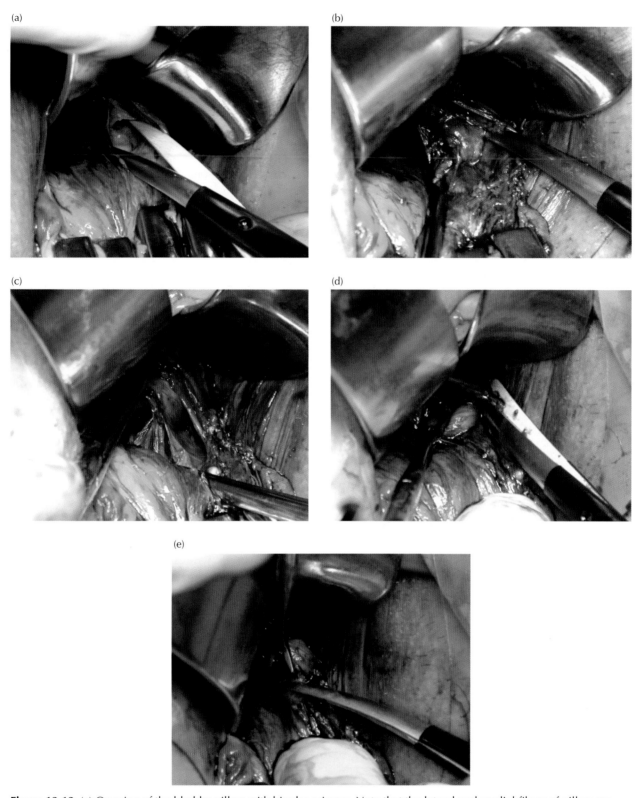

Figure 13.12 (a) Opening of the bladder pillars with bipolar scissors. Note that the lateral and medial fibers of pillars are separated and opened. (The use of bipolar scissors helps decrease bleeding from the pillars.) (b) Excision of the most distal pillars completed. Note the knee of the ureter appearing in the operating field. (c) A Babcock clamp can be used to retract and keep the ureter under tension while dissecting the pillars. (d) Excision of the most lateral fibers of the bladder pillars keeping the ureter under tension with the Babcock clamp. (e) Excision of the most medial fibers of the bladder pillars. This should be done carefully to avoid damage to the bladder base.

(a)

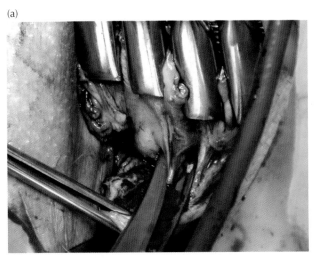

(b)

Figure 13.13 (a) Opening of the posterior cul de sac with Metzenbaum scissors. (b) Posterior cul de sac opened. Note the strands of the uterosacral ligaments on both sides laterally.

(a)

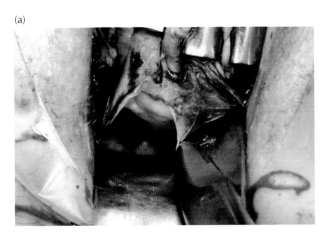

(b)

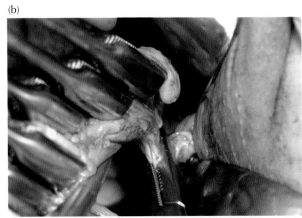

Figure 13.14 (a) Opening of the left pararectal space with Metzenbaum scissors. Note the peritoneal fold just medial to the scissors. (b) Clamping of the left uterosacral ligament with a curved Heaney.

not been incised too deeply at the 3 and 9 o'clock positions when defining the vaginal cuff at the beginning of the procedure. The lateral vaginal flap can now be incised deeper with the Chrobak clamps rotated to the right. One safe technique is clamping the paracolpos using a curved clamp applied just medial to the vaginal flap, excising and ligating with 2-0 Vicryl® (Figure 13.15).

The same procedure is done on the patient's right side. The dorsal phase preparation is now completed.

Lateral phase preparation (described for the patient's left side)

Excision of the parametrium

Before clamping the parametrium, the spaces should be redefined, i.e. the retractors replaced in the

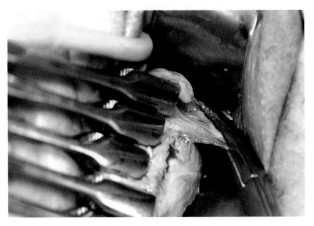

Figure 13.15 Clamping of the left paracolpos with a curved Heaney. Note that the specimen is rotated to the right of the patient.

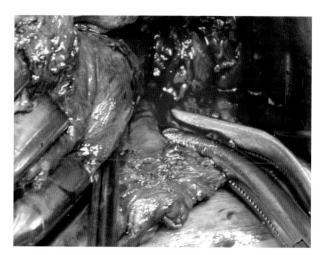

Figure 13.16 Clamping of the left parametrium with curved Heaneys. Note that a second clamp is placed higher just adjacent to the knee of the ureter to obtain a wider parametrium.

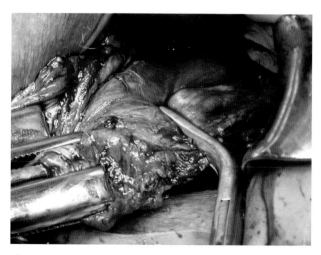

Figure 13.17 Clamping of the left cervicovaginal artery. Note that the right-angle clamp is applied directly at 90° to the isthmus just below the bulge of the arch of the uterine artery.

paravesical space and in the vesicovaginal space. The ureter should be precisely relocated. While the Chrobak clamps are pulled and rotated to the patient's right side, a curved clamp is placed proximally on the parametrium then a second clamp is placed higher and more lateral to obtain a wider section of parametrium. The second clamp should be placed almost in contact with the knee of the ureter, which can be further dissected if needed (Figure 13.16). However, the clamps should not be applied directly to the side of the uterus to avoid clamping the arch of uterine artery. The parametrial tissue is excised and ligated with 2-0 Vicryl®.

Excision of the cervicovaginal artery

As opposed to radical hysterectomy where the uterine artery is clamped at its origin, care is taken in the case of trachelectomy to selectively excise the cervicovaginal or descending collaterals of the uterine artery. The arch of the uterine artery is actually preserved to maintain optimal vascularization of the uterus in the event of a future pregnancy.

So, after precise localization of the isthmus and the arch of the uterine artery, the cervicovaginal vessels are clamped with a right-angle clamp placed at 90° and applied directly to the isthmus (Figure 13.17). The cervicovaginal vessels are now excised and ligated with 2-0 Vicryl®. Note the bulge of the arch of the uterine artery above the right-angle clamp. Another method to manage the cervicovaginal artery is to use a right-angle clamp with the tips entered posteriorly in the paraisthmic fossa and pushed anteriorly (described in the previous chapter).

Sealing the tissues included in the ligaments with the Biclamp is an alternative to the technique described

immediately above. It can also be used to manage the previous steps of the operation. Such a technique saves time, facilitates surgery and improves both postoperative comfort and radicality (see Chapter 12). However, it does not exempt the surgeon from the precise identification and preparation of anatomical spaces required for the precise identification and preparation of "ligaments" that are to be sealed and divided.

Again, the same procedure is done on the patient's right side. The trachelectomy specimen is now ready to be excised.

Excision of the specimen and closure

Excision of the specimen

The uterine isthmus and supravaginal cervix are precisely located by palpating the uterus ventrally and dorsally. In most cases the narrowing of the uterine isthmus is easily visible (Figure 13.18(a)). The cervix is amputated with a scalpel held perpendicular to the specimen about 1-cm distal to the isthmus (Figure 13.18(b)). As the specimen is excised, the cervical os appears gradually and the anterior lip can be grasped (Figure 13.18(c)). Care is taken not to angulate the scalpel to avoid removing too much cervix posteriorly. The specimen is completely excised in one single piece to facilitate pathological evaluation of the margins in particular, and the ventral aspect is identified with a suture.

Ideally, the specimen should be at least 1–2 cm wide, with 1 cm of vaginal mucosa and 1–2 cm of parametrium. In the case illustrated by Figure 13.19(a), the specimen is shorter because of prior conization. The endocervical cut surface appears normal (Figure 13.19(b)). Since the margins of the previous conization

(a)

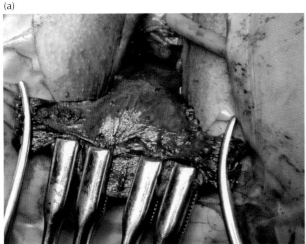

(b)

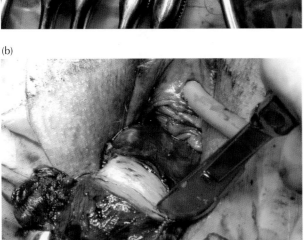

(c)

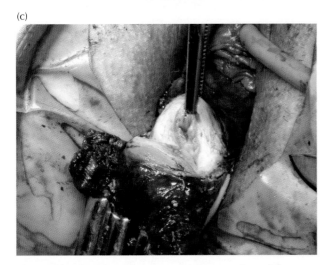

Figure 13.18 (a) Localization of the narrowing of the uterine isthmus. Note the arch of the uterine artery on the right side. The specimen is usually excised approximately 1 cm below the isthmus. Note also the presence of a parametrial node on the left side. (b) Excision of the specimen with a scalpel held at 90° to the specimen. (c) Excision of the specimen almost completed. Note the new cervical opening appearing.

(a)

(b)

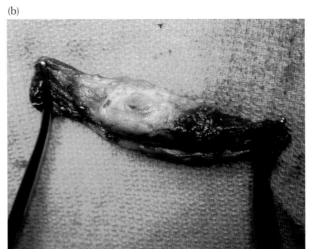

Figure 13.19 (a) Trachelectomy specimen (lateral view) with the parametrium stretched. Note the presence of a parametrial node on the left side. (b) Trachelectomy specimen (ventral view). Note again the presence of a parametrial node on the left side.

were clear, a frozen section is not performed in such a case. The specimen is kept intact for final analysis and is processed as a cone specimen. (See section "Patient with a macroscopic lesion" for the management of a patient with a macroscopic cervical lesion.)

Closure of the cul de sac

The final phase of the procedure begins with closure of the posterior cul de sac using a purse-string suture of absorbable 2-0 sutures. The suture is usually started at 6 o'clock posteriorly and continued counter-clockwise to include the peritoneum posteriorly and the peritoneum lining the back of the isthmus anteriorly (Figure 13.20). The stumps of the paracervical ligaments are included in the purse-string suture, which adds a "hysterosuspension effect" to the peritoneal suture.

Figure 13.20 Closure of the peritoneum of the posterior cul de sac with a purse-string suture.

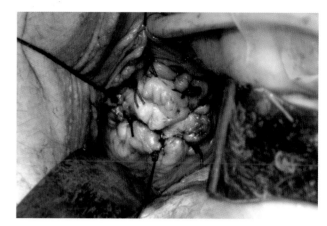

Figure 13.22 Closure of the vaginal mucosa to the new exocervix with interrupted sutures. The new cervix is obviously shorter but retains normal anatomical relationship. The cervical opening remains accessible for monitoring.

Closure of the vaginal mucosa

The procedure is completed by re-approximating the edges of the vaginal mucosa to the new exocervix. Stürmdorf stitches can be implemented. One can also use interrupted figure-of-eight sutures of 2-0 Vicryl. It is easier to place the suture at 12 and 6 o'clock first. The lateral sutures are then placed separately to include the vaginal mucosa and the lateral aspect of the cervix. Additional sutures can then be placed in between if necessary. Sutures should not be placed too close to the new cervical os to avoid burying the cervix making follow-up examinations more difficult. Sometimes, excess vaginal mucosa may need to be removed with the cautery to facilitate the closure. The final appearance of the cervix is actually quite normal (Figure 13.22). The cervix is obviously shorter but retains normal anatomical relationships. The new exocervix should remain accessible for monitoring with colposcopic examination and cytology.

At the end of the trachelectomy procedure, a "second-look" laparoscopy is performed to re-verify hemostasis in the pelvis and verify the integrity of the pelvic structures.

Patient with a macroscopic lesion

The diagnosis of patients with an exophytic visible lesion is frequently made with a cervical biopsy only. So if residual tumor is seen or suspected, the trachelectomy specimen is sent for immediate frozen section to assess the level of the tumor in relation to the endocervical resection margin. At least 8–10 mm of tumor-free tissue should be obtained between the level of the tumor and the endocervical cut margin, otherwise additional endocervix should be removed, or the trachelectomy should be aborted and a radical

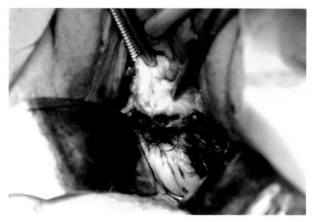

Figure 13.21 Placement of the permanent cerclage starting posteriorly at 6 o'clock, using a nonabsorbable suture such as Prolene-0 or Mersilene band.

Placement of the cerclage

In the case of a future pregnancy, a permanent cervical cerclage is placed with the hope of reducing the risk of second trimester losses secondary to cervical incompetence (see section "Obstetric outcome," p. 198). So, a permanent cerclage is placed at the level of the isthmus using a nonabsorbable strong suture starting posteriorly at 6 o'clock to leave the knot lying posteriorly (Figure 13.21). Prolene-0 or Mercilene band can be used. The sutures should not be placed too deeply into the cervical stroma as the cerclage can eventually erode into the endocervical canal and be expelled. When tying the cerclage knot, a uterine probe can be placed in the cervical os to avoid tightening the knot too much as this may cause cervical stenosis. The probe can also be used to measure the length of the residual endocervix. Ideally there should be about 1 cm of residual endocervix left.

vaginal hysterectomy (Schauta) completed instead. Two solutions are offered. The first is asking the pathologist to do a frozen section of the cervix with a section made longitudinally, i.e. from the ectocervix to the endocervix so he (she) can evaluate the level of the tumor in relation to the endocervical resection margin. The second solution is performing the first microscopic assessment just on the cranial edge of the specimen and postponing the final decision until assessment has been made after paraffin embedding. The procedure is more accurate and the decision of having to do a complementary hysterectomy or not is taken in safer conditions (such a strategy exposes a few, very few, patients to reoperation but it is less deleterious than removing the uterus unnecessarily).

Intraoperative difficulties

The most frequent difficulties and pitfalls associated with vaginal radical surgery have been extensively described in the previous chapter. Most difficulties are directly related to the opening of the spaces (vesicovaginal and paravesical spaces) and to the identification and de-roofing of the ureter. If those steps have been accomplished successfully, the rest of the procedure is actually quite simple.

For the radical trachelectomy specifically, special attention is directed to preservation of the arch of the uterine artery. Usually it is easily seen bulging anteriorly and just lateral to the isthmus. However, if there are some difficulties locating it precisely, one can proceed with opening the paraisthmic fossa as described in the previous chapter. Also, when excising the trachelectomy specimen with the knife, care is taken to avoid angulating the knife dorsally to avoid removing too much cervix dorsally. When placing the cerclage, care is taken not to place the sutures too deep into the cervical stroma and not too close to the edge of the cervix as the suture may tear. When tying the knot always check with a uterine probe that the knot is not too tight as this may cause cervical stenosis. Advise the patients that the first menses may be more painful because of residual swelling of the cervix.

Before re-approximating the vaginal mucosa to the new exocervix, it is important to verify hemostasis carefully, particularly at the base of the bladder and in the paravesical spaces, because these bleeders will not be accessible laparoscopically. Bleeding often comes from the edges of the vaginal walls and is controlled by suturing the vagina to the cervix. Avoid placing the sutures too close to the cervical os as this may bury the cervix and make follow-up evaluation more difficult. It is useful when placing the sutures to have an instrument such as a Crile in the cervical os to know at all times where the opening is. There is no need to pack the vagina at the end of the procedure. If there is concern about hemostasis the stitches must be cut and the bleeders identified and controlled.

At the end of the vaginal procedure, it is strongly recommended to take a few extra minutes to re-verify hemostasis in the pelvis by re-insufflating the abdomen and doing a "second-look" laparoscopy. Bleeding is sometimes encountered deep in the paravesical fossa or from the parametrial area. If a bleeder is identified it can be easily controlled with cautery or clip. If there is oozing, it may be safer to simply use a piece of surgicel inserted from the suprapubic port and to place it in the area of concern, then observe. Trying to control oozing in the parametrial area may in fact be worse and lead to more bleeding and frustration. One should not forget that oozing seen by laparoscopy always looks worse because of the magnification and that more oozing than that is often accepted when the operation is done abdominally.

Postoperative course

The postoperative course, intraoperative and postoperative complications have been extensively discussed in the previous chapter and are essentially identical to those seen after radical trachelectomy. Perhaps the only specific difference is the onset of painful menses early after surgery, in part because of a relative cervical stenosis probably secondary to some residual swelling of the cervical stroma. The pain rarely persists for more than the first or second cycle. Patients can resume normal sexual activities 4–6 weeks after surgery. The issue of cervical stenosis is also specific to the trachelectomy procedure. It is often secondary to the sutures used to re-approximate the vagina to the new exocervix that are placed too close to the os. Cervical stenosis may make follow-up examinations more difficult and the use of a cytobrush may be necessary to do a satisfactory Pap test, but it does not appear to be a major cause of infertility. Finally, difficult and painful intercourse is rarely a problem following a trachelectomy procedure as the uterosacral ligaments and pelvic supports are left undisturbed and the vagina is not significantly shortened.

Indications and contraindications

Indications

The indications for this procedure are not definitively established at this point as it is still a work in progress.

The eligibility criteria most commonly used are as follows:

1. Desire to preserve fertility
2. No clinical evidence of impaired fertility (relative contraindication)
3. Lesion size less than or equal to 2.0 cm
4. FIGO stage IA1 with presence of vascular space invasion, IA2 and IB1
5. Squamous cell or adenocarcinoma
6. No involvement of the upper endocervical canal as determined by colposcopy or MRI
7. No metastasis to regional lymph nodes.

As data accumulate, these criteria may change in the future. Of course, the trachelectomy procedure is technically feasible in patients with larger lesions. However, the risk of nodal metastasis and recurrence is higher. Whether patients wish to take additional risks to maintain their fertility is questionable and the issue should be thoroughly discussed with the patients.

Contraindications

Women with lesions greater than 2 cm in diameter should probably not be offered a trachelectomy procedure although this criterion may change in the future. Currently, there is very little data regarding the oncological outcome of this procedure in patients with larger lesions. However, if the tumor is purely exophytic the trachelectomy could probably be safely done in such cases, particularly by a surgeon experienced in radical vaginal surgery.

Patients with lesions that seem to extend deep into the cervical canal are always difficult cases. It is very important in these cases to obtain a pelvic MRI to have an accurate estimate of the extent of the lesion in relation to the isthmus, considering that at least 8–10 mm of normal cervix above the lesion should be obtained at surgery. In uncertain cases, it is always preferable to give patients the benefit of the doubt and offer them the option of trachelectomy with the clear understanding that if the endocervical margin is not clear, the procedure will be converted into a Schauta operation. The presence of lymph node metastasis discovered at the time of laparoscopy is another contraindication to trachelectomy and chemoradiation should be offered instead.

Finally, patients who present with high-risk histologies such as the small cell neuroendocrine type should probably not be offered this procedure as the risk of recurrence and death is so high that a combined chemoradiation approach is probably best indicated.

Oncological outcome

The recurrence rate with the most currently accepted indications is less than 5%. Most of the recurrences have been reported in the lymph nodes and very few in the parametrial area. Nodal recurrences are probably more a failure of the laparoscopic lymphadenectomy. Until the concept of the sentinel node is accepted in cervical cancer, a complete pelvic lymphadenectomy should be carried on with an average number of at least 20–25 pelvic nodes. It is also possible that some cervical cancers spread to unusual sites such as the presacral area and lower para-aortics or gluteal nodes. Again the sentinel node technique may help identify these unusual sites.

Recurrences in the parametrial area are more likely to be failures of the trachelectomy procedure itself. As described in the previous chapter, it is very useful after the lymphadenectomy is completed, to perform a laparoscopic parametrectomy to remove the most lateral and deep aspects of the parametria, which are difficult to remove vaginally. Good surgical technique with clear identification of the ureter should allow the removal of adequate proximal parametrium vaginally.

Interestingly, there have been no reports of recurrences in the residual cervix although transient low-grade cytologies have been reported. It is recommended that patients are followed up every 3 months for the first 2 years following trachelectomy, then every 6 months for the next 2 years, then annually. It is also prudent to wait at least 1 year before attempting pregnancy to let the cervix heal completely but also to a have few normal follow-up evaluations. At each visit, it is recommended that a Pap test is taken and detailed colposcopic evaluation performed. If needed, cytology specimens can be obtained with a cytobrush if the cervical opening is too stenotic.

Obstetric outcome

Most of the patients who become pregnant after radical trachelectomy deliver normal healthy babies. However, the overall fetal loss rate is around 40%. The rate of first trimester miscarriage does not seem to be higher than in the general population, but the rate of second trimester losses is higher. The inevitable shortening of the cervix after the trachelectomy procedure seems to prevent the formation of an efficacious mucous plug. The mucous plug is thought to be an important physiological barrier between the vaginal flora and the membranes preventing ascending infections. Hence, subclinical chorioamnionitis is thought to be responsible for premature rupture of membranes and premature labor. The Saling procedure (see Chapter 10) performed at 14 weeks of gestation is likely to be a good prophylaxis against second trimester losses. This assumption remains to be further investigated. Patients should be followed closely from 20 weeks on. A consultation with a high-risk obstetrician may be valuable in the second half of the pregnancy with more frequent evaluations of the cervical length by gentle digital examination or by ultrasound. Time off work and bed rest may be important as the uterus gets heavier. If the pregnancy evolves normally, delivery is planned at 38–39 weeks' gestation and because of the permanent cerclage women should be delivered by elective Cesarean Section.

The issue of fertility needs to be addressed with care. A history of infertility should not necessarily be considered a contraindication to the trachelectomy procedure. There have been reports of women with presumed infertility who became pregnant either naturally or with IVF after trachelectomy. Since the field of assisted reproductive technique evolves rapidly, a consultation with a fertility specialist may be valuable in patients with a history of infertility. Age should not be considered a contraindication either and the procedure can be offered to women over the age of 40 with the understanding that fertility potential is obviously less. Conversely, women with several children should not be denied this procedure as they may wish to have other children in the future. Finally, women's preferences should be taken into consideration. For some women the loss of the uterus is psychologically unacceptable and this should be respected. If the lesion is small and a good oncological outcome is expected, a trachelectomy may be an acceptable option for these patients.

Conclusion

Based on the collected data available thus far, the radical trachelectomy procedure truly offers a valuable alternative to young women with small early-stage cervical cancer who wish to preserve their fertility potential. Oncological outcomes are comparable to those for standard radical hysterectomy performed for similar sized lesions and the complication rate is low. Pregnancies are definitely possible after this procedure and overall obstetric outcome is good despite the rate of second trimester loss. The procedure requires good skills in radical vaginal surgery and in invasive laparoscopic procedures. The radical trachelectomy is probably the most important development in the surgical management of cervical cancer of the last century. Women can now have an alternative to cure their cancer while preserving their uterus and maintaining their childbearing potential.

14 Laparoscopic vaginal colpoplasty or colpopoiesis

Vaginal agenesis or Rokitansky Kuster Hauser (RKH) syndrome affects one in 3,000 female new borns. Despite its rarity it has raised a lot of therapeutic initiatives ranging from the simplest interventions (instrumental dilation) to the most sophisticated operations (intestinal colpoplasty). The procedure devised by the Russian gynecologist Davydov is a good compromise between the very simple but functionally unsatisfying interventions (cleavage procedures with insertion of molds) and the almost perfect but relatively dangerous operations (intestinal colpoplasty). It consists of separating the bladder and the rectum both from above and from below to create a cavity that will be covered by pelvic peritoneum. The laparotomy, which is part of the operation, allows mobilization of the peritoneum to lower it before stitching it to the vestibular mucosa. The second role of the laparotomy is to allow closure of the vault of the neo-vagina at the appropriate level. Laparoscopy can replace laparotomy making the operation even simpler.

Technique

The laparoscopic Davydov procedure has three constitutive steps. The first consists of opening the pelvic peritoneum under laparoscopic guidance. The second is performed with the patient in lithotomy position, which allows one to suture the pelvic peritoneum to the opened vulvar vestibule. The third and the last step uses the laparoscope once more to close the vault of the newly created vagina.

First laparoscopic step

The first aim of the laparoscopic step is to accurately assess the state of the pelvis. In most cases the uterus is absent and replaced by a transverse bundle joining two muscular ovoid structures located at the level of the pelvic inlet on top of which are two normal ovaries and tubes (Figure 14.1). This bundle is the tip of a transverse curtain that can be considered to be a rudiment of the absent vagina. The pathway between the bladder and the vagina can be sought either in front of this curtain and/or behind it. The latter is shorter.

The pelvic peritoneum is opened transversely at the bottom of the pouch of Douglas. The assistant produces traction on the centro-pelvic peritoneal curtain taken with a grasping forceps on the midline. The surgeon provides countertraction on the intestine taken with a Joan forceps. Drawing on the two instruments one identifies the point where the first incision should be made (Figure 14.2). Once the peritoneal incision has been performed one continues separating the intestinal wall from the pseudo-aponeurotic transverse membrane by alternating sharp and blunt dissection: the correct space is an avascular space; any bleeding signifies that one is too close to the intestine.

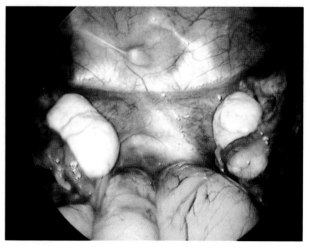

Figure 14.1 Laparoscopic view of the RKH syndrome.

201

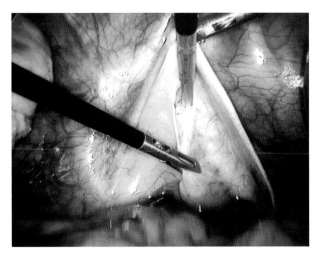

Figure 14.2 Incising the recto "uterine" peritoneum on the midline.

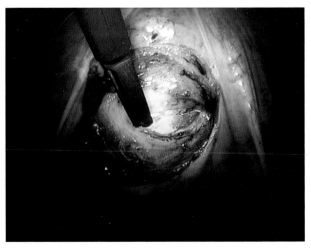

Figure 14.4 The vestibular vault is incised transversely.

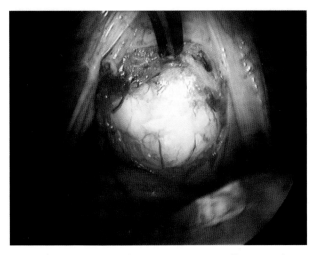

Figure 14.3 The tip of the transparent trans-illuminated Hegar dilator is visualized as the overlying bladder (ventral) and rectum (dorsal) are separated.

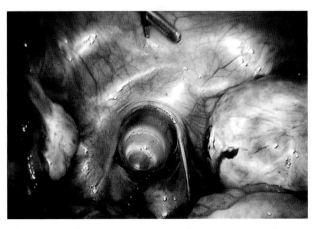

Figure 14.5 The 27–30 mm Hegar dilator arrives in the pelvic cavity.

We do not recommend putting a probe in the rectum. On the other hand, we place a transparent Hegar dilator 27-mm wide (to which we attach the end of a cold light cable) in contact with the vulvar vestibule. In mobilizing the intestine, the maximal risk is at the point of contact with this luminescent probe, i.e. the level where the anal canal follows, after a 90° bend, the rectal ampulla (Figure 14.3).

Once the fascia of the vestibular wall has been clearly identified by trans-illumination it is divided transversely using a monopolar beam (Figure 14.4) while maintaining pressure on the probe, which finally completely penetrates into the pelvic cavity (Figure 14.5). The first laparoscopic step of the operation is over. One can move on to the perineal approach.

Perineal step

Having placed the patient in the lithotomy position, two retractors are introduced through the transverse "vestibulotomy" made laparoscopically and the pelvic peritoneum is lowered. Each of the flaps is taken using a surgical forceps and stitched to the corresponding vestibular mucosal flap (Figure 14.6). If the vestibular vault has got some depth and width, 3–4 stitches can be put in place and the peritoneo-vestibular suture is deep enough and wide enough. The cavity created by the dissection is covered on four sides (Figure 14.7). In case of difficulty, the assistant exerts blind pressure from above to below with grasping forceps, to push the anterior and posterior flaps of the initial peritoneal incision, which lowers the pelvic peritoneum.

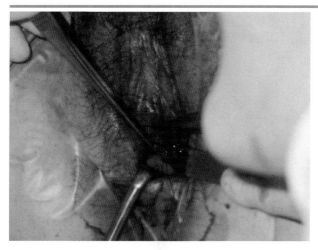

Figure 14.6 Vaginal step of the laparoscopic Davydov procedure: stitching the vestibular wall and the peritoneum at 12 o'clock.

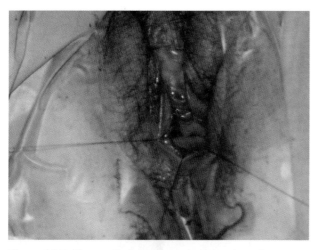

Figure 14.7 The vestibuloperitoneal stitches have been placed.

In some instances the vestibular vault is not adequately developed. The stitches joining the peritoneum and the vestibular mucosa are stretched and the raw surfaces are not completely covered. The depth and width of the mucosal part of the neo-vagina can be increased using a so-called nymphoplasty. The first step of nymphoplasty involves performing two vertical incisions at the extremities of the initial transverse vestibulotomy transforming the transverse incision into an H-shaped incision. This makes the vestibulotomy wider but not deeper.

In order to increase the depth of the mucosal part of the neo-vagina each of the labia minora can be duplicated. The gain will be proportional to the increased development of the labia minora (nympheal hypertrophy is not rare in individuals affected by RKH syndrome). The first step, in elevating the flap, is to perform two horizontal incisions at the extremity of the two vertical incisions of the H-shaped vestibulotomy. Actually the two incisions have to be divergently oblique making the flap wider at its base than

it is at its tip. The three incisions delineate the flap. To remove it, it is detached from its base by sharp dissection. During this dissection, the forefinger of the nonoperating hand pushes the deep aspect of the flap where it comes in contact with the cold knife to ensure that the dissection is in the right space: not too deep but not too close to the dermis. Once the flaps have been elevated their free extremities are stitched to the lateral edges of the incision made initially at the base of the pouch of Douglas. Interrupted sutures are inserted while taking care to leave sufficient space between the stitches to make the gap between the lower part and the upper part (the vestibular and the peritoneal part) of the neo-vagina wide enough.

Once the vestibuloperitoneal suture is finished the 27-mm Hegar probe is put in place again. One moves on to the second laparoscopic step of the operation.

Second laparoscopic step

Making the vault of the neo-vagina is the last step of the operation and is done from above. A purse-string suture is placed starting from the bladder dome and taking in succession its right lateral surface and then the medial pole of the right uterine rudiment. Afterwards, the stitch takes the "utero-ovarian ligament" and then the posterior sheet of the broad ligament taking care not to injure the underlying retroligamentous part of the ureter. The lateral rectal peritoneum, the lateral aspect of the rectal wall, and its anterior aspect are taken in turn and the same is done with the pelvic peritoneum in the left hemipelvis. Once finished (Figure 14.8), the purse-string suture is tied (Figure 14.9). We recommend using a 0 PDS suture and we prefer the extra corporeal knotting technique.

Postoperative course and complications

The immediate postoperative course after laparoscopic vaginal Davydov colpoplasty is uneventful as far as restoration of vital function is concerned. The bladder catheter can be removed immediately and bowel function returns to normal quickly. The patient could be discharged the day after surgery but the issue of care of the neo-vagina remains. In fact, without careful follow up the neo-vaginal cavity collapses spontaneously and, after the peritoneal serosa has been resorbed, adhesions form.

Inserting a double envelope prosthesis is the first answer to this problem. The size chosen must be the largest that will be acceptable and tolerable. As long as this is maintained *in situ* the bladder catheter must also be left in place. When the bowels first open the patient is taught how to remove the prosthesis before passing a motion and how to replace it after the bowels have moved. The bladder catheter can be removed at the same time and the patient must remove and replace the prosthesis each time she micturates or defecates. It is clear that the simplest approach is to keep the patient in hospital until these maneuvers are fully understood and appropriately executed. During the following weeks the patient must be assessed once a week either by the surgeon or by a specialist nurse who must control the healing process. This generally involves two steps: necrosis of the serosa and granulation of the underlying connective tissue followed by an

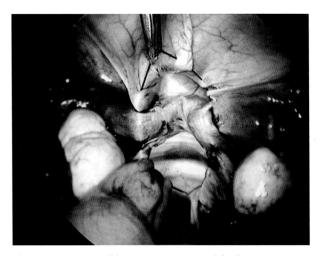

Figure 14.8 Second laparoscopic step of the laparoscopic Davydov procedure: a purse-string suture has been placed above the tip of the Hegar dilator using 0 PDS. Note that this suture takes in turn the bladder peritoneum, the rudimentary uterine horn, the "utero"-sacral ligament, the rectal peritoneum and the contralateral "utero"-sacral ligament and rudimentary uterine horn.

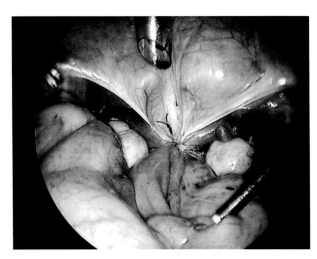

Figure 14.9 The stitch is tied.

ascending re-epithelialization starting at the vestibular part of the neo-vagina and growing progressively up to the vault of the peritoneal part. If a sexual partner exists, sexual intercourse is allowed (and encouraged) as soon as re-epithelialization appears, on visual assessment, to be adequately advanced.

Avoiding a prosthesis is best from a physiological perspective. The pressure of the prosthesis maintains physical patency of the neo-vagina but encourages necrosis of the serosa that covers it. For this reason, avoiding a permanent dilator may be better as long as instrumental dilation is performed at least three times a day. For patients who are able to perform this dilation correctly and regularly this second solution may be ideal as long as a careful follow-up schedule is in place. At the end of the healing process the neo-vagina can be catheterized easily with a 27-mm Hegar probe to a depth of 8–10 cm (Figure 14.10). On visual assessment the two parts of the neo-vagina usually appear quite different. The vaginal wall is thicker and more striated in its lower part (Figure 14.11). But

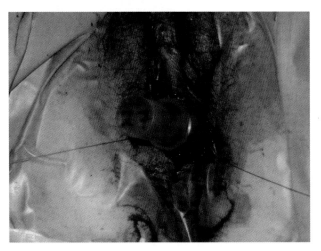

Figure 14.10 The full length of the 27-mm Hegar dilator can easily be introduced after the procedure.

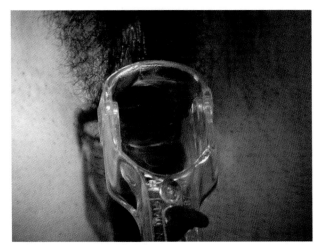

Figure 14.11 Appearance 12 weeks after the surgery using a standard Cusco's speculum.

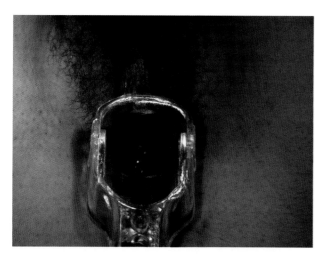

Figure 14.12 Iodine test 12 weeks after the surgery: the vaginal cavity is 8-cm long and is covered with iodine positive skin.

after staining with Lugol's iodine both parts appear equally iodine positive (Figure 14.12). The boundary between these two parts can often be appreciated on palpation but is not an obstacle to penetration.

During surgery the bladder and bowel are at risk. The advantage of the combined approach is that this risk is reduced. From this perspective laparoscopy is superior to laparotomy. Nonetheless, visceral injuries can occur either during laparoscopy or during the vaginal step of the operation. Although injury may be immediately apparent it can also escape immediate detection. In cases where doubt exists (particularly if abnormal bleeding occurred during the operation), it is recommended that a waterproof test be performed before finishing. If an injury is identified it must be fixed immediately (interrupted PDS sutures). Exceptionally, the injury becomes evident because of the abnormal leakage of urine or feces during the postoperative period. Faced with such a complication, removal of the prosthesis (or stopping dilation)

results in healing of the injury by formation of a spontaneous colpocleisis, but the patient returns to her preoperative state. Therefore, it is worth attempting to close the endovisceral orifice of the fistula (endovesical or endorectal approach).

Healing of the upper part of the neo-vagina is the main problem during the weeks following surgery. If postoperative care is not adequately assiduous either because of doctors' carelessness or patients' reticence, a contraction of the upper part can occur. If the warning signs of such an event are detected on time, forced dilation performed under general anesthesia can reverse the situation. If not, the final result will be reduced to that obtained with vestibuloplasty. This is an argument for using, as far as one can, the possibilities offered by nymphoplasty. It is also an argument for limiting the procedure to patients who already have a sexual partner.

Indications

All women affected by vaginal agenesis are candidates for laparoscopic vaginal colpoplasty. The most common indication is the RKH syndrome. Patients affected by pseudohermaphrodism may also be suitable candidates. Patients who have had vaginectomy should not be completely excluded. However, most of them have had radiotherapy and the technical difficulties and uncertainties regarding postoperative healing make other procedures preferable.

The most important issue is identifying the ideal timing of surgery. A lot of young people affected by RKH syndrome are slow to develop relationships with individuals of the opposite sex and as a result do not have a sexual partner. A prompt and normal sexual life postop is the best guarantee of a good result from the laparoscopic vaginal Davydov operation. This makes timing difficult, exceeding the competence of the isolated gynecological surgeon.

Index